LAW AND THE FORMATION OF MODERN EUROPE

Law and the Formation of Modern Europe provides an overview of the foundations of the modern European legal order, and it explores processes of legal construction in both the national and the supranational domains. In its supranational focus, it examines the sociological pressures which have given rise to European public law, the national origins of key transnational legal institutions and the elite motivations driving the formation of European law. In its national focus, it addresses legal questions and problems which have assumed importance in parallel fashion in different national societies and which have shaped European law more indirectly. Examples of this are the post-1914 transformation of classical private law, the rise of corporatism, the legal response to the post-1945 legacy of authoritarianism, the emergence of human rights law and the growth of judicial review. This two-level sociological approach to European law generates unique insights into the dynamics of national and supranational legal formation.

MIKAEL RASK MADSEN is Professor of European Law and Integration at the Faculty of Law and Director of iCourts, the Centre of Excellence for International Courts, University of Copenhagen.

CHRIS THORNHILL is Professor in Law at The University of Manchester.

LAW AND THE FORMATION OF MODERN EUROPE:

Perspectives from the Historical Sociology of Law

Edited by

MIKAEL RASK MADSEN

University of Copenhagen

and

CHRIS THORNHILL

University of Manchester

CAMBRIDGE
UNIVERSITY PRESS

CAMBRIDGE
UNIVERSITY PRESS

University Printing House, Cambridge CB2 8BS, United Kingdom

Cambridge University Press is part of the University of Cambridge.

It furthers the University's mission by disseminating knowledge in the pursuit of education, learning and research at the highest international levels of excellence.

www.cambridge.org
Information on this title: www.cambridge.org/9781107044050

First published 2014

Printed in the United Kingdom by Clays, St Ives plc

A catalogue record for this publication is available from the British Library

Library of Congress Cataloguing in Publication data
Law and the formation of modern Europe : perspectives from the historical sociology of law / edited by Mikael Rask Madsen, Chris Thornhill.
pages cm
ISBN 978-1-107-04405-0 (Hardback)
1. Law–Europe–History–20th century. 2. Law–Social aspects–Europe. I. Madsen, Mikael Rask, editor of compilation. II. Thornhill, Chris, editor of compilation.
KJC147.L37 2014
349.4–dc23 2014006240

ISBN 978-1-107-04405-0 Hardback

CONTENTS

CONTRIBUTORS

HAUKE BRUNKHORST is Professor of Sociology and Director of the Institute of Sociology, University of Flensburg, Germany.

YVES DEZALAY is Research Professor Emeritus at the National Centre for Scientific Research (CNRS), Paris, France.

BRYANT G. GARTH is Chancellor's Professor of Law at the University of California at Irvine, School of Law, and Affiliated Research Professor of the American Bar Foundation, United States.

POUL F. KJAER is a Professor at the Copenhagen Business School, Department of Business and Politics, Denmark.

JACEK KURCZEWSKI is Professor in charge of the Chair in Sociology and Anthropology of Custom and Law at the University of Warsaw, Institute of Applied Social Sciences, Poland.

MIKAEL RASK MADSEN is Professor of European Law and Integration and Director of iCourts – The Danish National Research Foundation's Centre of Excellence for International Courts, University of Copenhagen, Faculty of Law, Denmark.

THOMAS OLECHOWSKI is associate Professor for Legal History at the University of Vienna, Faculty of Law, and Director of the Federal Foundation 'Hans Kelsen-Institute', Austria.

IRENE STOLZI is Associate Professor of the History of Modern Law at the University of Florence, Faculty of Law, Italy.

DITLEV TAMM is Professor of Legal History and Director of the Centre for Studies in Legal Culture, University of Copenhagen, Faculty of Law, Denmark.

CHRIS THORNHILL is Professor of the Sociology of Law at The University of Manchester, School of Law, United Kingdom.

ANTOINE VAUCHEZ is Research Professor at the National Centre for Scientific Research (CNRS), Paris, and the Université Paris I – Sorbonne, France.

PREFACE

This book is the result of a long-term endeavour to understand the legal foundations and the processes of legal transformation that shape and underlie modern European societies. Our specific interest is to examine how law and legal institutions have reacted to and learned from the experiences of Europe's tumultuous century, the twentieth century. Further, the book is an attempt to contribute both to the promotion of new methods for exploring the legal structures of contemporary Europe and to the construction of original and distinctive paradigms for analysing how law has influenced the formation of twentieth-century European society. In pursuit of these goals, we here propose the concept of the historical sociology of law as a new and distinct way of making the interplay of law and European society intelligible.

Many of the chapters included in this book were first presented, in very preliminary form, at two conferences held in Copenhagen in 2010 and 2011, organized by the editors of this book, both of which were entitled *Law and the Formation of Modern Europe*. We would like to extend our gratitude to the institution which hosted these two conferences, The Centre for Studies in Legal Culture at the Faculty of Law, University of Copenhagen, and to the sponsor of both events, EURECO, a research excellence initiative for European studies at the University of Copenhagen. We also wish to thank all participants in these events for stimulating discussions and questions

In addition, we are indebted to Finola O'Sullivan at Cambridge University Press for her support throughout the process of turning a set of wide-ranging ideas into a book. Finally, we would like to offer very warm thanks to Katrine Meldgaard Kjaer, research assistant at iCourts – The Danish National Research Foundation's Centre of Excellence for International Courts – for her excellent editorial assistance.

1

Introduction: Law and the formation of modern Europe – perspectives from the historical sociology of law

MIKAEL RASK MADSEN AND CHRIS THORNHILL

1.1 Law and European society

At face value, the suggestion that we can comprehend the formation of modern European society from a perspective based in the historical sociology of law might appear counter-intuitive. There are several reasons for this. On one hand, the idea has become widespread that the legal order of contemporary Europe is founded in a categorical break with patterns of legal formation and authorization peculiar to the history of national states and national societies.[1] It is assumed, in particular, that the supranational process of European integration after 1945 marked a deep rupture with the previously prevalent belief, expressed most famously by Savigny (1814: 11), that law had its original foundation in, and drew its primary legitimacy from, its 'organic connection with the essence and character of the people'.[2] On the other hand, it is increasingly claimed that post-1945 European society has developed as a post-national society (Habermas 1998), marked by a highly distinctive and

[1] The principle of the distinctive autonomy of European law was strongly espoused in *Flaminio Costa v ENEL* [1964] and *Kadi & Al Barakaat Int'l Found v Council & Comm'n* [2008]. For excellent general discussion of the concept of the autonomy of European law in these cases and more widely see De Witte (2010). See also Azoulai and Maduro (2010).

[2] In the work of Montesquieu (1748) we can already find similar observations on the relations between land, culture and law. This historicist approach to law was of course widespread amongst legal theorists close to inter-war authoritarianism. Amongst prominent fascist legal theorists, see for example Karl Larenz's claim (1935: 19) that valid law results from the 'immanent structure and order' of the national community, and that 'community and law can never be separated from each other'. See also Hans Gerber's definition of law (1930: 56) as an 'unconditional obligation' born from an objective legal community of a historical people, and so 'rejecting natural law in any form'.

increasingly autonomous, *sui generis* legal system,[3] and that we need to renounce classical constructions of society, and of law's place in society, when we examine contemporary Europe.[4]

Quite evidently, there are justifiable grounds for such assumptions. From the outset, after 1945, the establishment of an overarching – categorically *European* – legal structure was driven by the express desire on the part of leading legal actors to draw a thick line between Europe in its contemporary form and European society in its pre-history of national statehood and national legal conflicts. This process involved the deliberate implementation of supranational norms by international actors, institutions and organizations in order to eradicate national legislative customs that had been contaminated by the rise of reactionary authoritarianism after 1918.[5] Moreover, as the process of European integration gathered momentum, leading judicial institutions enunciated the principle that European law was derived from 'an autonomous source', located outside national societies, and it needed to be fully distinguished from conventional state-based models of national statutory law and international law.[6] For these reasons, both 'history' and 'society' have become slightly controversial terms in analysis of modern European law. As a result, both historical sociology and – in particular – the historical sociology of law might easily appear rather obscure methodological

[3] For a very early variant on this see the claim in Badura (1966: 6) that the 'law of the EEC is an autonomous legal order *sui generis*' [*eine selbständige Rechtsordnung eigener Art*]. For later, more standard formulations see Ipsen (1970); Maduro (2005); de Witte (2012: 42). For reconstruction of the debate about autonomy see Bogdandy (2000: 231, 215, 223).

[4] For a critical discussion of the relative autonomy of European law see for example Weiler and Haltern (1996). On the end of methodological nationalism in sociology see for instance Beck (2003). For illuminating discussion see also Chernilo (2007).

[5] This was evident at the national level. In Germany, for example, new constitutional documents after 1945 showing continuities with corporate ideas were suppressed by the occupying forces. The most important example was the 1946 constitution of Hesse, Art 41 of which provided for the socialization of key industrial enterprises. This was opposed by the American military, and, partly for that reason, never applied. For documentation of this, see Berding (1996: 1068). Furthermore, Art 24(1) the German Basic Law declared that all statutes should accord with human-rights norms inscribed in international law. This was also evident at a transnational level. There is exhaustive documentation of the turn against nationalism in the formation of the Council of Europe and the European Convention on Human Rights. See for example Bates (2010: vii, 8). This is widely accepted as signifying a breach between pre-1945 and post-1950 legal presumptions. For recent comment see Williams (2011: 79); Pendas (2011: 215).

[6] This was the (in)famous ruling of the European Court of Justice in *Costa* in 1964. This principle of the distinctive autonomy of European law was equally strongly reiterated in *Kadi* (2008). For further discussion see the references mentioned *supra* note 1.

instruments for examining the development of modern transnational European society. The endeavour to account for the formation of modern European society as a historical-sociological process reflected – stage by stage – through the law and associated institutions involves challenging many presuppositions that are fundamental to the self-comprehension of modern European society.

Despite this, this book reflects the conviction that the distinction between the contemporary European supranational legal structure and the legal histories of different national societies in Europe is only – at most – partial. The formation of European society in its contemporary, partially integrated, form is not a historically disembedded legal phenomenon; instead, we argue, it is a process with sociological foundations in individual societies and European society at large. In consequence, this book advances the argument that historical examination of specific legal dilemmas and processes is a distinctively illuminating method for observing the emergence of modern European society as a whole. The overarching ambition of the book is, without adherence to one exclusive methodological approach, to elaborate a series of perspectives, which cut across traditional boundaries of discipline and thematic focus (for example, between law and politics, law and history, between the normative and the institutional, between the national and the transnational, or the supranational and the inner-societal), in order to address how deep social conflicts, systemic crises, group interests and historical dynamics of re-direction are reflected in the legal structure of modern European society.

In this introduction, first, we set out our primary arguments to support our framework of historical sociology of law for understanding twentieth-century Europe. Against this background, in the next section, we introduce some of the guiding lines of inquiry which have informed the analysis contained in the individual chapters. In the final section, we outline the individual contributions and discuss how they collectively contribute to the explanatory goals of the volume as a whole.

1.2 Towards a historical sociology of *European* law

On one hand, of course, it might be quite unnecessary to underline the importance of law in the emergence of contemporary society and contemporary Europe. It is self-evident that law is deeply embedded in the processes of state formation in modern European society, and a key characteristic of the national law of most European states is the fact that it is largely based in knowledge imported from other European states. It is well known that this Europeanization of law was originally influenced by the *peregrinatio academica* of individual jurists to Bologna, Paris and Oxford from the twelfth century onwards. This formed the foundation for a permanent transnational exchange of legal knowledge, which facilitated a convergence of notions of law and legal practices in large parts of Europe as early as the high medieval period. This was not merely an academic exchange, but a circulation both of systems of legal organization and of legal institutions and professional models, which was to mark the crucial interface between the formation of the European state and the emergence of the legal profession (Brundage 2008; Dezalay and Madsen 2012; Martines 1968).

Equally, it might be superfluous to make a particular case for the significance of distinctively sociological approaches to interpretation of law's importance in European society. The focus on law and history was clearly key to the first invention of sociology as a theoretical discipline; in fact, the rise of sociology was prefigured in part by theorists such as Montesquieu, Savigny, Hegel and Bentham, in whose works – however divergent in other respects – inquiry into law, history and society was inextricably interwoven. As modern sociology emerged as an academic discipline in the nineteenth century, then, the question of the role of law and legal practitioners in the construction of society – not surprisingly – assumed decisive importance for the pioneers of sociological research (see Banaker and Travers 2002). Marx, Tönnies, Durkheim and Weber all shared an interest in explaining the precise interface between law, legal technology and the formation of modern society. The defining works of both Durkheim (1960 [1893]) and Weber (1921) are emblematic of early attempts to develop a historical sociology of law which traces historical origins of solidified legal structures, and uses historical methods to clarify their impact on society at large. Despite this, however, the case for a historical-sociological analysis of European law needs to be re-asserted. Indeed, it is striking that the methodological centrality of the historical sociology of law in sociological inquiry in the nineteenth century and early twentieth century generally diminished in the latter part of the twentieth century. With few exceptions, none of the more recent traditions of socio-legal analysis, for example law and society, have tried to resume the quest for a genuine historical sociology of law.[7]

[7] For exceptions, however, see Dezalay and Garth (2010); Halliday and Karpik (1998); Madsen and Vauchez (2004).

This book takes inspiration from the many insights into the role of law in the formation of modern society which the classical sociology of law can offer. Yet, it does not form an attempt to analyse the long history of the creation of modern law, legal institutions and society. Instead the focus of the book is limited to assessing the influence of legal institutions, professionals and practices on the evolution of society in Europe in the longer twentieth century. Generally, two distinct convictions underlie the approach running through the book.

First, this book is guided by the view that the European legal structure, as it now exists in its relatively overarching form, displays deep continuities between different European societies, so that inquiry into specific inner-societal legal trajectories enables us to gain insights that reach well beyond national contexts and illuminate problems that are general across all of Europe (Dezalay and Madsen 2012). Throughout the twentieth century, conflicts regarding both the form and function of law have impacted deeply on European society across its national fault-lines, and different societies have experienced and been determined by parallel legal conflicts at different junctures: the law integrally refracts and discloses common dynamics connecting different social settings and conditions. For example, conflicts over the distinction between private law and public law (see for example Sacriste 2011), the legal order of state planning, and the foundations of social law and welfare rights (Castel 1995), were characteristic elements of all European societies in the inter-war era. These conflicts arose as European societies were confronted – in comparable manner, although to varying degrees – with acute problems caused by social mobilization, incubated nationalism, anxiety about revolution, and the material integration of volatile political constituencies, which had been posed initially by World War I and the resultant collapse of the liberal state and the liberal political economy (see Thornhill, Chapter 2 in this book). Likewise, debates over the extent of parliamentary authority and the need for constitutional checks and procedures for review of legislation have also figured, at different times, as important and relatively uniform legal contests, shaping the form of all European societies. These debates were originally stimulated by the emergence of federal polities caused by the collapse of late-feudal empires in the later nineteenth century, by the rapid expansion of parliamentary sovereignty after 1918, and by the accelerated ascription of new regulatory duties to public institutions. Debates about these questions persist today even in polities, such as the United Kingdom and France, that have a strong historical commitment to the supremacy of elected legislatures over other branches of government. Similarly, endeavours to implement solid guarantees for basic rights have played a crucial role in the political construction of all European societies: the conflict over rights, and over the conditions of their institutional protection, has proved one of the most enduring and universal features of modern European history (Madsen 2010). These debates have shadowed European history from 1789 to the present, but they have assumed particular prominence against the pan-European backdrop of extreme authoritarianism at different stages in the twentieth century and through the (in part) resultant emergence of a supranational legal order. On this basis, although large parts of this book are devoted to examining legal processes in particular national societies, these processes are selected because of their exemplary status in the broader formation of European law and European society.

Second, this book is guided by the view that contested legal processes in national societies have acquired vital significance in engendering a legal order that extends beyond the national context, and they have assumed catalytic importance in contributing to the formation of modern Europe. Such processes have punctuated modern European history, and they have acted as decisive causal factors in shaping the overall structure of European society in its contemporary extensive form (see Brunkhorst, Chapter 11). We can think here, by way of examples drawn from this book, of the wave of mass-democratic constitution writing after 1918; the crisis of classical liberal jurisprudence after 1918; the normative inclusion of multi-ethnic, pluralistic post-imperial societies; the judicial treatment of fascist collaboration in occupied societies after 1945; the legal dimensions of early welfare democracy; the wholesale transfer of populations after 1945; the incorporation of international human rights law after 1945; and the growth of judicial independence and constitutional review after 1945 and, especially, after 1989. In such processes, debates on law reflected and stimulated very far-reaching processes of structural re-direction in European society as a whole. Indeed, in these processes, problems addressed under national jurisdictions often assumed implications reaching beyond the national level, and solutions for such problems were widely shaped by the opening of national legal systems to comparative law and to transnational legal exchanges and communications (Dezalay and Madsen 2006; 2009). As a result, we can observe that certain legal controversies have historically possessed a tendency to transcend the national domain, and legal questions originating in national contexts have in many cases driven the construction of contemporary Europe and European law at a supranational level.

The disjuncture between the transnational reality of contemporary Europe and the national reality of earlier stages in the history of Europe, thus, is never fixed and categorical, and many legal phenomena in contemporary transnational European society have resulted from problems originally articulated in national legal fields. Indeed, the basic shared supranational normative structure of contemporary Europe – arising, for example, from the promotion of universal rights norms through the European Convention on Human Rights (ECHR) after 1950; from the increasing impact of the European Court of Justice (ECJ); and from the emergence of a constitutional design marked by powerful judicial actors in the democratic transitions of the mid-1970s and from the late 1980s to the early 1990s – can be clearly identified with historical causes embedded in national societies (see Olechowski (Chapter 3), Madsen (Chapter 9) and Vauchez (Chapter 4)). This view is reflected throughout this book in the fact that those chapters focusing on nationally specific questions always show regard for ways in which the phenomena under discussion also contain implications outside and above the specifically national context.

In consequence, in two quite separate respects – that is, both in its deep sequential and particularistic inter-societal continuities and in its more recent phase of rapid, catalytic global openness – it is possible to talk of a European law, and to outline a history of the law of modern European society. Moreover, it is possible to approach European society as a whole through inquiry into patterns of legal formation in different national settings. In fact, it is implicitly claimed throughout this book that law forms a particularly important prism for observing the formation of modern European society quite generally, and law is a field in which the transformative patterns underlying European society can be palpably discerned. Of course, law gives *particular visibility* to the linkages between the national and the transnational dimensions of European society: that is, it immediately refracts both the common sociological features of European society and the dynamics of international spill-over. So, to counter the suggestion that the evolution of modern Europe is primarily shaped by a disjuncture between the European legal structure and national legal dynamics, we maintain that a remarkable, although often temporally staggered, level of intersection can be identified between different tiers of the legal fields of European societies, and different dimensions of the European legal/political system are connected through an ongoing process of legal production and cross-fertilization. In other words, Europe is always produced at the crossroads of the national and the international (Dezalay and Madsen 2006).

On this basis, the primary intention of this book is to provide an explanatory overview of the main social factors impacting on the place of law in the formation of modern Europe. It attempts to throw light on these questions through the use of sociological methods, capable of accounting for the formative role of law and legal institutions in modern Europe at both a national, transnational and supranational level. Applying a variety of sociological approaches, the book aims to reconstruct some of the primary foundations of Europe's legal structure, and to examine the emergence of a distinctively European legal domain by observing the multiple causal pressures, both national and transnational, from which this domain results, and to which this domain forms a response.

1.3 The historical sociology of law as a framework for understanding Europe

In the following, we outline the ways in which we believe developing the historical sociology of law can assist our understanding of Europe, both historically and currently. We have singled out three distinct areas in which, we argue, the approaches suggested here make their most important contributions to scholarship concerning modern Europe and European integration in broad terms. These themes also reflect the distinct lines of inquiry which have shaped many parts of this book.

1.3.1 Sociology of constitutional law and state formation

The book contains a series of contributions which focus, in different ways, on what in broad terms can be called *the sociology of constitutional law and state formation*. Each chapter reflects an attempt to explain the social conflicts underlying the construction of normative order in the domain of European public law – at once in its national, international and supranational dimensions. Each chapter examines the correlation between social processes and the formation of public-legal norms in the sphere of constitutional law and international law, and in associated legal institutions, professions and practices. In this respect, the volume claims a certain distinction in the broader field of the sociology of law, and it extends the classical parameters of this sub-discipline. Above all, it contributes to consolidating *processes of constitutionalization* as objects of particular concern for sociological analysis.

As already suggested above, legal sociology in particular was first promoted as a sub-division of sociology by specialists with a distinct interest in private law. In fact, it is arguable that the emergence of legal sociology in its entirety was originally shaped by a critique of the abstracted normative apparatus of constitutional law, which emerged through the Enlightenment and assumed expression in the constitutional revolutions in the last decades of the eighteenth century. The first classical theorists of society tended to deride constitutional law as a somewhat chimerical normative order.[8] Later, legal sociologists, exemplified by Ehrlich, observed that the public/private dichotomy was misleading when law was seen in action: Ehrlich (1989 [1913]) argued that the claims to legal centralization and consolidation implied in the public law of even the most advanced states was a fiction, which could not withstand sociological inquiry. Of course, this focus on private law in legal sociology is not absolutely exclusive, and post-1945 sociology of law, for example in France, Scandinavia and the United States, has been deeply engaged with questions of public regulation and, more generally, with the welfare state. In addition, although his influence has been primarily felt in private law, Luhmann's *oeuvre* contains very important works on public law and constitutional law.[9] Generally, however, the constitutional dimensions of public law have not typically been able to acquire the same salience as private law as phenomena for sociological interpretation.[10] In more contemporary research, sociologists working on issues related to constitutional law (both national and international) have generally viewed constitutional law as providing only an illusory and socially segregated construction of legal order.[11] Similarly, sociologists have long been reluctant to engage in research on human rights, as rights were largely perceived as a philosophical or even ideological abstraction (see for discussion Madsen and Verschraegen 2013). Often, as exemplified by the later work of Jürgen Habermas, sociologists actually

[8] This proto-sociological hostility to formal public law connected such unlikely theorists as Bentham, Hegel, Burke and Marx. See also Turner et al. (1995: 26).

[9] For Luhmann's most important works on constitutionalism see Luhmann (1965; 1973; 1991).

[10] This is of course not to claim that research in, for example, socio-legal studies or law and society have not addressed public law and particularly regulatory aspects of the welfare state. However, they have rarely debated the foundational structures of law and society in categories derived from basic public law.

[11] See recently, for example, Hirschl (2000: 125; 2007: 723); Schneiderman (2008); Nicol (2010: chapter 4).

renounced sociological methods in thinking about rights, and they have tended to rely on analytical/philosophical methods to account for the significance of rights norms in public life and political order.

In recent years, however, we can witness a striking increase in interest in the explanatory possibilities offered by a sociological approach to foundational public law. This is evident in research on the functional abstraction of constitutional law (Thornhill 2011), in research on the conflictual and cognitive basis of constitutional norms (Brunkhorst 2002), and not least in research on the active producers of constitutional order (Madsen and Vauchez 2004; Sacriste 2011). It is in fact possible to discern a pronounced and consistent *turn* towards research on constitutional law in contemporary sociology. This volume relates expressly to this re-orientation in the sociology of law. Indeed, some of the leading exponents of this new direction in the sociology of law are represented here, and influential contemporary approaches to the sociological construction of constitutional order are elaborated and exemplified in different contributions. In different ways, this book is one of the first concerted attempts to subject the formation of constitutional law in modern European societies to diverse comparative sociological scrutiny.

1.3.2 Sociology of European integration

A second line of inquiry, which marks a number of the chapters in this book, is the attempt to deploy sociological methods for analysing what is typically referred to as European integration and/or as Europeanization. Examinations of the European Union (EU) have not generally, or at least conventionally, been marked by use of sociological methods and theory. The most penetrating inquiries into the construction of the EU *qua* polity have tended to be located in political science (strictly defined) or in law (strictly defined). Such approaches normally place emphasis – respectively – either on the abstracted institutional dynamics or on the semi-autonomous legal apparatus driving forward the process of integration.[12] As mentioned above, it can be said of the EU that it presents a distinctively difficult and challenging phenomenon for sociological inquiry (see Kauppi and Madsen 2013). By necessity, the EU has often appeared as a polity fabricated without a society, which is not easily explicable in

[12] See, for instance, Weiler (1991); Alter (2001); Stone Sweet (2004); Stone Sweet and Brunell (1998).

strict sociological categories or in reference to identifiable patterns of social formation (Bach 2008: 44–5).

To be sure, there are exceptions to this tendency. For some time, there has existed a body of more conventional sociological analysis of the EU; this usually focuses on motivational accounts of the EU, and it examines the EU from the perspective of opportunities for cosmopolitan identity construction (Habermas 1991: 25, 1998: 155). There also exists an (albeit relatively limited) quantity of sociological research with a more compact institutional focus; this has also tended, normally, to take the correlation of institution building, integration and socially embedded identities and attitudes as its primary concern.[13] In very recent years, moreover, it has become clear that a more encompassing sociological approach to the European integration process is emerging. Sociology of the EU, or – more accurately – the sociology of European integration and European structural formation, has clearly begun to establish itself as a distinct, diverse, and often programmatically defined field of inquiry.[14] This book positions itself as a contribution to these debates. In offering a range of sociological perspectives for comprehending the national, transnational and international processes underpinning European integration, it seeks to add momentum to the growing importance of sociological research on the fabrication of Europe as far more than a set of narrow legal and political processes evolving in and around Brussels.

This book adds to this research strand in two ways. *First*, for all the recent expansion of the sociology of European integration, the methodological emphasis of such inquiry is not widely extended to incorporate the specific legal dimension of the EU and of European society as a whole. Of course, some of the contributors to this book have already begun to formulate distinct sociological methodologies for capturing the historical and societal dynamics impacting on the distinctive *judicial constitution* of contemporary Europe (see Vauchez 2008a; 2008b; Madsen 2010; 2011; Thornhill 2012). Moreover, some sociologists have attempted to elaborate, in outline, a neo-Durkheimian model to assess the transnational division of labour underscoring the phenomenon of

[13] See Medrano (2003: 233, 241); Delanty (2005); Delanty and Rumford (2005: 104–5); Bartolini (2005: 215, 220); Fligstein (2008: 138); Madsen (2011) and Kauppi (2013). Note however the powerful critique of integration as dominant paradigm in Favell (2003). This view stands somewhat remote from law, but might challenge legal perceptions in a number of ways.

[14] See, for example, Beck and Grande (2007); Parsons (2010); Saurugger (2008); Kauppi and Madsen (2013). For an overview see Favell and Guiraudon (2009).

judicial integration in the EU (Münch 2001: 196; 2008: 522; Frerichs 2008: 67). Other researchers have developed new sociological paradigms to account for the position of the EU within the global constitutional order (see Sand 2010; Frerichs 2010). With regard to the existing literature, however, this book has distinctive status as it generally approaches the European legal structure, including both the legal fields of single states and the European legal-political space as a whole, from a comprehensive socio-legal sociological standpoint. That is, as discussed, it attempts to interpret the structural forces underlying and giving rise to the changing legal order of European society in an encompassing perspective, and it refuses to focus on juridical phenomena formalized by the EU or the Council of Europe (mainly the ECHR) as the sole dimension of the European legal order. Most crucially, this book aims to comprehend the supranational European construction and the single European societies, together, as conjoined elements of a sociologically inclusive European legal structure, which remains embedded in longer, still formative, histories.

Using this approach, we break with the typical legalistic postulate of the 'autonomy' of European law, as instituted through the growth of the EU.[15] We deploy instead a more macro-sociological analysis of the European legal order, which examines European law as a *legal structure*, incorporating both national and transnational dimensions and generated by inner-societal pressures. In this respect, different theoretical standpoints are proposed throughout the volume to explain the processes and structural motivations giving impetus to the legal construction of Europe, both in national settings and as part of the unification process following World War II. In other words, we analyse the transformation of Europe within an overarching, socially produced legal structure, in which the EU obviously plays a prominent role, but in which it is by no means the sole expression of the complex factors which underpin the European transnational legal structure of today.

A *second* way in which this book adds a distinct dimension to scholarship on the sociology of Europe is by virtue of its pronounced historical-sociological focus. While using the approach detailed above, we preserve a strong focus on formative legal processes that historically pre-date and underlie the dynamics of European polity building (see for instance Thornhill (Chapter 2), Dezalay and Garth (Chapter 10) and Stolzi

[15] For discussion on the 'autonomy' of European law see *supra* notes 1 and 6.

(Chapter 6)). To accomplish the wider objective of explaining the legal structure of contemporary Europe using law as an analytical point of entry, the volume opts for a *longue-durée* approach. As discussed, for example, it examines the origins of European constitutionalism through a historical reconstruction of older genealogies of constitutionalism and older genealogies of legal formation, re-orientation and collapse. This allows us to appreciate the emergence of a European legal domain as an occurrence prefigured by legal processes dating from well before 1945. In some cases, it views the European legal order as at once building on, reacting to problems implied in, and reflecting tensions specific to, processes of legal construction and institution building reaching back into the classical age of constitutionalism and formation of the modern state. In promoting a historical-sociological approach to European law, therefore, the volume also adds a very pronounced historical dimension to the sociology of European integration more generally.

1.3.3 *Sociology of transnational processes in law and society*

The two lines of inquiry already described – the sociology of law and state formation and sociology of European integration – both form part of what can be termed the sociology of transnational processes, a third line of inquiry which has also guided the development of this book. Because of the interdisciplinary and simultaneously national/transnational focus of this book, we have selected a number of chapters which address legal processes that, at least *prima facie*, are primarily of relevance to single (national) European societies. As discussed, however, these chapters are included either because they illuminate processes of institutional formation ultimately having far-reaching implications for the evolution of a European legal structure or because they describe dramatic processes of legal transformation, which provide exemplary and transferable insights into the nexus between social formation and legal reflection extending across boundaries between European societies. Examples of this are the chapters by Stolzi (Chapter 6) on the legal apparatus of Italian fascism, by Olechowski (Chapter 3) on late- and post-Habsburg judicial politics in Vienna, and by Kurczewski (Chapter 8) on the legal principles shaping the democratic transition in Poland.

A further set of chapters seek, in a transnational framework, to explain how legal-institutional problems have shaped the formation of modern Europe. Examples of this are Madsen (Chapter 9), which explores the complex interplay of national and international law and politics in the formation of human rights as a legal and political force in contemporary Europe, Dezalay and Garth (Chapter 10), examining how the legal profession – a key motor of European state formation since the twelfth century – has come to play very different yet generally comparable roles across Europe, and Kjaer (Chapter 5), analysing the interface of law and corporatism in European society. Similarly, Thornhill (Chapter 2) analyses how fascism influenced European state building and ultimately necessitated the rise of supranational models of legitimacy and public law, and Brunkhorst (Chapter 11) discusses how crises in legal justification have contributed to the evolution of Europe.

While, for the reasons already stated, the book contributes to two important bodies of literature – that is, the sociology of constitutional law (broadly speaking), and the sociology of European legal formation –, its most novel contribution in many ways results from a fusion of both these approaches. In fact, in combining both these strands of research, we examine societal pressures leading to the construction of public-legal order in the *transnational domain*. Analysis of inter- and transnational constitutionalism has become a prominent area of theoretical inquiry in recent years. This literature varies greatly between research that promotes a stable normative account of international constitutional law,[16] and research that opts for a relativized, pluralistic account of post-national legal order.[17] Across the board, however, such inquiry only rarely engages in analysis of inter- or transnational law in relation to its national, inner-societal origins and it typically ignores the sociological pressures leading to the emergence of such law. Such inquiry, moreover, normally postulates a deep rupture between national and transnational constitutional conditions.[18] In these respects, with this book we seek to provide a counterpart to more established lines of argument, and we stake out a new position in debates concerning the rise of transnational order. First, we approach the emergent legal/normative design of transnational society as the result, not of rationally acceded principles and norms, but of embedded processes of legal adaption, societal

[16] See Dupuy (1997); Petersmann (2001: 22); Peters (2005); Fassbender (2007: 309); Habermas (2008: 369). For comment see Maus (2011: 285). See also the arguments in Höffe (1999).

[17] For example, Teubner (2006). See also Zumbansen (2006: 747; 2010: 187) and Fischer-Lescano (2003).

[18] See also, for example, Kuo (2010: 329); Krisch (2010: 17). See for general reflections the papers collected in Dobner and Loughlin (2010).

restructuration and protracted contest. Second, we are very attentive to the close correlation between the national and the transnational dimensions of legal formation, that is, the ways in which transnational legal structures originate in historical problems of national law. While there is a growing literature on so-called transnational constitutionalism and a good deal of literature on the specific constitution arising from the dynamics of transnational polity building in the EU and in European society as a whole, our approach is probably the first attempt to examine these processes in a historically embedded sociological framework. It thus explains transnational law as law generated by historical pressures registered in national law, which run – literally – across the boundaries between national societies.

1.4 Outline of the book

To incorporate these variations in focus and this encompassing approach to European legal formation outlined in the previous sections, we have divided the book into three parts, each of which elucidates our objectives with different theoretical or contextual emphasis. The first part is entitled 'Legal institutions and European state formation'. It contains a set of chapters that in most cases are focused on explaining the historical problems and preconditions, within comparative political settings, that ultimately impacted on, and in fact *gave rise to*, the legal process of Europeanization after 1945. The second part has the title 'Law and Europe's ideological transformations'. This part examines the dynamics of national political transformation and alignment, which flanked the emergence of a European legal domain. On one hand, this section reconstructs ways in which the legal order of different European societies, reflected through salient ideological forms, adapted to exigencies arising at different junctures during the course of the twentieth century. On the other hand, it elucidates the transformation of national legal systems after 1945, which cleared the ground for the emergence of a European legal structure. Part III is entitled 'Law and the supranational reinvention of Europe'. This part takes stock of the state of sociological research on the formation of a European legal order. It contains a series of chapters offering diverse, yet also complementary, accounts of the sociological prerequisites of the construction of a European legal structure and proposing alternative macro-sociological perspectives for the comprehension of these prerequisites.

1.4.1 *Part I – Legal institutions and European state formation*

In this part, Chris Thornhill (Chapter 2) proposes an encompassing sociological account of the formation of authoritarian regimes in different societies (especially Germany, Italy, Spain, Portugal and Austria) in interwar Europe. He explains the triumph of reactionary extremism at that time as a crisis of statehood, induced in particular by the constitutional designs emerging from World War I, which dramatically altered the status of constituent power in constitution writing. In this approach, he identifies constitutions as central sociological objects in the overall composition of society, and he outlines a sociological methodology based in *historical functionalism* to explain the constitutional weaknesses, adaptive crises and problems of depleted autonomy afflicting European state institutions after 1918. He draws the conclusion that the increasingly transnational constitutional design of post-1945 European states can be viewed as a reaction to the over-inflation or the *excessive inclusivity* of national sovereignty in European political systems established after 1918. He sets out the provocative thesis that constitutional democracy was never fully established in national-state settings in pre-1945 Europe. Democracy, he claims, in fact presupposed the rise of an international legal domain for its effective and enduring realization.

Also focusing on legal conditions in interwar Europe, Thomas Olechowski (Chapter 3) examines how the institution of judicial review was established after 1918 in the constitutions of Czechoslovakia (1920) and the First Republic of Austria (1920). He argues that the principle of jurisdiction by constitutional court resulted from the specific legal conditions of the late Habsburg Empire, and this principle was designed as a means for accommodating problems of linguistic and cultural diversity and federalist centrifugalism in post-Habsburg states. He traces the controversies surrounding principles of constitutional jurisdiction in the 1920s, notably the famous disputes between Carl Schmitt, Heinrich Triepel and Hans Kelsen. Against this background, he explains how the Austrian model of the *Staatsgerichtshof* established a dominant template for later patterns of constitutional formation, notably in Germany, Italy, many Eastern European states, France and Europe (including the EU) as a whole.

Chapter 4 by Antoine Vauchez focuses on socio-legal processes of a later period, roughly from the inauguration of the French Fifth Republic to present-day Europe, but it also explores the ways in which judicial review has gained an important position in European society.

The chapter thus connects with Olechowski's analysis of the innovative nature of this new legal institution, yet it provides an empirical analysis of reasons why the judiciary has come to play a prominent role in contemporary European society. Vauchez argues that although the overriding process of 'judicialization' can be traced back to the 1960s as part of modernist movements in law, it was not until the 1990s that it experienced a complete breakthrough in Europe. There are a number of processes that underpin this rising power of the judiciary, some of them directly linked to inter- and supranational European courts and their development of judicial review as a cornerstone of European law and politics. Vauchez demonstrates how the increased salience of judicial institutions in Europe is caused by factors that go far beyond constitutional reform, and can be linked to attempts, for example, to combat organized crime and political corruption.

Combining a focus on public institutions with a concern with the transformation of private-legal relations, Poul Kjaer (Chapter 5) sets out an expansive account of changes in the functions of law throughout the longer twentieth century, which he explains as results of changes in the dominant pattern of regulatory relation between polity and economy. Using concepts of legal positivization and hybridity derived from systems theory and governance theory, he argues that, in their essential political-economic design, modern European societies are marked by an evolutionary trajectory which passes through three stages: corporatism, neo-corporatism, and governance. He then explains that this trajectory is refracted in changes in the juridical form of society, and each stage in the process of economic transformation is reflected in a different form of positive law. Corporatism is correlated with the more formal rule of law; neo-corporatism is marked by the use of law as a medium of democratic interventionism; governance is marked by the proceduralization of law. On this basis, Kjaer offers a new overarching, semi-causal model for explaining the positivization of law and for addressing the formative functions of law in the changing economic structure of European society.

1.4.2 Part II – Law and Europe's ideological transformations

In this part, Irene Stolzi (Chapter 6) examines the legal order of fascism and its implications for democratic politics after 1945. She reconstructs fascist doctrines of statehood as elements of a legal response to the initial rise of mass democracy and welfare democracy in European society, especially in Italy, after World War I. She explains how at this time theories of the corporatistic state, integrating social organizations and delegations of labour and business within the political system, formed a framework in which societies fundamentally altered the legal principles for the organization of economy and society inherited from nineteenth-century jurisprudence, and in which they ultimately projected a new basic conception of politics. She also elucidates how the legacy of corporatism proved contradictory for the post-war Italian legal order and for Italian democracy as a whole, and she examines the ambiguous residues of corporatistic thinking in contemporary democratic debates. At one level, she explains how the post-authoritarian consensus in Italy was intent on abandoning corporatistic ideas. This, however, obstructed the formation of new, non-authoritarian models of social law and collective rights. In this respect, Stolzi tentatively proposes that corporate ideals require re-consideration, and may, even in the European dimension, provide useful instruments for the design of social legislation.

Ditlev Tamm (Chapter 7) examines the role of political trials for the consolidation both of national political systems and, more broadly, of the European legal system after 1945. In particular, he discusses the trials of collaborators which were conducted after World War II in most of the European countries that had suffered German occupation. He examines the impact of the 'purges' conducted at this time on the structure of different societies and on the political status and self-perception of the judiciary, and he considers ways in which, in occupied societies, judicial actors were exposed to, and in turn reflected, deep tensions in society. He connects these processes with contemporary analysis of transitional justice, and examines how the purges established preconditions for post-war social order and also produced judicial and more general institutional foundations for European convergence.

Jacek Kurczewski (Chapter 8) describes the socio-legal forces underlying the collapse of Communism in Eastern Europe. He focuses on the process of social modernization in Poland that culminated in the 'Solidarność' movement. The movement giving rise to 'Solidarność' is interpreted as representing the third wave in a longer trajectory of modernization underlying Polish society: it was the only stage in this process that developed from the bottom through to the top of society, and which effected a transformation of the ruling elite and the rules determining the exercise of power. The chapter argues that the rapid recovery of legal-state institutions after the end of Communism was facilitated by inherited elements of Polish legal culture; especially by the hidden continuity between the tradition of an independent judiciary, law professions and high legal culture in the pre-Communist and pre-authoritarian Poland. Most notably, the chapter deploys a sociological model to account for ways in which the resurrection of rights in public debate led to the reintroduction of rights as basic concepts in official legal discourse. It proposes a typology to explain how rights impact on democratic structure, and so traces the contours of democratization in post-transitional Poland through reference to the consolidation of rights at a more general European level.

1.4.3 Part III – Law and the supranational reinvention of Europe

In the first chapter of this part (Chapter 9), Mikael Rask Madsen examines the formation after 1945 of a new normative order – 'Europe of Human Rights' – and he considers how the rise of this new legal order was influenced by a global transformation of European societies after World War II. He situates the emergence of a European system of human rights within the larger structural and geopolitical process in which Europe was transformed from its dominant past as a conglomerate of imperial societies into the new overarching form of an integrated polity. Using this approach, he demonstrates how the growth in importance of European human rights for European society remains a global process, but one possessing increased intra-European implications. Deploying the Bourdieusian notion of social field, his chapter explores the social spaces, or fields, of human rights in Europe, and it examines the interconnections between more specific practices – notably the legal practice(s) of human rights by courts – and the structural evolution of society. In a first section, he shows how European human rights initially acted as an ordering device for Western Europe in a world marked by Cold War tension. In a second section, focusing on the period post-1989, he shows human rights becoming deeply societally embedded norms for ensuring, at one and the same time, public order and individual rights via a new transnational order of legal institutions.

Yves Dezalay and Bryant Garth (Chapter 10) focus on the ways in which the legal professions, and the changing interests of professional groups, have shaped the legal arena in Europe in a specific configuration of law, politics and economics. In particular, they argue that the rapid internationalization of the markets for corporate consulting and services, triggered to a large degree by the construction of the Single Market, has impelled legal actors to move towards a strategy of concentration and international deregulation. Whereas, from its beginning in medieval and Renaissance Italy, the professionalization of lawyers was deeply embedded in the politics of the modern nation state, in contemporary European society legal professions are determined by dynamics of international competition, resulting from relations of hegemony and patterns of state formation shaped by the Cold War. This argument is developed through a focus on the social and political histories of lawyers in the United States, England, Italy, France and Germany and through analysis of professional relations between different levels of the legal hierarchy and associations between lawyers and academics.

In the last chapter of the book (Chapter 11), Hauke Brunkhorst examines the formation of European legal order in a broad historical-sociological perspective, and he proposes a method derived from a fusion of neo-Marxist critical theory and post-Parsonian evolutionary functionalism to account for the forces shaping constitutional construction in Europe. He argues that in most societal contexts constitutions are formed through a two-stage process: that is, through periods of revolutionary foundation, followed by periods of gradual consolidation and evolutionary equilibration. This model is then applied to the constitutional order of the EU, from its foundation through to the present. However, the chapter concludes that only those constitutions that establish fully inclusive political rights succeed in obtaining enduring legitimacy. This source of legitimacy has been obscured by the primarily judicial focus of the EU constitution, and as a result the EU remains exposed to an endemic crisis of legitimacy, which becomes acute under conditions of financial crisis.

Bibliography

Alter, Karen (2001). *Establishing the Supremacy of European Law. The Making of an International Rule of Law in Europe*. Oxford: Oxford University Press.

Azoulai, Loïc and Miguel Maduro (eds) (2010). *The Past and Future of EU Law: Revisiting the Classics on the 50th Anniversary of the Rome Treaty*. Oxford: Hart.

Bach, Maurizio (2008). *Europa ohne Gesellschaft. Politische Soziologie der europäischen Integration*. Wiesbaden: VS Verlag.

Badura, Peter (1966). 'Bewahrung und Veränderung demokratischer und rechtsstaatlicher Verfassungsstruktur in den internationalen Gemeinschaften', *Veröffentlichungen der Vereinigung der Deutschen Staatsrechtslehrer* 23: 34–96.

Banakar, Reza and Max Travers (eds) (2002). *Introduction to Law and Social Theory*. Oxford: Oxford University Press.

Bartolini, Stefano (2005). *Restructuring Europe. Centre Formation, System Building, and Political Structuring between the Nation State and the European Union*. Oxford: Oxford University Press.

Bates, Ed (2010). *The Evolution of the European Convention on Human Rights. From its Inception to the Creation of a Permanent Court of Human Rights*. Oxford: Oxford University Press.

Beck, Ulrich (2003). 'Toward a New Critical Theory with a Cosmopolitan Intent', *Constellations* 10: 453–68.

Beck, Ulrich and Edgar Grande (2007). *Das kosmopolitische Europa: Gesellschaft und Politik in der Zweiten Moderne*. Frankfurt: Suhrkamp.

Berding, Helmut (ed.) (1996). *Die Entstehung der Hessischen Verfassung*. Wiesbaden: Historische Kommission für Nassau.

Bogdandy, Armin von (2000). 'A Bird's Eye View on the Science of European Law: Structures, Debate and Development Prospects of Basic Research on the Law of the European Union in a German Perspective', *European Law Journal* 6(3): 208–38.

Brundage, James A. (2008). *The Medieval Origins of the Legal Profession: Canonists, Civilians, and Courts*. Chicago: University of Chicago Press.

Brunkhorst, Hauke (2002). *Solidarität. Von der Bürgerfreundschaft zur globalen Rechtsgenossenschaft*. Frankfurt am Main: Suhrkamp.

Castel, Robert (1995). *Lés métamorphoses de la question sociale. Une chronique du salariat*. Paris: Fayard.

Chernilo, Daniel (2007). *A Social Theory of the Nation State: The Political Forms of Modernity beyond Methodological Nationalism*. London: Routledge.

Delanty, Gerard (2005). 'The Idea of a Cosmopolitan Europe: On the Cultural Significance of Europeanization', *International Review of Sociology* 15(3): 405–21.

Delanty, Gerard and Chris Rumford (2005). *Rethinking Europe. Social Theory and the Implications of Europeanization*. London: Routledge.

De Witte, Bruno (2010). 'European Union Law: How Autonomous is its Legal Order', *Zeitschrift für öffentliches Recht* 65: 141–55.

(2012). 'The European Union as an International Legal Experiment', in Gráinne de Búrca and J.H.H. Weiler (eds). *The Worlds of European Constitutionalism*. Cambridge: Cambridge University Press, pp. 19–56.

Dezalay, Yves and Bryant G. Garth (2010). *Asian Legal Revivals: Lawyers in the Shadow of Empire*. Chicago: University of Chicago Press.

Dezalay, Yves and Mikael R. Madsen (2006). 'La construction européenne au carrefour du national et de l'international', in Antonin Cohen, Bernard Lacroix and Phillippe Riutort (eds). *Les formes de l'activité politique: Éléments d'analyse sociologique XVIIIè–XXè siècle*. Paris: Presses Universitaires de France.

(2009). 'Espaces de pouvoir nationaux, espaces de pouvoir internationaux', in Antonin Cohen, Bernard Lacroix and Phillippe Riutort (eds). *Nouveau manuel de science politique*. Paris: La Découverte.

(2012). 'The Force of Law and Lawyers: Pierre Bourdieu and the Reflexive Sociology of Law', *Annual Review of Law and Social Science* 8: 433–52.

Dobner, Petra and Martin Loughlin (eds) (2010). *The Twilight of Constitutionalism?* Oxford: Oxford University Press.

Dupuy, Pierre-Marie (1997). 'The Constitutional Dimension of the Charter of the United Nations Revisited', *Max Planck Yearbook of United Nations Law*: 1: 1–33.

Durkheim, Émile (1960 [1893]). *De la division du travail sociale*, seventh edition. Paris: Presses Universitaires de France.

Ehrlich, Eugen (1989 [1913]). *Grundlegung der Soziologie des Rechts*, fourth edition. Munich: Duncker und Humblot.

Fassbender, Bardo (2007). 'The Meaning of International Constitutional Law', in Nicholas Tsagourias (ed.). *Transnational Constitutionalism. International and European Models*. Cambridge: Cambridge University Press, pp. 307–28.

Favell, Adrian (2003). 'Integration Nations: The Nation-state and Research on Immigrants in Western Europe', *Comparative Social Research Yearbook* 22: 13–42.

Favell, Adrian and Virginie Guiraudon (2009). 'The Sociology of the European Union: An Agenda', *European Union Politics* 10(4): 550–76.

Fischer-Lescano, Andreas (2003). 'Die Emergenz der Globalverfassung', *Zeitschrift für ausländisches öffentliches Recht und Völkerrecht* 63: 717–60.

Fligstein, Neil (2008). *Euroclash. The EU, European Identity, and the Future of Europe*. Oxford: Oxford University Press.

Frerichs, Sabine (2008). *Judicial Governance in der europäischen Rechtsgemeinschaft. Integration durch Recht jenseits des Staates*. Baden-Baden: Nomos.

(2010). 'Constitutional Ideal Types in the Global Age: A Sociological Review', in Kaarlo Tuori and Suvi Sankari (eds). *The Many Constitutions of Europe*. Farnham: Ashgate, pp. 69–88.

Gerber, Hans (1930). *Die Idee des Staates in der neueren evangelisch-theologischen Ethik*. Berlin: Juncker und Dünnhaupt.

Habermas, Jürgen (1991). *Staatsbürgerschaft und nationale Identität. Überlegungen zur europäischen Zukunft*. St Gallen: Erker.

(1998). *Die Postnationale Konstellation*. Frankfurt am Main: Suhrkamp.

(2008). 'Konstitutionalisierung des Völkerrechts und die Legitimationsprobleme einer verfassten Weltgesellschaft', in Winfried Brugger, Ulfrid Neumann and Stephan Kirste (eds). *Rechtsphilosophie im 21. Jahrhundert*. Frankfurt am Main: Suhrkamp, pp. 360–79.

Halliday, Terence C. and Lucien Karpik (eds) (1998). *Lawyers and the Rise of Western Political Liberalism: Europe and North America from the Eighteenth to Twentieth Centuries*. Oxford: Oxford University Press.

Hirschl, Ran (2000). 'The Political Origins of Judicial Empowerment through Constitutionalization: Lessons from Four Constitutional Revolutions', *Law and Social Inquiry*: 25(1) 91–149.

(2007). 'The New Constitutionalism and the Judicialization of Pure Politics Worldwide', *Fordham Law Review* 75: 721–53.

Höffe, Otfried (1999). *Demokratie im Zeitalter der Globalisierung*. Munich: Beck.

Ipsen, Hans Peter (1970). *Verfassungsperspektiven der Europäischen Gemeinschaften*. Berlin: Walter de Gruyter.

Kauppi, Niilo (ed.) (2013). *A Political Sociology of Transnational Europe*. Colchester: ECPR Press.

Kauppi, Niilo and Mikael Rask Madsen (eds) (2013). *Transnational Power Elites: The New Professionals of Governance, Law and Security*. London: Routledge.

Krisch, Nico (2010). *Beyond Constitutionalism: The Pluralist Structure of Postnational Law*. Oxford: Oxford University Press.

Kuo, Ming-Sung (2010). 'The End of Constitutionalism as We Know It? Boundaries and the State on Global Constitutional (Dis)ordering', *Transnational Legal Theory* 1(3): 329–69.

Larenz, Karl (1935). *Rechtsperson und subjektives Recht. Zur Wandlung der Rechtsbegriffe*. Berlin: Juncker und Dünnhaupt.

Luhmann, Niklas (1965). *Grundrechte als Institution. Ein Beitrag zur politischen Soziologie*. Berlin: Duncker und Humblot.

(1973). 'Politische Verfassungen im Kontext des Gesellschaftssystems, I', *Der Staat* 12(2): 1–22.

(1991). 'Verfassung als evolutionäre Errungenschaft.' *Rechtshistorisches Journal* 9: 176–220.

Madsen, Mikael Rask (2010). *La genèse de l'Europe des droits de l'Homme Enjeux juridiques et stratégies d'État (France, Grande-Bretagne et pays scandinaves, 1945–1970)*. Strasbourg: Presses Universitaires de Strasbourg.

(2011). 'The Protracted Institutionalization of the Strasbourg Court: From Legal Diplomacy to Integrationist Jurisprudence', in Jonas Christoffersen and Mikael Rask Madsen (eds). *The European Court of Human Rights between Law and Politics*. Oxford: Oxford University Press, pp. 43–60.

Madsen, Mikael R. and Antoine Vauchez (2004). 'European Constitutionalism at the Cradle. Law and Lawyers in the Construction of a European Political Order (1920–1960)', *Recht der Werkelijkheid* 25: 15–36.

Madsen, Mikael R. and Gert Verschraegen (2013). 'Making Human Rights Intelligible: An Introduction to Sociology of Human Rights', in M.R. Madsen and G. Verschraegen (eds). *Making Human Rights Intelligible: Towards a Sociology of Human Rights*. Oxford: Hart, pp. 1–22.

Maduro, Miguel Poiares (2005). 'The Importance of Being Called a Constitution: Constitutional Authority and the Authority of Constitutionalism', *International Journal of Constitutional Law* 3(2–3): 332–56.

Martines, Lauro (1968). *Lawyers and Statecraft in Renaissance Florence*. Princeton: Princeton University Press.

Maus, Ingeborg (2011). *Über Volkssouveränität. Elemente einer Demokratietheorie*. Frankfurt am Main: Suhrkamp.

Medrano, Juan Díez (2003). *Framing Europe. Attitudes to European Integration in Germany, Spain, and the United Kingdom*. Princeton: Princeton University Press.

Montesquieu, Charles-Louis de Secondat (1748). *De l'esprit des lois*. Genève: Barillot.

Münch, Richard (2001). *Offene Räume. Soziale Integration diesseits und jenseits des Nationalstaats*. Frankfurt am Main: Suhrkamp.

(2008). 'Constructing a European Society by Jurisdiction', *European Law Journal* 14(5): 519–41.

Nicol, Danny (2010). *The Constitutional Protection of Capitalism*. Oxford and Portland, OR: Hart.

Parsons, Craig (2010). 'How – and how much – are sociological approaches to the EU distinctive?', *Comparative European Politics* 8(1): 143–59.

Pendas, Devin O. (2011). 'Toward World Law? Human Rights and the Failure of the Legalist Paradigm of War', in Stefan Ludwig Hoffmann (ed.). *Human Rights in the Twentieth Century*. Cambridge: Cambridge University Press, pp. 215–36.

Peters, Anne (2005). 'Global Constitutionalism in a Nutshell', in Klaus Dicke *et al.* (eds). *Weltinnenrecht. Liber amicorum Jost Delbrück*. Berlin: Duncker und Humblot, pp. 535–50.

Petersmann, Ernst-Ulrich (2001). 'Human Rights and International Economic Law in the 21st Century: The Need to Clarify their Interrelationships', *Journal of International Economic Law* 4(1): 3–39.

Sacriste, Guillaume (2011). *La République des constitutionnalistes. Professeurs de droit et légitimation de l'État en France (1870–1914)*. Paris: Sciences-Po. Les Presses.

Sand, Inger-Johanne (2010). 'Constitutionalism and the Multi-Coded Treaties of the EU: Changing Concepts of Constitutionality', in Kaarlo Tuori and Suvi Sankari (eds). *The Many Constitutions of Europe*. Farnham: Ashgate, pp. 49–67.

Saurugger, Sabine (2008). 'Une Sociologie d'integration européenne', *Politique européenne* 25: 5–22.

Savigny, Friedrich Carl von (1814). *Vom Beruf unserer Zeit für Gesetzgebung und Rechtswissenschaft*. Heidelberg: Mohr.

Schneiderman, David (2008). *Constitutionalizing Economic Globalization. Investment Rules and Democracy's Promise*. Cambridge: Cambridge University Press.

Stone Sweet, Alec (2004). *The Judicial Construction of Europe*. Oxford: Oxford University Press.

Stone Sweet, Alec and Thomas Brunell (1998). 'Constructing a Supranational Constitution: Dispute Resolution and Governance in the European Community', *American Political Science Review* 92: 63–81.

Teubner, Gunther (2006). 'Die anonyme Matrix: Zu Menschenrechtsverletzungen durch "private" transnationale Akteure', *Der Staat: Zeitschrift für Staatslehre und Verfassungsgeschichte, deutsches und europäisches öffentliches Recht* 44: 161–87.

Thornhill, Chris (2011). *A Sociology of Constitutions: Constitutions and State Legitimacy in Historical-Sociological Perspective*. Cambridge: Cambridge University Press.

(2012). 'The Formation of a European Constitution: An Approach from Historical-Political Sociology', *International Journal of Law in Context* 8(3): 354–93.

Turner, Bryan S., Robyn Rowland, R.W. Connell, Malcolm Waters and J.M. Barbalet (1995). 'Symposium: Human Rights and the Sociological Project', *Journal of Sociology* 31: 1–44.

Vauchez, Antoine (2008a). '"Integration-through-Law": Contribution to a Socio-history of EU Political Commonsense', *EUI Working Papers RSACS 2008/10*.

(2008b). 'The Force of a Weak Field: Law and Lawyers in the Government of the European Union (For a Renewed Research Agenda)', *International Political Sociology* 2: 128–44.

Weber, Max (1921). *Wirtschaft und Gesellschaft. Grundriss der verstehenden Soziologie*. Tübingen: Mohr.

Weiler, Joseph (1991). 'The Transformation of Europe', *The Yale Law Journal* 100: 2403–83.

Weiler, Joseph and Ulrich Haltern (1996). 'The Autonomy of the Community Legal Order: Through the Looking Glass', *Harvard International Law Journal* 37: 411–48.

Williams, Andrew (2011). 'Burying, not Praising the European Convention on Human Rights: A Provocation', in Neil Walker, Jo Shaw and Stephen Tierney (eds). *Europe's Constitutional Mosaic*. Oxford: Hart, pp. 75–96.

Zumbansen, Peer (2006). 'Transnational Law', in Jan Smits (ed.). *Encyclopedia of Comparative Law*. Cheltenham: Edward Elgar, pp. 738–54.

(2010). 'Transnational Legal Pluralism', *Transnational Legal Theory* 1(2): 141–89.

PART I

Legal institutions and European state formation

2

Fascism and European state formation: the crisis of constituent power

CHRIS THORNHILL

2.1 Constitutions, rights and state autonomy

Many European states of the pre-1914 era were either marked by high levels of residual privatism or they in fact remained structurally half-privatistic. That is to say, although by this time European states contained institutions typical of an advanced level of state building, they had not yet fully developed the definitive hallmarks of statehood as a fully differentiated pattern of public order. *Internally*, for instance, many European states struggled to extract a constitutional apparatus of statehood from the day-to-day functions of government. In particular, owing to high levels of patronage and privilege, states were in many cases only weakly qualified to separate public responsibilities from private actors. As a result, they were unable, in differentiated fashion, to project a constitution to facilitate the rotation of office, as part of a public apparatus, between different persons, or even to detach public authority from personal and local monopolies.[1] *Externally*, likewise, many European states of this era remained structurally limited by the remnants of patrimonial authority. In many cases, clientelism was a vital pillar

[1] In Imperial Germany, for example, it is documented that private actors had easy access to government, so that the 'boundaries between private and public interest almost entirely disappeared' (Winkler 1972: 12). Of note in Bismarckian and post-Bismarckian Germany, moreover, was the power of cartels. Germany had a highly cartelized economy (25 per cent of the economy was cartelized by 1907). Cartels, situated originally in the domain of private law, assumed 'half-public character' (Pohl 1979: 230) at the fringes of government. In Spain, public power was sustained through a system of *caciquismo*, in which public offices, especially in localities, were sustained and allocated through privilege and egregious patronage. The term *caciquismo* in fact originates in private relations of feudal vassalage in Latin America. On this, see Tusell (1976: 75); Ortega (1977: 353–4). Similarities to this existed in the governmental strategy of *trasformismo* in Italy initiated in the 1880s and culminating under Giolitti, in which the highest offices were exchanged and secured through private deals.

of state authority at a local level and the general use of power across society was only possible because state power was propped up by private actors in different functional spheres. As a result, state executives, to differing degrees, were porous to disparate private interests, and they were often required to co-ordinate social and economic policy via informal arrangements with select organizations, which formed a highly diffuse and influential political periphery. One consequence of this vestigial inner and outer privatism at the core of European statehood before 1914 was that pre-1914 states were widely marked by *low levels of differentiation and autonomy*.[2] This was manifest in the fact that they depended on private co-operation at a local level, they applied their power in very uneven fashion across territories and gradations of socio-structural status, and, owing to their obligation to powerful private persons, groups

[2] It needs to be noted here that this claim implies a distinct principle for assessing state autonomy. It is often asserted that state autonomy can be measured by the extent to which states are able to act against powerful interest groups, often utilizing social entrenched resources of influence, or by the extent to which states possess capacities of *directiveness* for the mobilization of society. For an established view on state autonomy as the ability of a state to determine its own preferences against societal actors, see Nordlinger (1981: 22). On the state's embeddedness in an international conjuncture as a source of relative autonomy, see Skocpol (1979: 32). On infrastructural power as a sign of state autonomy, see Mann (1984). On autonomy as reflected in the state's directiveness, see Gurr *et al.* (1990: 88). On autonomy and state capacity, see Barkey and Parikh (1991: 526). On autonomy as evident in the state's mobilization of resources, see Gurr (1988: 45); Davidheiser (1992). However, my suggestion here is that we require a simpler and more generic indicator of state autonomy: the most reliable index of state autonomy is whether states contain capacities for utilizing power as a positive and inclusive social phenomenon and, in particular, for amplifying or even generating reserves of power *from within their own internal structure*. This, then, is likely to presuppose that states are capable of holding their own functions at a level of relative internal differentiation, of delineating a political sphere and a set of politicized contents as distinct from the rest of society, and of cementing clear boundaries between what is and what is not essentially political. For the idea that a political system is required to produce power and that modern societies are required to meet inflationary demands for power, and that the relatively autonomous 'differentiation of political power' leads to conditions of advanced social order; see Luhmann (1988: 91). For more extensive discussion of my construction of power, see Thornhill (2010). On this account, state autonomy is normally evident in circumstances where states can include societal actors and exchanges relatively evenly in political power, where they can apply power in approximately uniform fashion across distinctions of status and geography, and – most vitally – they can apply power as an iterable and internally reproducible object: that is, they can *produce sufficient power* to make and enforce decisions without recruiting and being both obligated to and determined by powerful external actors. This condition of state autonomy of necessity means that states can autonomously generate a distinction, in one societal conjuncture, between those exchanges in society that are and those exchanges in society that are not *eminently political*.

and interests, many social exchanges marked by high controversy could not be easily assimilated under state jurisdiction. Of key importance in this respect was taxation: especially inheritance and progressive income tax. In many states, public revenue could only be generated in a very selective manner, and some potential sources of revenue were excluded because of the interest groups which they touched.[3]

The dynamics of constitution writing underlying most European societies in the course of the nineteenth century were integrally related to these problems of state autonomy. Indeed, the incremental implementation of constitutional law in European society throughout the long nineteenth century intimately reflected the tortuous process in which states tentatively evolved towards a condition of public autonomy. It is notable in fact that the rise of constitutional rule in Europe did not involve a simple imposition of a legal order upon states that were already formed, fully constructed, and able to use their power at a high degree of independence. On the contrary, constitution writing formed an intrinsic part of the functional trajectory of state construction in modern Europe, and constitutions played a vital sociological role in gradually enabling societies to overcome potentially destabilizing problems of *weak public authority* and *weak political abstraction and differentiation*. Contrary to more conventional and literal assumptions, constitutional formation did not occur as a simple normative circumscription of the more despotic tendencies in the exercise of monarchical power (Grimm 2001: 183; Bartolini 2005: 162). Instead, constitution writing was an incremental process of political-systemic construction, in which the progressive intensification of constitutional rule elevated the *effective power* of public institutions (see Luhmann 1984: 40). Step-by-step, the process of constitutional formation facilitated a regular and legally ordered co-opting of social actors to extend political power across large distances, it brought about a diminution in the standing of countervailing local actors, and it effected a concentration of political power in delineated institutions. It thus gradually promoted an exclusion of the sources of patrimonial authority obstructing the differentiated consolidation of public institutions, it formed a vital instrument for the de-privatization of public authority, and, above all, it made possible the concerted and regular inclusion of disparate and varied societal actors under the rule of

[3] In Imperial Germany, for example, it was almost impossible effectively to force the aristocracy to pay inheritance tax, and governments that attempted to do so, notably the Bülow bloc (1907–9), were brought to collapse (Witt 1970: 272–3).

law. European constitution making, in consequence, can be seen as an objective sociological or socio-functional process, in which the boundaries of state power were progressively structured and rendered consistent, actors using political power were able to pre-determine the conditions under which they utilized power, and private groups were prevented from obtaining and isolating for themselves large volumes of power. In each respect, constitution making was central to the formation of the state as a part of an abstract, differentiated and relatively autonomous political domain in society.

Of fundamental significance in the sociological status of constitutions as institutions promoting state formation and rising state autonomy is the relation between *constituent power* and *constitutional rights*. Indeed, the connection between constituent power and rights is crucial for the comprehension of the abstractive and politically consolidating function of constitutions more generally. To explain this point, it is necessary briefly to consider the conceptual position of constituent power in constitutional theory, and to elucidate this concept in light of its specific functions within the political system and its functional resonance for society as a whole.

Classical theories of constitutionalism are typically underscored by an antinomy between *constituent power* and *constitutional rights*. That is, it is widely claimed in constitutional theory that constitutions originate through primary acts of constituent power, which is activated in a distinctively *pre-legal* space, so that the decisions of the constituent power, categorically prior to all other objective norms, generate the legal order by which the people is subsequently, in its most essential public dispositions, constituted and obligated.[4] On this account, constitutional rights belong to the *constituted* elements of the polity, and their binding status depends on the fact that they give expression to non-derogable elements of the original will of the people, so that, as such, they can be invoked to limit subsequent pursuit of popular interest. This notion of constituent power gathered impetus in the first wave of revolutionary constitution writing in America after 1776, and it assumed consummate expression in the first months of the French Revolution.[5]

[4] See the formulations in Carré de Malberg (1920–22: 490–1); Schmitt (1928: 76).

[5] The theory of constituent power was spelled out by Sieyès in and after 1789. But this theory was already quite clear in *Federalist* 53, where Madison made the key distinction between 'a Constitution established by the people and unalterable by the government, and a law established by the government and alterable by the government' (Madison *et al.* 1987 [1787–88]: 327).

Subsequently, the emergence of constituent power was widely reflected as a defining formulaic caesura between pre-modern and modern societies and pre-modern and modern conceptions of legitimate political authority. In contemporary constitutional discourse, constituent power is commonly invoked as an irreducible norm to capture both the legitimacy of the constitution and other institutions in the polity, and the founding political self-comprehension of modern society more widely. Indeed, the concept of constituent power, to a greater extent than rights or other determinate legal norms, is often envisioned as tracing in broad strokes the basic emancipatory, self-legislative logic of modern socio-political order.[6]

If observed from a more sociological perspective, however, this primary formula of modern politics – that is, the normative image of constituent power as the original *alegal* source of all legitimate order – appears rather paradoxical. In fact, it can be observed from the outset that the space of constituent power never conformed to its dominant theoretical description. Constituent power was always subject to prior legal constraint and pre-formation. Constituent power became a formative political principle, not as a *pre-juridical* source of norms, but precisely in consequence of its *internally juridical* configuration.

To give support to this claim, on one hand, in the period before the founding of the first revolutionary constitutions between 1776 and 1791, in which constituent power initially became active,[7] rights had already begun pervasively to shape, to determine, and to subject to certain conceptual constraints, the demands of actors assuming entitlement to constituent authority.[8] Historically, in fact, the principle of constituent power was suffused with rights before it was first expressed or even theoretically envisaged. In the revolutions at the origins of contemporary societal structure, it was never considered possible that the exercise of constituent power could occur *without a deep inner juridical reference to rights*: to exercise constituent power meant, in principle, to exercise claims over rights. In revolutionary America, for example, the impulse

6 Dieter Grimm for example sees the distinctive novelty of constitutional law as residing in the fact that it binds 'the power of the state in legally obligatory fashion' to recognize certain principles (2001: 83).

7 Note though that the English Convention Parliament in 1688 was also by any reasonable definition a bearer of constituent power (Pincus 2009: 283–6).

8 This was especially the case in America, where rights were already articulated as a defence of colonial liberties within the transatlantic constitution. See on this point Reid (2003: 4); Bradburn (2009: 27–9).

towards the formative exercise of constituent power was shaped by a demand for subjective rights as instruments to resist the perceived depredatory taxes imposed by the British parliament. In this context, constituent power was built around a contested assertion of rights in cases in which particular laws or court rulings were perceived as repugnant to an inherited British common-law ideal of constitutional inviolability, habitually explicated in a vocabulary of rights. The first elementary space of constituent power, which evolved as the American colonies split apart from Britain, was not lastly the outcome of the fact that judicial actors insisted on rights to query and invalidate imperial edicts. The logic of rebellion against the Stamp Act and other coercive statutes, in consequence, was expressed, typically through courts of law, as justified by strict and demonstrable rights (Rakove 1999: 1940). The resultant logic of *constituent assembly*, in which claimants to rights began to found new centres of government in different British colonies, was motivated by similar principles (Amar 1998: 29, 122).[9] In France, analogously, the impulse towards the revolutionary assertion of constituent power after 1789 was shaped by a widespread demand for equal juridical entitlements, abrogating the uneven and highly privileged rights structure of the *ancien régime*. Although rights had less formative importance in revolutionary France than in America, the norm of shared and equal rights in law impelled the assault on singular and corporate legal privilege which first gave rise to the idea of republican sovereignty and constituent power in the summer months of 1789 (Sieyès 1839 [1789]: 45).[10]

Notably, in fact, in these revolutionary settings rights did more than simply open the political landscape for the exercise of constituent power. In addition, rights immediately began to act as institutes that curtailed the extent and potency, and pre-defined the substance, of constituent power, and they placed strict limits both on the procedures for the activation of constituent power and the selection of those persons entitled to exercise it.[11] In revolutionary America, at one level, bills of

[9] The Declaration of Independence itself stated that if any 'Form of Government becomes destructive' it is 'the Right of the People to alter it and abolish it, and to institute new Government'.

[10] For the social background to the use of rights in the French Revolution, in which singular subjective rights were applied to eliminate collective corporate rights, see Fitzsimmons (2010: 11).

[11] On anxiety about the revolutionary potency of constituent power amongst members of the Federal Convention see Rakove (1997: 107).

rights were proclaimed (in Virginia and other states in and after 1776) before the main constitutional documents of the revolution were drafted.[12] This meant that the content of the leading constitutional texts was to some degree pre-formulated by rights. Moreover, the principle was established in America well before 1787, albeit in highly inchoate fashion, that judiciaries applying norms derived from rights could assume power to review legislative acts of parliaments, and even to reduce the scope of constituent power.[13] Before the Federal Convention was convoked, it was accepted that some norms, standing above or prior to specific acts of constituent power, were subject to singularly elevated constitutional extraction, and the principle that acts of constituent power were exposed to implicit rights-based filtration had been clearly sanctioned (at least in inchoate manner). Then, after the passing of the Judiciary Act in 1789, the introduction of the Bill of Rights in 1791, and the ensuing controversy over judicial competence in 1803, the power of actors in the state assuming custody of rights was increased.[14] In particular, although this is of course a matter of wide and intense dispute, rights were often implemented in America after 1789 as institutions designed to prevent the dramatic re-articulation of constituent power, and to obviate or mollify conflicts likely to provoke a fundamental re-examination of the Federal Constitution.[15] In each of these respects, rights stood in for, pre-defined, and they in many respects *effectively enacted*, constituent power.

This integral nexus between rights and constituent power in founding-era America provided a vital source of legitimacy for the nascent federal state. The fact that, in the early republic, the rights-based constitution was, to some degree at least, placed in the custody of the courts acted, albeit dialectically, to construct and maintain within the state a reference to constituent power as the deepest foundation of political authority,

[12] The Virginia Bill of Rights has signal importance in this debate. It was adopted over two weeks prior to the Virginian Constitution of 1776 and in many respects formed a separate document (Rakove 1997: 307).

[13] See most notably Gerber (2011: 93, 204, 222). Both historically and in contemporary politics in the United States, the power of judicial review is of course highly contested (Tarr 1998: 76–7).

[14] I find little evidence to sustain the common view that *Marbury v. Madison* established judicial review. It was already provided for by the Judiciary Act, and had antecedents in state legislation. In agreement see Graber (2003: 610–12); Treanor (2005: 457, 473).

[15] The Bill of Rights was enacted in 1791 as a means, not lastly, to avoid renewed convention in Philadelphia. See Maier (2010: 285, 295, 421, 444); Amar (1998: 289).

so that constituent power remained a symbolically *live* source of legitimacy in particular acts of legislation. That is to say, the fact that the constitution incorporated a strong judiciary able to subject laws to second-order judicial review *in respect of rights* meant that a perennial image of constituent power was conserved or enshrined within the political system.[16] The idea of the constituent people as an aggregate of rights holders was stabilized at the core of the political system, and it could be constantly invoked to authorize new statutes. The result of this was that, in concrete statutory acts, the political system was able constantly to reach beyond the factually existing *electoral people* demanding particular laws or particular policies, and to justify its laws by claiming to derive founding legitimacy from the *constituent people* itself, represented in the normative guardianship of the courts.[17] This meant that judicial actors were able, to all intents and purposes, to position themselves within the political system in a location situated *between* constituted and constituent power, and the state could mine from resources of judicially prepared and conserved constituent power (attached to rights), which the courts purported to represent and make available for the state.[18] This meant in turn that the political system as a whole acquired heightened legitimacy for new laws through reference to an internally devised projection of its constituent source (the constituent people *qua* rights holders), and courts were used to symbolize the constant presence of the original people, the primary constituent corpus, as a recurrently authorizing premise for single acts of legislation. Above

[16] It is typically argued that, because the Bill of Rights was not incorporated in state legislation until the passing of the Fourteenth Amendment, the post-founding Supreme Court did not apply rights as basis for review (Lewis and Trichter 1981; Stone Sweet 2008: 230: Maier 2010: 463–4). It seems to me that this misses the vital point that the constitution in its entirety was seen by the founders as expressing rights. The system of review established under the Judiciary Act was quite clearly meant as rights review in a generic sense, including, but not exclusive to, enforcement of the Amendments passed in 1791. Note John Marshall's comments on *Marbury v. Madison*: 'But where a specific duty is assigned by law, and individual rights depend upon the performance of that duty, it seems equally clear that the individual who considers himself injured, has a right to resort to the laws of his country for a remedy' (Hobson and Teute 1990: 174).

[17] Building on Hamilton's famous earlier argument in *Federalist* 78, Marshall argued that the Supreme Court spoke for the 'original and supreme will' of the constitution (Hobson and Teute 1990: 182). For excellent related comment, see Patterson (1949: 451); Eijsbouts (2010: 219).

[18] This is of course vehemently disputed by opponents of judicial review, who typically argue for constituted democratic will formation against courts. For a small sample, see Tushnet (1999: 9); Kramer (2004: 233).

all, the judicial dimension of the new American Republic after 1789 meant that, in referring to those from whom it derived power as an aggregate of *rights holders*, the state could reproduce its laws through society as endlessly reflecting the needs of, and strictly proportioned to, the people in that pre-defined quality. Rights thus implanted a static formula of constituent power inside the political system. This formula was then ceaselessly summoned or in fact subliminally instilled within the medium of power itself in order to support, differentiate and give plausibility to single acts of legislation.

The relation between rights and constituent power in revolutionary France was marked by partial contrast with the early American Republic. In France, of course, the Declaration of the Rights of Man was completed two years before the first constitution. However, in France, the final distinction between constituent and constituted power was not settled until after 1795. Early revolutionary parliaments continued to act in essence as constituent assemblies in permanent session,[19] so that the juridical restriction of constituent power was notably weaker than in America. Moreover, in France the revolution as a whole expressed a vehement dislike of autonomous judicial power, which was observed as a corrosive remnant of corporate particularism,[20] acting to fracture the legitimate will of the state. The periods of most intense revolutionary upheaval were thus infused with a strong Rousseau-inspired scepticism on the part of legislators towards antecedent or constitutionally external norms, including rights. Despite this, nonetheless, throughout revolutionary-era France, rights retained the capacity to shape acts of constituent power. In the constitutions of 1791 and 1795, rights were clearly invoked as devices to pre-define and selectively to assimilate the legitimating force of constituent power.[21] It was only in the highly exceptionalist period of intensified Jacobin rule that rights were not admitted as objective checks on the political presence of constituent power (see Halperin 1987).

Beneath its typical constructions in constitutional theory, in consequence, constituent power first became politically formative in modern societies in a form that was inextricably *conjoined* with rights. If observed sociologically, the classical separation of constituent and constituted power is not tenable:

[19] This was acknowledged by Sieyès (17–: 97).

[20] See as background Carré (1912: 201); Badinter (1989: 19); Burdeau (1995: 47); Lafon (2001: 102).

[21] In 1795 Sieyès even advocated the creation of a constitutional jury to oversee legislation.

rights always pre-constituted constituent power. In fact, if, following the pattern of analysis proposed above, constitutions are viewed as instruments of differentiation and abstraction acting inside the political system, the antinomy between rights and constituent power appears singularly redundant. If constitutions are approached from a functionalist standpoint, it is no exaggeration to suggest that the common separation of constituent power and rights obscures the most fundamental sociological dimension of constitutionalism, and the interdependence of rights and constituent power needs to be appreciated as the central mainspring of modern constitutional rule. It was the intense inner configuration of rights and constituent power that, as described above, first enabled constitutions to play their formative role in abstracting society's political domain. It was the formal coalescence of rights and constituent power that underscored the emergence of the modern state as an aggregate of institutions endowed with a certain degree of structural autonomy. The rise in state power, which was promoted by constitutional formation in general terms, was most specifically and distinctively induced by the functional interrelation of these two concepts.

These interlinked functions of constitutional rights and constituent power in contributing to the early abstraction and autonomy of modern society's political domain became manifest in several different ways. In each respect, however, the convergence of these concepts formed a more general functional template for the organization of the modern political system as a differentiated and autonomous arena.

First, the fact that revolutionary constitutions were formed by constituent actors constrained by rights and that constitutional laws were assigned legitimacy by virtue of their consonance with prior rights norms dramatically simplified the state's ability to apply power in abstract, positive fashion across society. The fact that under most post-1789 constitutions laws intrinsically referred to rights as their inner founding justification meant that the political system, once centred around a constitution, incorporated an internal construction of its legitimating source in reference to which it was able, relatively simply, to support and authorize its laws at a high level of stability against external variations. This construction endowed the state with highly positive and flexible legislative powers, and it greatly alleviated the generalized use of power across the increasingly varied terrains of modern, differentiated society. The reference to rights thus imprinted a vital residual store of legitimacy within the legal apparatus: this simultaneously reduced the volume of legitimacy which states were required to produce and consume in the application of single laws, and it internally simplified the justification and transmission of particular laws through society. In fact, as discussed, the reference to rights meant that states explained themselves as applying power to persons who were already internally reflected, *qua* rights holders, in the structure of power, and who thus received power from the state as *their own power*.[22] This also greatly augmented the facility with which power could be explicated and distributed across the structurally varied environments of society.

Second, the internal relation of constituent power and rights meant that the number of activities throughout society which needed to be constructed as specifically relevant for the state's legitimacy was restricted. That is to say, the fact that the state projected itself as *constituted by a people willing rights* meant that the exchanges in society defined by rights were invariably vindicated, authorized and essentially depoliticized: activities covered, for instance, by rights of economic freedom, rights of free speech, rights of autonomous scientific endeavour, rights of aesthetic self-expression, etc., were removed from the intense cycles of politicization around the state, and the actions of persons in pursuit of such rights were not constantly expressed through the state, and they only rarely required exercise of state jurisdiction.[23] This meant that the state was able to attach its legitimacy only to a rather limited and strictly defined set of objectives, and, although declaring itself as legitimized by an expansive *pouvoir constituant*, the state was able to curtail the volume of society's exchanges and conflicts needing to be directly legitimized by this power.[24] Rights pre-selected the dimensions of social exchange assuming relevance for the state and requiring legitimacy produced by the state. Although symbolically present as the foundation of the state, thus, constituent power did not need to be invoked in many acts of law, and the mass of exchanges authorized specifically by such power was internally diminished. Through rights, constituent power was located symbolically *within* the state. Yet the factual bearers of constituent power (the people in their manifold social activities) were always held *outside*

[22] For example, Kant (1976 [1797]: 569) argued that the source of the state's autonomy and legitimacy was its recognition of persons as endowed with rights: in particular, the right to be treated in accordance with rationally generalizable principles. In applying law to persons as rights holders, the state could automatically account for itself and each of its laws as generally legitimate, and rights could be used to authorize laws for all people and in all social locations.

[23] For background to this conception, see Luhmann (1965: 135).

[24] In France, notably, Sieyès applied Adam Smith's conception of the division of labour to activities and membership of constituent bodies, so reserving their powers for specialized elites (Sieyès 17–: 138–9).

the state, and the extent to which the state was expected to channel an amorphous factual will through state institutions was radically reduced. Indeed, through reference to rights, the state was able precisely to define the exchanges in which constituent power needed to be invoked and consumed.

As a result, third, the configuration of constituent power and rights meant that nascent modern states were able to define themselves as relatively indifferent to controversy over specifically private exchanges, and they excluded many private conflicts (in all but *exceptional* cases) from the centre of state power. This meant that private actors, or actors asserting private rights, progressively lost the capacity to infiltrate state power and to render state power porous to private interests, which had debilitated statehood in the course of its pre-revolutionary or pre-constitutional formation.

In sum, the fusion of constituent power and rights spelled out in post-1789 constitutions produced the dialectical form underlying the functional emergence of modern society's political system as a relatively autonomous arena of exchange. The basic structure of the state as both *inclusive and expansive* in respect of its legitimation yet also *exclusive and selective* in respect of its functional reach and its practical obligations was elaborated on this conceptual foundation. This structure obtained its first articulation in the constitutional revolutions of the late eighteenth century. Yet, with many variations, it remained fundamental to the interrelated processes of state building and constitution making that persisted through the nineteenth century and beyond. At the very centre of the fusion of these concepts was the fact that the intersection of rights and constituent power meant that the state could authorize laws as immediate expressions of constituent power, although constituent power always remained a managed, internally controlled and in fact *factually absent* commodity within the political system.

2.2 World War I and the material constituent power

Despite the state-building impetus of early constitutional concepts, by 1914 neither the process of state building nor the process of constitution writing underlying the differentiated form of modern European societies had approached completion. In the decades before 1914, as discussed, many European states had not concluded their formation as strictly public orders, and they only possessed constitutions enabling them to utilize political power at a relatively low level of differentiated autonomy and inner abstraction. Most distinctively, most European states remained marked by structural weaknesses (high internal privatism, and low autonomy) precisely because they had struggled to balance the dialectical elements of rights and constituent power, which had originally surfaced as a template for political autonomy in classical revolutionary constitutions. On one hand, for instance, few European constitutions in the age of high Imperialism effectively enshrined constituent power as a principle of legitimacy. Instead of this, they founded their public order in half-imposed ultra-positivistic constitutions, designed marginally to placate proto-democratic movements in society without enshrining full popular accountability for the political system. These constitutions generally provided sediment for a political order based in a fragile accord between private privilege and public obligation at the core of the state. Even the more democratic states, such as France and, to a lesser degree, the United Kingdom (UK), had failed to generate a constitutional order founded in constituent power, and they had opted either for thinly positivistic (France 1875) or gradualistic/organic constitutional orders (UK 1832, 1867, 1884). On the other hand, the constitutions implemented in the age of high Imperialism typically either weakened the content of rights developed in earlier processes of constitution making, or they contained no catalogue of rights at all. This formed part of a strategic attempt, in softened Bonapartist style, to guarantee aggregates of private rights in order dualistically to detach the thin edifice of the state administration from the sphere of private exchange and private antagonism, and so to harden the state executive against potential destabilization caused by its internalization of societal conflicts.[25] Earlier revolutionary constitutions, thus, had acted generally to promote state autonomy (that is, to generate positively usable, differentiated, and inclusive reserves of political power within existing states). In contrast, the constitutions of the later nineteenth century adopted a model of statehood, based in a deep compromise between personalistic and inclusive processes for the production and concentration of political power, which fostered a weak and weakly differentiated model of statehood, in which state power interlocked haphazardly with private agency in society. This was in no small part conditioned by the fact that such states opted only for a deeply depleted construction of rights and constituent power.

The European constitutional landscape, however, was fundamentally and irreversibly transformed by World War I. The years 1914–1918 saw a

[25] The Savoyard Constitution of 1848 and the Spanish Constitution of 1876 contained limited provisions for rights. The German Constitution of 1871 and the French Constitution of 1875 contained no separate catalogue of rights.

far-reaching and entirely unprecedented expansion in the functions of statehood, and they witnessed a dramatic intensification of the institutional contours of the state. In many respects, it was only between 1914 and 1918 that the classical Weberian idea of state formation as a process in which one group of institutional actors obtained full and conclusive territorial control began to become reality. On one hand, the years of warfare saw an increase in the public/inclusionary functions of the state, as states assumed a primary role in mobilizing industrial production and controlling employment and import policies relevant to the war effort. In particular, the war years witnessed a dramatic growth in the amount of revenue transacted through the state, as states were forced exponentially to raise levels of taxation and other borrowing to fund military activities.[26] One outcome of this, clearly, was an exponential growth of the administrative capacities of the state and an increase in the dimensions of public authority: the inclusionary capacities of the state increased beyond all precedent between 1914 and 1918. On the other hand, however, the war also had the consequence that in extending the inclusionary apparatus of the state it led to a significant lowering of *the threshold of the political*. That is, in order to sustain its newly assigned administrative and distributive functions, the state was forced to negotiate with previously marginalized bargaining organs (i.e. trade unions, socialist parties, big-business delegations), and it began immediately to co-opt multiple private and economic actors into its periphery. In consequence of this, the political system, its primary objectives dictated by war, was forced to define itself to a large degree as an arbitrational mediator in conflicts traditionally construed as pertaining to the private sphere – usually in conflicts over conditions of industrial production and mobilization for the war effort. The ability of the state to perform its designated obligations thus increasingly depended on the manifold brokering of private agreements and the expansionary widening of the state periphery to intersect with private organizations positioned on different sides of the military/industrial production process.[27]

[26] The statistics provide quite startling evidence of this revolutionary transformation of state activity. It is only possible to give an illustrative sense of this. In France, however, public spending increased from 10 to 50 per cent of GDP in the war (Hautcoeur 2005: 183). In the UK, by 1918 two-thirds of all employees were directly or indirectly employed by the state (Tawney 1943: 3). Moreover, in some countries (Germany and France) only around 2 per cent of war expenditures was covered by revenue (Forsyth 1993: 69).

[27] This is discussed in individual cases below. But for general analysis see the classic account in Maier (1975: 19–87).

As a result of these two over-layered processes, World War I created a new and wholly distinctive *constitutional conjuncture* in most European societies. The war articulated a paradox of constitutional design, which stands at the beginning of, and still overshadows, the structure of contemporary statehood. Following the age of classical constitutionalism (1776–1791 or – arguably – 1776–1848) and the age of imperial constitutionalism (1848–ca.1900), 1914 marked the beginning of a distinctive *third wave* of constitution writing, whose implications were far more transformative and revolutionary and far more complex than those of earlier patterns of constitutional formation.[28] Most obviously, the war dramatically increased the density in the public apparatus of the state, it augmented the mass of societal exchanges requiring political legislation, and – commensurately – it intensified the need for a constitution to support the expansionary co-ordinating autonomy of the state. In these respects, the war induced an accelerated constitutional revolution, which perpetuated and intensified the sociological functions of classical constitutions in underpinning state power as a system of inclusion and societal control. Yet, at a different level, the war also contained constitutional implications that cut against the primary abstractive tendency of classical constitutionalism. The war also led to the intensified formation of European states around an internally privatistic political structure, in which disparately convergent elements of public/private order were haphazardly integrated into and stabilized within the political system. In most countries, these processes of integration were sustained in the years of combat through a coercive climate of social cohesion, in which military adversity and its ideological dimensions allowed governing elites to assume counterfactual social unity, and to paper over divergent interests and class fissures in their subordinate constituencies. In many settings, moreover, these processes of integration were bolstered by additional rafts of prerogative labour-market legislation.[29] Indeed, the expanded war-time state apparatus was typically held together by the almost untrammelled use of emergency powers and the widespread

[28] I agree here with Orlando, Prime Minister of Italy in 1918, who described the war 'as the greatest political and social revolution history records' (quoted from Wrigley 1990: 13). This view remains accurate today.

[29] Major examples are the Munitions of War Acts in the UK (1915–17), the Auxiliary Service law in Germany of 1916, and the Military-Economic Enabling Law in Austria. Italy and France also witnessed similar prerogative attempts to stabilize labour conflicts and introduce conditions close to industrial conscription. On the series of emergency laws introduced in the UK see the contemporary commentary in Lester (1919).

reliance on only thinly checked executive authority. None of this could obscure the fact, however, that the accelerated rise in public power after 1914 was purchased through a profoundly uneasy incorporation of private actors and organizations. In effect, post-1914 constitutionalism led at once to a rapid extension of state power and to an implicit dissipation of the (already precarious) reserves of public autonomy that states had hitherto acquired through their constitutional formation.

In this respect, World War I marked, paradoxically, both a culmination and a contradiction in the conjoined process of constitution writing and state building, which had shaped the structural form of European societies through the nineteenth century. Between 1914 and 1918, states underwent a quite radically expedited process of concentration and expansion, which promoted the growth of states as repositories of autonomous public authority. As discussed, classically, the rise in public power had originally been organized through a conceptual design based in a fusion of constituent power and rights, which acted to abstract the state against its residual privatism and to harden the state against claims for social inclusion that could not easily be politicized. As discussed, further, most pre-1914 European states realized only highly attenuated versions of this design, and their constitutional construction as fully public orders remained partial and truncated. At one level, clearly, the previous processes of constitutional formation culminated in World War I: the war gave rise to an intensified dynamic of constitutional formation to support the extended functions of the public domain and the higher levels of societal penetration assumed by state organizations. At a different level, however, under the conjuncture described above, the war stimulated an alternative pattern for the formation of public power, bearing only distorted resemblance to previous constitutional models. This can be characterized as follows. In the war, first, a constitutional structure emerged in which many classical rights were weak: many civil and political rights (including rights of freedom of movement, freedom of labour, freedom of contract, and political expression) were widely suspended through prerogative laws aimed to regulate industrial conscription and military mobilization. Yet, second, material rights (including rights of contract protection, trade-union delegation, and well-being at work) were subject to a rapid and far-reaching consolidation and entrenchment: states, owing to their dependence on organized labour for military production, were transformed into organs of corporate integration, required to purchase support for the war by establishing favourable production and bargaining conditions for the labour force, by assuming adjudicative functions in industrial conflict, and so by absorbing originally private actors and organizations as bearers of actionable private/material rights. To this degree, between 1914 and 1918 the classical function of rights in regulating the integration of societal exchanges in the state was inverted: rights began to act, not as organs of sensibly measured systemic exclusion, but as organs of programmatic political inclusion.

On these grounds, the transformation of constitutional order after 1914 meant that the principle of constituent power, which had remained under-elaborated in most European societies before 1914, became a dramatically pervasive constitutional formula within most European states. After the outbreak of hostilities, states began to draw legitimacy from their rapid incorporation of a diffuse constituent power, expressing its will through numerous half-public/half-private bargaining associations, focused largely on demands for material rights, and channelled through somewhat *ad hoc* and legally unstructured processes of material inclusion. Most notable in this was the fact that the war deeply unsettled the functional relation between constituent power and rights. In classical constitutionalism, as discussed, constituent power became politically constitutive as a juridically pre-constructed founding force, whose demands were controlled and moderated by the constraining force of limited civil and political rights. By contrast, in World War I constituent power became active within the state specifically through intensified collective claims over private/material rights. Through this, in fact, the state lost its defining ability, by virtue of rights, to moderate the extent of its internalization of constituent power. This meant that in World War I the deeply dialectical fabric of inclusion and exclusion at the centre of modern constitutionalism and its functions of political abstraction and consolidation was recast. As a result, states, rapidly transformed from their pre-1914 legal-state minimalism, were *saturated with constituent power*, which, often articulated in highly erratic and privatistic fashion, they were forced by their recognition of positive/programmatic rights to assimilate as a constantly active source of legitimacy.

To summarize, World War I stimulated a rapid, far-reaching and deeply revolutionary constitutional experiment. Pre-1914 constitutions had assumed legitimacy for their power on the basis of abstracted representation and rather thin processes of rights-based legal inclusion, in which rights holders were observed from within the state as singular generic persons. In contrast, states established in World War I began to conceive their legitimacy as a result of their *total inclusion* of the citizen, in which rights holders were defined, through party, professional or class affiliation, as collective persons, entitled to demand incessant, societally encompassing, *quasi-plebiscitary* incorporation in the nervous system of the state (see Smend 1968 [1928]: 182). Tellingly, this re-designing of state legitimacy in World War I found its most condensed expression in a transformation of the rights-fabric of constitutional law, and it had at its centre a conversion of the classical form of singular subjective rights into group rights or programmatic objective rights. In the period 1914–18, the dominant principle of public law switched from inclusion of the citizen as holder of series of private formal rights situated outside the state to inclusion of the citizen as holder of private material rights situated within state. The private yet collective material will of citizens, in short, became the inner constituent legitimating basis for the state, and the legitimate exercise of state power became conditional on the state's ability to internalize and reconcile, through material rights, the private interests of citizens in their quality as members of objective social groups and organizations. This meant that the state internalized those practical and volitional dimensions of society that it had previously, through subjective rights, been able to hold outside its own structure. Indeed, given its internal obligation to these stratified interests, the state committed itself constitutionally to represent a constituent power which was *collectively organized* and *endlessly active* within the political system, and whose force could not be mollified or eradicated from constituted power through the force of rights.

This deep war-time re-direction at the centre of constitutional law did not come to an end in 1918. On the contrary, after 1918, a number of processes came together to ensure that it was still further accentuated. First, the war-time transformation of constitutional law was intensified through the staggered crisis of international capitalism, beginning in 1918 and continuing effectively until after 1945. At the onset of this crisis, states, in the process of demobilizing vast military populations, were exposed to deeply destabilizing industrial conflicts, and as a result they were – to a large degree – expected to sustain policies of material integration established in the war: they were unable to reduce the expectations fermented in the war in respect of collective rights and social and material inclusion.[30] The transformation of constitutional law was then further heightened, second, by the fact that the early stages of

[30] Though for an alternative view see Tawney (1943).

the economic crisis were overshadowed by the threat of widespread Bolshevik-style revolution. This meant that states not opting for the Bolshevik brand of state capitalism tried to purchase support from their constituencies, often in an atmosphere of high alarm about their revolutionary preferences, by pursuing redistributive strategies of material compensation. The result of both these facts was that the constitutional model of war-time political economy and expansionary yet pluralistic public/private inclusion was carried over into, and had to be functionally adjusted to, the conditions of peace. Owing to high levels of industrial agitation after 1918, the states emerging from World War I were compelled to retain the private/collectivistic constituent basis formed in the period of conflict. That is, they could not exclude trade unions and other private parties from bargaining positions in trilateral economic negotiating frameworks, and, in many cases, they even devolved responsibilities for producing statutes to corporate actors in the economic arena. In particular, however, post-1918 European states were obliged to give more permanent constitutional formality to the conditions in which they pursued inclusion of material constituent power during the war. After armistice, the invocation of military necessity and the use of prerogative laws to bring cohesion to private war-time corporate alliances could not be used enduringly to sustain the constitutional system of material pluralism. Consequently, states confronted the paradoxical problem that they were required to found themselves in private material arrangements, yet also constitutionally to translate these arrangements into a distinctively *public and political will*, able to solidify the pluralistic foundations of post-war statehood in a solidified and normatively robust fashion. Indeed, states were widely expected to assimilate war-time patterns of economic management into an autonomous constituent force, capable of elevating the state above the pluralistic arena of private/material protagonists, from which it drew legitimacy (see pp. 51–55 below).

In consequence, as Benjamin Constant might well have appreciated, the dominant constitutional system of post-1918 Europe reflected a perpetuation of the pattern of *military constitutionalism* instituted in the war.[31] This system was founded in a substructure of unfiltered and immediately articulated constituent power, which was not differentiated or abstracted against its private/material origins and could not easily be

[31] Constant saw Jacobinism as militarized constitutionalism, unsuitable for large societies (1997 [1819]). The same might be said of post-1918 constitutionalism.

represented or even contained in the state. This constituent power was evident, on one hand, in the fact that post-1918 constitutions were typically based in a direct and vertical relation between legislative and executive institutions. This meant that horizontal counterweights to the transfusion of power through the political system were weak, and the volume of power condensed in executives was high (see Mirkine-Guetzevitch 1950: 608). This was expressed in the presidential bias of many post-1918 constitutions. Most particularly, this constituent power was evident in the fact that most constitutions after 1918 imagined states as deriving legitimacy through their corporate inclusion of a dynamic and multi-layered social will, or even through their recognition of a *society as a whole* as an endlessly active material constituent body, whose constitution-building power remained permanently alive within the constituted state structure as a result of its claims to material rights and material incorporation.[32]

2.3 The crisis of state autonomy: patterns of reaction to the military constitution

The ability of European states to cement strong material foundations for their power by integrating, as their constituent base, the diffuse volitional associations assuming organizational power in the war presupposed both a high level of structural hardness in state institutions and a high level of state integrity and autonomy. As discussed, however, in 1914, most European states possessed only low or moderate levels of state autonomy, and most were compelled during the war to build up their integrative functions from a pre-1914 position of partial privatism, uncertain internal density, and low autonomy. In consequence, the defining constitutional challenge of interwar Europe revolved around the fact that states were required, from a basis of internal diffuseness and low structural integrity, to secure and display legitimacy through the public solidification of a live, pluralistically volatile, and unfiltered constituent power, articulated through often antagonistic material demands. Interwar Europe was politically dominated by a series of divergent responses to this defining constitutional challenge. Across Europe, this challenge

[32] This was exemplified in particular by the constitutional writings of Hugo Sinzheimer, who, as one of the drafters of the German constitution of 1919, defined state legitimacy as derived through the gradual transposition of civil society, in its political and material dimensions, into the state (Sinzheimer 1916: 35).

formed the basic sociological determinant of statehood after 1918. The fashion in which states responded constitutionally to this conjuncture was vital for their future stability. Indeed, the pattern of reaction to this challenge defined the structural landscape of different European societies from 1918 until 1945.

The next sections of this chapter are intended to examine different lines of constitutional reaction amongst European states both to the socio-material constellation and to the legal/legitimatory expectations created by World War I. In this regard, the analyses below attempt to complement and extend existing sociological paradigms for examining and explaining the rise of fascism.[33] Distinctively, these analyses offer principles for the analysis of fascism from the perspective of *constitutional sociology*. That is to say that, on one hand, the remainder of this chapter, using the framework proposed above, accounts for constitutions as reflexive instruments within the political system, whose primary function, as discussed, is to enable a political system to construct its reserves of power at a level of sustainable abstraction and to preserve its autonomy in a form adapted to an objective societal constellation. Therefore, it rejects the classical sociological suggestion that constitutions are mere formal elements of a political superstructure with little bearing on society as a whole.[34] It argues that, as mechanisms of state autonomy, constitutions are vitally implicated in the cohesion of society as a whole. On the other hand, however, in the sections below fascism is interpreted as a political phenomenon both involving and resulting from a sequence of *sui generis* constitutional crises, and the causes of the widespread transition to authoritarianism (be this in the form of pure fascism, semi-fascism, clerico-fascism, or National Socialism), which featured in many European societies in the 1920s and 1930s, are examined (in part) as the result of malfunctions and adaptive problems

[33] The dominant sociological patterns of analysis challenged here might include Marxist accounts of fascism as class hegemony or as a 'conjuncture of class struggle' (Poulantzas 1974); Parsonian analysis of fascism as resulting from dominant patterns of social structure or 'imperfect structural integration' (Parsons 1942: 144; Gerhardt 1996: 306); analysis of socio-demographic profiles of fascist sympathizers (see, classically, Lipset 1963: 149; and, in general, Muhlberger 1980); analysis of societal cleavages as preconditions of fascism in the manner of Lipset and Rokkan; analysis of fascism as a response to 'problems of modernization' (Mann 2004: 353). Instead of these approaches, this chapter proposes an analysis of fascism that observes fascism as a critical condition of the political system of society itself, and it approaches the pathologies attached to fascism as distinctive problems regarding the production of political power.

[34] Most obviously see Marx (1958–68 [1844]).

in the constitutional apparatus of society. From this perspective, in particular, fascism is analysed as a social phenomenon occurring within a societal constellation marked at once by constitutional failure and, resultantly, by low state autonomy. This leads to the claim that the emergence of fascism found propitious preconditions in constitutional systems not capable of engendering adequate degrees of autonomy in the political system. This approach to fascism views fascism, in a manner more typical of pure legal analysis, as a primarily constitutional disorder or pathology. As such, however, it proposes the more strictly sociological claim that fascism emerged as a phenomenon reflecting the failure of the political system of a society, in one given conjuncture, to find a manageable legal construction to abstract and to utilize its political power as a societally differentiated and internally autonomous medium.

2.3.1 Britain and France

After 1918, Britain and France possessed states that managed to adapt to the inclusionary pressures generated by the war without a full constitutional transformation, and they reacted to the war and its aftermath by intensifying capacities for autonomous inclusion and institutional construction already formed before 1914. Both states experienced quasi-corporate expansion in the war: that is, both witnessed government by emergency laws, the co-opting of unions into the political process, and a resultant dramatic increase in state-sector density.[35] However, both were able after 1918 to adjust to this expansion within the constraints of an existing constitutional order, and on the basis of existing reserves of state autonomy. One key cause of this relatively high level of adaptive autonomy which the state possessed in these societies was that liberalism or republicanism had emerged as a politically integrative movement by the middle of the nineteenth century. As a result, in both Britain and France, liberalism or a broadly equivalent doctrine of middle-class integrationism had exercised powerful cross-class force before Marxism developed as a strong ideology. This meant that, by 1900, liberalism had been able to create an (albeit strained) collaborative working framework between the more moderate aspects of the labour movement and

[35] See on this Lorwin (1954: 50); Middlemas (1979: 151); Horne (1991: 15); Turner (1992: 12, 52, 334–5, 369).

the increasingly consolidated middle class.[36] If taken together, these factors meant that the radically inclusionary construction of material citizenship stimulated by World War I could be more easily absorbed within the public order of the state and mediated through existing political fora and existing ideological alliances.[37] In both France and the UK, the aftermath of the war entailed deep structural changes at a sub-constitutional level. For example, in the UK, it saw (as closely related events) the division of the Liberal Party, the growing impact of the Labour Party, and the final extension of the male franchise (Cowling 1971: 224). However, in both cases the public-legal apparatus was able, both at the level of political integration and labour-market legislation, to devise patterns of inclusion to accommodate an adequate proportion of widening societal expectations without exposing itself to extreme destabilization.

2.3.2 Germany in the Weimar Republic

The political system of the Weimar Republic expressed a model attempt to construct a body of constitutional law designed to help the state to adapt, from a position of only moderate autonomy, to the constituent absorption of semi-collectivized public/private agents occurring in the course of World War I.[38] Fundamental to the legal order of the Weimar Republic were, on one hand, packages of *political* legislation, enacted in the *Weimarer Reichsverfassung* of 1919, that: (a) implemented a mass franchise, whose delegates had comprehensive legislative powers (Arts 32, 68); (b) removed restrictions on parliamentary access to the legislature

[36] It is widely argued that in the UK Lloyd George had effected a partial integration of labour before 1914 and the assimilationist attitude to labour amongst pre-1914 Lloyd George liberals had acted to *decelerate* the emergence of a powerful labour movement (Wrigley 1976: 43–4; Burgess 1980: 107). Integration of labour in France was more fitful, and syndicalism remained a powerful influence. As late as 1906, the syndicalist unions rejected collaboration with the parliamentary system. However, independent socialists were active in government by 1900, and Radicalism was open to the left from 1876 onwards. On labour integration as a vital factor in strengthening late-liberal states against authoritarianism, see Luebbert (1987); Zimmermann and Saalfeld (1988: 326).

[37] For still illuminating reflection on this, see Halévy (1938: 95–133). Also very helpful is Gerber (1988: 104, 125).

[38] On the dimensions of collectivization during World War I in Germany, and its implications for relations between trade unions and the state, see the near contemporary analysis in Umbreit (1928: 148–52) and also Varain (1956: 117, 151); Kocka (1973: 115); Feldman and Steinisch (1985: 19–20); Bender (1988).

and opened binding channels of accountability between elected legislatures and ministerial authorities (Arts 54, 57, 59); (c) gave the labour movement (represented by the SPD) previously prohibited access to both legislative and executive power. On the other hand, this legal order was shaped by the introduction (never fully complete) of a raft of *social* legislation, partly formed by the constitution itself and partly contained in subsequent subsidiary statutes, pertaining to the sphere of labour law. This legislation was designed to ensure that the political unity of the state was cemented in the material unity of society, and that the legitimacy of the state, conventionally based in private and political rights, was extended to incorporate material rights, allowing the will of state to draw support and legitimacy through its representation and inclusion of its subjects in all aspects of their lives. This social legislation entailed: (a) the legalization of collective bargaining (acknowledged in late 1918, and eventually formalized in Arts 159 and 165 of the constitution); (b) provisions for the (tentative and incomplete) establishment of council democracy, for (after 1920) fora for self-determination at the place of work (Art 165), and even for basic structures for the constitutional organization of the economy;[39] (c) the partial internalization of labour conflicts in state power via arbitration tribunals and procedures for state mediation in industrial conflict; (d) the ascription to parties (i.e. union, business delegations) acting outside the legislature of quasi-statutory force in labour legislation (Bohle 1990: 14, 23). This last point was shaped by the belief that, if integrated into the state under the equal rule of law, even the most hostile economic adversaries would be inclined to produce and articulate a consensual cross-class will, bilaterally beneficial to business and labour.

The early Weimar Republic, in short, was underscored by a constitutional endeavour, effective both at the level of constitutional law and at the sub-constitutional level of labour law, to transform the design of the state emerging in the 1914–1918 war into a fully public system of political order, in which the material will of the people was actualized as a politically *live* constituent power. That is, the Weimar Republic was based in the attempt to transpose war-time arrangements into an order of state in which private/material elements of societal volition could be

[39] This was based in Sinzheimer's idea that a system of labour legislation to provide a legitimizing material basis for the state could be produced through the 'social self-determination' of the workforce (1976 [1919]: 67). See the discussion offered by Brunkhorst (Chapter 11 in this book).

mediated, through the integration of society as a constituent force seeking to balance diverse collective/material rights, into one encompassing will, expressed both at the macro-political level of the constitution and through subsidiary institutions of private conflict resolution. This was shaped by the belief, echoing Marx's quasi-existential laments in *On the Jewish Question* regarding the division between the *homo economicus* and the *homo politicus* in modern society, that the modern political system had previously been split into two separate, yet equally relevant spheres of will formation (the political constitution and the material will of society). The legitimacy of the new democratic state, accordingly, depended on its ability to reconcile and re-harmonize these two dimensions through the construction of a rights-based constitution shaped both by an organically evolving political, and a constantly integrated material, constituent power. In fact, it was widely argued by the various social-liberal *Verfassungsväter* of 1919 that the formation of the German state as a national welfare democracy had a crucial role to play in the final consolidation of the German state as a fully public and fully inclusive state, and they saw material democracy as marking the endpoint in the hitherto tortuous and thwarted construction of German statehood as a distinctively public order (see Preuß 1926).

It is vital to note, however, that the endeavour, underlying the German constitutional experiment of 1919, to translate the pluralistically privatized will of hostile societal actors into a public constitutional will was soon undermined by a shift in the factual power of economic bargaining groups and political parties. This in itself was induced by the hyperinflation and other economic crises which afflicted the Weimar Republic in the early 1920s. After 1923, the elements representing labour in the construction of the state's material constitution became weaker, and deputations of business became at once stronger and less inclined to accept the consensus-oriented negotiating positions allotted to them in the constitution (Maier 1975: 364; Blaich 1979: 64). This meant that the corporate principle of cross-class will formation that had been fundamental to the Weimar Republic was eroded. Because of this, the original founding vision of the constitution remained out of line with (i.e. to the left of) factual constitutional reality, and the idea of a political order produced through the constant translation of material rights into political will formation transpired as a mirage.[40] In fact, a creeping process of

[40] This is the view implied in Kirchheimer (1981 [1930]).

selective re-privatization, entailing a deep fragmentation of the agreed terms of constitutional order, was initiated. The original constitution notionally gave a number of private parties similar access to statutory power, and it opened the state periphery to delegates of different private organizations, located at different points in the economic production process. After 1923, however, one party or one linked aggregate of parties rapidly assumed privileged and uneven capacities for approaching state power through corporate negotiating channels, and this bloc increasingly used such access to influence policy decisions to its own advantage.[41] This process was dramatically intensified after the formal suspension of democratic procedure in 1930. The presidential interim instituted by Hindenburg in 1930, in fact, was marked by the fact that the state executive lost its structural connection with the legislature, and it abandoned its intended mediating position vis-à-vis different societal organizations. As a result, the constitutional presumption that the executive was founded in a societally embedded relation to agents of constituent power was (to a large degree) dissolved. After 1930, the coercive resources contained in the state executive were transformed into unilateral instruments of more business-friendly policies, which, prompted by powerful economic actors, suppressed the corporate material rights designated under the constitutional arrangements of 1919.[42] Commencing with the Chancellorship of Brüning, a situation emerged in which the attempt to elevate the corporate will of the state above fragmented particularistic prerogatives began palpably to fracture. The legislature was largely suspended, the executive apparatus was increasingly transformed into an instrument for balancing, prioritizing and consolidating privilege through society, so that the corporate agreements underlying Weimar social legislation were unilaterally abrogated (see Petzina 1985: 63). Notably, this re-orientation was reinforced through the far-reaching use of emergency laws, which were derived originally in part from the military system of rule by fiat pioneered in the war.

The late-Weimar constitutional system embodied a deep failure of state autonomy: a failure of the state constitutionally to solidify the dimensions of constituent power that it had internalized. In many respects, in fact, the

[41] Given its broad base, the last democratic cabinets of the Grand Coalition (1928–29/30) were notorious for their porosity to acts of private lobbying. This tendency was exacerbated under Brüning after 1930.

[42] For background commentary, see Grübler (1982: 187, 189, 199); Mommsen (1990: 370); Golla (1994: 96).

formation of the late-Weimar executive signalled a return to the haphazardly constructed constitutional order of pre-war statehood. After 1930, the German state reverted to a privatistically fragmented condition, characterized at once by low autonomy and by policies of social integration based selectively in executive coercion and filtered privilege. As such, the state began to assume a constitutional form adapted to its weak reserves of autonomy. That is, the late-Weimar Republic developed a constitution which allowed the state, lacking cohesive powers of *public integration*, to perform residual functions of societal regulation and legal inclusion through the use of private political instruments and broadly privatized political resources. The constitution evolved, in short, as a compensatory constitution, creating a skeletal framework for the use of state power at a deeply depleted level of autonomy.

2.3.3 *Spain under Primo de Rivera, Portugal and Austria*

Partial similarities to the constitutional structure that emerged during the last years of the Weimar Republic can be identified in Spain between 1923 and 1930, under the moderate dictatorship of Primo de Rivera. To be sure, this system did not grow directly out of the war. Spain had been non-belligerent in World War I. However, as a beneficiary of military conflict in other states owing to inflated demand for its industrial products, Spain experienced many of the same problems as belligerent societies. In particular, after 1918, Spain witnessed industrial mass-mobilization, intensely problematic conflicts over labour integration, and the push for widened political and social democracy that shaped other European polities (Ben-Ami 1983: 20).[43] Notably, moreover, these problems were experienced against the background of a singularly weak state structure. In Spain, for the combined duration of both dictatorships (1923–1930, 1939–1975) and the quasi-democratic interlude of the Second Republic (1931–1939), public authority remained vested to an unusual degree in local institutions; private power was widely preserved outside the state; and the state as a whole could not lay claim to institutional integrity (see Sánchez 1998: 128, 130). Like other societies at this time, therefore, the post-1918 Spanish state entered a process of rapid political/constitutional intensification, through which it was required, from a position of very low autonomy, to absorb pressures caused by deep societal polarization, to integrate extremely

[43] After 1918 'Spain rose to fourth among European countries in strikes and numbers of workdays lost' (Martin 1990: 211).

antagonistic actors with claim to constituent authority, and to preserve operative autonomy in an environment marked by high material expectations and rising societal density.

In the first instance, this conjuncture stimulated a deep reactionary backlash, and it gave rise, under de Rivera, to what might be defined as a constitutional system of *balanced authoritarian pluralism*. Distinctive in this case was that, after 1923, a regime evolved which was marked at once by the consolidation of a relatively suspended executive structure, comprising military and economic elites, and by the expansion of collective/material rights in the economy. Under the political apparatus created by de Rivera, in fact, an authoritarian and half-detached executive came to co-exist with a programme of far-reaching economic co-ordination, in which various social groups, including at once the army, trade unions, and industrialists, were co-opted into the state periphery and obtained certain privileges and even enhanced collective rights because of this. Although it did not have an elected legislature, the Spanish state under de Rivera retained a certain element of legislative pluralism through the support of Roman Catholic associations and commercial bodies (Ben-Ami 1983: 82), and through the partial co-option of trade unions and delegates of the labour movement, who were encouraged to preserve informal negotiating fora in matters regarding industrial production and monetary policy.[44] Notably, organizations of labour were admitted to the legislative process through personal invitations from executive actors, and they contributed to policy on the basis of informal arrangements and calculations. The post-1923 Spanish state thus obtained a loose constitution, in which diverse private interests in society were selectively permitted to assume a degree of legislative influence (i.e. to impact on policy and economic distribution). The result of this was the formation of an informally pluralistic legislative system, containing a number of haphazardly equilibrated private groups, situated beneath a disconnected, personally authorized executive, which at once presided over, gave formal leadership to, and sustained with its coercive force, the arrayed private actors obtaining a stake in legislation. These arrangements culminated in de Rivera's projected constitution of 1929. Although reinstating the legislative functions of the elected *Cortes*, this document (which was never enforced) placed restrictions on independent legislative power (Art 62). However, it also contained institutes to place labour under

[44] On the ambiguous links between de Rivera and the labour movement both in Spain and internationally, see Meaker (1974: 476–7); Martin (1990: 274).

special protection of the state. For instance, Article 80 provided for state-led co-ordination of industry and even partial nationalization if required for 'social utility'.

In general, the overall constitution of de Rivera's dictatorship evolved on a pattern which resulted from the inability of the Spanish state to construct a public order to integrate, balance and respond to the pressures directed to it, externally, by different social factions. From the outset, it reflected an acceptance that political power was to be used largely as an object of private transaction, and the essential function of the state was to sustain a residual stratum of coercive authority in society by filtering private access to state power. Vitally, the de Rivera regime created a precedent for a model of statehood, in which fully public contours of statehood were difficult to discern and in which political power was constructed and applied through a loose balance between an authoritarian executive and a broad informal state periphery. Quasi-fascist government thus initially emerged in Spain as a system of highly pluralistic and privatistically weakened statehood. This system was designed, either strategically or inadvertently, to create a model of government which compensated for its own debility by allowing private actors, not yet bound together in a distinctive public will, to serve as diffuse supports to facilitate the societal transmission of power. This was, notably, replaced in 1931 by a constitutional model, that of the Second Republic, which owed much to the left-oriented corporatism of the early Weimar Republic.

Similarities with these features were evident in the Portuguese state cemented by Salazar. In this setting, a governmental system also emerged in which the republican model of state was replaced by a pluralistic and semi-privatized legislature, under the control of a powerful and militarized executive. This system also had the characteristic that it at once parcellated political authority for potent societal actors and allocated compensatory collective/material rights to different parties in the economic arena. Distinctive in Salazar's governmental order was the fact that rights were primarily assigned to group bodies such as guilds, corporations, and other civil and economic associations, who were then, as collective persons, actively incorporated in legislation. Membership in these associations was seen as formative for rights entitlements (Wiarda 1977: 85), and classical subjective rights were diminished in scope and strength. Furthermore, notably, although it is often disputed whether these corporate principles ever became operative as anticipated (see Wheeler 1978: 251; Costa Pinto and Rezola 2007: 361), the constitution of Salazar's *Estado Novo* of 1933 was based in a model of active material constituent power. The constitution claimed to establish a state that was formed through a constituent 'equilibrium' between the active demands of labour and capital, which (at least in declared intention) interacted through the state to form a balanced political system, above the economic arena (Art 31). In consequence, the constitution committed the state to promote a 'national corporate economy'; to limit unrestricted economic competition (Art 34); and to police relations of property, capital and labour so that their 'social function' was preserved (Art 35). Despite this corporate orientation, however, the constitution was enacted after free trade unions had been outlawed via repressive labour legislation imposed through the National Labour Statute (1933), which meant that only select actors could freely avail themselves of the rights offered by the constitution. The collective rights enshrined in the constitution, although purporting to enshrine principles of a common economy, were thus utilized mainly for promoting the interests of specifically privileged actors in economic production. Group rights, albeit enabling sufficient distribution of state rewards to exercise a palliative influence through society, were employed, not to integrate broad-based social groups in the state, but both coercively to regiment labour and to consolidate the access of private elites to the state (see Machado 1991: 7–9, 57–9; Madureira 2007: 84). Indeed, in view of the small size of Portuguese society and the fact that a closed group of families exercised a dominant position within this society, the constitution of the *Estado Novo* acted to underpin a legal order in which control of state institutions was partly ceded to potent actors in society, such that these actors obtained the coercive support of the state at a constitutional level in order to cement their position at a socio-material level. In consequence, the constitution of the *Estado Novo* formed the classical example of a state in which typically public institutions of state were partly re-privatized, and in which deployment of state power was facilitated for, and brought palpable benefit to, distinctively privileged social groups. As in cases discussed above, the primary characteristic of this state resided in the fact that it possessed a low level of autonomy, and it surrendered reserves of state power to private actors as a condition of its assumption of operative autonomy in a small number of specific and strictly delineated functions. As in Spain under de Rivera, the quasi-fascist constitution instituted under Salazar acted as an arrangement for enabling a state, which was structurally defined by diminished reserves of autonomy, to mobilize a certain limited volume of power across society.

A similar phenomenon can be observed in the constitution of Austria proposed by the Dollfuß government in 1934. Notable in this context is the fact that the democratic constitution of the First Republic of Austria (1920), written partly by Hans Kelsen, had contained a particular strategy for avoiding the privatistic fragmentation of public offices, and for converting the privatistic aggregate of war-time interests into a stable political order. Although it was initially (rather loosely) supported by a concept of the state as residing in a balance of class forces,[45] in which different group interests were integrated into the will and material constitution of the state, Kelsen's constitution avoided making distinct provision for corporate rights.[46] In fact, it did not contain a separate list of rights, and it referred to earlier constitutions for rights norms. Most importantly, however, the 1920 constitution provided for a constitutional court (Art 137), which was supposed to filter legislation, review statutes and ensure procedural integrity in parliamentary acts.[47] The court was intended, presciently, to insulate the state against the endemic tendency towards privatistic and regional annexation, and to solidify the state as a singular and categorically *public order*. Indeed, as discussed in the earlier case of the United States, the Austrian Constitutional Court was designed, implicitly, to stabilize a formula (*Grundnorm*) for the exclusive concentration of law's authority within the public order,[48] and expressly to obviate any expectation that the state should integrate constituent power in *live* form as the basis for legislation. Nonetheless, the ideal of the state as a public order constitutionally hardened and procedurally delineated by a court standing outside the normal judiciary did not withstand the concerted mobilization of reactionary forces against the constitution, which assumed potency in Austria in 1929, and culminated in the suspension of democratic normalcy in 1933/34. Like other semi-fascist constitutions, the constitution arising from this reactionary backlash in 1934 had the distinction that it provided for the allocation of legislative power to private actors, and it granted corporate collective rights as instruments for cementing the authority of structurally prominent social groups. This constitution, although purporting to guarantee liberal principles of uniform parity before the law and

45 See the argument to support this theory in Bauer (1980 [1924]).

46 For discussion of background see Ermacora (1980: 60); Gerlich (1980: 245); Owerdieck (1987: 125); Berchtold (1998: 165).

47 See Olechowski, Chapter 3 in this book.

48 Kelsen argued (1922: 93–4) that 'the ground of validity of a sovereign coercive order' resides, not in the factual will of the people, but in 'an original norm' which is accepted as valid and forms 'the ultimate source' for the authority of the state.

equal entitlement to basic rights (Arts 16, 19), instituted a model of group-managed federal rule (Art 2), based in sectoral estates, which substantially weakened political rights and blurred the distinction between public and private office and authority. As in Germany after 1930, moreover, the process of re-orientation away from the democratic constitution was accelerated through the use of prerogative legislation derived from the war,[49] and the Austrian state reverted in part to a system of coercion fusing private corporate agency and military authoritarianism, patterned on the material constitution developed in World War I.

In parallel to the constitutional model that emerged in the latter stages of the Weimar Republic, therefore, the semi-fascist constitutions of Spain in 1923–30, Portugal after 1926–28/1933 and Austria after 1933–34 were constitutions that acted primarily to privatize the inner dynamics of the legislative process. In these states, to a greater degree than in late-Weimar Germany, the executive, although lending its coercive force in selective manner to certain groups obtaining a stake in the legislative process, remained anchored within a pluralistic legislature: the executive was not fully stripped away from the legislative apparatus, and it was still forced to some degree to mediate between groups seeking economic rewards and privileges from the state (see Giner 1982: 187). Nonetheless, as in Germany between 1930 and 1933, in these states the executive was transformed into a banker for a partially privatized political order, which selectively purchased support from group actors in society. Most notably, as in late-Weimar Germany, a constitution was formed in which the privatization of state power and the widening of the state periphery acted as preconditions for the inclusionary use of power and indeed for the basic persistence of statehood. That is, the essential institutional substructure of government, which is typically enclosed within the state under democratic constitutions, was partly released from state control and re-located to societal positions (i.e. large families, local actors, professional bodies, the military) outside the state. The distribution of state power across society came to depend upon an array of bargains between the state and actors occupying legally protected locations in its margins. The state began to collapse into a dualistic aggregate of arrangements between formal institutions and externally privileged social groups. High privatization of public goods became the precondition for the

[49] The constitution was ultimately suspended, in 1933, through use of emergency laws dating from the last years of the war (Hasiba 1981).

use of state power in a sociological conjuncture in which the abstract autonomy of state power was extremely curtailed.

2.3.4 *Italy*

Italy provides a further example of a post-1918 state that faced insoluble problems in translating the privatistic constituent model of war-time statehood into a system of public order. Indeed, in Italy the attempt to construct a uniform political order from the quasi-collectivism resulting from World War I encountered (at least arguably) the greatest obstacles. This circumstance was caused by two factors.

First, as in other countries, in Italy, the war had given rise to a high level of trade-union incorporation in the political process; in fact, this was accompanied by particularly repressive acts of labour-market legislation (Tomassini 1991). By 1918, this promoted a strong and widespread expectation of corporate will formation and governance. Building on pre-1914 syndicalist ideas, perspectives at greatly divergent points in the post-war Italian political spectrum expressed the view that governments capable of maintaining legitimacy in a mass-democratic system needed to be defined both by a political and by a material constitution:[50] legitimate government required a deeply founded material-democratic will, able to apply collective rights to integrate and unify all members of society in their different dimensions as participants in political formation. After 1918, the principle that the state must obtain legitimacy from an unstructured everyday material constituent force was intensely pervasive, and it was commonly presumed that the formation of a system of political-economic organization based in some variant on state corporatism was inevitable (Adler 1995: 123).

Second, the introduction of the mass franchise in Italy, beginning in 1912, created a legislative apparatus which, after 1918, was polarized between two (loosely) democratic factions, which refused to co-operate in forming a coalition government (the Roman Catholic PPI and the Socialist PSI) (see Horowitz 1963: 132). The result of this was that, as no party or enduring coalition could control parliament, executive power could scarcely be supported by a comprehensive majority mandate established in the legislature. In consequence, executive power was increasingly opened to persons lacking representative or even publicly mandated authority and

[50] For differences between left-leaning and right-leaning syndicalism, and on the complex fusion of the two promoted initially by fascism, see Cordova (1974: 4–5).

using private or personalistic influence to consolidate their position, and actors in the executive, without a cohesive link with parliament, began to act in near autonomy in their relation to the legislature. The absence of clear parliamentary support for the government soon led to a stripping-out of the executive structure, so that mandates for use of executive power were increasingly established, not by electoral strength, but by quasi-private deals, in fact strongly modelled on the earlier half-privatistic regime of patronage and brokerage [*trasformismo*], which had been characteristic in pre-1914 Italy (see Procacci 1968: 176; Knox 2007: 395).

The confluence of these two phenomena meant that the post-1918 Italian state was susceptible to two corrosive processes of systemic privatization, impacting on political formation at both a societal and at an executive level. This predicament was exacerbated by the fact that the state barely possessed an effective monopoly of political violence, and it lacked the ability to mobilize reserves of power either to solidify private factions in society or to control private bodies seeking a stake in the executive.

This tendency towards dual fragmentation, already evident before this point, culminated in the assumption of power by Mussolini in 1922. After this point, a constitutional order was established in which the executive fused – in part – with a single political party, strongly bolstered by potent economic interests. Lacking a basis either in the elected legislature or in society more broadly, Mussolini's executive sustained its power through society by securing informal accords with an extensive array of half-private and half-public organs and informal groups, often showing particular reliance on private support in localities where the general purchase of state power was weak.[51] In addition to this, Mussolini's regime was based in a system of rights allocation and corporate co-option, in which certain social groups (outside the state) claimed collective rights to influence socio-economic policy, but in which the allocation of such rights acted specifically to preserve and insulate established economic positions: rights, distributed by the state, acted primarily as objective instruments of material/economic stabilization, enabling the regime to exercise judicial power through tribunals at the place of work. At one level, ideologically, Mussolini and his legal advisors promoted a corporatistic definition of the fascist state as an aggregate of

[51] An important article on this argues that the PNF acted in government as a 'body among bodies', using state power to broker semi-public, semi-private bargains which served the solidification of its own power and the private interests of other associations (Bersani 2002: 186).

institutions integrating, through objective collective rights, all society within the state. In reality, however, fascist corporatism assigned rights as devices designed quite specifically to provide judicial insulation for certain privileged actors, and to underwrite the positional security (outside the state) of social groups favouring the regime. This organizational structure was exemplified by corporate legislation passed by Alfredo Rocco in 1926 and then in the *Carta del Lavoro* (Charter of Labour) of 1927. These laws were designed to bind economic actors into the political system by means of industrial arbitration courts and collective rights yet also to ensure that the inclusionary power of rights was applied in highly selective fashion, so enabling select economic groups privileged access to, and disposition over, reserves of state power.[52] The *Carta del Lavoro*, notably, was introduced after trade unions had been made illegal and it specifically acknowledged the primacy of business representatives in economic negotiating processes.

In consequence, the defining constitutional characteristic of the state evolving under Mussolini was that it was based on one hand in a suspended executive. But this executive was porous to – it in part fused with – and it was in turn diffusely supported by, a range of private actors, primarily located either outside the state or in the margins of state power, who, in the exercise of corporate rights, assumed quasi-public force in certain functions and certain localities (Mellis 1996: 367). In other words, Mussolini's regime was characterized by a two-level process of political re-privatization and selective re-corporation. Central to this regime model was a transformation of group rights into rights of instrumental coercion, in which private and economic activities were selectively brought under state control and dominant social positions were stabilized both within and outside the state. As in other cases, Mussolini's regime reflected a constitutional condition of statehood defined by the fact that the state had not been able to internalize and structurally to solidify the mass of actors and interests absorbed during the war, and it had reverted to obtaining support from diverse sources located within an extended public/private periphery. In this setting, too, aspects of constitutional design reflected a re-emergence of the structure of war-time arrangements, and emergency legislation, flanked by a dramatically escalating politicization of criminal law, was used to secure industrial support and to mobilize private actors for the state. Above all, Mussolini's regime

[52] For further discussion of these points see Stolzi, Chapter 6 in this book and more generally Stolzi (2007). See also Cordova (1974: 424–34).

again provided an example of a state marked by a low level of autonomy and differentiation, which was forced to utilize private actors to circulate its power at a reasonable level of consistency through society.

2.3.5 Germany and the National Socialist German Workers' Party (NSDAP)

The pattern of constitutional formation emerging in Germany after 1933 was initially marked by a rather heady enthusiasm for the re-establishment of corporate-style governance, which promised to re-position the executive (reduced to a thin coercive body by emergency laws passed between 1930 and 1933) in a direct relation to societal organizations. The months after the take-over of the NSDAP were witness to wide declarations of enthusiasm for a return to a political system with deep collective/material foundations. Some National Socialist theorists even proclaimed that the party, having abolished the apparatus of parliament, aspired to create an organic state founded in political-economic estates (*Ständestaat*), which resolved the divisions of class society by finally establishing social rights with regard to ownership of property and material rights with regard to professional representation (Bülow 1934: 61). In this period, a number of strategic laws concerning industrial design were introduced, which together established a broad quasi-constitutional material structure for the new political order. In particular, the first years of Hitler's regime witnessed the introduction of various laws to regulate conditions of production, to maintain stability in the production process, and to obviate industrial conflicts. First, notably, in May 1933 the German Labour Front (*Deutsche Arbeitsfront*: DAF) was formed. The DAF was originally heralded as a corporate forum for syndical co-ordination of productive forces, and in its initial functions it was considered a mechanism for securing material rights at the workplace and ameliorating general conditions of employment. In fact, however, the plan for a corporatistic organization of the economy was soon abandoned and economic decision making was brought strictly under control of the party (van Eyll 1985: 76). In consequence, although it remained an intermittent platform for labour dissent, the operations of the DAF were soon re-specified, and it acted mainly as an organ of social indoctrination and pacification.[53] The establishment of the DAF was

[53] See the account of this in Mason (1966).

followed in 1933 by a law for the forcible creation of industrial cartels, which was designed to facilitate price setting and general economic co-ordination. Additionally, these institutes were soon accompanied by a further package of labour-market legislation: notably, the Law for the Organization of Labour (*Arbeitsordnungsgesetz*) of 1934, which was designed to organize industrial relations in a (highly authoritarian) corporate structure.

These packages of corporate law constructed a political and material constitution to underpin the Nazi regime, which mirrored the selective dimensions of corporatism in other fascist states. In particular, this legislation provided for a system of industrial arbitration that, although notionally based in a delegatory system, privileged specified groups and was strongly biased against the class of employees (see Stolleis 1974: 115; Kahn 2006: 15). As in Italy in 1926–1927, the *Arbeitsordnungsgesetz* had been preceded by the proscription of free trade unions, and the position of union representatives was taken by appointees of the NSDAP. Moreover, this law stressed that the workforce owed obedience to the factory leader, whose authority had normally been established under the laws of the free market before 1933. Further, it stipulated that the resolution of conflicts within factories or companies was the responsibility of appointed trustees of labour (*Treuhänder*), whose duty it was to ensure that conflicts were resolved in accordance with the wider macroeconomic prerogatives of the regime. As in Italy, this legislation also foresaw an expansion of the judicial power of the state into industrial activity, and it established tribunals at the place of work to apply effective political sanction for professional misdemeanours (absenteeism, alcohol abuse, etc.). From the late 1930s onwards, these acts of legislation were followed by further laws to promote labour-market regulation. These subsequent laws strengthened the power of the NSDAP to channel investment, to pump-prime certain areas of production, to determine prices for commodities and for labour, and even to regulate labour flows. On this basis, the Nazi regime implemented a constitutional system which purported to draw legitimacy for executive decisions from collective representations of private groups. *De facto*, however, the coercive power of the party was deployed to prioritize specific categories of embedded socio-economic interest, and the party was itself sustained by bearers of such privilege positioned outside the (strictly defined) political system.

Some aspects of the material constitution of Nazi Germany were modelled indirectly on the material constitution of Italy. The principle that the coercive force of the party could be selectively allocated to strengthen private positions, especially those of negotiators representing business, was salient in this respect. At the same time, however, the political/economic dimension of the Nazi constitution differed significantly from that of Mussolini's Italy. In the political order emerging under Hitler, the state executive had little of the formal independence that was characteristic of Mussolini's regime, and Mussolini's relatively straightforward division of power between a formal (residually late-liberal) executive and a mass of public/private bodies at the periphery of the state was not replicated. Instead, under Hitler the remnants of the state executive were effectively absorbed within the structure of the NSDAP, which, after its assumption of power, proceeded at once to dismantle, partly to re-privatize, and erratically to replicate and reproduce the offices originally contained within the state.[54] The regime of the NSDAP retained only a rather fluidly public status, and powers of government were exercised in a diffuse, and often internally duplicated, system of coercion, in which special authorities, with personally imputed commissions, arrogated high levels of public authority for themselves.[55] The governmental techniques of the NSDAP were to a large degree founded in the personal distribution of office for private motives and the co-option of private actors in order to enact the imperatives set by the party. A pattern of government thus began to emerge that was capable of mobilizing diverse actors in society because, in addition to its extensive use of violence (also, as in other cases, typically effected through a politicization of criminal law), it could rely on a coercive fusion of private and public power, and it was able to spread directives and recruit structural support through society in a twilit amalgam of public and private authority. As in other cases of interwar authoritarianism, therefore, the political constitution of the NSDAP regime developed as an essentially dualistic model for the mobilization of power. As in other

[54] My (rather controversial and unfashionable) view of the Nazi system, not as resulting from an inflation of state power or an 'interwar surge' of statism (Mann 2004: 90), but as a quasi-patrimonial dissolution of distinctively state-centred power, is accepted by some of the classic treatises on the public law of the NSDAP. See Schmitt (1995 [1938]: 118); Neumann (1944). For historical research supporting this analysis see similar reflections in Diehl-Thiele (1969: 294). More recently see Costa Pinto (2011: 206–7). The absence of statehood as a feature of Hitler's regime was expressly proclaimed by Alfred Rosenberg, a leading ideologue of the NSDAP, who stated: 'The National Socialist state developed into a *legal centralism* and into a *practical particularism*' (quoted in Ruck 1996: 99).

[55] There is a vast literature on this. But helpful here is Costa Pinto (2002: 45).

cases, this was adapted to a conjuncture in which power could only be generated with private assistance, at a restricted level of autonomy.

2.4 Conclusion

Fascism in its broadest definition developed as a system of government involving a quasi-corporate political and material constitution that was produced by a crisis of state autonomy. This crisis of state autonomy was induced by a constitutional conjuncture that evolved in World War I, in which states, without the protective filters classically provided by rights, integrated a *live and materialized constituent power* into their inner structure. As a result, states began to imagine their legitimacy and autonomy as dependent on their capacities for the immediate, uncontrolled and unconstructed inclusion of all society. In most cases, the constitutions of fascism reflected the fact that states were overburdened by the expectations of integration directed towards them after 1914, and they failed to construct their constituencies as a balanced, integrated and *meaningfully public* foundation for legislation. Fascist constitutions evolved as alternatives to constitutions founded in fully formed state autonomy, and they projected compensatory patterns for the use of power in societies in which power was articulated at a very low level of general abstraction and where experiments in deeply founded pluralistic constitutional inclusion had been unsuccessful. In other words, fascist constitutions were hastily pieced together as default constitutions, which were designed to make possible the general use of power in societies where the comprehensive and even inclusion of society in political power had, owing to institutional debility, systemic opposition, and residual private monopolies, proved very improbable.[56] Throughout the nineteenth century, the process of constitutional formation can be seen as correlated with a progressive, albeit halting and inconclusive, rise in state autonomy. States began finally to assume socially monopolistic features close to those intuited by Weber during World War I. Yet they were not able to sustain the level of autonomy required to perform functions of statehood, and they were not able to adopt a constitutional order able to consolidate themselves as fully

[56] If the corporate structure characterizing much fascist governance can truly be seen as giving rise to 'enhanced autonomy' (Hearn 1984: 139), this autonomy occurred only at a very low starting level.

sovereign and fully autonomous actors. Totalitarianism, often perceived as the dilation of party-states to incorporate an improbably large mass of social exchanges, was induced by the inability of states to translate the war-time corporate order into an effectively integrated public/constitutional will. Fascism developed where state autonomy fractured.

On these grounds, it can be concluded that the modern state (i.e. the state as an organ of territorial control and positive legal inclusion) never reached a stage of final construction.[57] Fascism can be viewed as the tragedy of the non-emergence of statehood. European states approached a condition of near monopolistic power in the period 1914–1918. At this moment, they, to an unprecedented degree, began to apply power inclusively across all dimensions of society. After 1945, then, states renounced the impetus towards undiluted national sovereignty, and they were re-designed as institutions ceding segments of their autonomy to international bodies, courts and tribunals. Initiating a *fourth wave* of constitution writing, in fact, post-1945 European states implemented a distinctive constitutional model in which courts of law, functionally interlocking with a transnational normative arena expressed through UN Treaties and the progressive consolidation of a system of human rights through the European Convention on Human Rights, checked and stabilized the invocation of constituent power in national constitutional settings. The construction of state power within a system of supranational norms ultimately did much to stabilize the autonomy of national state institutions, and it was only at this time that most European states assumed reliable public control of their primary functions.[58] Contrary to the arguments of globalization theorists, in fact, modern European states only became autonomous democratic states in conjunction with the rise and consolidation of a powerful trans- or supranational legal domain. The trajectory of European state building can, in consequence, be divided into two periods: the period up to 1914, in which state power was internally shared between state institutions and dominant private actors, and the period after 1945, in which national state power was over-layered by trans- or supranational norms. In neither of these periods did states act in a condition close to monopolistic autonomy in society. The period in the middle was the period of fascism, when states experienced a radical failure – or perhaps

[57] This expands a theory first proposed in Thornhill (2011).
[58] See my development of this point in Thornhill (2013).

impossibility – of sovereign statehood based in full societal inclusion and supported by a fully internalized constituent will. In this period, the attempt of states to act fully as states and to include all dimensions of society in their power resulted in a catastrophic constitutional crisis of state autonomy, to which fascism formed a compensatory constitutional reaction.

Bibliography

Adler, Franklin Hugh (1995). *Italian Industrialists from Liberalism to Fascism. The Political Development of the Industrial Bourgeoisie, 1906–1934*. Cambridge: Cambridge University Press.

Amar, Akhil Reed (1998). *The Bill of Rights. Creation and Reconstruction*. New Haven, CT: Yale University Press.

Badinter, Robert (1989). 'Introduction. Naissance d'une justice', in Robert Badinter (ed.). *Une autre justice 1789–1799*. Paris: Fayard, pp. 9–25.

Barkey, Karen and Sunita Parikh (1991). 'Comparative Perspectives on the State', *Annual Review of Sociology* 17: 523–49.

Bartolini, Stefano (2005). *Restructuring Europe. Centre Formation, System Building, and Political Structuring between the Nation State and the European Union*. Oxford: Oxford University Press.

Bauer, Otto (1980 [1924]). 'Das Gleichgewicht der Klassenkräfte', in *Werkausgabe* edited by the *Arbeitsgemeinschaft für die Geschichte der österreichischen Arbeiterbewegung*, in 9 vols. Vienna: Europaverlag, IX: pp. 55–71.

Ben-Ami, Shlomo (1983). *Fascism from Above. The Dictatorship of Primo de Rivera in Spain 1923–1930*. Oxford: Clarendon.

Bender, Gerd (1988). 'Vom Hilfsdienstgesetz zum Betriebsrätegesetz. Zur rechtlichen Regulierung des industriellen Verhandlungssystems zwischen Reform und Revolution (1916–1920)', *Ius Commune*, Sonderheft 37: *Revolution, Reform, Restauration. Formen der Veränderung von Recht und Gesellschaft*. 191–210.

Berchtold, Klaus (1998). *Verfassungsgeschichte der Republik Österreich*. Vol. I: *1918–1933*. Vienna: Springer.

Bersani, Carlo (2002). 'Gli enti pubblici tra stato e società 1926–1943', in Aldo Mazzacone (ed.). *Diritto, economia e istituzioni nell'Italia fascista*. Baden-Baden: Nomos, pp. 165–92.

Bilder, Mary Sarah (2004). *The Transatlantic Constitution: Colonial Legal Culture and the Empire*. Cambridge, MA: Harvard University Press.

Blaich, Fritz (1979). *Staat und Verbände in Deutschland zwischen 1871 und 1945*. Wiesbaden: Steiner.

Bohle, Thomas (1990). *Einheitliches Arbeitsrecht in der Weimarer Republik: Bemühungen um ein deutsches Arbeitsgesetzbuch*. Tübingen: Mohr.

Bradburn, Douglas (2009). *The Citizenship Revolution. Politics and the Creation of the American Union 1774–1804*. Charlottesville, VA: University of Virginia Press.

Bülow, Friedrich (1934). *Der deutsche Ständestaat. Nationalsozialistische Gemeinschaftspolitik und Wirtschaftsorganisation*. Leipzig: Alfred Kröner.

Burdeau, François (1995). *Histoire du droit administratif (de la révolution au début des années 1970)*. Paris: Presses Universitaires de France.

Burgess, Keith (1980). *The Challenge of Labour. Shaping British Society 1850–1930*. London: Croom Helm.

Carré, Henri (1912). *La fin des parlements*. Paris: Hachette.

Carré de Malberg, Raymond (1920–22). *Contribution à la théorie générale de l'État*. Vol. II. Paris: Sirey.

Constant, Benjamin (1997 [1819]). 'De la liberté des anciens comparée à celle des modernes', in Benjamin Constant. *Écrits politiques*. Paris: Gallimard, pp. 589–619.

Cordova, Ferdinando (1974). *Le origini dei sindicati fascisti 1918–1926*. Bari: Laterza.

Costa Pinto, António (2002). 'Elites, Single Parties and Political Decision-making in Fascist-era Dictatorships', *Contemporary European History* 11(3): 429–54.

(2011). 'Ruling Elites, Political Institutions and Decision-Making in Fascist-Era Dictatorships: Comparative Perspectives', in António Costa Pinto (ed.). *Rethinking the Nature of Fascism. Comparative Perspectives*. Basingstoke: Palgrave, pp. 197–226.

Costa Pinto, António and Maria Inácia Rezola (2007). 'Political Catholicism, Crisis of Democracy and Salazar's New State in Portugal', *Totalitarian Movements and Political Religions* 8(2): 353–68.

Cowling, Maurice (1971). *The Impact of Labour 1920–1924. The Beginnings of Modern British Politics*. Cambridge: Cambridge University Press.

Davidheiser, Evelyn B. (1992). 'Strong States, Weak States: The Role of the State in Revolution', *Comparative Politics* 24(4): 463–75

Diehl-Thiele, Peter (1969). *Partei und Staat im Dritten Reich. Untersuchungen zum Verhältnis von NSDAP und allgemeiner innerer Staatsverwaltung 1933–1945*. Munich: Beck.

Eijsbouts, Willem T. (2010). 'Wir sind das Volk. Notes about the notion of "The People" as occasioned by the *Lissabon Urteil*', *European Constitutional Law Review* 6: 199–222.

Ermacora, Felix (1980). 'Die Grundrechte in der Verfassungsfrage 1919/20', in Rudolf Neck and Adam Wandruszka (eds). *Die österreichische Verfassung von 1918 bis 1938*. Vienna: Verlag für Geschichte und Politik, pp. 53–61.

Feldman Gerald D. and Irmgard Steinisch (1985). *Industrie und Gewerkschaften 1918–1924. Die überforderte Zentralarbeitsgemeinschaft*. Stuttgart: Deutsche Verlagsantalt.

Fitzsimmons, Michael F. (2010). *From Artisan to Worker. Guilds, the French State, and the Organization of Labor, 1776–1821*. Cambridge: Cambridge University Press.

Forsyth, Douglas J. (1993). *The Crisis of Liberal Italy. Monetary and Financial Policy, 1914–1922*. Cambridge: Cambridge University Press.

Gerber, Larry G. (1988) 'Corporatism in Comparative Perspective: The Impact of the First World War on American and British Labor Relations', *The Business History Review* 62(1): 93–127.

Gerber, Scott Douglas (2011). *A Distinct Judicial Power. The Origins of an Independent Judiciary 1606–1787*. Oxford: Oxford University Press.

Gerhardt, Uta (1996). 'Talcott Parsons and the Transformation of German Society at the End of World War II', *European Sociological Review* 12(3): 303–25.

Gerlich, Rudolf (1980). *Die gescheiterte Alternative. Sozialisierung in Österreich nach dem ersten Wetlkrieg*. Vienna: Braumüller.

Giner, Salvador (1982). 'Political Economy, Legitimation and the State in Southern Europe', *The British Journal of Sociology* 33(2): 172–99.

Golla, Guido (1994). *Zielvorstellungen und Auswirkungen der Brüningschen Sparmaßnahmen*. Cologne: Botermann und Botermann.

Graber, Mark A. (2003). 'Establishing Judicial Review: *Marbury* and the Judiciary Act of 1789', *Tulsa Law Review* 38: 609–50.

Grimm, Dieter (2001). *Die Verfassung und die Politik. Einsprüche in Störfällen*. Munich: Beck.

Grübler, Michael (1982). *Die Spitzenverbände der Wirtschaft und das erste Kabinett Brüning: Vom Ende der Großen Koalition1929/30 bis zum Vorabend der Bankenkrise 1931*. Düsseldorf: Droste.

Gurr, Ted Robert (1988). 'War, Revolution, and the Growth of the Coercive State', *Comparative Political Studies* 21: 45–64.

Gurr, Ted Robert, Keith Jaggers and Will J. Moore (1990). 'The Transformation of the Western State: The Growth of Democracy, Autocracy, and State Power since 1800', *Studies in Comparative International Development* 25(1): 73–108.

Halévy, Élie (1938). *L'ère des tyrannies: études sur le socialisme et la guerre*. Paris: Gallimard.

Halperin, Jean-Louis (1987). *Le tribunal de cassation sous la révolution (1790–1799)*. Paris: Pichon et Durand-Auzias.

Hasiba, Gernot (1981). 'Das kriegswirtschaftliche Ermächtigungsgesetz (KWEG) von 1917. Seine Entstehung und seine Anwendung vor 1933', in *Aus Österreichs Rechtsleben in Geschichte und Gegenwart. Festschrift für Ernst C. Helbling*, edited by the Rechtswissenschaftliche Fakultät der Universität Salzburg. Berlin: Duncker und Humblot, pp. 543–65.

Hautcoeur, Pierre-Cyrille (2005). 'Was the Great War a Watershed?: The Economics of World War I in France', in Stephen Broadberry and Mark Harrison (eds). *The Economics of World War I*. Cambridge: Cambridge University Press, pp. 169–205.

Hearn, Frank (1984). 'State Autonomy and Corporatism', *Contemporary Crises* 8: 125–45.

Hobson, Charles F. and Fredrika J. Teute (eds) (1990). *The Papers of John Marshall*. Vol. VIII. Chapel Hill, NC: University of North Carolina.

Horne, John N. (1991). *Labour at War. France and Britain 1914–1918*. Oxford: Clarendon.

Horowitz, Daniel L. (1963). *The Italian Labor Movement*. Cambridge, MA: Harvard University Press.

Kahn, Daniela (2006). *Die Steuerung der Wirtschaft im nationalsozialistischen Deutschland. Das Beispiel der Reichsgruppe Industrie*. Frankfurt am Main: Klostermann.

Kant, Immanuel (1976 [1797]). 'Metaphysik der Sitten', in Wilhelm Weischedel (ed.). *Werkausgabe*. Vol. VIII. Frankfurt am Main: Suhrkamp, pp. 309–634.

Kelsen, Hans (1922). *Der soziologische und der juristische Staatsbegriff: Kritische Untersuchung des Verhältnisses von Staat und Recht*. Tübingen: J.C.B. Mohr.

Kirchheimer, Otto (1981 [1930]). 'Weimar – und was dann? Analyse einer Verfassung', in Otto Kirchheimer *Politik und Verfassung*. Frankfurt am Main: Suhrkamp, pp. 9–56.

Knox, MacGregor (2007). *To the Threshold of Power, 1922/33. Origins and Dynamics of the Fascist and National Socialist Dictatorships*. Vol. I. Cambridge: Cambridge University Press.

Kocka, Jürgen (1973). *Klassengesellschaft im Krieg. Deutsche Sozialgeschichte 1914–18*. Göttingen: Vandenhoeck und Ruprecht.

Kramer, Larry D. (2004). *The People Themselves. Popular Constitutionalism and Judicial Review*. Oxford: Oxford University Press.

Lafon, Jacqueline Lucienne (2001). *La révolution française face au système judiciaire d'ancien régime*. Geneva: Droz.

Lester, H. Geraldine (1919). 'British Emergency Legislation', *California Law Review* 7: 323–39.

Lewis, Peter W. and Joseph Gary Trichter (1981). 'The Nationalization of the Bill of Rights: History, Development and Current Status', *Washburn Law Journal* 20: 195–240.

Lipset, Seymour Martin (1963). *Political Man*. London: Heinemann.

Lorwin, Val R. (1954). *The French Labor Movement*. Cambridge, MA: Harvard University Press.

Luebbert, Gregory M. (1987). 'Social Foundations of Political Order in Interwar Europe', *World Politics* 39(4): 449–78.

Luhmann, Niklas (1965). *Grundrechte als Institution. Ein Beitrag zur politischen Soziologie*. Berlin: Duncker und Humblot.

(1984). 'Widerstandsrecht und politische Gewalt', *Zeitschrift für Rechtssoziologie* 5(1): 36–45.

(1988). *Macht*, 2nd edition. Stuttgart: Enke.

Machado, Diamatino P. (1991). *The Structure of Portuguese Society. The Failure of Fascism*. New York, NY: Praeger.

Madison, James, Alexander Hamilton and John Jay (1987 [1787-88]). *The Federalist Papers*. London: Penguin.

Madureira, Nuno Luís (2007). 'Cartelization and Corporatism: Bureaucratic Rule in Authoritarian Portugal, 1926–45', *Journal of Contemporary History* 42(1): 79–96.

Maier, Charles S. (1975). *Recasting Bourgeois Europe. Stabilization in France, Germany, and Italy in the Decade after World War I*. Princeton, NJ: Princeton University Press.

Maier, Pauline (2010). *Ratification. The People Debate the Constitution 1787–1788*. London: Simon and Schuster.

Mann, Michael (1984). 'The Autonomous Power of the State: Its Origins, Mechanisms and Results', *European Journal of Sociology* 25: 185–213.

(2004). *Fascists*. Cambridge: Cambridge University Press.

Martin, Benjamin (1990). *The Agony of Modernization. Labor and Industrialization in Spain*. Ithaca, NY: ILR Press.

Marx, Karl (1958–68 [1844]). 'Zur Judenfrage', in Karl Marx and Friedrich Engels. *Werke*. Vol I. Berlin: Dietz, pp. 347–77.

Mason, Tim (1966). 'Labour in the Third Reich, 1933–1939', *Past and Present* 33: 112–41.

Meaker, Gerald H. (1974). *The Revolutionary Left in Spain, 1914–1923*. Stanford, CA: Stanford University Press.

Mellis, Guido (1996). *Storia dell'amministrazione italiana 1861–1993*. Bologna: Mulino.

Middlemas, Keith (1979). *Politics in Industrial Society. The Experience of the British System since 1911*. London: Deutsch.

Mirkine-Guetzevitch, Boris (1950). 'Le régime parlementaire dans les récentes Constitutions européennes', *Revue internationale de droit comparé* 2(4): 605–38.

Mommsen, Hans (1990). *Die verspielte Freiheit. Der Weg der Republik von Weimar in den Untergang 1918 bis 1933*. Frankfurt am Main: Propyläen.

Muhlberger, Detlef (1980). 'The Sociology of the NSDAP: The Question of Working-Class Membership', *Journal of Contemporary History* 15(3): 493–511.

Neumann, Franz (1944). *Behemoth. The Structure and Practice of National Socialism 1933–1944*. New York, NY: Harper and Row.

Nordlinger, Eric A. (1981). *On the Autonomy of the Democratic State*. Cambridge, MA: Harvard University Press.

Ortega, José Varela (1977). *Los amigos políticos. Partidos, elecciones y caciquismo en la Restauración (1875–1900).* Madrid: Alianza Editorial.

Owerdieck, Richard (1987). *Parteien und Verfassungsfragen in Österreich. Die Entstehung des Verfassungsprovisoriums in der Ersten Republik 1918–1920.* Munch: Oldenbourg.

Parsons, Talcott (1942). 'Some Sociological Aspects of the Fascist Movements', *Social Forces* 21(2): 138–47.

Patterson, Perry C. (1949). 'The Supreme Court as a Constituent Convention', *Tulane Law Review* 23(4): 431–51.

Petzina, Dietmar (1985). 'Soziale und wirtschaftliche Entwicklung', in Kurt G.A. Jeserich, Hans Pohl and Georg-Christoph von Unruh (eds). *Deutsche Verwaltungsgeschichte.* Vol. 4: *Das Reich als Republik und in der Zeit des Nationalsozialismus.* Stuttgart: Deutsche Verlags-Anstalt, pp. 39–66.

Pincus, Steve (2009). *1688. The First Modern Revolution.* New Haven, CT: Yale University Press.

Pohl, Hans (1979). 'Die Entwicklung der Kartelle in Deutschland und die Diskussionen im Verein für Socialpolitik', in Helmut Coing and Walter Wilhelm (eds). *Wissenschaft und Kodifikation des Privatrechts im 19. Jahrhundert,* Vol. IV: *Eigentum und industrielle Entwicklung. Wettbewerbswerbordnung und Wettbewerbsrecht.* Frankfurt am Main: Klostermann, pp. 206–35.

Poulantzas, Nicos (1974). *Fascism and Dictatorship: The Third International and the Problem of Fascism.* London: New Left Books.

Preuß, Hugo (1926). *Staat, Recht und Freiheit.* Tübingen: J.C.B. Mohr.

Procacci, Giovanna (1968). 'From Interventionism to Fascism, 1917–1919', *Journal of Contemporary History* 3(4): 153–76.

Rakove, Jack (1997). *Original Meanings. Politics and Ideas in the Making of the Constitution.* New York, NY: Vintage.

(1999). 'The Super-Legality of the Constitution, or a Federalist Critique of Bruce Ackermann's Neo-Federalism', *Yale Law Journal* 108: 1931–58.

Reid, John Phillip (2003). *Constitutional History of the American Revolution: The Authority of Rights.* Madison, WI: University of Wisconsin Press.

Ruck, Michael (1996). 'Zentralismus und Regionalgewalten im Herrschaftsgefüge des NS-Staates', in Horst Möller (ed.). *Nationalsozialismus in den Regionen.* Munich: Oldenbourg, pp. 99–122.

Sánchez Cazorla, Antonio (1998). 'La vuelta a la historia: Caciquismo y franquismo', *Historica social* (3): 119–32.

Schmitt, Carl (1928). *Verfassungslehre.* Berlin: Duncker und Humblot.

(1995 [1938]). *Der Leviathan in der Staatslehre des Thomas Hobbes. Sinn und Fehlschlag eines politischen Symbols.* Stuttgart: Cotta.

Sieyès, Emmanuel (1839 [1789]). *Qu'est-ce que le tiers-état?* Paris: Pagnerre.

(17–). *Collection des écrits.* Vol. I. Paris: C.F. Cramer.

Sinzheimer, Hugo (1916). *Ein Arbeitstarifgesetz. Die Idee der sozialen Selbstbestimmung im Recht.* Munich: Duncker & Humblot.

(1976 [1919]). 'Die Neuordnung des Arbeitsrechts', in Hugo Sinzheimer. *Arbeitsrecht und Rechtssoziologie: Gesammelte Aufsätze und Reden.* Frankfurt am Main: Europäische Verlags Anstalt. Vol. I, pp. 62–9.

Skocpol, Theda (1979). *States and Social Revolutions. A Comparative Analysis of France, Russia and China.* Cambridge: Cambridge University Press.

Smend, Rudolf (1968). 'Verfassung und Verfassungsrecht', in Rudolf Smend, *Staatsrechtliche Abhandlungen und andere Aufsätze,* 2nd edition. Berlin: Duncker und Humblot, pp. 119–277.

Stolleis, Michael (1974). *Gemeinwohlformeln im nationalsozialistichen Recht.* Berlin: Schweitzer.

Stolzi, Irene (2007). *L'ordine corporativo. Poteri organizzati e organizzazione del potere nella riflessione girudica dell'Italia fascista.* Milan: Giuffrè.

Stone Sweet, Alec (2008). 'Constitutions and Judicial Power', in Daniele Caramani (ed.). *Comparative Politics.* Oxford: Oxford University Press, pp. 217–39.

Tarr, Alan H.G. (1998). *Understanding State Constitutions.* Princeton, NJ: Princeton University Press.

Tawney, Richard H. (1943). 'The Abolition of Economic Controls, 1918–1921', *The Economic History Review* 13: 1–30.

Thornhill, Chris (2010). 'Legality, Legitimacy and the Form of Political Power: On the Construction of a False Antinomy', *The Journal of Political Power* 3(3): 293–316.

(2011). 'The Future of the State', in Poul Kjaer, Gunther Teubner and Alberto Febbrajo (eds). *The Financial Crisis in Constitutional Perspective: The Dark Side of Functional Differentiation.* Oxford: Hart.

(2013). 'National Sovereignty and the Constitution of Transnational Law: A Sociological Approach to a Classical Antinomy', *Transnational Legal Theory* 3(4): 394–460.

Tomassini, Luigi (1991). 'Industrial Mobilization and the Labour Market in Italy during the First World War', *Social History* 16(1): 59–87.

Treanor, William Michael (2005). 'Judicial Review before *Marbury*', *Stanford Law Review* 58: 455–562.

Turner, John (1992). *British Politics and the Great War. Coalition and Conflict 1915–1918.* New Haven, CT: Yale University Press.

Tusell, Javier (1976). *Oligarquia y caciquismo en Andalucia (1890–1923).* Barcelona: Planeta.

Tushnet, Mark (1999). *Taking the Constitution away from the Courts.* Princeton, NJ: Princeton University Press.

Umbreit, Paul (1928). *Die deutschen Gewerkschaften im Krieg.* Stuttgart: Deutsche Verlags-Anstalt.

van Eyll, Klara (1985). 'Berufsständische Selbstverwaltung', in Kurt G.A. Jeserich, Hans Pohl and Georg-Christoph von Unruh (eds). *Deutsche Verwaltungsgeschichte*, Vol. 4: *Das Reich als Republik und in der Zeit des Nationalsozialismus*. Stuttgart: Deutsche Verlags-Anstalt, pp. 66–77.

Varain, Heinz Josef (1956). *Freie Gewerkschaften, Sozialdemokratie und Staat. Die Politik der Generalkommission unter der Führung Carl Legiens (1890–1920)*. Düsseldorf: Droste.

Wheeler, Douglas L. (1978). *Republican Portugal. A Political History 1910–1926*. Madison, WI: University of Wisconsin Press.

Winkler, Heinrich August (1972). *Pluralismus oder Protektionismus? Verfassungspolitische Probleme des Verbandswesens im deutschen Kaiserreich*. Wiesbaden: Fr. Steiner.

Witt, Peter-Christian (1970). *Die Finanzpolitik des deutschen Reiches von 1903 bis 1913. Eine Studie zur Innenpolitik des Wilhelminischen Deutschlands*. Düsseldorf: Droste.

Wrigley, Chris (1976). *David Lloyd George and the British Labour Movement*. Hassocks: Harvester.

(1990). *Lloyd George and the Challenge of Labour. The Post-War Coalition 1918–1922*. New York, NY: Harvester.

Zimmermann, Ekkart and Thomas Saalfeld (1988). 'Economic and Political Reactions to the World Economic Crisis of the 1930s in Six European Countries', *International Studies Quarterly* 32(3): 305–34.

3

The beginnings of constitutional justice in Europe

THOMAS OLECHOWSKI

3.1 Introduction[1]

Until recently, courts of law were not typically constructed as primary objects of sociological study, and even political scientists only rarely examined the role of courts.[2] Recent sociological research, however, has begun to direct attention towards courts, and many legal and political sociologists now place emphasis on courts as key phenomena in the transformation of modern social order. Most notably, sociologists have begun to evaluate the prominent role of Constitutional Courts in contemporary societies, and they have increasingly identified the polity-building role of such courts as a new and distinctive feature of contemporary society. For this reason, contemporary sociology has begun to develop a variety of models for accounting for the *judicial review of statutes* as a defining characteristic of modern social and political organization, and a number of sociologists now conduct research on the reasons why judicial review is currently so widespread and why it apparently brings stability to new political systems.

This new interest has produced a body of sociological research that addresses, in very general terms, the increasingly widespread *judicialization* of democratic legislative procedures,[3] and which devises sociological perspectives to explain the growing proliferation of constitutional designs that give particular weight to judicial authority.[4] One commentator has neatly described this general feature of contemporary democracy, arguing that: 'If

[1] Note that the introductory sections of this chapter were added by the editors. Some of these sections reproduce material that was first published in Thornhill (2012).

[2] A famous exception is Dahl (1957).

[3] For background regarding the development of this concept, see Tate (1995: 27).

[4] It is commonly observed that the classical features of political democracy have been transformed in recent years by the rising power of judicial institutions, and it is widely suggested that traditional patterns of democratic governance have been redesigned through a *rights revolution* or even a *constitutional-court revolution*, as a result of which rights are constitutionally extracted as institutions that curtail the authority and autonomy of

the Nineteenth century was a century of parliaments, and the Twentieth was a century of governments, then the Twenty-first will be that of courts and judges' (Wellens 2004: 180–1). Some of the literature concerning the rise of courts is very critical in tenor, and some sociological theorists of judicial power allege that the growing status of courts reflects a strategy for the protection of international economic elites (Hirschl 2004, 2007: 723; Ferejohn 2002: 41, 44). However, much of this literature is more neutral and descriptive in tone. It includes anthropological analysis of the increasing influence of courts, observing how courts embed acceptance for constitutions in different political settings (Scheppele 2003). It includes research focused on the composition of high-court judiciaries (Schnapper 2010), research on the internal systemic functions of Constitutional Courts (Gawron and Rogowski 2007; Hesse 2006), and research examining the functions of courts in particular processes of regime change (Schatz 1998; Miller 1997). It also includes a large body of research which analyses the rising judicialization of political decision making and legitimization as reflecting broader societal patterns of transnational convergence in the increasingly globalized political arena (Commaille, Dumoulin and Robert 2010). In general terms, in short, the sociology of courts is a rapidly expanding area of sociological inquiry, and judicialization is widely perceived as an important object for sociological scrutiny.

Against this background, it is notable that sociological research on the judicial review of statutes has very particular relevance in sociological work on the formation of contemporary Europe. At one level, this is the case because the process of national democratization in Europe in recent decades has been based – in part – around powerful Constitutional Courts. The re-establishment of democracy in post-1989 Eastern Europe was, to some degree at least, led by Constitutional Courts, and the unprecedented role of judicial actors in the promotion of democracy in these societies has not escaped sociological attention (Skapska 2011; Blokker 2013). In addition, however, this is the case because of the importance of judicial institutions, conducting processes of *de facto* constitutional review, in the formation and enlargement of the European Union (EU). As is widely recognized, the relatively autonomous role of courts, and of the European Court of Justice (ECJ) in particular, has assumed vital importance in the process of supranational constitutional construction in contemporary Europe. Indeed, it is often argued that the

legislatures. Note the use of the term 'judicial review revolution' to describe recent changes in democratic design (Renoux 1994: 892).

ECJ created a constitution for the EU effectively *ex nihilo*.[5] In consequence, the incrementally judicialized form of the EU constitution is an object of increasing interest for sociologists, and the constitution-making role of judicial actors is seen as marking a deep change in the political structure and sources of political agency in European society. Sociological literature addressing the status of judicial power in the construction of the EU includes a growing body of historical-sociological research, which follows Bourdieu in examining the elite actors originally giving impulse to the formation of the European system of human-rights legislation (Vauchez 2008; Madsen 2010). This research includes neo-Durkheimian functional analysis, which addresses the 'court democracy' resulting from the generalization of EU law through the ECJ as part of a transnational process of functional differentiation and resultant *individualization* (Münch 2008: 522). This also includes historical-functionalist literature on the inclusionary role of courts in systemic formation (Thornhill 2012). Across these different lines of investigation, the basic foundations for a sociological construction of judicial integration have emerged as important elements in research on European polity building. Each of these avenues of research attempts to uncover the social causes for the distinctively judicial constitution of the EU, and research in each body of work focuses on the distinctive functions of courts in creating diffusely centred and loosely federalized polities. In these respects, too, therefore, the sociological assessment of courts has striking and increasing explanatory relevance.

Absent to date in the more sociologically oriented work on judicial review and the role of courts, however, is an historical account of the initial origins of judicial review and constitutional jurisprudence in Europe. Indeed, the extent to which the recent and contemporary rise of courts was prefigured by earlier debates about polity building, legal uniformity, federalism, and the functions of the judicial branch is rarely considered as a background to contemporary judicial politics. This chapter attempts to rectify this gap in the literature. To this end, in particular, it discusses the historical origins of judicial review, giving due weight to the United States, but focusing on Austria in the late nineteenth and early twentieth centuries: that is, on a society that confronted questions relating to federalism, multiculturalism, linguistic diversity, and complex integration not dissimilar to contemporary legal pressures, and where, partly in response to such

[5] See the classic analyses of this in Stone Sweet (2004); Alter (1998); Burley and Mattli (1993).

challenges, the principles of judicial review were first fully formalized and the first fully operative Constitutional Court was established.[6] In describing the Austrian background to court-led democracy, this chapter aims briefly to reconstruct the controversies surrounding early constitutional jurisprudence, and so to illuminate the historical beginnings of what has become a core institution in constitutional law, both in single national societies and in modern Europe as a whole.

3.2 The American paradigm

When Thomas Jefferson was inaugurated as third President of the United States on 4 March 1801, he noted that his predecessor John Adams had nominated justices of the peace literally up to the very last minute of his term, but that all the documents of appointment had not been successfully delivered to the persons in question. So Jefferson instructed his new Secretary of State, James Madison, not to deliver these documents of appointment although they bore the signature of the former President. At this, one of the not-appointed-after-all justices, William Marbury, complained to the Supreme Court of the United States. However, on 24 February 1803, the Supreme Court dismissed the complaint on grounds that it was not competent to hear the case. Although the Judiciary Act of 1789 decreed that the Supreme Court was the competent court for such cases, this legal regulation was in contradiction to the constitution, whose exclusive function was to determine the competences of the Supreme Court, and it therefore could not be applied.[7]

The above-mentioned facts of the case *Marbury v. Madison* have been widely forgotten in the meantime. The argument, however, which the Supreme Court used in arriving at its decision became famous, because for the first time the question had been posed before the Supreme Court as to how to treat laws contradictory to the constitution. The question ran as follows:

> The constitution is either a superior, paramount law; unchangeable by ordinary means, or it is on a level with ordinary legislative acts, and, like other acts, is alterable when the legislature shall please to alter it. If the

[6] The remainder of this chapter contains results of my project, with the title: *Kelsen's Life in America and the Diffusion of his Legal Theory across the Globe*. This project has been funded by the Austrian Science Fund (FWF, project no. P 23747). My special thanks are due to Ms Patricia Haeusler for the translation of large parts of the text.

[7] Stourzh (1989: 66 ff); Paulson (2003: 226); Haase and Struger (2009: 22 ff); Heller (2010: 37).

> former part of the alternative be true, then a legislative act contrary to the constitution is not law: if the latter part be true, then written constitutions are absurd attempts, on the part of people, to limit a power in its own nature illimitable. Certainly all those who have framed written constitutions contemplate them as forming the fundamental and paramount law of the nation, and consequently, the theory of every such government must be that an act of legislature, repugnant to the constitution, is void.[8]

Having ascertained the nullity of unconstitutional law, the ruling in *Marbury v. Madison* is generally seen as the origin of the American model of constitutional justice. Of course, one has to bear in mind that this origin has a long prehistory itself, reaching back to seventeenth-century England, and already in 1766 a county court in Virginia had decided that a statute (in this case: the famous Stamp Act 1765) does not bind the people if it is unconstitutional (Stourzh 1989: 37; Paulson 2003: 225). The importance of *Marbury v. Madison*, however, is that this time it was the Supreme Court of the United States who had to decide about 'judicial review' and that the Supreme Court found a formulation for a principle, which has remained practically unchanged until today.

The American model of judicial review accords American courts a very significant political role and one which soon came to play a part in discussions in Europe. Only a few other countries established a similar type of constitutional justice, however, one of them being Norway, where the Supreme Court – the Højesteret – already reached a decision in the American style in 1814. In Denmark, the Højesteret recognized the principle of judicial review from 1912 on, but the first judgment including a decision that a statute of the Danish parliament was null and void was not delivered until 1999 (Haase and Struger 2009: 229, 232). Otto von Bismarck was one of the many notable opponents of judicial review: in 1863 during the Prussian constitutional crisis he stated that the 'political future of a country should on no account depend on one single subjective decision taken by a court' (Triepel 1929: 9). Ultimately, however, the principle of judicial review did become established in Germany. Gradually, starting in 1921, then, categorically, in 1925 the *Reichsgericht*, the Supreme Court for civil and criminal affairs, declared that constitutional regulations 'require that the judges must ignore subsequent statutes which are in contradiction to the original laws'.[9]

[8] US Supreme Court, *Marbury v. Madison*, decision from 24 February 1803, quoted after Urofsky and Finkelman (2002) No. 46; see also Paulson (2003: 228).

[9] Reichsgericht, decision from 4 November 1925, in *Entscheidungen des Reichsgerichts in Zivilsachen* 111 (1926: 320–35, here 323).

In fact, this had no practical consequences: no law was ever declared unconstitutional by the *Reichsgericht*, neither in the case in point, nor in any other case up until 1933.[10]

3.3 The Austrian Constitutional Court and Hans Kelsen

In the field of constitutional jurisdiction a second model was opposed to the US model, originating markedly later and sometimes referred to as 'the European model', sometimes as 'the Austrian model' and sometimes as 'the Kelsenian model' (Haase and Struger 2009: 37; Schulz 2010: 2 ff; Stourzh 2011: 171). This clearly refers to the Austrian Federal Constitution of 1920, largely developed by Hans Kelsen, which provided for constitutional jurisdiction of a very different nature to the American model, with constitutional justice concentrated at one single court only.

It has been objected, however, that the Austrian Federal Constitution of 1 October 1920 is not the oldest constitution of this kind. The constitution of Czechoslovakia of 29 February 1920 originated seven months earlier, and likewise foresaw one Constitutional Court, forbidding the other courts to exercise powers of judicial review (Spáčil 2008: 16; Schelle and Tauchen 2009: 22; Heller 2010: 186). It is well known that Kelsen's school of legal theory, the Pure Theory of Law, had many adherents in Czechoslovakia, especially in Brno, the subsequent seat of the Czechoslovakian Constitutional Court. But, as has been discussed in the recently published doctoral thesis of Jana Osterkamp, these people did not play a substantial role in establishing the Czechoslovakian Constitutional Court. The true 'father' of these regulations was Jiři Hoetzel, a declared opponent of Kelsen (Osterkamp 2009: 10).[11]

There must, however, be deeper underlying reasons why, at the same time, the Republic of Austria and the Czechoslovakian Republic should introduce constitutional jurisdiction that differed so markedly from the American model. In fact, the roots of this development can be traced back to the constitutional law of the Habsburg monarchy from which both republics emerged (Osterkamp 2011: 276). When we examine this, only the Austrian half of the Austro-Hungarian monarchy needs to be taken into account.[12] The Kingdom of Hungary – like the United Kingdom of

[10] See in detail Stolleis 2003; see also Sellert 1990: 1053; Haase and Struger (2009: 78).

[11] Here, Osterkamp refutes a widespread opinion that is shared by many authors, like Haase and Struger (2009: 58).

[12] See for a general overview of the constitutional situation Rumpler and Urbanitsch (2000), with further references.

Great Britain and (Northern) Ireland – did not have a formal constitution at all, and it lacked the preconditions for the establishment of constitutional jurisdiction. In fact, a Constitutional Court was only established in Hungary in 1989, and the United Kingdom of Great Britain and Northern Ireland is one of the few European states where there is neither a formal constitution nor a system of constitutional justice (Haase and Struger 2009: 134, 267).[13] In the Austrian Empire, five *Staatsgrundgesetze* (Basic Laws) were enacted in 1867, which together formed the constitution. Changes to this constitution could only be made if at least half the members of parliament were present and a two-thirds majority vote was cast in both houses. Laws enacted by parliamentary majority in this way were considered part of the constitution; consequently, by the end of the monarchy, constitutional law as a whole was already dispersed over countless laws stipulating more and more details. This state of affairs not only continued, but was in fact intensified, under the Austrian Republic, with the result that up until today Austrian constitutional law is uniquely fragmented (Heller 2010: 95; see also Stourzh 2011: 170). At face value, one might think that a distinction between simple laws enacted by a simple majority and constitutional laws, enacted by a qualified majority, would have the effect that laws contradictory to constitutional laws would be void. This was not the case. On the contrary, the courts were explicitly forbidden to examine laws.[14] What was seen as the deplorable American custom of judicial review was well known in Austria, but it was rejected.[15] And so the distinction between constitutional laws and simple laws became legally meaningless (Kelsen 1914: 202, 390).

As early as 1885, the legal scholar Georg Jellinek had criticized this fact and demanded a 'Constitutional Court for Austria' (Jellinek 1885; see Olechowski 2010: 35; Osterkamp 2011: 280). He put forward various examples of cases where members of parliament had claimed that a draft law was unconstitutional and that it therefore needed to be passed with

[13] However, not even the UK is immune to the rise of judicial sovereignty. Note the recent tendency in the UK towards the consolidation of constitutional jurisprudence, and the resultant shift in power from politicians to judges. This is partly induced by the direct effect of European law, but still more by the Human Rights Act of 1998. See for example Woodhouse 2004: 152–3; Elliott (2003: 35).

[14] Staatsgrundgesetz über die richterliche Gewalt, 21 December 1867, Article 7. In: *Reichsgesetzblatt für das Kaiserthum Oesterreich*, No. 144/1867.

[15] A rather unknown, but important episode of the history of judicial review in Austria is reported by Stourzh (2011: 13).

a two-thirds majority in order to make it a constitutional law. But the decision as to which kind of vote should be taken was reserved for the President of the Parliament, who was elected by simple majority vote! Thus, it remained *de facto* in the hands of a simple majority of the members of parliament to enact laws which were unconstitutional but – as there was no provision for judicial review – incontestable. Georg Jellinek was of the opinion that parliament infringed its competences if it decreed laws for which a qualified majority would be necessary with a simple majority, and, in order to rectify this, he called for a court that would settle such a quarrel about competences (Jellinek 1885: 20; Heller 2010: 131; Olechowski 2010: 36).

This was understandable insofar as a court for resolving conflicts regarding partition of competence already existed in Austria at that time: the *Reichsgericht* (Imperial Court), founded in 1869 (Heller 2010: 99; Olechowski 2010: 32). This institution had already been named *Verfassungsgerichtshof* (Constitutional Court) on another occasion (Heller 2010: 127; Jabloner 2011: 220). It had no right of judicial review, although it was endowed with various other functions which were intended to safeguard the constitution. In addition to the power to decide conflicts of competence, the power to examine administrative acts with regard to their constitutionality is significant. However, it is precisely in this respect that all the attendant problems of a non-existent constitutional justice came to the fore. For example, in 1883, a newspaper editor had lodged a complaint with the Imperial Court, because the authorities had deprived him of the right to sell his newspaper at newsagents, and he pleaded for the freedom of the press guaranteed by the constitution. But the Imperial Court declared that the authorities could support their view, citing a relevant regulation from the Press Act 1862, and it did not examine whether the Press Act 1862 itself was contradictory to the constitution, so the newspaper editor's plea was unsuccessful (Olechowski 2010: 34). It was obvious, therefore, that the rule of law had a gap in this respect. However, Jellinek was the first one who captured the essence of the problem in its totality.

In 1918, when Hans Kelsen was charged by the new state chancellor Karl Renner with responsibility for preparing a law that would delegate the competences of the former Imperial Court to a new republican court, he suggested *Verfassungsgericht* (Constitutional Court) as the name for this institution. In addition, he declared that there was a real need for a court that would be able to protect the constitution in every way possible (Stourzh 1989: 314; Schmitz 2003: 244; Olechowski 2009: 214). As a first step, the new Constitutional Court was only charged with the competences of the former Imperial Court,[16] but its competences were gradually increased in the ensuing reforms up until 1920.

The main problem with this constitutional development was linked to the simultaneous transformation of the Austrian state into a federal republic.[17] Renner had already entertained the idea of Austria as a federal state during World War I: the state and the provinces were to be given their own parliaments, which made the question of defining competences more acute. Renner was in favour of establishing a federal Constitutional Court, which would, when requested by the government, decide whether a law fell under the jurisdiction of the state or the provinces (Öhlinger 2003: 211; Schmitz 2003: 242; Jabloner 2011: 221). In the intervening period between the proclamation of the Republic in 1918 and the decision regarding the *Bundes-Verfassungsgesetz* of 1920 (Federal Constitution Act 1920), a two-year provisional constitution was in force. Austria was not a true federal state, but was already split up into federal provinces, which had their own parliaments, with their own competences.[18] Under instructions from Renner, Kelsen produced a report for the state chancellery in January or February of 1919, in which he set out the plan to transform Austria into a federal state and considered various possible alternatives. In this context, he proposed creating a federal Constitutional Court which should be authorized to declare provincial laws null and void if they were in contradiction to the national laws. Shortly before the report was published in the *Zeitschrift für Öffentliches Recht* (Journal for Public Law) (Kelsen 1919), the *Konstituierende Nationalversammlung* (Constituent National Assembly) took up this suggestion and amended the provisional constitution in such a way that legal decisions of the provincial parliaments had to be announced to the national government prior to their enactment, and that for a fortnight the national government had the right to plead unconstitutionality before the Constitutional Court.[19] In the course of the one and a half

16 Gesetz über die Errichtung eines deutschösterreichischen Verfassungsgerichtshofes, 25 January 1919, *Staatsgesetzblatt für die Republik Deutschösterreich*, No. 48/ 1919; see for details Heller (2010: 149).

17 Öhlinger (2003: 212) holds the discussion about federalism as essential for the beginnings of constitutional justice in Austria and says that the 'power of the Constitutional Court was obviously designed as an instrument to resolve conflicts between federal and state law'.

18 See for details Merkl (1919).

19 Gesetz über die Volksvertretung, 15 March 1919, Article 15, *Staatsgesetzblatt für die Republik Deutschösterreich*, No. 179/1919; see Schmitz (2003: 247).

years in which this provision was valid, there were in fact two such cases (Öhlinger 2003: 211; Olechowski 2009: 215–16; Jabloner 2011: 224). They were problematic insofar as they furnished the national government with the opportunity to plead against provincial laws, but did not accord the same right to provincial parliaments to appeal against national laws. The Tyrolean legal scholar, Stephan Falser, drew attention to this problem; in October 1919, he himself drew up a draft constitution with a strongly *federalist* character, which foresaw the reciprocal right of federal government and provincial parliaments to challenge each other's legislation (Stourzh 1989: 332; Olechowski 2009: 227). This last provision was included in the final text of the *Bundes-Verfassungsgesetz* of 1920 (Art. 140). This provision is still valid and it retains considerable theoretical significance in relation to Austria's federal structure. In practice, however, it has only been applied in a few cases. The real reason for the late acceptance of the Austrian model of constitutional legislation has to be sought elsewhere. In Article 140, the Constitutional Court was also empowered to annul a law when it would have – in a pending suit – to apply a regulation which might be deemed unconstitutional.

The final formulation of the jurisdiction of the Constitutional Court derives from Hans Kelsen. Kelsen's decisive influence on Austrian constitutional law is attributable in part to the fact that in the summer of 1919 he produced the drafts which formed the basis for further work on the constitution (Stourzh 1989: 317; Olechowski 2009: 216). In addition, however, in July 1920, he was co-opted as an independent constitutional expert to the parliamentary sub-committee, which by October of that year had drawn up the final text of the constitution. It was in this sub-committee that on 31 August Kelsen proposed that the Constitutional Court could initiate a judicial review *ex officio* (Öhlinger 2003: 213; Olechowski 2009: 227). But the members of parliament felt this measure went too far and was unacceptable. The Constitutional Court would have been empowered to submit all and any laws to judicial review whenever it desired. Consequently Kelsen changed the wording on 23 September. The final wording was as follows: 'The Constitutional Court shall decide on application by the federal government whether state laws are unconstitutional and likewise on application by a state government whether federal laws are unconstitutional, but ex officio in so far as the Court would have to apply such a law in a pending suit.' This was literally a last-minute initiative: one week later, on 1 October, the resolution was formally adopted by the Constitutive National Assembly, and the regulation was included in the content of Article 140.[20]

The practical significance of this can be demonstrated by referring once more to the case of the newspaper editor previously mentioned. If a newspaper editor appeals to the freedom of the press, although the authorities are of the opinion that their measures were in accordance with the Press Act 1862, the first thing the Constitutional Court does is to examine the measures taken by the authority. But if the judges are in any doubt as to the constitutionality of the Press Act, they have to stop their examination of the administrative measures and *ex officio* initiate a fresh examination of the Press Act 1862 to see if it violates the constitutional principle of the freedom of the press. Only on the completion of this second examination can the first examination be continued; should the law have been annulled in the meantime, the administrative decision is declared unlawful.

The nature of this case is reminiscent of the American system. Yet, it must be stated that the emergence of the Austrian system had a markedly different background and originated from a dispute concerning the federalization of Austria. This is also the main reason why the Constitutional Court was established as the only court in Austria to decide on the constitutionality of laws, as other courts were still forbidden to initiate judicial review. If the Constitutional Court ruled that a law was unconstitutional, then it declared it null and void, which was announced in the Federal Law Gazette. But the law remained in force until the ruling was made – although it was unconstitutional, it was not really 'void' but simply open to contest, not absolutely null and void but relatively so.[21]

Parallel developments in respect of constitutional jurisdiction in Czechoslovakia diverged from those in Austria on many counts.[22] Although Czechoslovakia was made up of diverse parts of the former Habsburg monarchy, it was not a federal state but a centralized state. There was no need to examine provincial or national laws to see if they conformed to the constitution. Furthermore, the organization of the courts of law in Czechoslovakia as well as in the Republic of Austria had been taken over from the Habsburg monarchy, although in 1918 the

[20] Gesetz womit die Republik Österreich als Bundesstaat eingerichtet wird (Bundes-Verfassungsgesetz), 1 October 1920, Article 140, *Bundesgesetzblatt für die Republik Österreich*, No. 1/1920; see Öhlinger (2003: 213); Olechowski (2009: 227).

[21] Kelsen (1929: 71 (41)).

[22] A good comparison is given by Osterkamp (2011, see esp. 281 ff.).

Czechoslovakian legislators had opted not to create a court which would assume the competences of the former Imperial Court, but rather to accord these competences to the Supreme Administrative Court (*Nejvyšší správní soud*).[23] When in 1920 the Czechoslovakian Constitutional Court was established,[24] its sole function was to examine and rule on the constitutionality of laws, whereas in Austria this is merely one, albeit central, competence of the Constitutional Court (Haase and Struger 2009: 60). What distinguished Czechoslovakia from Austria, then, was the material, or the cases upon which the Court could base its decisions. In the case of Czechoslovakia, only a few authorities were entitled to submit a request for examination, and for various practical reasons these legal instances had little interest in mobilizing the Czech constitutional justice system. Indeed, the activities of the Constitutional Court were absolutely minimal, with the result that in the literature it was not clear until recently whether the Court ever actually took action. The aforementioned doctoral thesis by Osterkamp has thrown some light on this matter: after one single judgment concerning a governmental ordinance in 1922, there was one case, in 1939, in which a law was annulled. This occurred after protracted proceedings, and – grotesquely – at a time when Czechoslovakia had already ceased to exist as a sovereign state (Osterkamp 2009: 184)!

3.4 'The Guardian of the Constitution'

Within the European constitutional law system the Austrian Constitutional Court was seen as the only one of its kind, and it attracted a good deal of attention. When the Association of German Constitutional Jurists met in Vienna in 1928 the question of *Staatsgerichtsbarkeit* (state jurisdiction) was dealt with by two speakers: the host Kelsen delivered a paper, but the constitutional expert Heinrich Triepel from Berlin was also invited to speak on the subject. However, the expected éclat did not take place. Triepel had interpreted his subject quite differently and spoke at length about impeachment proceedings (*Ministeranklagen*). He only touched marginally upon questions of unconstitutional laws. Together with Kelsen he admitted that the two of them had opened up ways

[23] Zákon o nejvyšším správním soudě, 2 November 1918, *Sbírka zákonů a nařízení*, No. 3/1918.

[24] Zákon kterým se uvozuje Ústavní listina Československé republiky, 29 February 1920, *Sbírka zákonů a nařízení*, No. 121/1920.

through the woods from two different sides, but without their paths crossing (Triepel 1929; Kelsen 1929).[25]

However, the most significant controversy broke out one year later, when Carl Schmitt, at that time Professor at the Berlin School of Economics (who had not attended the Vienna meeting), published an essay with the title: 'The Guardian of the Constitution'.[26] In this piece Schmitt roundly refuted the possibility that a court of law could decide on constitutional matters. The task of justice was to rule in individual cases and to apply laws to facts. But in decisions on constitutional matters there are no facts that can be subsumed under a law (Schmitt 1931: 36 ff). Moreover, Schmitt suspected – like Triepel before him – that questions of law and questions of politics were starkly opposed: a law court that ruled on political matters was a court of justice no longer. Kelsen reacted to this article in 1931 with the counter-question: 'Who should be the Guardian of the Constitution?' (Kelsen 1931). Together with the published version of his 1928 speech, this article became a general-theoretical justification of the Austrian Constitutional Court system. Kelsen raised the legal system created for Austria to an abstract level, which then became a paradigm for many other legal systems (van Ooyen 2008: VIII).

The image of the guardian used by Kelsen is reminiscent of the description of the US Supreme Court given at the beginning of this chapter. The court referred to the constitution as a 'superior, paramount law'. In the same way Kelsen saw the constitution as a paramount norm (Kelsen 1929: 36 (7)). He extended the image still further by structuring the entire legal order hierarchically into higher norms and lower norms and explained that the constitution was superior to statute law in the same way as statute law was superior to the judgment of a court. Both when parliament passed a new law and when a judge gave a ruling, it was the higher-ranking norms that made the enacting of a new law or a fresh judicial decision possible that had to be reviewed first. On Kelsen's account, these higher-ranking norms provide a kind of framework, which is partly open-ended and gives the competent legal institutions a certain space to manoeuvre. The actual nature of the decision that the legal instance reaches is discretionary. Here one leaves the domain of legal interpretation and enters the realm of expediency – of a political nature. Both of these aspects, legal interpretation

25 See to the controversy in general Olechowski 2013: 15 ff.

26 The article, first published in 1929 in the *Archiv des öffentlichen Rechts*, became extended to a monograph later (Schmitt 1931). See to the controversy in general Diner and Stolleis (1999).

and the political considerations, are always present when a legal act is carried out. Executing the law and delivering a legal opinion are therefore one and the same thing (Kelsen 1931: 586 (67)).

The political background which gave rise to the controversy between Schmitt and Kelsen becomes evident if we consider whom Schmitt regarded to be the true Guardian of the Constitution: the Reich President, who was the democratically elected representative of the entire nation and holder of a 'neutral power' within the state (Schmitt 1931: 132). In former times it was the task of the monarch; now, for Schmitt, it was the task of the Reich President to protect the constitution. Kelsen answered that the President was very powerful and that it should be obvious that nobody should be judge of his own affairs, that the task of examining whether the due adherence was shown to the constitution must not be surrendered to someone who primarily intends to infringe it and who is politically motivated (Kelsen 1931: 618 (96)).

These remarks – made in 1931 – were imbued with almost prophetic wisdom. Even at that time Kelsen noted that the political power of the Reich President had been steadily growing. Less than two years later, in February 1933, the democratic system of Weimar would be abolished: this occurred through the Presidential Order for the Protection of People and State – the so-called Reichstag Fire Decree. Kelsen, who had been lecturing in Cologne at that time, lost his professorial chair in April 1933, whereas Schmitt joined the National Socialist German Workers' Party (NSDAP) in May. Almost at the same time the Austrian Federal Government carried out a *coup d'état*, partly hoping to stop the triumphant advance of National Socialism in Austria, partly because it rejected the democratic system itself. In March 1933, the Austrian parliament was dispensed with and in June 1933 the Constitutional Court was abolished (Walter 1997). Perhaps these events of 1933 demonstrate more clearly, and better than any theoretical discussion ever could, the intrinsic connection between democracy and the Constitutional Court system.

3.5 Developments after 1945

After the end of World War II, the centralized Constitutional Court system embarked on a triumphant takeover throughout much of Europe (Heller 2010: 74).[27] The Austrian Constitutional Court was already re-established

[27] The overview given here is following Haase and Struger (2009: 69 ff). See for Germany also Borowski (2003) with further references.

in 1945; a year later a Constitutional Court, based on this model, was created in Bavaria in 1946, becoming in its turn the model for the Federal Constitutional Court of Germany, which took up its activities in 1951. Likewise, the Italian Constitution of 1948 foresaw a Constitutional Court, which began its activity only in 1956. Eight years later, in 1964, Yugoslavia followed as the first state led by a socialist government to introduce the Constitutional Court system. In Czechoslovakia, the return to the Constitutional Court system did not take place before 1991;[28] after its dissolution into a Czech and a Slovakian Republic, the common tradition of constitutional jurisdiction is now independently perpetuated in Brno and in Bratislava. Meanwhile, there is hardly a European state without a Constitutional Court, a Supreme Court with constitutional competences or some other type of judicial control of the constitution; most of them follow the Kelsenian model.

And what about Europe itself? It is well known that the Treaty establishing a Constitution for Europe has not been realized. Nevertheless, if examined from the legal point of view, the Treaties of Rome and Maastricht with their amendments, such as the Treaty of Lisbon, can be seen as a sort of constitution. Moreover, in some aspects, the ECJ can be seen as a Constitutional Court.[29] In particular, the procedure of nullity, which enables the annulment of legal acts contradictory to the European Treaties, shows many parallels to the legal examination process at the Austrian Constitutional Court.

European law literature often describes the Commission as 'guardian of the treaties'.[30] This image is as inappropriate as that of the Reich President being the Guardian of the Constitution. The Guardian of the Treaties is clearly the ECJ, and for this reason it is justifiable to describe it as a European Constitutional Court.

On this basis, it is observable that one of the core institutions of contemporary politics, and one of – if not *the* – most noteworthy institution in the European Union can be traced to a series of policies and controversies originating in Austria in the later Habsburg period

[28] The Constitutional Court of the Czech and Slovak Republic existed for only ten months: Spáčil (2008: 26).

[29] The status of the ECJ as a Constitutional Court is often disputed (Shapiro and Stone 1994: 411); O'Neill (2009: 7). However, its classification as a Constitutional Court began in the late 1970s and was generally established by the 1980s (Weidmann 1985: 294). This view, although still not universal, is now common. Note the recent description of the ECJ as a 'comprehensive Constitutional Court' in Bauer (2008: 174).

[30] This common phrase appears to originate in Ipsen (1972: 361).

and the First Republic. Some questions regarding the contemporary role of judicial review cannot easily be answered through historical analysis of the Austrian context. For example, the reasons for the prominence of rights-based jurisprudence in modern constitutional review after 1945 need a separate explanation (see Madsen, Chapter 9 in this book), as Kelsen was of the opinion that parliament ought to have primary responsibility for deciding how fundamental rights must be understood. He claimed that a Constitutional Court could only exceptionally rescind a law in contravention of fundamental rights. Nonetheless, many socio-political functions performed by Constitutional Courts in contemporary society, for example their role in stabilizing loosely integrated democracies, their role in establishing higher norms for new federal polities, and even their ability to link national jurisprudence to international law, can be observed, however inchoately, in the Austrian setting at the beginning of the twentieth century.

Bibliography

Alter, Karen J. (1998). 'Who are the "Masters of the Treaty"? European Governments and the European Court of Justice', *International Organization* 52(1): 121–47.

Bauer, Lukas (2008). *Der Europäische Gerichtshof als Verfassungsgericht?* Baden-Baden: Nomos.

Blokker, Paulus (2013). 'Constitutions and Democracy in Post-national Times: A Political-sociological Approach', *Irish Journal of Sociology* 20(2): 68–90.

Borowski, Martin (2003). 'The Beginnings of Germany's Federal Constitutional Court', *Ratio Juris* 16: 155–86.

Burley, Anne-Marie and Walter Mattli (1993). 'Europe before the Court: A Political Theory of Legal Integration', *International Organization* 47(1): 41–76.

Commaille, Jacques, Laurence Dumoulin and Cécile Robert (2010). *La juridicisation du politique*. Paris: L.G.D.J.

Dahl, Robert A. (1957). 'Decision-Making in a Democracy: The Supreme Court as a National Policy-Maker', *Journal of Public Law* 6: 279–95.

Diner, Dan and Michael Stolleis (eds) (1999). *Hans Kelsen and Carl Schmitt: A Juxtaposition*. Gerlingen: Bleicher.

Elliott, Mark (2003). 'Embracing "Constitutional" Legislation: Towards Fundamental Law?', *Northern Ireland Legal Quarterly* 54(1): 25–42.

Ferejohn, John (2002). 'Judicializing Politics, Politicizing Law', *Law and Contemporary Problems* 65(3): 41–68.

Gawron, Thomas and Ralf Rogowski (2007). *Die Wirkung des Bundesverfassungsgerichts. Rechtssoziologische Analysen*. Baden-Baden: Nomos.

Haase, Gudrun and Katrin Struger (2009). *Verfassungsgerichtsbarkeit in Europa.* Wien: Verlag Österreich.

Heller, Kurt (2010). *Der Verfassungsgerichtshof. Die Entwicklung der Verfassungsgerichtsbarkeit in Österreich von den Anfängen bis zur Gegenwart.* Wien: Verlag Österreich.

Hesse, Hans Albrecht (2006). 'Das Bundesverfassungsgericht in der Perspektive der Rechtssoziologie', in Robert Christian van Ooyen and Martin H.W. Möllers (eds). *Das Bundesverfassungsgericht im politischen System.* Wiesbaden: VS Verlag, pp. 87–98.

Hirschl, Ran (2004). *Towards Juristocracy. The Origins and the Consequences of the New Constitutionalism.* Cambridge, MA: Harvard University Press.

(2007). 'The New Constitutionalism and the Judicialization of Pure Politics Worldwide', *Fordham Law Review* 75: 721–53.

Ipsen, Hans Peter (1972). *Europäisches Gemeinschaftsrecht.* Tübingen: Mohr Siebeck.

Jabloner, Clemens (2011). 'Die Gerichtshöfe des öffentlichen Rechts im Zuge des Staatsumbaues 1918 bis 1920', *Beiträge zur Rechtsgeschichte Österreichs* 1: 213–27.

Jellinek, Georg (1885). *Ein Verfassungsgerichtshof für Österreich.* Wien: Hölder.

Kelsen, Hans (1914). 'Reichsgesetz und Landesgesetz nach der österreichischen Verfassung', *Archiv des öffentlichen Rechts* 32: 202–45 and 390–438.

(1919). 'Die Stellung der Länder in der künftigen Verfassung Deutschösterreichs', *Zeitschrift für öffentliches Recht* 1: 98–122.

(1929). 'Mitbericht [zum Beratungsgegenstand: Wesen und Entwicklung der Staatsgerichtsbarkeit]', in *Veröffentlichungen der Vereinigung der Deutschen Staatsrechtslehrer.* Vol. 5. Berlin/Leipzig: de Gruyter, pp. 30–84. Reprinted in Robert Christian van Ooyen (ed.) (2008). *Wer soll der Hüter der Verfassung sein?* Tübingen: Mohr Siebeck, pp. 1–57.

(1931). 'Wer soll der Hüter der Verfassung sein?' *Die Justiz* VI, pp. 576–628. Reprinted in: Robert Christian van Ooyen (ed.) (2008). *Wer soll der Hüter der Verfassung sein?* Tübingen: Mohr Siebeck, pp. 58–105.

Madsen, Mikael R. (2010). *La genèse de l'Europe des droits de l'homme. Enjeux juridiques et strategies d'état (France, Grande-Bretagne et pays scandinaves).* Strasbourg: Presses universitaires de Strasbourg.

Merkl, Adolf (1919). *Die Verfassung der Republik Deutschösterreich. Ein kritisch-systematischer Grundriß.* Wien, Leipzig: F. Deuticke.

Miller, Jonathan (1997). 'Judicial Review and Constitutional Stability: A Sociology of the U.S. Model and its Collapse in Argentina', *Hastings International and Comparative Law Review* 21: 77–176.

Münch, Richard (2008). 'Constructing a European Society by Jurisdiction', *European Law Journal* 14(5): 519–41.

Olechowski, Thomas (2009). 'Der Beitrag Hans Kelsens zur österreichischen Bundesverfassung', in Robert Walter *et al.* (eds). *Hans Kelsen: Leben – Werk – Wirksamkeit.* Wien: Manz, pp. 211–30.

(2010). 'Grundrechte und ihr Schutz in der Habsburgermonarchie', *Österreichische Richterzeitung* 88: 30–7.

(2013). 'Hans Kelsen als Mitglied der Deutschen Staatsrechtslehrervereinigung', in Matthias Jestaedt (ed.). *Hans Kelsen und die deutsche Staatsrechtslehre*. Tübingen: Mohr Siebeck, pp. 11–27.

O'Neill, Michael (2009). *The Struggle for the European Constitution. A Past and Future History*. London: Routledge.

Öhlinger, Theo (2003). 'The Genesis of the Austrian Model of Constitutional Review of Legislation', *Ratio Juris* 16: 206–22.

Osterkamp, Jana (2009). *Verfassungsgerichtsbarkeit in der Tschechoslowakei (1920–1939). Verfassungsidee – Demokratieverständnis – Nationalitätenproblem*. Frankfurt am Main: Vittorio Klostermann.

(2011). 'Verfassungshüter ohne politischen Rückhalt. Das tschechoslowakische Verfassungsgericht nach 1920 im Vergleich mit Österreich', *Beiträge zur Rechtsgeschichte Österreichs* 1: 275–90.

Paulson, Stanley (2003). 'Constitutional Review in the United States and Austria: Notes on the Beginnings', *Ratio Juris* 16: 223–39.

Renoux, Thierry S. (1994). 'Le Conseil constitutionnel et le pouvoir judiciaire en France dans le modèle européen de contrôle de constitutionnalité des lois', *Revue internationale de droit comparé* 46(3): 891–9.

Rumpler, Helmut and Peter Urbanitsch (eds) (2000). *Die Habsburgermonarchie 1848–1918*. Vol. VII: *Verfassung und Parlamentarismus*. Wien: Verlag der Österreichischen Akademie der Wissenschaften.

Schatz, Sara (1998). 'A Neo-Weberian Approach to Constitutional Courts in the Transition from Authoritarian Rule: The Mexican Case (1994–1997)', *International Journal of the Sociology of Law* 26: 217–44.

Schelle, Karel and Jaromír Tauchen (2009). *Grundriss der Tschechoslowakischen Rechtsgeschichte*. München: Verlag Dr. Hut.

Scheppele, Kim Lane (2003). 'Constitutional Negotiations. Political Contexts of Judicial Activism in Post-Soviet Europe', *International Sociology* 18(1): 219–38.

Schmitt, Carl (1931). *Der Hüter der Verfassung*. Tübingen: Mohr Siebeck. Reprinted Berlin: Duncker & Humblot (1996).

Schmitz, Georg (2003). 'The Constitutional Court of the Republic of Austria 1918–1920', *Ratio Juris* 16: 240–65.

Schnapper, Dominique (2010). *Une sociologue au Conseil constitutionnel*. Paris: Gallimard.

Schulz, Martin (2010). 'Verfassungsgerichtsbarkeit im globalen Kontext', *giga-focus* 5: 1–8.

Sellert, Wolfgang (1990). 'Richterliches Prüfungsrecht', in Adalbert Erler *et al.* (eds). *Handwörterbuch zur Deutschen Rechtsgeschichte*. Vol. IV. Berlin: Erich Schmidt Verlag, pp. 1050–4.

Shapiro, Martin and Alec Stone (1994). 'The New Constitutional Politics of Europe', *Comparative Political Studies* 26(4): 397–420.

Skapska, Grażyna (2011). *From 'Civil Society' to 'Europe'. A Sociological Study on Constitutionalism after Communism*. Leiden: Brill.

Spáčil, Michal (2008). *Ústavní Soud České Repbuliky. The Constitutional Court of the Czech Republic*. Brno: published by the Czech Constitutional Court.

Stolleis, Michael (2003). 'Judicial Review, Administrative Review, and Constitutional Review in the Weimar Republic', *Ratio Juris* 16: 266–80.

Stone Sweet, Alec (2004). *The Judicial Construction of Europe*. Oxford: Oxford University Press.

Stourzh, Gerald (1989). *Wege zur Grundrechtsdemokratie*. Wien, Köln: Böhlau.

(2011). *Der Umfang der österreichischen Geschichte*. Wien, Köln, Graz: Böhlau.

Tate, C. Neal (1995). 'Why the Expansion of Judicial Power?' in C. Neal Tate and Torbjörn Vallinder (eds). *The Global Expansion of Judicial Power*. New York, NY: New York University Press, pp. 27–38.

Thornhill, Chris (2012). 'The Formation of a European Constitution: An Approach from Historical-Political Sociology', *International Journal of Law in Context* 8(3): 354–93.

Triepel, Heinrich (1929). 'Bericht [zum Beratungsgegenstand: Wesen und Entwicklung der Staatsgerichtsbarkeit]', in *Veröffentlichungen der Vereinigung der Deutschen Staatsrechtslehrer*. Vol. 5. Berlin, Leipzig: de Gruyter, pp. 2–28.

Urofsky, Melvin I. and Paul Finkelman (eds) (2002). *Documents of American Constitutional and Legal History*. Vol. I, 2nd edition. Oxford: Oxford University Press.

van Ooyen, Robert Christian (2008). 'Die Funktion der Verfassungsgerichtsbarkeit in der pluralistischen Demokratie und die Kontroverse um den "Hüter der Verfassung"', in Robert Christian van Ooyen (ed.). *Wer soll der Hüter der Verfassung sein?* Tübingen: Mohr Siebeck, pp. vii–xxiii.

Vauchez, Antoine (2008). 'The Force of a Weak Field: Law and Lawyers in the Government of the European Union (For a Renewed Research Agenda)', *International Political Sociology* 2: 128–44.

Walter, Robert (1997). 'Die Ausschaltung des Verfassungsgerichtshofes im Jahre 1933', in Verfassungsgerichtshof der Republik Österreich (ed.). *Verfassungstag 1997*. Wien: Austrian Constitutional Court, pp. 17–34.

Weidmann, Klaus W. (1985). *Der Europäische Gerichtshof auf dem Weg zu einem europäischen Verfassungsgerichtshof*. Frankfurt am Main: Lang.

Wellens, Karel (2004). 'Fragmentation of International Law and Establishing an Accountability Regime for International Organizations: The Role of the Judiciary in Closing the Gap', *Michigan Journal of International Law* 25: 1159–81.

Woodhouse, Diana (2004). 'The Constitutional and Political Implications of a United Kingdom Supreme Court', *Legal Studies* 24: 134–55.

4

Judicialization: A sociohistorical perspective (lessons and questions from the French Fifth Republic)

ANTOINE VAUCHEZ

> Whereas the values of the Republic and the values of public service are at the core of the teaching dispensed in the elite institutions of higher education in the [French] Republic, whereas Alain Juppé was trained in precisely these institutions, subsequently served as a high civil servant, and later played a prominent role in public life, notably as a member of Parliament, precluding that he was ignorant of the letter of the law regarding the acts of which he is declared guilty [...] Whereas in the terms of article 4 of the Constitution 'political parties and groups contribute to the expression of the public will. They are formed and exercise their activity freely. They are bound to respect the principles of national sovereignty...'; and hereby is in particular reiterated their submission to the law, the expression of national sovereignty before which 'all citizens' are equal; whereas Alain Juppé, in search of the human resources that he deemed necessary to the action of the RPR, deliberately opted for a certain efficiency, through recourse to illegal arrangements [...] Whereas the nature of the acts committed is intolerable for the body politic, being contrary to the general will expressed by the law; in acting thusly Alain Juppé, at the time invested with a public elective mandate, betrayed the confidence of the sovereign people. [...].[1]

4.1 A judicial revolution?

Since the early 1990s, Europe has been in the throes of a veritable judicial revolution. From the first major investigations of political corruption in

[1] 'Les principaux attendus du premier procès Juppé', *Le Nouvel Observateur*, 20 October 2004. Personal translation. This quote is taken from the judgment of the tribunal of Nanterre that in January 2004 found former prime minister Alain Juppé guilty in the political scandal related to the illegal financing of the Gaullist party at the time presided over by Jacques Chirac.

the early 1990s to the present, the scope of the judicial control exercised by magistrates over the political body has extended further up the hierarchy of positions in society, and has become more intense and pervasive over the period. First and foremost, this domination has expanded through the proliferation of judicial enquiries concerning political personnel and practices. The creation of teams of specialized investigators grouped in economic and financial judicial poles and the resulting strategies aimed at materially joining cases have fostered an unprecedented increase in the range and time of investigation. This is illustrated in France by the gigantic Elf case, relating to kickbacks connected to large French oil contracts in Africa, and in Italy by a variety of anti-mafia trials, starting with the one against former Prime Minister Giulio Andreotti (cf. Briquet 2007).

The reach of judicial review extends even farther, as legal investigations have moved up the ladder of the political hierarchy, rising from political 'spade men' and supporters to the very highest level of parties and government (Vauchez 2005; Roussel 2002). Judges have thus gradually penetrated a series of 'political sanctuaries'. This has been the case in France, from the first searches conducted in the headquarters of political parties, an event which was labelled at the time a 'judicial burglary' by Georges Kiejman, a lawyer who represented the Socialist Party at the beginning of the 1990s, to the Clearstream case, which implicated Dominique de Villepin and Nicolas Sarkozy, who were at the time respectively Prime Minister and *ministre de l'intérieur* (Home Secretary) under Jacques Chirac. More than anything else, the latter incident clearly illustrates the extent to which it has become commonplace to search and subpoena witnesses at the very heart of the state.[2] Indeed, over the years no ministry has escaped searches, whether it be the ministry of Finance, Health, Foreign Affairs, Defence or the Home Office. Only once has this judicial penetration been brought to a halt in France: this was in March 2001, when President Jacques Chirac refused to respond to a subpoena summoning him as an 'assisted witness' in an investigation of embezzlement of funds related to the attribution of public housing contracts by the City of Paris, of which Chirac had been mayor from 1977 to 1995.

In addition, judicial power has also become more intense, as enquiries now extend well beyond the cases of political corruption that had

[2] At the time, in 2006, the questioning of sitting Prime Minister Dominique de Villepin lasted one entire day.

traditionally been their purview; the very ways in which public action is conducted are now subject to scrutiny, nationally as well as locally. The 'contaminated blood' affair (referring to the failure of the government and the administration in the mid-1980s to consider the risk that the HIV virus could be transmitted via blood transfusions), as well as the 'straw huts' affair (concerning political and bureaucratic accountability regarding the 1999 explosion of a restaurant illegally built on a beach in Corsica), triggered deep-digging investigations into the political/bureaucratic chain of command, ultimately implicating both ministers and directors of the civil service (Beaud 2000). There is no aspect, not even 'the dark side of politics' – the 'secret funds' that used to be distributed by the prime minister's office until the early 2000s; the 'black cabinet' of the secret services at the presidential offices and its illegal activities in controlling François Mitterrand's major critics – that can now avoid the risk of being exposed to the light of investigation.

4.2 'Judicialization' as a grid for sociohistorical analysis

The concept of 'judicialization' is a classic tool used within political science to describe the historical transformations of the place occupied by justice and designate the incremental expansion of judicial power (see for example Tate and Vallinder 1997; Guarnieri and Pederzoli 1996; Cichowski and Stone 2003). Other related terms such as 'jurocracy' (Horowitz 1977), 'juristocracy' (Hirschl 2004) or 'courtocracy' (Scheppele 2003) have also emerged, but the notion of 'judicialization' is the most widely employed term – so much so that it has become a catch-all category, which is used to describe the increasing control judges enjoy in determining and regulating a broad range of public policies in the fields of medicine, politics and economics – in India, France (Commaille and Kaluszinsky 2007; Stone 1994), the European Union (Cichowski 2007; Kelemen 2011), the World Trade Organization (Stone and Brunell 2013), and the United States (Shapiro 1994). All these authors note a general shift in the balance of power and in the sources of legitimacy, both nationally and internationally. As the notion was becoming a sort of a meeting point for legal studies and political science focusing on justice, it became a vague term with as many definitions as there are authors in the field: some writers use it to refer only to constitutional courts, others look to all 'judicial' powers regardless of their great diversity within and among countries (on this point see Vauchez 2004), and still others have an even broader vision of the dissemination of a 'judicial model' via the growing recourse to quasi-judicial procedures in government administration and the economy. The different typologies produced clearly reveal this to be a polysemic field. For Alessandro Pizzorno (1998), a historical figure in Italian sociology, 'judicialization' embraces five phenomena:

1) the growing participation of the judge in the process of creating the law;
2) the trend whereby legislative and administrative bodies increasingly delegate powers to the judiciary;
3) wider access of citizens to justice for resolution of conflicts that were traditionally resolved by various social authorities;
4) the institution of oversight regarding constitutionality;
5) the emergence and expansion of the practice of oversight of political rectitude or 'supervision of virtue' by judges.

This analysis touches simultaneously upon the place of judicial decisions in public action, the professional model for judges, and the political, social and also moral functions that are granted to them in a given society, etc. The Canadian legal specialist Ran Hirschl (2006), however, evokes just three situations:

1) the spread of legal discourse, jargon, rules, and procedures into the political sphere and policy-making forums and processes;
2) judicialization of public policy-making through 'ordinary' administrative and judicial review; and
3) the judicialization of 'pure politics' – the transfer to the courts of matters of an outright political nature and significance including the issue of core regime legitimacy.

Without further pursuing this inventory, which could in any case never be exhaustive, when looking at the prolific development of work within this field, we cannot avoid observing that these very different studies share one common point: that is, all, or nearly all (see *a contrario* Roussel 2003; Commaille and Dumoulin 2009), proceed as if the term were simply a popular academic categorization that can be used to describe transformations of society from the outside. Contrary to this impression, however, all evidence indicates that the use of the term 'judicialization' has developed in academic circles, not as an external description, but *in parallel* with a multitude of other social spheres, which means that the theory is not an *ex post* explanation of the practice. Quite the contrary, in fact, the scholarly discourse on 'judicialization' was constructed at the same time, and sometimes in the same context, as observations of practices in the judicial field itself. We cannot ignore the fact that 'judicialization' is also a *mot d'ordre* for the actors in the social spheres that this term claims to describe. A host of think-tanks, professional groups (of magistrates, lawyers, etc.), para-public research centres, expert committees and other bodies have elicited, or themselves fashioned, discourses and definitions, often competing with each other, on this subject. Indeed, since the 1990s, a vast lexical field has developed around the related and frequently used notions 'juridictionnalization', 'juridicization', 'procéduralization', 'giustizialismo', 'giuridizionalizzazione', etc. Some of these terms have even found their way into dictionaries – *judiciariser* and *judiciarisation*, for example, became entries in the Larousse in 2002 (Commaille and Dumoulin 2009). Actors in differing social positions have thus taken up these words and transformed them into 'discursive arms' to serve the causes and sectoral conflicts in which they are mobilized (doctors/patients, employers/employees, government majority/opposition, professors/students, companies/consumers, etc.). The term is today an 'object-frontier', sufficiently malleable and adaptable to be easily circulated from one social sphere to another, but also sufficiently robust and coherent to bind together a stable set of meanings (Griesemer and Star 1989). Unsurprisingly, as a result of this, the term is very normatively charged – positively or negatively, depending on the cases and social groups involved. For some, it describes a desirable development, an essential lever for social progress, which will check the arbitrary character of traditional social powers (patriarchal, professorial, etc.) and make way for the full empowerment of individual rights. For others, this development brings with it a major risk that a 'government by judges' could emerge, a trend in the development of a 'litigation society', or even an 'Americanization' of society. Whether they fear or favour this 'development', these actors nonetheless share a common arsenal of arguments – that of 'judicialization' – that has by now come to be the central set of arguments when discussing the role of judges in society (Commaille and Dumoulin 2009). One of the characteristics of this concept is its hybrid nature, specifically in relation to the way in which the descriptive and the prescriptive are interwoven at all times. It is descriptive of a historical movement that is seen to be ineluctable, and by means of which 'justice', understood as a homogeneous 'actor' endowed with a single unique and transhistorical rationality ('the law'), is progressively established in all social spheres as the central space for mediation and arbitration. But it is also prescriptive, because this movement signals, depending on the individual case, a 'progress' or, on the contrary, a 'deterioration' of democratic societies, marked by a growing individualization of rights. In this sense, the concept bears similarities to ideology as defined by the Marxist French philosopher

Louis Althusser: that is, it maintains a double relationship to the real, through *allusion*, in the mode of empirical observation, and through *illusion*, in the mode of historical prophecy.

When confronted with this type of frequently found discourse (the terms 'modernization', 'financiarization', 'managerialization', etc. come to mind), it is not the sociologist's role to separate the 'true' from the 'false', and even less to decree what would be 'well founded' or 'lacking substance' in fact. In fact, by the consequences of belief that they engender, or simply by virtue of their 'cognitive saliency' in the public debate, these notions are 'well founded illusions', to use the celebrated expression of Emile Durkheim. In a way, it hardly matters whether these developments are 'substantiated' or 'mythologized' if there are social actors who believe in them and feel obliged to adjust to their 'reality'. In other words, the notion of 'judicialization' is itself a *mythe agissant*, which has a very real impact on the social sphere: by grounding new anticipations, diagnoses or claims, it helps bring about the development that it has described itself. To gain evidence of this, it is enough simply to observe the political field, where 'judicialization' is taken to be a 'reality' that justifies 'political reactions' and 'public policies' that are intended to promote this trend: 'upholding the Constitution', 'combating political corruption' by bolstering the instruments at the disposal of the judiciary, 'defending independent justice' – or, inversely, countering it – by restoring 'the primacy of democratic legitimacy', 'the sovereignty of the people', etc. This underscores the essential importance of representations, and especially of academic or quasi-academic theorizations of the growing role of judges, because these contribute to the transformation of disparate facts in various domains (a spectacular judicial ruling, a reform of the justice system, etc.) into indicators of an overall movement and of a new 'context of action' marked by a 'judicialization' of cross-sectoral or even global scope.

At this point, the nature of the sociological question changes: it is no longer a matter of providing a supplementary definition of 'judicialization', but rather a matter of tracking the historical and social conditions in which this concept has come to be established as a template for deciphering situations or events and as a set of justificatory arguments that are applicable to a multitude of social spheres – so much so that this 'judicialization' is today taken to be a self-evident social fact. This means that the question for sociologists is now a matter of tracing the collective and circular dynamics of the social transformation of identities, institutions and instruments that, from sector to sector, have given judicial rulings and, more broadly, judicial powers this saliency in the public sphere. A few examples come to mind: the creation or reinforcement of legal departments in government administrations (Colera 2009); the exponential development of insurance contracts that cover 'legal risks'; the adoption of policies offering broader access to the justice system via legal aid as a new component of citizenship; the development of 'rights' for various categories of users, consumers (class action), victims and patients; and the proliferation of polls concerning a 'demand for justice' or 'the right to reparation'. The objective of a political sociology of 'judicialization' thus lies in tracing the historical process – always contested, always situated, always reversible – that triggers and consolidates this movement of circular reinforcement between the effects of belief in 'judicialization' as an ineluctable global phenomenon on the one hand and the concrete social practices that ground their legitimacy and authority in this judicial teleology on the other hand.

In this sense, the sociology of 'judicialization' necessarily calls for a historical study of the conditions under which this 'theory effect' is fostered. This sociology is meaningful only in relation to an *earlier* period, in which the law and legal practitioners were marginalized in political, administrative and economic spheres, as illustrated in the next section (4.3). It cannot be understood without discussing the work of engagement and enrolment that a number of 'entrepreneurs of law' undertook starting in the 1970s (4.4). It requires tracing the social conditions that fostered the emergence of this movement (4.5). Finally, it calls for a mapping of the power struggles in various sectors of society concerning the reality of this 'new deal' and its necessary consequences (4.6).

4.3 A starting point: the instauration of the Fifth Republic in France and the 'Crisis of Law'

A discussion of 'judicialization' only makes sense if it is viewed in relation to the period when, unlike today, France was 'unjudiciarized'. In this respect, the situation in France in the 1960s can serve as a starting point. This period witnessed the culmination of a process of marginalization of the law and legal professions that had begun in the first decade of the century. We can read, for instance, this diagnosis written by an observer in 1964:

> When one seeks to describe the position of the legal profession in society today, one is struck by the flight from the legal system of the subjects of the law, as well as by the tangible diminution of the courts' functions and a profound transformation of the role of the judge. Regarding the flight from justice, the figures are eloquent: in 1892 there were 621,000 cases per year

> in France, for 38 million inhabitants. In 1956 there were only 457,000 cases for a population of 43 million. [. . .] Recruitment for the legal profession is poor. It does not seem to match the aspirations of the young generation. [. . .] In our industrial society the legal professional meets with nothing but scorn from the rich and hate from the poor. [. . .] Scorned on one side, hated on the other, the legal profession seems to have ceased to be necessary, politically, socially and economically. (Jacob 1964: 1 and 6)

The conclusion is brutal: French society accords only a marginal role to the judiciary and its professionals.

Indeed, already largely undermined in the post-World War II period, the conditions surrounding the creation of the French Fifth Republic a few years earlier had confirmed the decline of the 'law-centred model'. This dominant model of political legitimacy upheld both a balance of power favourable to Parliament – a system for producing laws in which parliamentary committees and legal corporations have the leading roles – and a form of political elite incarnated in the figure of the lawyer-member of Parliament (Sacriste 2012). We now know, building on two decades of research in political sociology, that this model was definitively abolished by the establishment of the Fifth Republic. The new frameworks conferring intelligibility on the government called into question the basic pillars of the law-centred model (Vauchez 2005). This new regime, born at the intersection between the Gaullist stance (power restored to central state government, plebiscite as a form of legitimization) and the move to reform the bureaucracy in order to steer the economic and political rebirth of the country through planning and modernization, etc., was expressly founded in opposition to the law-centred government of the Third and Fourth Republic. The rejection of the '*régime d'assemblée*' (namely the overall ascendancy of the Parliament) was accompanied by a critique of legal formalism (Dulong 1997), which was deemed incapable of grounding 'modern' public action and unable to face the challenges of a rapidly evolving French society. In this context, legal knowledge had largely lost its currency within the structures of the state (in the definition of the requisite qualities of the 'high civil servant' and that of the 'figure of state' alike), and it was replaced by the bureaucratic expertise of the top functionaries of the *Commissariat général du Plan* and the 'vital forces' of the country, i.e. high-level civil servants, 'reformist' trade unions and corporate business leaders, and representatives of social sciences, in particular economics and sociology. This can be seen in the very drafting process of the new Constitution adopted in October 1958, which demoted law faculties to a secondary role as engineers of political institutions (François 1997). It can also be seen in the legislative procedure, in which legal expertise was ostracized, even in the most traditional domains of civil law such as family and personal law. Here, public policy was now instead pre-empted by new specialists, new knowledge (demographic, statistical, etc.) and new institutions (Lenoir 1990; Vauchez 2005).

This decline in the esteem of legal expertise was mirrored in the changes in the channels and pathways through which the political and administrative elite were recruited. The dissolution of lawyers' networks of influence and access to careers in politics that had begun in the post-war period suddenly accelerated.[3] From 30 per cent in 1910, only 12.8 per cent of MPs from 1945 to 1958 were lawyers, a figure which fell again to 7.5 per cent by 1958 (Le Beguec 2003). The most senior deputies and senators elected before the war were the last to have known the *République des avocats* that had been so decisive in establishing the Third Republic (Le Beguec 2003).[4] Generally speaking, we can observe a movement ostracizing law faculties in the training of the elite for the political and for government administration. This decline, which commenced in part under the Third Republic with the development of the *Ecole libre des science politiques* (Sacriste 2012), accelerated because of the inability of law professors to block the creation of an *Ecole national d'administration*, and later to wield any influence over access to this institution and its teachings. The emergence of business schools and the increasingly autonomous status of the study of economics also deprived law faculties of their traditional career opportunities in banking and finance, so that law schools no longer had any purpose other than to train future professionals in legal and judicial fields. Indeed, enrolment in law schools stagnated and even dropped in the post-war period to 32,000 students in 1959–60 compared to close to 40,000 ten years earlier, showing a certain disaffection with law studies, whereas the opposite was true within literary and scientific studies. The attractiveness of legal professions also suffered, as attested

[3] Gilles Le Beguec in *La République des avocats* (2003) notes, however, that it was above all the elite of the Paris Bar that seemed to lose interest in political careers, while the profession of lawyer apparently continued to represent a valid resource at the local level (at least up to the end of the 1960s).

[4] The same is true for government ministries, but came later in time. Much more than for Parliament, 1958 was the moment of collapse – only two ministers in the Debré government were lawyers, with a total of nine lawyers appointed minister between 1959 and 1967 (Le Beguec 2003). This confirmed the ebb tide for ministerial cabinets (11% in 1944–46, 7% under the Fourth Republic, 2% under the Fifth Republic).

by the unprecedented difficulties encountered in recruiting judges during this period. The number of candidates for the *Ecole nationale de la magistrature* (ENM) fell steeply from 280 in 1958 to 202 in 1963 and to 98 in 1964 (Bodiguel 1991). As the ultimate proof of this loss of status, the major reform of the judiciary undertaken by the Minister of Justice, Michel Debré, in January 1958 called for the creation of a magistrates' school with a single competitive entrance exam modelled after ENA as the only possible way out of this crisis (Boigeol 1989). Moreover, the sense of decline remained very much present in legal debate, which was often tinged with pessimistic humour, for instance in the writing of tutelary figures such as George Ripert (*Déclin du droit*, 1949) and René Savatier (*Métamorphoses économiques et sociales du droit*, 1948), as well as in the significant reform of the law curriculum in 1954, which henceforth included non-judicial subject matter (political science, legal sociology, criminology) in the hopes of boosting the credibility of legal training (Vauchez 2005).

4.4 Historical conditions of possibility: the *aggorniamento* of the legal professions

It is important to understand the historical conditions that made it possible for the legal and judicial professions to rise from this marginal position. To this end, I will in this section present the unexpected consequence of the exclusion of legal specialists from political and administrative spheres in the post-war period: namely that this exclusion encouraged the development of a variety of strategies to *reinvest* in legal jobs and positions from the 1960s onwards, a process which was accompanied by a profound *aggiornamento* of professional knowledge and practices. In this respect, legal professionals fostered new relationships with the political and economic spheres, in which judges were used as mediators and even social regulators *par excellence.*

The first part of this process was the invention of new forms of political engagement on the fringes of conventional party politics in the 1960s and 1970s. Legal activism emerged in a series of causes and struggles such as women's rights, support for foreign workers, defence of the rights of employees, environmental protection, regional autonomy movements (Basque, Corsican, Brittany, etc.) and human rights, for which recourse to law and legal proceedings had critical importance. This new alliance between social activism and the law was, of course, born in the new political context of the post-1968 years, in which 'new social movements' emerged in Europe and became progressively independent of the parties attached to the labour movement.[5] This 'cause-lawyering' (Sarat and Scheingold 1998) was also the product of the challenges traditional models of excellence within the legal professions faced with the *Syndicat de la magistrature* (Devillé 1992) among judges, the *Syndicat des avocats français* (SAF, cf. Tonneau 2011) among lawyers, and the *Critique du droit* movement (Kaluszinsky 2010) among professors. While these groups' denunciation of the false-front apolitical stance of 'bourgeois law' and of professional orders was fairly typical of the left, their contestation was innovative in that it simultaneously questioned the idea, previously prevalent in Socialist and Communist parties, that the law could *only* be a 'reflection of the dominant classes'. In direct contrast, they suggested that this instrument of the state could be usefully turned against the state itself, thereby becoming a subversive force (Israël 2009b; Madsen 2011; Agrikolianski 2003). In doing so, they rehabilitated legal knowledge and know-how and elevated them to tools that were indispensable for militants, both in defence against eventual penal prosecution and in seizing chances to change the law in the courts. An example of this would be the small group of high-level civil servants and law professors who in the early 1970s created the *Groupe d'information et de soutien des immigrés* (GISTI) and became specialists in defending the rights of foreign workers, being the engineers of a multitude of legal notes, advisory services and proceedings before the *Conseil d'Etat* (Israël 2009a). Likewise, the mobilization of lawyers within the SAF and the legal department of the *Confédération française démocratique du travail* (CFDT) trade union helped progressive magistrates develop a broad spectrum of new jurisprudence in the area of labour law (Cam 1978). Together, these various movements fostered the emergence of a new repertory of legal action, for which the law and the judicial arena became essential levers for social protest, and, more broadly, for driving demands addressed to the state. One example among others is the 'Ornano cabinet', which was formed in the 1970s around a collective of lawyers working 'full-time' to defend militants of a diverse range of causes – Basque and Corsican nationalists, labour activists, feminists, foreign workers, etc. This group is emblematic of the development of different forms of specialization in the defence of activists (Madsen 2011). The growing *professionalization* of the defence of these causes (environment, human rights, consumers, etc.) in the late 1970s also helped consolidate the new roles of both the law and the judge, as exemplified by

[5] On this point see Donatella Della Porta (1995); Isabelle Sommier (1998).

the emergence of specialized legal departments within non-governmental organizations (NGOs), trade unions and social movements.

However, this *aggiornamento* of legal professions was not limited to the sphere of legal activism. In fact, a move towards the conquest of the market of corporate consulting services can also be observed during this time. Heirs to an aristocratic conception of their role as being to emphasize the lawyer's vocation and disinterested motivation (Osiel 1990), the representatives of the French Bar had long been keen to close their profession to legal specialists who were closest to the commercial sector, i.e. corporate lawyers, legal advisors, business agents, etc. (Boigeol and Dezalay 1997). The acceptance of the 'business lawyer' as a professional member of the Bar came late and is inseparably linked to the contestation of the 'classic' Bar model that began in the 1960s (Karpik 1995). The most internationalized segments of the Paris Bar, bolstered by support from figureheads in the profession, such as Bar President René-William Thorp, recommended a taking back of the field of corporate legal advice that had been left to all sorts of competitors (legal and fiscal advisors, commercial court proxies, notaries, business agents, fund managers, etc.).[6] Drawing upon the 'promises' held in the rise of the Common Market (Vauchez 2013), they called for the birth of the 'business lawyer' or *avocat d'affaires*, a neologism[7] used to describe a legal practitioner who would 'no longer be exclusively a pleader of cases, a specialist in procedure, a man of litigation and lawsuits', but who would claim a position of 'permanent collaboration to provide advisory services relevant to the problems and plans of company executive management' (Jeantet 1964: 1 and 5). The arrival of this new type of lawyer coincided with the invention of a new kind of law – 'business law' (Jeantet 1957: 7) – which aspired to bring together all streams of legal knowledge useful to companies (fiscal, commercial, penal, etc.), and sought to break with an archaic system of commercial law that was perceived as belonging to the bygone era of 'shopkeepers'.[8]

This reform agenda led to the 1967 publication of the important *Livre bleu* by the *Association nationale des avocats*, calling for 'the [disappearance] of legal or fiscal advisors, so-called corporate consultants, legal services of so-called fiduciary companies, proxies before the commercial

[6] On this point see Boigeol and Dezalay (1997).

[7] This word was coined by René-William Thorp in a speech, 'La réforme du barreau', given at the solemn opening session of the lawyers' conference on 26 November 1955, in Thorp 1962: 213. Goldsmith (1964).

[8] On this point see the dissertation by Laurent Gueguen (2005).

courts, business agents, fund managers, real estate agents whose activity is to prospect for clients and negotiate contracts between parties' (Tinayre and Ricci 1967), to the benefit of a 'single, legal and judicial profession, independent and endowed with a monopoly' that would be fully capable of exercising its role within the world of business (Sialelli 1987: 151). This reform project successfully made its way to the political agenda and was implemented in the so-called 'fusion' laws in 1971 and 1990, under which, first, the profession of the *avoués* and, later, even more importantly, the corporate legal advisors (the so-called *conseillers juridiques*) were accepted into the Bar. Professional barriers and bans on activity thus became the favourite targets of the representatives of the 'business Bar'. The report *Rapport sur les professions du droit* submitted in 2008 to then-President Nicolas Sarkozy by Jean-Michel Darrois, a leading figure in this movement, took up this cause and called for the elimination of professional exclusions (in particular for activities as partner/manager of a commercial company) in order to allow lawyers to compete with 'service vendors such as banks, insurance companies, complementary health insurance providers, legal advisory services, debt recovery companies, as well as with chartered accountants and management consultants' (Sialelli 1987: 46). This gradual expansion of the scope of the legal profession with the 1971 law (absorbing advocates) and the 1991 law (absorbing legal advisors) went hand in hand with a far-reaching transformation of a number of French law firms, who now more than ever shaped their activity in entrepreneurial terms of management and profitability – the only way to fend off the increasing competition from British and American law firms. The rise of national and international competition (from corporate jurists, chartered accountants, etc. within the country and from British and American law firms) motivated new forms of 'corporate' organization within the Bar, particularly in the firms most confronted with international competitors. These corporate firms could employ up to several hundred people.[9] Thus, a 'business Bar' emerged around a cluster of large law firms with significant corporate client rosters, both French (August & Debouzy, Gide, Jeantet, Berlioz, Lefebvre, Fidal, etc.) and Anglo-American (Baker McKenzie, Cleary Gottlieb, Orrick, Willkie Farr & Gallagher, Weil & Gotschall, etc.). These firms now offered a wide range of 'services' to their clients, from litigation and 'legal advice' to management and lobbying on business law and fiscal issues.

[9] On this transformation, see Dezalay 1992.

Thus cause lawyers and business lawyers very concretely redefined professional practices, and, in this way, they proposed new models that underscored the social utility of the law. This undertaking was strengthened by new scholarly work within the field of legal doctrine in the late 1970s (Vauchez and Willemez 2007). With the introduction of new sources of jurisprudence from the Constitutional Council, the Court of Justice of the European Communities and the European Court of Human Rights, a group of 'entrepreneurs in doctrine' invested renewed interest in the subject of 'fundamental rights' in various ways ('constitutionalism', 'State of Law', 'fair trial', etc.) and they used this to found a new model to explain the legitimacy of law and judges (whether European, constitutional or judicial) as based in their functions as social and political regulators. Bastien François (1997) has shown that the work of the 'constitutionalist' professors who, from the late 1970s, reinvented French constitutional law aimed more at developing a case law grounded in fundamental freedoms more than just basic rules about the functioning of political institutions. The emergence of concepts such as 'Etat de droit' or 'constitutionalism' highlighted the importance of the jurisdictional function in limiting the power of the state. In this academic work the judge was thus henceforth the key to a renewed democracy.

4.5 Conditions of coalescence: 'judicialization' as social configuration

Until the 1990s, however, the theme of 'judicialization' was either absent or remained restricted to a few narrowly circumscribed social spheres. Indeed, the various movements focusing on the modernization of law mentioned above were not seen as constituting a 'system'. The emergence of 'judicialization' was first of all intimately tied to the fact that judicial actors had attained a new status of credibility in the public forum. The new place acquired by justice from the 1990s on was greatly reinforced by the fact that it coincided with a process of depoliticization of the public space, which underlined the value attributed to new 'virtues' such as expertise, objectivity and independence. The 1980s were a time of a simultaneous devaluation of political resources in the functioning of certain social networks (journalism, legal doctrine, not-for-profit and trade union activism, the judiciary) and ramping up of new canons of professional and sectoral excellence that strongly resonated with the criticism of the political universe (Briquet and Garraud 2001). The independence and objectivity of these sectoral transformations were highlighted and upheld in multiple ways, thus modifying the view of justice in the public eye. The decline of the model of 'advocacy journalism' in favour of investigative journalism, which, as a matter of principle, sought to treat the political sphere in the same way as other social universes, is of course inscribed in the internal dynamics of the media (the retreat of forms of political control, greater competition), but it also had the effect of bringing into anti-corruption judicial enquiries a new light (Marchetti 1996). Likewise, the commitment of national and international organizations (OECD, IMF, World Bank) and NGOs (Transparency International) to the fight against corruption in the 1990s (Bezes and Lascoumes 2005); the renewed interest in judicial regulation of the economy shown by modernist segments in the entrepreneurial sphere and by the ministry of the economy (Dezalay 1992); and the emergence of 'moral entrepreneurs' who called for a 'political renovation' were all, while relatively independent of each other, movements that converged around a common denunciation of 'irregular elites' (Lascoumes 1997) and a new willingness to assign political and social functions to judicial institutions (Commaille and Kaluszynski 2007). At the same time, the state partly redefined its forms of action according to a post-modern paradigm in which the state is conceived as a regulator, and is no longer a producer directly in charge of the management and development of economic units. These quasi-jurisdictional structures, i.e. independent administrative authorities, experienced an exceptional expansion in the 1980s, particularly in sectors such as finance regulation and public administrations' transparency.

However, it was on the political scene that the judicial issue made its most spectacular entrance. The first judicial enquiries into political corruption were launched at the beginning of the 1990s. As has been demonstrated by Violaine Roussel (2002), the transformation of 'what is judicially possible and feasible when facing the political' was effected not in one single blow but through a series of 'micro reversals of the state of play'. The unanticipated validation by the Angers Court of Appeals in 1991 of the pre-trial investigation conducted by Thierry Jean-Pierre in an iconoclastic fashion (judicial search at the Socialist Party headquarters in the Urba case in April of the same year) made other enquiries and moves possible. But it was the impetus of the 'moral entrepreneurs' (Becker 1963) that raised the wide-ranging *political* stakes of these one-off individual judicial decisions. It was the strategies of distinction of these entrepreneurs within the political sphere that linked the give-and-take of politics to judicial dynamics, progressively turning the judicial cases into political scandals and the political scandals into new rules of the political game. The 1995 law instating the loss of eligibility to political office for certain offences made 'judicial purity' a necessary prerequisite for running for election in France. Likewise, following the political custom known as the 'Bérégovoy–Balladur jurisprudence', which was adopted in 1992 against Bernard Tapie, government ministers are 'obliged' to resign from their cabinet posts if they are indicted (seven ministers were thus forced to resign between 1992 and 2007). These conditions and customs anchor judicial reasoning at the very heart of the political arena (Israël *et al.* 2005).

This rehabilitation of the judicial function ('*le pouvoir judiciaire*') is inscribed within and upheld by a parallel renewal of liberal political theory that redefined the state around the pillar of its judiciary (Chevallier 1993). During this time, there ensued a proliferation of writings in political philosophy that rationalized and theorized the new position of a justice system that would no longer be in the service of the state, but on the contrary would serve only the 'subjects of the law' and 'civil society' in order to protect them from the excesses and miscarriages of the state and the political sphere. In the wake of the anti-totalitarian criticisms of the 1970s, the criticism of the Jacobin French Republic and the law-centred republicanism that structured its liberal thinking led to a rehabilitation of the figure of the 'third power', now embodied by the judiciary. Faithfully following the notion that sovereignty today takes on a variety of forms and is manifested through the judiciary rather than being controlled by the voice of Parliament alone, these theories position magistrates as referees between civil society and the state. Elevated to the status of 'keeper of promises' (Garapon 1996) contained in the constitutional pact, the 'judiciary power' was henceforth endowed with a direct political legitimacy (Gauchet 1995). The development of procedural theories of democracy further shored up this rehabilitation of the judiciary, which emerged as the locus *par excellence* of 'communicative action' – a vector and essential factor for political and social integration in otherwise increasingly conflictual and fragmented societies (Habermas 1997).

Because these various sector-specific developments concurred in claiming that this evolution of the judiciary was the transformation they had hoped for, i.e. the advent of a 'judiciary power', they were natural allies for one another, and they formed a social platform for the judiciary in the public sphere (Vauchez and Willemez 2007). These enterprises in various sectors contributed to making the judiciary the locus of many expectations – renovation of politics, modernization of government administration, liberalization of the economy, empowerment of social and political minorities, promotion of gender balance, etc. Although they were very different, even antagonistic, these different groups pursued the same redefinition of the powers of state – of the actors authorized to participate in social regulation, of competencies, of conditions of legitimacy and the exercise of power, etc. – that transformed the judiciary into a cardinal political institution, ultimately responsible for a broad range of specific sectoral problems. Naturally, these movements in different sectors were met with resistance from many fronts, as illustrated by the multiple controversies regarding the respective places of the penal responsibility and the political accountability of elected officials (Bezes and Lascoumes 2005); the relationship between 'historical truth' and 'judicial truth' (*Droit et société* 1998); the line between 'investigative journalism' and the 'confidentiality of judicial enquiry' (Marchetti 1996); or the role of medical authority and 'patients' rights' (Barbot 2008). These are all debates that raise, sector by sector, the question of the place of the judiciary and judicial reasoning in society. All in all, 'judicialization' represents much more than just a greater presence of judges in the social sphere. It represents a configuration of social actors – legal specialists, of course, but also NGOs, employer organizations, social movements, advocates and entrepreneurs of morality, interest groups, segments of the state, European and international institutions, etc. – all of which are subject to specific dynamics in their own sphere of action, but which all have an interest in the authority and power of the judiciary. 'Judicialization' designates a set of sectoral struggles that have crystallized around the place of judicial regulation, judges and legal knowledge. In this sense, 'judicialization' is the code name for a series of sectoral battles that call into question the balance of powers as much as the types of authority on which the Fifth Republic grounds its legitimacy.

Bibliography

Agrikolianski, Eric (2003). *La Ligue des droits de l'homme (1947–1990). Pérennisation et transformations d'une entreprise de défense des causes civiques*. Paris: L'Harmattan.

Barbot, Jeanine (2008). 'Soigner en situation de risque judiciaire. Refus de transfusion et responsabilité médicale', *Revue française de science politique* 58(6): 985–1014.

Becker, Howard (1963). *Outsiders: Studies in the Sociology of Deviance*. New York, NY: The Free Press.

Bodiguel, Jean-Luc (1991). *Les magistrats: un corps sans âme?* Paris: PUF.

Beaud, Olivier (2000). 'La responsabilité politique face à la concurrence d'autres formes de la responsabilité des gouvernants', *Pouvoirs* 92: 17–30.

Bezes, Philippe and Pierre Lascoumes (2005). 'Percevoir et juger la corruption politique', *Revue française de science politique* 55(5–6): 757–85.

Boigeol, Anne (1989). 'La formation professionnelle des magistrats: de l'apprentissage sur le tas à l'école professionnelle', *Actes de la recherche en sciences sociales* 76–7: 49–64.

Boigeol, Anne and Yves Dezalay (1997). 'De l'agent d'affaires au barreau', *Genèses* 27: 49–68.

Briquet, Jean-Louis (2007). *Mafia, justice et politique en Italie*. Paris: Karthala.

Briquet, Jean-Louis and Philippe Garraud (2001) (ed.). *Juger le politique. Entreprises et entrepreneurs critiques de la politique*. Rennes: PUR.

Cam, Pierre (1978). 'Juges rouges et droit du travail', *Actes de la recherche en sciences sociales* 19: 2–27.

Chevallier, Jacques (1993). 'Le discours sur l'Etat de droit', *Politiques* 6: 13–20.

Cichowski, Rachel (2007). *The European Court and Civil Society. Litigation, Mobilization and Governance*. Cambridge: Cambridge University Press.

Cichowski, Rachel and Alec Stone (2003). 'Participation, representative democracy and the courts', in Bruce E. Cain, Russell J. Dalton, and Susan E. Scarrow (eds). *Democracy Transformed? Expanded Political Opportunities in Advanced Industrial Democracies*. Oxford: Oxford University Press, pp. 192–202.

Colera, Christophe. (2009). *Les services juridiques des administrations centrales*. Paris: L'Harmattan.

Commaille, Jacques and Laurence Dumoulin (2009). 'Heurs et malheurs de la légalité dans les sociétés contemporaines. Une sociologie politique de la judiciarisation', *L'année sociologique* 59(1): 107.

Commaille, Jacques and Martine Kaluszynski (eds) (2007). *La fonction politique de la justice*. Paris: La découverte.

Della Porta, Donatella (1995). *Social Movements, Political Violence and the State*. Cambridge: Cambridge University Press.

Devillé, Alain (1992). 'L'entrée du syndicat de la magistrature dans le champ juridique en 1968', *Droit et société* 22: 639–71.

Dezalay, Yves (1992). *Marchands de droit*. Paris: Fayard.

Droit et société (1998). Special issue: 'Vérité judiciaire et vérité historique' 38: 9–67.

Dulong, Delphine (1997). *Moderniser la politique. Aux origines de la Cinquième République*. Paris: L'Harmattan.

François, Bastien (1997). 'Le Conseil constitutionnel et la Vème République. Réflexions sur l'émergence et les effets du contrôle de constitutionnalité en France', *Revue française de science politique* 3–4: 377–403.

Garapon, Antoine (1996). *Le gardien des promesses. Justice et politique*. Paris: O. Jacob.

Gauchet, Marcel (1995). *La révolution des pouvoirs. La souveraineté, le peuple et la représentation*. Paris: Gallimard.

Goldsmith, Jean-Claude (1964). *L'avocat d'affaires*. Paris, Liège: Beranger.

Griesemer, James and Susan Leigh Star (1989). 'Institutional Ecology, "Translations" and Boundary Objects', *Social Studies of Science* 19(3): 387–420.

Guarnieri, Carlos and Patrizia Pederzoli (1996). *La puissance de juger*. Paris: Michalon.

Gueguen, Laurent (2005). *L'invention du droit des affaires. La construction doctrinale d'un savoir spécialisé alliant la rationalité gestionnaire au langage juridique*, Dissertation in political science, Université Paris I.

Habermas, Jürgen (1997). *Droit et démocratie entre faits et normes*. Paris: Gallimard.

Hirschl, Ran (2004). *Towards Juristocracy. The Origins and Consequences of the New Constitutionalism*. Cambridge, MA: Harvard University Press.

(2006). 'The New Constitutionalism and the Judicialization of Pure Politics Worldwide', *Fordham Law Review* 75: 721–56.

Horowitz, Donald (1977). *Courts and Social Policy*. Washington, DC: The Brookings Institution.

Israël, Liora (2009a). 'Un droit de gauche? Rénovation des pratiques professionnelles et nouvelles formes de militantisme des juristes engagés dans les années 1970', *Sociétés contemporaines* 1: 47–71.

(2009b). *L'arme du droit*. Paris: Presses de Sciences Po.

Israël, Liora, Guillaume Sacriste, Antoine Vauchez and Laurent Willemez (eds) (2005). *Sur la portée sociale du droit. Usages et légitimité du registre juridique*. Paris: PUF, coll. CURAPP.

Jeantet, Fernand-Charles (1957). *Droit des affaires*. Les cours du droit, Institut d'études politiques de Paris.

(1964). 'Le rôle de l'avocat, conseil des entreprises', *La vie judiciaire* 977: 1–5.

Kaluszinsky, Martine (2010). 'Sous les pavés, le mouvement "Critique du droit" ', *Droit et société* 3: 523–41.

Kelemen, Daniel (2011). *The Rise of Eurolegalism. The Transformation of Law and Governance in Europe*. Cambridge, MA: Harvard University Press.

Lascoumes, Pierre (1997). *Élites irrégulières: essai sur la délinquance d'affaires*. Paris: Gallimard.

Le Beguec, Gilles (2003). *La République des avocats*. Paris: Belin.

Lenoir, Remi (1990). 'L'Etat et la construction sociale de la famille', *Actes de la recherche en sciences sociales* 91: 20–37.

Madsen, Mikael (2011). *La genèse de l'Europe des droits de l'homme. Enjeux juridiques et stratégies d'Etat*. Strasbourg: Presses Universitaires de Strasbourg.

Marchetti, Dominique (1996). 'La genèse médiatique du "scandale du sang contaminé"', in Ethique, sida et société. *Rapport d'activité du Conseil national du sida*. Paris: La Documentation française, pp. 327–468.

Jacob, Nicolas (1964). 'La profession judiciaire devant l'Etat contemporain', *La vie judiciaire* 21–26 December: 1 and 6.

Karpik, Lucien (1995). *Les avocats entre l'Etat, le public et le marche XIII–XXème siecle*. Paris: Gallimard.

Osiel, Mark (1990). 'Lawyers as Monopolists, Aristocrats and Entrepreneurs', *Harvard Law Review* 103(9): 2009–66.

Pizzorno, Alessandro (1998). *Il potere dei giudici. Stato democratico e controllo della virtu*. Bari: Laterza.

Roussel, Violaine (2002). *Affaires de juges. Les magistrats face aux scandales politiques*. Paris: La Découverte.

(2003). 'La judiciarisation du politique, réalités et faux-semblants', *Mouvements* 29: 13–18.

Sacriste, Guillaume (2012). *La République des constitutionnalistes*. Paris: Presses de Sciences Po.

Sarat, Austin and Stuart Scheingold (1998). *Cause Lawyering: Political Commitments and Professional Responsibilities*. Oxford: Oxford University Press.

Scheppele, Kim (2003). 'Democracy by Judiciary (or why can courts be sometimes be more democratic than Parliaments)', in Adam W. Czarnota, Martin Krygier and Wojciech Sadursk (eds). *Rethinking the Rule of Law in Post-Communist Europe*. Budapest: CEU Press.

Shapiro, Martin (1994). 'The Juridicalization of Politics in the United States', *International Political Science Review* 15(2): 101–12.

Sialelli, Jean-Baptiste (1987). *Les avocats de 1920 à 1987*. Paris: Litec.

Sommier, Isabelle (1998). *La violence politique et son deuil. L'après 68 en France et en Italie*. Rennes: Presses Universitaires de Rennes.

Stone, Alec (1994). *The Birth of Judicial Politics in France*. Oxford: Oxford University Press.

Stone, Alec and Thomas Brunell (2013). 'Trustee Courts and the Judicialization of International Regimes: The Politics of Majoritarian Activism in the ECHR, the EU, and the WTO', *Journal of Law and Courts*, 1(1): 61–88.

Tate, Neal and Torbjorn Vallinder (1997). *The Global Expansion of Judicial Power*. New York, NY: New York University Press.

Thorp, René (ed.) (1962). *Vues sur la justice*. Paris: Julliard.

Tinayre, Alain and Denis de Ricci (eds) (1967). *Au service de la justice. La profession juridique de demain*. Paris: Dalloz.

Tonneau, Jean-Philippe (2011). 'Du projet politique au projet syndical: Le Syndicat des avocats de France (1973–1981)', *Politix* 96(4): 97–114.

Vauchez, Antoine (2004). *Une institution remotivée. Le processus d'institutionnalisation d'une 'nouvelle justice' en Italie (1960–2000)*. Paris: LGDJ.

(2005). 'Le droit en transitions. L'invention d'un art législatif dans la Vème République naissante', in *Sur la portée sociale du droit*. Paris: Presses Universitaires de France.

(2013). *L'Union par le droit. L'invention d'un programme institutionnel pour l'Europe*. Paris: Presses de Sciences Po.

Vauchez, Antoine and Laurent Willemez (eds) (2007). *La justice face à ses réformateurs (1980–2006). Entreprises de modernisation et logiques de résistance*. Paris: PUF.

5

Towards a sociology of intermediary institutions: the role of law in corporatism, neo-corporatism and governance

POUL F. KJAER

5.1 Introduction

The central ambition of this chapter is to develop dimensions of a theoretical and conceptual framework for the study of intermediary institutions, such as corporatist, neo-corporatist and governance institutions, in the European context. As such, it is designed to create a framework that is capable, not only of delineating intermediary institutions as an independent object of study and of increasing our understanding of their contribution to the integration of society, but also – more specifically – of illuminating the pivotal role of law in their evolution. This ambition is derived from the insight that intermediary institutions are the hinges of modern society insofar as they serve as central sites for the stabilisation of relations between multiple social spheres, most notably between the economic and the non-economic spheres, of society. Intermediary institutions might therefore be considered to be particularly dense forms of the structures characterising society as such, in the same way that changes in the design of intermediary institutions might reflect particularly clear illustrations of the transformations which society in its entirety has undergone. Developing a new understanding of the role of intermediary institutions will, therefore, provide a direct contribution to our understanding of modern European states, and it implicitly contains the promise of increasing our understanding of society in a broader sense.

The distinction between the economy and other segments of society is one of the central cleavages characterising modernity.[1] For this reason,

[1] The work on this chapter was made possible through support from the European Research Council. I would like to thank Chris Thornhill for extensive comments on an earlier draft. Full responsibility remains with the author.

this distinction has been one of the most important objects of study within law and the social sciences. [2] In the past two decades, the institutional form through which the relations between the economy and the wider society are framed has, however, experienced a paradigmatic shift through the 'turn to governance'. The governance concept refers to a particular type of intermediary institutions, which are characterised by multiple, partly overlapping, and partly colliding, frameworks for the co-ordination of public as well as private activities (Rhodes 2007). In the European setting, in particular, this development has been associated with a concordant decline of (neo-)corporatist intermediary institutions (Streeck 2009), which is taken to indicate a deep-seated change in the organisational design and self-understanding of contemporary society (Crouch 2005).

Law and social sciences have grappled with this development throughout the last two decades. This has resulted both in an intense level of conceptual innovation and in a large volume of empirical studies related to specific regions and economic sectors (see, for instance, Levi-Faur 2006; Schuppert 2006). However, the academic debates of the past two decades suffer from two central shortcomings. First, the endeavour to explain why the governance phenomenon emerged is still lacking an understanding of why its predecessors experienced decline. In the European settings, corporatist frameworks emerged in the middle of the nineteenth century and retained their vigour until the middle of the twentieth century, neo-corporatist institutions assumed dominance in the immediate post-war period, and patterns of governance have been increasingly vibrant from the 1980s onwards. European society thus seems to have undergone substantial consecutive transformations in terms of its organisational and normative setup. However, a systematic illumination of the process of successive transformation which led, first, from corporatism, via, second, neo-corporatism to, third, governance, which unfolded in Europe and other areas from the mid-nineteenth century up to today, has not been developed. Consequently, contemporary governance research remains fundamentally a-historical in nature. Second, in political economy and economic sociology, the role of law in the evolution from corporatism through neo-corporatism to governance has not received sufficient attention. Legal scholars have of

[2] As examples, see Bourdieu (2000); Durkheim (2007); Foucault (2004 [1979]); Habermas (1981); Luhmann (1988); Marx (2009 [1867–94]); Parsons and Smelser (2001 [1956]); Polanyi (2001 [1944]); Schumpeter (1976); Simmel (2009 [1900]); Tönnies (2005 [1887]); Weber (1976).

course dealt extensively with these phenomena. Yet, a strict sociological analysis of the role of law, and of legal instruments covering all three types of institution, has not yet emerged. This is a remarkable gap in the literature, for juridification is a factor that plays a decisive role in enabling a successful stabilisation of relations between the economic and non-economic spheres of society through corporatist, neo-corporatist and governance institutions. This is the case because, as we will return to, the primary contribution of law to society is simultaneously to separate and to reconnect different societal spheres, including, yet not restricted to, the economic and the political spheres. Conversely, the absence or erosion of legal stabilisation mechanisms might be considered the single most important reason for the outbreak of profound societal crises. This was, for example, the case in the interwar period (Thornhill 2008), and it is also the case in the ongoing financial crisis (Kjaer 2011).

In the following, an attempt is made to illuminate the central role of law in the stabilisation of exchanges between economic processes and the rest of society through the advancement of five propositions, which will make it possible for us to obtain an increased understanding of the independent contribution of law in the stabilisation of societal exchanges in general and intermediary institutions in particular. First, it is proposed that corporatism, neo-corporatism and governance fulfil identical societal functions, albeit under altered structural conditions, since each of them is simultaneously oriented towards the internal stabilisation of economic processes and the establishment of external compatibility with non-economic segments of society. Second, it is proposed that the relationship between the economic and the political spheres of society is characterised by a relation of reciprocal enhancement. This is a relation in which, in contrast to a zero-sum game, more of one implies more of the other. Third, the claim is advanced that the widespread attempt to reduce the relation between economic spheres to the rest of society to the binary relation between economy and politics severely simplifies the nature of the relations between economic and non-economic processes in society. Fourth, it is proposed that the process of evolutionary transition from corporatism, through neo-corporatism, to governance is closely linked to deeper transformations of societal structures, which unfolded within the European setting, and which are reflected in the continued transformation of the spatial reach of intermediary institutions. Corporatism is mainly to be understood as a localistic phenomenon insofar as corporatist institutions typically were limited to a specific city and its immediate surroundings. Only with the emergence of neo-corporatism did fortified and generalised national frameworks emerge; this is analogous to contemporary governance frameworks, which were in many instances characterised by a Europe-wide or even global reach. Fifth, it is proposed that these structural transformations implied, not solely a change in organisational composition as reflected in the fundamentally different design of corporatist, neo-corporatist and governance institutions, but also a transformation in the function of law and legal instruments within these compositions. This transformation can furthermore be traced back to an increased temporalisation of society, understood as an increase in the speed of societal change, as embodied in the increased proceduralisation of law.

5.2 A methodological and theoretical recalibration

Before we turn our attention to the above propositions, a methodological and theoretical recalibration is needed. The methodological premise advanced here resides in the claim that the corporatist, neo-corporatist and governance institutions themselves and the legal instruments on which they rely should be considered the primary object of study. To this degree, the primary object of study is not the market, the organisations such as firms and public administrations, or the broader social groupings such as social classes, against which these institutions are oriented. Instead, corporatist, neo-corporatist and governance institutions need to be understood as autonomous social phenomena, producing independent reserves of power and norms, and following independent patterns of evolution (Morgan 2005). This perspective is quite different from the understanding which has usually dominated the academic stage, as corporatist, neo-corporatist and governance institutions have at best been treated as 'intermediate variables' located in-between state and society with society de facto being equated to the economic system (Schmitter and Lembruch 1979).

In addition to the strategic move towards a focus on the independent impact of corporatist, neo-corporatist and governance these institutions need to be embedded in a broader theoretical architecture capable of combining several strands of research.

Corporatism, neo-corporatism and governance have to date been approached and analysed from numerous different angles and perspectives, and none of these approaches have succeeded in providing a complete picture. In theories of social differentiation, the emphasis has been placed on the multifaceted relationship between segmentary, stratificatory, centre/periphery, territorial and functional forms of differentiation. Such models have been advanced on the basis of an essentially actor-based perspective (e.g. Rueschemeyer 2009); a structural perspective, which does not exclude an actor perspective (e.g. Münch 2004); and a systemic perspective (e.g. Luhmann 1997). Common to the perspectives emerging from these approaches, however, is that the emergence and evolution of corporatist, neo-corporatist and governance institutions can be understood as closely linked to increases in the division of labour and functional specification within society as a whole. A different strand of research is the meso-level approach in historical institutionalism, which combines an emphasis on historical development paths with a focus on institutions in the form of rules and norms, and on their impact on outcomes and behaviour (Evans *et al.* 1985; Steinmo *et al.* 1992). The historical focus increases the reference points for analysis just as the explicit orientation towards the time dimension implies a strong emphasis on explaining change. Although not originally described by the term historical institutionalism, the neo-corporatist school, prominent in the 1970s and 1980s, and which focused on the role of centralised bargaining and the triangular relationship between employers, employees and the state[3] is closely related, both in its methodology and its conclusions, to the approach promoted by historical institutionalism. A further, today somewhat marginalised, perspective, which also emphasises the time perspective, is social evolution theory. In order to explain the driving forces and outcomes of social change, evolutionary theory originally focused on the impact of exogenous conditions on internal selection (e.g. Weber 1976). But in recent decades evolutionary theory has heightened its focus both on endogenous factors (Luhmann 1997) and on the reciprocal relations between exogenous and endogenous structures over time (see for example Amstutz 2001), thereby increasing its capacity for explaining co-evolutionary developments. If we retain our focus on the independent status of corporatist, neo-corporatist and governance institutions, the latter perspective is particularly important, as it provides a basis for an understanding of these institutions as formations which enable co-evolutionary developments of the economic and other spheres of society. The study of corporatism, neo-corporatism and governance has, furthermore, played a central role within the multifaceted regulation approach, which is aimed at developing a critical political economy emphasising economic as well as extra-economic factors in

[3] See Berger (1981); Goldthorpe (1984); Schmitter (1974), Schmitter and Lehmbruch (1979).

capitalist development (Boyer 2003; Hirsch 2005; Jessop and Sum 2006). The regulation approach is essentially constituted around the distinction between economic production and non-economic reproduction processes. As will be discussed in the following section, this distinction is compatible with the distinction between internal stabilisation and external compatibility of economic processes on which corporatist, neo-corporatist and governance institutions are reliant, in that the central function of these institutions is to stabilise exchanges between economic and non-economic social processes. Especially since the 1990s, organisational studies and network theory, loosely connected with the regulation school, have attempted to include a wider range of institutions and actors in the study of corporatist, neo-corporatist and governance institutions. This has been pursued through a stronger focus on sectorial regimes, flexible modes of production and the relationship between localised, national, regional (e.g. European) and global frameworks (e.g. Gilson *et al.* 2009). This, again, implies a gradual increase in the emphasis on the firm as the central object of study. The emphasis on the firm is further strengthened within the varieties of capitalism perspective, which seeks to develop a relational perspective on the firm while emphasising the importance of national frameworks (Hall and Soskice 2001). For the governance phenomenon, the political science literature on new and multilevel governance has conducted a similar exercise taking the political system as its point of departure (Heritier 2007; Hooghe and Marks 2001; Kohler-Koch 2003) in the same way that efforts have been made to combine the two perspectives (Mayntz 2007). In legal discourse, the same developments have been captured by the still ongoing debate about the transformation in the function of law. A new understanding of the role of law has emerged through an emphasis on 'reflexive law' and 'learning law' which is seen as providing modalities for the handling of new knowledge in society (Ladeur 1997; Teubner 1983; Zeitlin and Trubek 2003). This development has, on the other hand, triggered a reaction amongst legal scholars who continue to emphasise the importance of formalised normative stabilisation as the central task of law (see for example Joerges 2010).

While drawing on aspects from the approaches outlined above, the perspective that is advanced here differs markedly from other methods in a number of respects. As becomes clear below, in my approach the focus on the function of intermediary institutions is reinforced and a multi-dimensional perspective capable of going beyond binary state/economy perspectives is developed. This again indicates the need to proceed from a theory of society rather than from particularistic theories of capitalism and the state when seeking to understand the evolutionary processes underpinning the formation of modern Europe.

5.3 The common function of corporatism, neo-corporatism and governance

The three types of institutional formation considered here possess the common feature that they combine private and public elements. That is the case insofar as they are simultaneously oriented towards the internal stabilisation of economic processes and the establishment of compatibility between such processes and non-economic social processes through the construction and enforcement of overarching frameworks leading to the formation of (legal) norms and expectations as well as concordant social roles and categories within a limited spatial context. As a result, the three types of institutional formation share the feature that they serve as interfaces between economic production and the reproduction of the societal conditions enabling production.

As mentioned, corporatist institutions emerged from the mid-nineteenth century onwards and maintained their vigour until the middle of the twentieth century. In the same period, a multifaceted but distinct body of corporatist social thought emerged. Common to, for example, Catholic, socialist, syndicalist and fascist forms of corporatist thinking was their holistic approach (Wiarda 1997). These approaches shared the objective of (re-)establishing institutional arrangements capable of (re-)integrating the social practices of economic production with, for example, religious and family-based structures as well as a wide range of other social functions, relating to areas such as education, policing and health. Such an approach was for example consciously advanced by Pope Leo XIII (Wiarda 1997). As such, the emergence of corporatist structures can be understood as a reaction against the increased differentiation (*Ausdifferenzierung*) of the economic sphere and the concordant breakdown of holistic universes of meaning in the emerging modern society as described and analysed by authors as different as Hegel, Marx and Polanyi. In consequence, it was common to most forms of corporatist thinking that they possessed a 'reactionary' dimension. Yet, rather than possessing a simple, one-dimensional reactionary character, corporatist institutions fulfilled a dual modernising and stabilising function for society. They acted internally to stabilise new forms of economic process, which were characterised by an increase in the division of labour, the establishment of monopolistic structures, the ramification of quasi-feudal stratified orders of social class, and by the institutionalisation of wage bargaining. At the same time, corporate institutions were oriented towards the establishment of compatibility with other increasingly functionally delineated segments of society, possessing, for example, a political or religious character. In consequence, corporatist institutions can be understood as structures which simultaneously fortified and transformed existing institutions.

The emergence of European neo-corporatism in the post-1945 period also took the dual form of a real-life phenomenon and a distinct body of social thought (see for example Schmitter and Lembruch 1979). In practice, neo-corporatism took the form of complex negotiation systems (Willke 1992), which relied on highly centralised peak-organisations. The organisational form of neo-corporatism was thus fundamentally different from earlier forms of corporatism, which to a high extent relied on a continuation of earlier forms of feudal types of organisation. The core characteristic of both variants of corporatism, however, remained the dual function of internal stabilisation and external compatibility of economic processes as outlined above. Neo-corporatist structures internally frame the relationship between employers and employees in relation, not only to wage bargaining, but also to general working conditions. As such, the core function of neo-corporatism is very closely related to the question of the maintenance of stability in the economic system. Although great regional variations can be observed, the task of internal ordering has in many cases been extended to functions such as the organisation of education (for example, vocational training), the administration of unemployment benefits, health and safety at work, and also, in some national settings, most notably Germany, the workforce participation in management through work councils and co-determination. At the peak level, tripartism between the state, employers and employees emerged as a central form of (economic) policy co-ordination between the state and neo-corporatist institutions in the post-war period. Both internal ordering in the economic sphere, and the stabilisation of relations between the economy and other spheres of society, thereby became prominent aspects of neo-corporatism.

Governance, a phenomenon that emerged in the 1980s and which has continued its expansion ever since, implies a partial move towards firm- or sector-specific internalisation of the functions originally associated with corporatism and neo-corporatism through the emergence of complex intra- and inter-firm co-ordination and control mechanisms and thus internal bodies of (legal) norms. Four dimensions can be distinguished in this process. These are:

1) The establishment of internal coherence between mother companies and subsidiaries and the framing of relations between employers and employees operating within them;
2) The co-ordination of increasingly complex supply and distribution chains involving a large number of different firms;
3) Industry-wide collaboration via trade associations and self-regulatory arrangements;
4) The establishment of compatibility with the non-economic spheres through, for example, corporate social responsibility and lobbying frameworks.

Due to technological developments, however, the internal focus of governance has increasingly been shifted from labour relations to more abstract knowledge- and capital-intensive processes. In addition, a reduction of (nation) state-centredness in relation to the establishment of compatibility with the segments of society which are external to the economic system can be observed. Lobbying, for example, is increasingly oriented towards non-state political structures such as the European Union and the World Trade Organization. Even more fundamentally, partnerships are increasingly being established directly between companies and their non-political environment, through stabilised relations with scientific and educational institutions and environmental groups. This development creates novel links circumventing the binary relationship between economy and politics, which was the defining feature of neo-corporatism at the same time as the dual function concerning internal stability and external compatibility remains at the forefront.

5.4 Beyond the state/society dichotomy

The development of new types of institutional linkages between economic processes and non-political segments of society means that the distinction between internal stability and external compatibility cannot, as is the case in mainstream political economy, be reduced to the distinction between state and society. The dual formation of a specialised system of political rule in the form of the modern state and the formation of a distinct modern capitalist economic system implied a breakdown of the kind of intermediate structures, in the form of guilds and more generally the institution of the household, which was a central characteristic of the feudal form of social order (Hegel 1971 [1800–02]; Polanyi 2001 [1944]). A gradual replacement of these forms of feudal organisation took place through the emergence of corporatist, neo-corporatist and governance institutions. Although this is hardly recognized in the liberal understanding of the economy as a spontaneous order (von Hayek 1994), however, the state clearly played a pivotal role in the emergence of modern capitalism (Block 1994). Similarly, transformations in the mode of economic production had a profound effect on the societal expectations directed towards the state, on the fiscal foundation of the state, and thereby on the form of political rule which prevailed in different settings (Anderson 1985 [1974]). However, neither the one-dimensional state-centric perspective nor the perspective shared by economic liberals and structural Marxists, which asserts the categorical supremacy of economic structures, offers convincing tools for explaining the relation between polity and economy. In fact, the relations between these two spheres of society have normally been characterised by versatile interaction and mutually constitutive engagement: that is, by a relation, in which, as discussed, more of one implies more of the other. This insight has, however, to date not assumed a dominant position.

First, by way of example, the neo-corporatist school of thought mainly advanced by Schmitter emphasised the 'societal' and thus 'normatively superior' character of neo-corporatism as opposed to the alleged state-centredness of early corporatism (Schmitter 1974). But the location of (neo-)corporatism in one or the other sphere (i.e. in either polity or economy) does, first of all, not in itself offer any intrinsic information concerning the normative quality of such structures. The arbitrariness of power relations is a characteristic of all social interactions and not just of those which are located within the state. Normative perspectives which are aimed at countering arbitrary deployments of power therefore need to take a broader societal perspective into account and go beyond the state/society dichotomy (Sciulli 1992).

Second, and more fundamentally, the neo-corporatist approach misunderstands the very function of intermediary institutions insofar as they are not located in a singular sphere, but rather serve specifically as frameworks of transfer and stabilisation, which are located in-between different societal spheres. They stabilise expectations between different societal spheres such as, but not only, the economic and political spheres and they enable the transmission of condensed social components such as political decisions, legal judgments, financial capital, economic products, scientific knowledge and technologies between these spheres.

Third, the neo-corporatist approach advanced by Schmitter relies on false historical-sociological premises. Early forms of corporatism, maintaining strong pre-modern features, did not, as Schmitter argued (Schmitter 1974), evolve primarily in settings marked by strong states, but, on the contrary, in settings marked by weak states. As essentially localistic forms of order, they usually emerged in contexts in which strong characteristics of modern statehood were absent or in contexts where newly formed states had yet to find a stable form (e.g. Austria, Germany and Italy). Thus, the idea that the existence of highly centralised and autocratic forms of political rule of the kind which often promoted corporatist approaches indicates the existence of strong states can fruitfully be replaced by an alternative conception of statehood, in which 'strong states' are seen as characterised by self-limitation. On this account, strong states are states which have an organisational and legal form that allows for the maintenance of a distinction between 'state and society' and thereby a condensed and autonomous form of political power which, through an activation of legal mechanisms, is protected from arbitrary manipulation by privatistic interests operating outside the state. From this perspective, even totalitarian regimes which promoted specific strands of corporatism such as National Socialist Germany and fascist Italy cannot be characterised as strong states. Such totalitarian regimes combined extremely arbitrary forms of privatistic rule with elements of modern organisation in a manner which implied dissolution of the distinction between the state and the rest of society. Accordingly, the 'total state' means the absence of a state, not a strong state (Neumann 1983 [1944]: 467 ff.).

However, even the claim that the relationship between economy and politics is characterised by a relationship of mutual increase rather than being a zero-sum game does not go far enough. The idea that the differentiation of the economic system developed primarily in conjunction with the establishment of a specialised system of political rule greatly simplifies the actual historical processes through which the differentiation of the economic system took place. The modern economic system emerged through far more complex processes, which involved, not only a severing of ties to traditional forms of political authority, but also a reduction of the linkages between the emerging economic system and other segments of society. In particular, the severing of ties to religious belief systems and the move away from dependence on customary law and towards a novel linking with modern positive law seems to have been just as important a feature as the differentiation between economy and politics (Kjaer 2009). This is also confirmed by the historical development path of corporatist, neo-corporatist and governance institutions. These institutions have always taken the form of conglomerates which fulfil the function of tying a whole range of societal spheres together. Neo-corporatism, for example, does not only stabilise relations between the economy and the state. It also stabilises relations towards areas such as health and education, which rely on their own social practices, norms and objectives. In a similar manner, contemporary governance arrangements imply a stabilisation of relations between the economy and a whole range of social formations. This occurs in areas such as science through risk regulation frameworks. It occurs in art and sports through new types of sponsorships. It might even be seen to occur in religion through Islamic banking.

5.5 Structural transformations

Corporatist institutional arrangements grew out of already existing feudal institutions. In many cases, already existing feudal structures merely assumed new labels while in actuality a considerable degree of continuity could be observed between feudal and corporatist institutions. That was, for example, the case in relation to the development of new corporatist-based frameworks of skill formation in Germany in the late nineteenth century, which relied heavily on already existing frameworks developed within the framework of the guild system and various other voluntary artisanal associations (Thelen 2004: 41 ff.) Although the actual emergence of corporatist structures was characterised by significant regional differences, a common feature was that they materialised, not via a clear-cut break with, but rather through impalpable evolution from, already existing conditions. New logics, organisational forms and semantics gradually emerged while, at least initially, these structures remained reliant on the institutional arrangements which preceded them. Similar processes can be observed in relation to the subsequent switches to neo-corporatism and governance (Mayntz 2006). In this specific sense corporatist, neo-corporatist and governance structures can also be characterised as Eigenstructures, which rely on already existing structures for their emergence, but over time marginalise the structures on which they rely (Stichweh 2006). Thus, behind the immediate changes loom far more fundamental structural transformations (Habermas 1973), which over time have built up pressures that at certain stages provide the structural possibility for contingent but drastic changes in development paths (Sassen 2006). This again provides the possibility for different types of transformations, such as displacement, layering, drift, conversion or exhaustion (Streeck and Thelen 2005; Thelen and Mahoney 2010), to occur on the basis of different combinations of endogenous and exogenous factors. In relation to displacement,

Colin Crouch and Maarten Keune have, for example, analysed the shift from Keynesianism to Thatcherism in the United Kingdom in the 1980s as a process where pre-existing diverse institutional setups were captured and deployed in order to promote fundamentally different policy objectives than those previously promoted (Crouch and Keune 2005).

In terms of exogenous factors, additionally, a central, but so far under-explored, element in corporatism seems to be the relation between structural transformations and increased acceleration of time structures. As also reflected in the move towards proceduralisation of legal arrangements, the increased speed of societal change (Rosa 2005; Scheuerman 2004; Virilio 1977) has created a functional pressure for enhanced adaptability and in so doing provided a basis for the emergence of increasingly reflexive and flexible institutional forms through which societal compatibility can be maintained.

In a similar manner, each of the evolutionary shifts from corporatism, via neo-corporatism, to governance implied an expansion in spatial reach and concordant increases in the abstraction of social processes. The vast majority of existing approaches are characterised by 'methodological nationalism' (Chernilo 2007): that is, they proceed from an ontological assumption concerning the existence of static national spaces and the assumption that nation states are the 'container' of society. That is, for example, the case for the 'varieties of capitalism' approach (Hall and Soskice 2001) as well as for evolutionary approaches, which continue to subscribe to a 'holistic' understanding of national societies (Steinmo 2010). However, the evolution from corporatism, via neo-corporatism, to governance illustrates the dynamic character of spatial compositions (Lefebvre 1974). Corporatism was first and foremost, not a national, but a localistic phenomenon. Although considerable variations can be observed in this regard, corporatist institutional formations were typically centred on a city and its immediate catchment area and as such never gained the status of fortified and generalised state-based frameworks. Only with the emergence of neo-corporatism in the post-war period did fortified frameworks characterised by a high level of concurrence with national boundaries emerge. This type of concurrence, however, was not only an evolutionary coincidence, but it also only assumed reality for a very short period of time in the middle of the twentieth century. In fact, this type of concurrence disintegrated almost immediately after its manifestation due to the emergence of new types of transnational frameworks as most notably expressed in the emergence of the European Coal and Steel Community in the 1950s and the Common Agricultural Policy in the 1960s within the framework of the European integration process. This process was further intensified through the launch of the Internal Market in the 1980s. This was a development that was materialised through a compromise which foresaw a division of labour between national and European settings with market regulation being communised while social regulation and welfare provisions remained a predominantly national prerogative. This was in turn a compromise, however, which never led to the stable equilibrium sought by its advocates (Scharpf 1988). Instead, the launch of the internal market entailed an almost immediate spill-over of regulatory responsibility into areas such as labour law and social regulation, just as current efforts to increase the coherency of the euro area imply an attempt to re-structure and unify the organisational framework of national regulatory regimes in relation to economic and social regulation. In spite of this development, however, the European Union does not (yet) possess the internal coherence associated with modern statehood, but is rather a conglomerate of partially overlapping, sometimes mutually supportive and sometimes contradictory, functional regimes (Kjaer 2010). Acting as functionally delineated micro-polities, each of these regimes has its own organisational infrastructure, and all these regimes generate their own sense of purpose, which makes it possible for them to assume the status of separate epistemic communities. As a result, national boundaries seem to be in the process of losing their centrality through the emergence of sectorial governance frameworks with a European (and increasingly global) reach, despite the fact that at the same time no single coherent framework has emerged (Kjaer 2010).

However, in addition to the fragile state of the regulatory conglomerate called the European Union, the development described above also illustrates that evolutionary transformations in most cases do not imply an outright eradication of preceding types of institutional formations. On the contrary, each evolutionary switch from corporatism, via neo-corporatism, to governance rather illustrates the surprising resilience of the preceding types of institutional formation. The local production regimes developed within the framework of early forms of corporatism, for example, continue to be of central importance in areas such as northern Italy and southern Germany (see Crouch *et al.* 2004), just as the restructuring of the German neo-corporatist model in the first decade of the new millennium illustrated the ability of a national framework successfully to adapt to changed structural conditions. Instead of a linear move from one type of spatial reality to another the evolutionary trajectory from corporatism, via neo-corporatism, to governance instead highlights the existence of a multilevel spatial reality, which is characterised by versatile and constantly changing relations between local, national, regional (and global) configurative processes as being a central characteristic of European society.

5.6 The organisational infrastructure: organisations, networks and social roles

Modern society is above all an 'organisational society', and the organisational revolutions, which unfolded through the emergence and radical expansion of modern forms of formal-legal organisation from the sixteenth century onwards, are one of the central characteristics of modernity (Harste 1997). One consequence of this is that the modern state and the modern capitalist economy to a large extent rely on the same organisational model. Historically speaking, the state bureaucracy served as the organisational role model of the modern firm just as the contemporary expansion of New Public Management implies a reorganisation of public bureaucracies on the model of the firm. Organisations, moreover, become formal organisations when they are legally structured on the basis of formal and generalised rules and norms (Kjaer 2009). Against this background, formal organisations can be understood as the central type of social organisation, to which corporatist, neo-corporatist and governance institutions are attached insofar as they are internally orientated towards the stabilisation of relations between management and workers and externally oriented towards the stabilisation of relations between firms and other organisations, such as public administrations, educational organisations and (mainly historically) religious organisations. In consequence, whereas the firm has been the central focus of political economy in the last decade (Hall and Soskice 2001), a historical perspective seeking to understand corporatist, neo-corporatist and governance institutions as oriented towards maintaining the dual function of internal stability and external compatibility between the economic sphere and other sections of society indicates that, not only firms, but rather a far broader set of formal organisations, need to be taken into account.

This is also apparent from the evolutionary trajectory from corporatism to governance. As previously indicated, corporatist institutions typically emerged in settings characterised by amalgamations of pre-modern forms of social order, relying on the institution of the household and emerging forms of modern bureaucratic organisation. Neo-corporatist negotiation systems are, on the other hand, located in-between hierarchical organisations such as firms and state organisations, in the same way that neo-corporatist organisations themselves tend to rely on hierarchical and strongly formalised forms of organisation. As such, neo-corporatist frameworks are often regarded as the embodiment of a society relying on formal organisation. In relation to governance arrangements, this is seemingly very different insofar as a common argument in the governance discourse is that a 'breakdown of hierarchy' is taking place (e.g. Ladeur 1997; Piore and Sabel 1984). But to the extent that governance frameworks are defined as heterarchical frameworks that rely on networks as their central organisational form and which are oriented towards facilitating the transfer of dense social components such as products, capital, scientific knowledge, political decisions or legal judgments between formal organisations, the emergence of the governance phenomenon points in the opposite direction (Kjaer 2010). From this perspective the governance phenomenon in fact emerged because the existing neo-corporatist frameworks did not provide sufficient channels of transfer in increasingly complex and temporalised societal settings. An increase in social complexity, furthermore, implied a massive increase in the reliance on formal organisation as exemplified through the emergence of the multinational firm as a central form of business organisation and the expansion in welfare state arrangements relying on formal organisation from the middle of the twentieth century onwards.

However, the expansion in formal organisation does not imply that heterarchical networks are not of great importance. In fact, all three types of institutional formation under scrutiny are characterised by a reliance on the network form. But, at the same time, substantial transformations and variations can be observed in relation to this dimension. In corporatism, networks played an essential role as instruments of exclusion in the sense that they were forms through which social entities detached themselves from other spheres of society through normatively based ramification processes. One example of this can be found in the construction of cartels and the regulation of inclusion and exclusion of labour into specific segments of the economy. This was for example the case in the German setting both before and after 1933 (Neumann 1983 [1944]: 235). In relation to neo-corporatism, the network element was increasingly marginalised through formal organisation leaving only policy networks of the kind which tend to surround the hierarchical peaks of all formal organisations. Nonetheless, in this limited function networks still played a pivotal role in the stabilisation of expectations between different societal spheres (Grabher 1993). In relation to contemporary forms of governance, networks have in contrast become a central instrument for the stabilisation of relations between formal organisations. That is not only the case in relation to inter-firm relations through supply, production and distribution networks but also in relation to formal organisations operating within other areas, as exemplified by the centrality of lobbying networks, Corporate Social Responsibility Networks and network-based public–private partnerships. In contrast to corporatist networks, which were oriented towards the maintenance of their own normative closure, contemporary governance networks are primarily oriented towards the establishment of cognitive openness in the sense that their function is to increase the observational capacities of the organisations involved and their capacity of transfer of social components such as political decisions and rights-based social demands from one sphere to another, thereby establishing a basis for a higher level of mutual adaptability. Thus, one might argue that the societal function of networks has been inverted through the trajectory from early corporatism to contemporary governance.

Like the transformation in the network function, each of the three types of institution relies on specific sets of dually constituted social roles (see for example Dahrendorf 2010 [1954]), as apparent in the distinctions between master craftsmen and apprentices, between employers and employees, and between experts and laymen. Social roles fulfil a dual internal/external role within all three types of institutional formation at the same time as the substantial form differs quite dramatically. Externally, social roles are deployed as inclusion/exclusion mechanisms that delineate the section of society which a given institution reflexively observes and against which it orients its actions, through reference to generalised semantic categories such as 'the working class', 'professions' and 'expertise'. A central function of such categories is to provide a basis for developing rules of inclusion through membership. To a large degree, early forms of corporatism mirrored the feudal form of the guilds in the sense that membership was provided on the basis of specific criteria, relating to, for example, apprenticeship and inheritance. Contemporary governance arrangements, on the other hand, tend to rely on specific criteria regarding expert knowledge as their central criteria of inclusion, as for example is apparent within risk-regulating frameworks. Internally, the construction of social roles fulfils a stabilising function. For example, the distinction between employers and employees in neo-corporatism may at a first glance seem to reflect a conflictual relation, but this distinction also serves as a formula for mediation between the two sides in the sense that the distinction is the condition for a mutual stabilisation and institutionalisation of the relationship between them. Social roles thereby become formulae for the mutual construction and advancement of legitimate claims through the development of 'justifying narratives' which are aimed at advancing, for instance, 'economic freedom' and 'social justice' within neo-corporatist setups or 'evidence based' decisions within risk regulatory frameworks.

5.7 The transformation of law

The development described above has been accompanied by a substantial transformation in the design and function of law. In a general manner, the three different types of institutional formation were mirrored in corresponding phases of juridification. The three phases of juridification can be categorized using the following concepts: (1) rule of law; (2) democratic interventionist law; (3) legal proceduralisation. In this context, the concept of the rule of law implies the emergence of a type of positive law which is increasingly detached from earlier forms of customary law and which is deployed in a generalised manner across an increasingly coherent spatial setting. Democratic interventionist law was, on the other hand, linked to an understanding of law as a medium which was intrinsically linked to the production of legislation through democratic procedures and an understanding of legally mediated politics as a framework enabling a correction of societal development paths or even a substantial steering of society as such. As a reaction to increased societal complexity, the move towards proceduralisation was also invoked as a way to maintain an ambition of 'second-order guidance', understood as an indirect form of societal steering, while at the same time renouncing the idea of a substantial regulation through legal means.[4]

These legal transformations are intrinsically linked to the institutional transformations from corporatism to governance. In fact, a certain degree of hybridity can be detected insofar as these forms of law largely emerged within the institutional formations under scrutiny here. Each of these formations was faced with a functional need internally to develop condensed normative frameworks in order to achieve internal coherency and stability. This in turn triggered the activation of law and legal instruments, as law came to serve as a formalised version of the norms produced within these formations, thereby enabling the law to provide a secondary stabilisation of these structures. Externally, the reliance on formalised legal instruments is the central mechanism through which the dual function of simultaneously maintaining the separation and mutual stabilisation of economic and non-economic processes while

[4] See Habermas (1981); Habermas (1992); Luhmann (1983 [1969]) and Wiethölter (1968).

simultaneously establishing a possibility of transfer is achieved. This is particularly evident in relation to rights and rights-based frameworks. As the form through which liberties are secured *and* obligations imposed, rights are instruments which simultaneously safeguard the autonomy of, and impose obligations upon, legal subjects. Not surprisingly, as a result the thrust of rights-based legal scholarship has been characterised by an intrinsic tendency to focus upon the impact of rights on individuals (for example Rawls 1999 [1971]). This perspective, however, underplays the more general and abstract contribution of rights regimes to the facilitation of exchanges between social spheres. From a societal perspective, rights can be understood as frameworks which establish the modalities through which social components are delineated and transposed between social spheres while simultaneously safeguarding the integrity and autonomy of the spheres involved. Rights-based frameworks are, however, not a free-standing phenomenon. Instead, the persistent existence of intermediary institutions rather indicates that rights tend to be embedded in broader organisational setups, since it is through the coupling with such setups that rights gain systemic relevance for society (Kjaer 2014).

The dual internal and external role of law becomes evident if one observes periods of profound societal crisis. The breakdown of the Weimar Republic, for example, was inherently linked to a suspension of the legal infrastructure enabling a separation and a limited formalised re-connection of societal spheres (see for example Thornhill 2008). In a similar manner, the move, in recent decades, towards increased deregulation and reliance on (self-regulatory) governance frameworks operating outside formalised law has led to novel forms of coalescence and de-differentiation between economic and non-economic processes, as also illustrated by the 2008 financial crisis (Kjaer 2011). This is evident in particular in relation to the transformation in the network function outlined above. The increased emergence of network-based frameworks, such as those associated with social corporate responsibility institutions, has led to the emergence of (embryonic) legal frameworks that are aimed at stabilising relations between economic processes and non-economic processes (Callies and Zumbansen 2010). But, at the same time, traditional concerns regarding the de-differentiating character of networks and their tendency to produce coalescence were increasingly thrown overboard in the decades preceding the financial crisis. Especially within the framework of the European integration process, 'soft law' mechanisms were hailed as more efficient mechanisms, which had the distinctive ability to secure adequate levels of normative condensation (Dawson 2011). The reliance on soft law has, however, had profound de-differentiating effects. In European Research and Development Policy, for example, the introduction of soft law engendered a process through which the advancement of science was captured by an economistic logic concerned with the enhancement of competitiveness (Kjaer 2010: 104 ff.). Also at the local and national level, equally the attempt to reduce the transaction costs associated with economic exchanges through deregulation implied a move towards coalescence. In Spain, for example, the legal frameworks for the sale of public land, typically owned by local communes, the granting of building permits by local authorities and the rules for mortgage lending were relaxed at the turn of the millennium. Initially, this development unleashed massive amounts of energy in the form of an immense building boom that seemingly confirmed the economistic regulatory philosophies which guided the move towards increased deregulation. Yet, the basis for this development was the emergence of informal networks of coalescence between local politicians, politically appointed civil servants, the politically appointed or politically connected management of local savings banks and local building entrepreneurs. Over time, this led to a process of mutual decay through which the integrity and rationale guiding both political as well as economic decisions became increasingly eroded, paving the way for an increasingly unsustainable economic development. The short-term unleashing of energy therefore turned out to have disastrous consequences for both state and economy in the long term.

Although the contexts differ substantially and the outcome was far more catastrophic, the short-term unleashing of an economic boom in the wake of the National Socialist takeover in Germany in 1933 was, as described by Franz Neumann, characterised by a similar logic of coalescence (Neumann 1983 [1944]).[5] This indicates that times of structural transition, due to changes in the level of social complexity, the speed of social development and the spatial reach of social processes, tend to lead either to an outright suspension of, or at least to increased pressure on, the legal frameworks which are aimed at stabilising societal exchanges. Both the transformations from corporatism to neo-corporatism and the subsequent switch from neo-corporatism to governance seem to confirm that substantial divergence between societal structures and the internally developed legal stabilisation mechanism, which is aimed at stabilising these structures, can also create preconditions for unsustainable development, and they highlight the need

[5] One might speculate whether it would be possible to analyse the economic explosion currently taking place in China with a similar vocabulary.

for a move towards a re-stabilisation of society within a new legal and organisational framework which corresponds to the contemporary structural setting.

5.8 Conclusion

European society underwent consecutive waves of structural transformation through the twentieth century. This was epitomised in the evolutionary shifts from corporatism, via neo-corporatism, to governance. These transformations fundamentally changed the social reality of European society, although, at the same time, at a deeper structural level, the core societal tensions and cleavages very much remained the same. This dynamic permanence is most clearly expressed in the continued relevance of the dual function of corporatist, neo-corporatist and governance institutions: namely, in the orientation towards stabilising economic production processes and establishing compatibility between these processes and non-economic reproduction processes. This indicates that intermediary institutions are central to our understanding of the composition and integration of society. The continued striving towards a stabilisation of intermediary setups is, furthermore, a central, if not the central, function of law in modern society. The law is both the central medium through which transfers of condensed social components such as products, capital, formal decisions and judgements between social spheres are structured, and it is also the medium charged with responsibility for ensuring that such transfers do not lead to coalescence and de-differentiation. However, this task has not always been successfully fulfilled, a fact testified by the continued re-emergence of periods of profound societal crisis.

Bibliography

Amstutz, Marc (2001). *Evolutorisches Wirtschaftsrecht. Vorstudien zum Recht und seiner Methode in den Diskurskollisionen der Marktgesellschaft*. Baden-Baden: Nomos.

Anderson, Perry (1985 [1974]). *Lineages of the Absolutist State*. London: Verso.

Berger, Suzanne (ed.) (1981). *Organizing Interests in Western Europe*. Cambridge: Cambridge University Press.

Block, Fred (1994). 'The Roles of the State in the Economy', in Neil J. Smelser, and Ricard Swedberg (eds). *The Handbook of Economic Sociology*. Princeton, NJ: Princeton University Press, pp. 691–710.

Bourdieu, Pierre (2000). *Structures Sociales de l'Économie*. Paris: Seuil.

Boyer, Robert (2003). *Théorie de la régulation: L'Etat des savoirs*. Paris: La Découverte.

Callies, Gralf-Peter and Peer Zumbansen (2010). *Rough Consensus and Running Code. A Theory of Transnational Private Law*. Oxford: Hart Publishing.

Chernilo, Daniel (2007). *A Social Theory of the Nation-state: The Political Forms of Modernity beyond Methodological Nationalism*. London: Routledge.

Crouch, Colin (2005). *Post-democracy*. Cambridge: Polity Press.

Crouch, Colin and Maarten Keune (2005). 'Changing Dominant Practice. Making Use of Institutional Diversity in Hungary and the United Kingdom', in Wolfgang Streeck and Kathleen Thelen (eds). *Beyond Continuity: Institutional Change in Advanced Political Economies*. Oxford: Oxford University Press, pp. 83–102.

Crouch, Colin, Patrick Le Galès, Carlo Trigilia and Helmut Voelzkow (eds) (2004). *Changing Governance of Local Economies. Responses of European Local Production Systems*. Oxford: Oxford University Press.

Dahrendorf, Ralf (2010 [1954]). *Class and Class Conflict in Industrial Society*. London: Routledge.

Dawson, Mark (2011). *New Governance and the Transformation of European Law: Coordinating EU Social Law and Policy*. Cambridge: Cambridge University Press.

Durkheim, Émile (2007 [1893]). *De la division du travail social*. Paris: Presses Universitaires de France.

Evans, Peter B., Dietrich Rueschmeyer and Theda Skocpol (eds) (1985). *Bringing the State Back In*. Cambridge: Cambridge University Press.

Foucault, Michel (2004 [1979]). *Naissance de la biopolitique*. Paris: Gallimard/Seuil.

Gilson, Ronald J., Charles F. Sabel and Robert E. Scot (2009). 'Contracting for Innovation: Vertical Disintergration and Interfirm Collaboration', *Columbia Law Review* 109(3): 431–502.

Goldthorpe, John H. (ed.) (1984). *Order and Conflict in Contemporary Capitalism*. Oxford: Clarendon Press.

Grabher, Gernot (ed.) (1993). *The Embedded Firm*. London: Routledge.

Habermas, Jürgen (1973). *Legitimationsprobleme im Spätkapitalismus*. Frankfurt am Main: Suhrkamp Verlag.

(1981). *Theorie des kommunikativen Handelns Bd. 1–2*. Frankfurt am Main: Suhrkamp Verlag.

(1992). *Faktizität und Geltung. Beiträge zur Diskurstheorie des Rechts und des demokratischen Rechtsstaats*. Frankfurt am Main: Suhrkamp Verlag.

Hall, Peter A. and David Soskice (2001). *Varieties of Capitalism. The Institutional Foundation of Comparative Advantage*. Oxford: Oxford University Press.

Harste, Gorm (1997). *Modernitet og Organisation*. Copenhagen: Politisk Revy.

Hegel, Georg W.F. (1971 [1800–02]). *Die Verfassung Deutschlands, Werke 1*. Frankfurt am Main: Suhrkamp Verlag.

Héritier, Adrienne (2007). *Explaining Institutional Change in Europe*. Oxford: Oxford University Press.

Hirsch, Joachim (2005). *Materialistische Staatstheorie: Transformationsprozesse des kapitalistischen Staatensystems*. Hamburg: VSA Verlag.

Hooghe, Liesbet and Garry Marks (2001). *Multilevel Governance and European Integration*. Lanham, MA: Rowman & Littlefield.

Jessop, Bob and Ngai-Ling Sum (2006). *Beyond the Regulationist Approach*. Cheltenham: Edward Elgar.

Joerges, Christian (2010). 'Rechtsstaat and Social Europe', *Comparative Sociology* 9(1): 65–85.

Kjaer, Poul F. (2009). 'Post-Hegelian Networks', in Marc Amstutz and Gunther Teubner (eds). *Networks: Legal Issues of Multilateral Cooperation*. Oxford: Hart Publishing, pp. 75–85.

(2010). *Between Governing and Governance. On the Emergence, Function and Form of Europe's Post-national Constellation*. Oxford: Hart Publishing.

(2011). 'Law and Order within and beyond National Configurations', in Poul F. Kjaer, Gunther Teubner and Alberto Febbrajo (eds). *The Financial Crisis in Constitutional Perspective: The Dark Side of Functional Differentiation*. Oxford: Hart Publishing, pp. 395–430.

(2014). *Constitutionalism in the Global Realm. A Sociological Approach*. London: Routledge.

Kohler-Koch, Beathe (ed.) (2003). *Linking EU and National Governance*. Oxford: Oxford University Press.

Ladeur, Karl-Heinz (1997). 'Towards a Legal Theory of Supranationality – The Viability of the Network Concept', *European Law Journal* 3(1): 33–54.

Lefebvre, Henri (1974). *La production de l'espace*. Paris: Gallimard.

Levi-Faur, David (ed.) (2006). 'Varieties of Regulatory Capitalism: Sectors and Nations in the Making of a New Global Order, Special issue of Governance', *Governance* 19(3).

Luhmann, Niklas (1983 [1969]). *Legitimation durch Verfahren*. Frankfurt am Main: Suhrkamp Verlag.

(1988). *Die Wirtschaft der Gesellschaft*. Frankfurt am Main: Suhrkamp Verlag.

(1997). *Die Gesellschaft der Gesellschaft*. Frankfurt am Main: Suhrkamp Verlag.

Marx, Karl (2009 [1867–94]). *Das Kapital. Kritik der politischen Ökonomie*. Köln: Anaconda Verlag.

Mayntz, Renate (2006). 'Governance Theorie als fortentwickelte Steurungstheorie?', in Gunnar Folke Schuppert (ed.). *Governance-Forschung*. Baden-Baden: Nomos Verlag, pp. 11–20.

(2007). 'The Architecture of Multi-Level Governance of Economic Sectors', *MPIfG Discussion Paper* 13.

Morgan, Glenn (2005). 'Institutional Complementarities, Path Dependency, and the Dynamics of Firms', in Glenn Morgan, Richard Whitley and Eli Moen (eds). *Changing Capitalisms? Internationalization, Institutional Change, and Systems of Economic Organization*. Oxford: Oxford University Press, pp. 415–46.

Münch, Richard (2004). *Soziologische Theorie. Bd 3: Gesellschaftstheorie*. Frankfurt am Main: Campus Verlag.

Neumann, Franz L. (1983 [1944]). *Behemoth: The Structure and Practice of National Socialism 1933–1944*. London: Octagon Press.

Parsons, Talcott and Neil J. Smelser (2001 [1956]). *Economy and Society*. London: Routledge.

Piore, Michael J. and Charles Sabel (1984). *The Second Industrial Divide*. New York, NY: Basic Books.

Polanyi, Karl (2001 [1944]). *The Great Transformation. The Political and Economic Origins of our Time*. Boston, MA: Beacon Press.

Rawls, John (1999 [1971]). *A Theory of Justice*. Cambridge, MA: Harvard University Press.

Rhodes, Roderick A.W. (2007). 'Understanding Governance: Ten Years On', *Organization Studies* 28(8): 1243–64.

Rosa, Hartmut (2005). *Beschleunigung: Die Veränderung der Zeitstrukturen in der Moderne*. Frankfurt am Main: Suhrkamp Verlag.

Rueschemeyer, Dietrich (2009). *Usable Theory*. Princeton, NJ: Princeton University Press.

Sassen, Saskia (2006). *Territory, Authority, Rights: From Medieval to Global Assemblages*. Princeton, NJ: Princeton University Press.

Scharpf, Fritz W. (1988). 'The Joint-Decision Trap. Lessons from German Federalism and European Integration', *Public Administration* 66(2): 239–78.

Scheuerman, William E. (2004). *Liberal Democracy and the Social Acceleration of Time*. Baltimore, MD: Johns Hopkins University Press.

Schmitter, Philippe C. (1974). 'Still the Century of Corporatism?', in Frederich B. Pike and Thomas Stritch (eds). *The New Corporatism*. Notre Dame, IN: University of Notre Dame Press, pp. 85–131.

Schmitter, Philippe C. and Gerhard Lehmbruch (eds) (1979). *Trends toward Corporatist Intermediation*. New York, NY: Sage Publications.

Schumpeter, Joseph A. (1976 [1942]). *Capitalism, Socialism and Democracy*. London: George Allen and Unwin.

Schuppert, Gunnar F. (Hrsg) (2006). *Governance-Forschung*. Baden-Baden: Nomos Verlag.

Sciulli, David (1992). *Theory of Societal Constitutionalism. Foundations of a Non-Marxist Critical Theory*. Cambridge: Cambridge University Press.

Simmel, Georg (2009 [1900]). *Philosophie des Geldes*. Köln: Anaconda Verlag.

Steinmo, Sven (2010). *The Evolution of Modern States: Sweden, Japan, and the United States*. Cambridge: Cambridge University Press.

Steinmo, Sven, Kathleen Thelen and Frank Longstreth (eds) (1992). *Structuring Politics: Historical Institutionalism in Comparative Analysis*. Cambridge: Cambridge University Press.

Stichweh, Rudolf (2006). 'Strukturbildung in der Weltgesellschaft - Die Eigenstrukturen der Weltgesellschaft und die Regionalkulturen der Welt', in Thomas Schwinn (ed.). *Die Vielfalt und Einheit der Moderne*. Wiesbaden: Verlag für Sozialwissenschaften, pp. 239–57.

Streeck, Wolfgang (2009). *Re-Forming Capitalism: Institutional Change in the German Political Economy*. Oxford: Oxford University Press.

Streeck, Wolfgang and Kathleen Thelen (eds) (2005). *Beyond Continuity: Institutional Change in Advanced Political Economies*. Oxford: Oxford University Press.

Teubner, Gunther (1983). 'Substantive and Reflexive Elements in Modern Law', *Law and Society Review* 17: 239–85.

Thelen, Kathleen (2004). *How Institutions Evolve. The Political Economy of Skills in Germany, Britain, the United States, and Japan*. Cambridge: Cambridge University Press.

Thelen, Kathleen and James Mahoney (eds) (2010). *Explaining Institutional Change: Ambiguity, Agency, and Power*. Cambridge: Cambridge University Press.

Thornhill, Chris (2008). 'Towards a Historical Sociology of Constitutional Legitimacy', *Theory and Society* 37(2): 161–97.

Tönnies, Ferdinand (2005 [1887]). *Gemeinschaft und Gesellschaft*. Leipzig: Fues's Verlag.

Virilio, Paul (1977). *Vitesse et Politique: essai de dromologie*. Paris: Galilée.

von Hayek, Friedrich A. (1994). *Freiburger Studien: Gesammelte Aufsätze*. Tübingen: Mohr Siebeck.

Weber, Max (1976). *Wirtschaft und Gesellschaft*. Tübingen: Mohr Siebeck Verlag.

Wiarda, Howard J. (1997). *Corporatism and Comparative Politics: The Other Great 'Ism'*. Armonk, NY: M.E. Sharpe.

Wiethölter, Rudolf (1968). *Rechtswissenschaft*. Frankfurt am Main: Fischer Verlag.

Willke, Helmut (1992). *Ironie des Staates. Grundlinien einer Staatstheorie polyzentrischer Gesellschaft*. Frankfurt am Main: Suhrkamp Verlag.

Zeitlin, Jonathan and David Trubek (eds) (2003). *Governing Work and Welfare in a New Economy*. Oxford: Oxford University Press.

PART II

Law and Europe's ideological transformations

6

Private, public and collective: the twentieth century in Italy from fascism to democracy

IRENE STOLZI

6.1 Looking for a new order

A few preliminary statements are necessary in order to clarify the limits and approach of this chapter. First and foremost, it is necessary to explain the chronological framework. In this chapter, we attempt summarily to reconstruct the modalities in which Italian legal thought responded to the demands posed by the complex historical situation which followed World War I, and in which it projected conditions of legal order which were adapted to post-1918 society more broadly. Then, proceeding from a series of reflections on the legal concepts underlying the doctrines of *corporatism* in Italian fascism, we aim, by way of conclusion, to look beyond 1945, and to present a composite picture of post-war Italy, which, marked both by new legal forms and the persistence of old ones, drew part of its (democratic) identity from interpretations of corporatism as it had been historically experienced. At a methodological level, further, we intend in this chapter to disentangle the complex legacy of interwar Italian legal theory. In particular, we examine ways in which under fascist rule in Italy both trade unions and the political party began to acquire new meaning as essential instruments for organizing social life and for enabling social participation in the governance of public affairs, albeit within the framework of a very authoritarian conception of coexistence. Under fascism a new conception of politics began to take shape: politics was seen as a dimension of society, in which a comprehensive project of coexistence could be elaborated, and in which the activities of all public and private actors, channelled and expressed through the political party, could be given direction. This expanded concept of politics meant that social organizations acquired a specific and distinct role: social organizations were entrusted with internal responsibilities for governance, connected with the organization of their members' everyday lives (it was in the fascist period, for instance, that the first organizations for sport and leisure were born). It is in this respect that the complexity of the legacy of fascism becomes apparent. Clearly, some of the organizational processes pioneered under fascism were not connected with developments specific to fascism, but were rooted in a process of historical evolution and widespread transformation that was evident in many states and many societies, ruled by different political regimes. For this reason, after the fall of fascism these organizational innovations did not have to be abolished, but could be made compatible with life in the new democratic state, after 1945. Often, however, the weight of history – that is, the fact that many legal theorists from a liberal background associated corporatism with authoritarianism – meant that the conversion of corporatist ideas into democratically formative principles was obstructed. For instance, after 1945 political parties and trade unions were allowed to retain the status of private associations, even though they were responsible for tasks of great importance and undeniable public relevance. For this reason, this chapter addresses the legacy of fascism from a twofold sociological perspective. It examines the corporate legal ideals of fascism as reflecting a deep transformation of Italian society (and other societies) in interwar Europe. Yet it also addresses the problematic legacy of these ideals for the consolidation of democracy in post-war Italy. In the conclusion, we address attempts to find remedies for the weaknesses of merely private-legal ideas of societal membership, and we propose ways in which the corporatist theoretical lexicon might be re-opened.

It is probably unnecessary to re-examine the reasons for the legal complexity of post-1918 Italy. At the risk of simplification, we can say that after World War I it became increasingly difficult to ascribe autonomy to the private sphere in its relation to the public sphere. In general terms, it became difficult to assert the autonomy of law in relation to politics, and to the economy. More particularly, it became increasingly difficult to portray private law as a legal horizon inhabited by single and unrelated individual actors, defined by the primacy of their single wills, and to depict public law as a horizon inhabited solely by the state, a power that remained abstracted against underlying socio-economic dynamics, which, for this reason, was considered capable of perpetuating its indisputable sovereign substance *ad aeternum*. This 'harmonious' and 'schematic' idea of a legal order 'in which everything is (was) reduced to the concepts of sovereignty and individual freedom' was overturned, after 1918, by a combination of various factors (Capograssi 1959 [1922]: 409), which are also well known and can be summed up through various diffuse ideas of *crisis*. On one hand, this crisis was seen as a crisis of the state, in which the state was besieged by the proliferation of organized interests, so that this new society of parties, unions and concentrated economic organizations experienced a crisis in its capacity for producing powers not finally reducible to relations between private parties (see Ornaghi 1984). However, private law was also afflicted by crisis. This was due to the fact that it was forced to come to terms with a state that, from the beginning of the war onward, had intervened heavily on the economic terrain, even invading the strongholds of nineteenth-century private law (property and contract). Notably, the state had done this through expropriations and requisitions of farmlands and industrial plants, through restrictions and obligations intended to determine the quality and quantity of production, and through binding imperative interventions in future or already stipulated contracts, thus bearing witness to the growing difficulty of identifying private law with the area of 'free individual decisions' (Vassalli 1960 [1918]: 341; Cesarini Sforza 1929: 119). Nonetheless, private law, to the same degree as public law, was also pushed into a crisis due to the growing importance of organized interests, as these interests seemed to absorb the individual and its autonomy and risked transforming personal affiliation – that is, affiliation to a group, an organization – into the decisive precondition for the attainment of a full and fully realized legal subjectivity.

Imagining a new order, therefore, meant tackling a set of multifarious challenges. It required an attempt to delineate the contours of the private and the public spheres, of law, politics and the economy, in a manner that reflected an awareness of the ways in which they had become unavoidably connected. It is not superfluous to note that this was neither exclusively an Italian problem nor a problem limited solely to the climate between the two world wars. What was specifically Italian, however, was the debate engendered by the promised emergence of a corporatistic civilisation, one that was intended to promote a fully twentieth-century society, for which fascism aspired to become the historical standard-bearer.

While the chronological limits of this chapter have been clarified, a few words must be dedicated to explaining what the corporatistic order was or, more accurately, what it was intended to be. In the twenty-year period between the wars, references to corporatism alluded to an overall project of social, political and economic reform, a project that was supposed to develop in two successive and interdependent phases. The first phase, termed 'union corporatism', and the only one, we might add, which received an adequate normative and institutional expression, was based on the legal recognition of associations of workers and employers. This recognition was intended to enable trade unions and employers' associations to oversee and discipline labour relations: primarily through the stipulation of collective labour agreements with *erga omnes* effect, but also through the assumption of responsibilities in respect of assistance and supervision towards the members of their respective professional categories.[1] In contrast to this, the second, more authentically corporatistic, phase provided for the formation of corporations: that is, organs of the state made up of elements drawn from unions, the administrative apparatus of the state, and the National Fascist Party (PNF). These organs were intended to constitute what was emphatically defined as the General Staff of the Italian economy. In particular, corporate groups were to be entrusted with the task of promoting and realizing a so-called third way model of economic organization: that is to say, they were intended to promote a system of economic-production relations capable of combining the continued respect for property and private initiative with various patterns of public intervention in economic matters (from direct intervention with restricted scope, to the imposition of qualitative and quantitative results on productive activities,[2] which was intended to become the general rule).

In this brief and summary description, I have used some verbs in the conditional mode. This is because we know – clearly – that corporatism was only practically realized to a very limited practical degree. Despite its disastrous results, however, it was capable of animating a debate possessing important theoretical depth (Gagliardi 2010; Stolzi 2007). Alongside a large host of sceptics who attempted to reduce new corporate ideas to traditional images of legal order, a significant number of legal theorists identified in corporatism a theoretical system that might

[1] See the contents of the law promulgated 3 April 1926, no. 563.

[2] Declarations VII and IX of the Labour Charter of 1927, which was intended to form the platform for the new Fascist Corporate State, have this express meaning. Declaration VII states (emphasis added): 'The Corporate State considers private initiative in the field of production as the most effective and most useful tool in the interest of the Nation. As the private organisation of production is a function of national interest, *the company organiser is responsible before the State for production policy*. The collaboration of production forces generates reciprocity of rights and duties among them. The employee, technician, clerk and labourer are active collaborators of the economic concern, whose management and responsibility are entrusted to the employer.' Declaration IX states: 'The intervention of the State in economic production occurs only when private initiative is either lacking or insufficient or when political interests of the State are at stake. This intervention can assume the form of control, encouragement or direct management.'

have made it possible to move beyond nineteenth-century legal models and instruments. These theorists saw corporatism as a legal order that was able both to outline a conception of society capable of confronting the problem of legal citizenship demanded by the bodies and organizations typical of the new mass society, and of addressing the problem of the necessary interaction between private parties and the state in the economic arena.

In reconstructing this scenario, and moving on to our more general approach, we shall examine how legal science articulated a series of responses to these conditions. In consequence, we will at times be forced to move outside the history of institutions and society, and we will develop our argument through reconstruction of the history of legal thought. This focus is important, in general terms, if we consider how, historically, the cultivation of certain images of society has proven capable of conditioning the direction of a legal system's development. This focus is most particularly important, however, in the context of European society in the early twentieth century. At this time, it was widely perceived that the restrictive boundaries which had permitted modern European society to articulate the difference between disciplinary universes – that is, between law, politics, economy, sociology, etc. – as well as to formulate the distinctions within the legal universe itself (that is, primarily, the distinctions between private and public law, but also the distinctions between law in force and living law, between procedures for the production and the application of laws, and so on) had a markedly archaic character. In order to avoid a situation in which the collapse of these traditional barriers meant abdicating all hope of a future order, it became indispensable to find a conceptual model capable of defining and disciplining relations between all the levels of society, and to identify the specific legal trajectory for twentieth-century social order.

From a similar point of view, the diffuse references to the function of government and the primacy of politics represented a call for a synthesis designed to identify the contours of a given project of society. This was conceived as a project that could be formulated by a wide range of authors and could integrate the most disparate contents, but that in any event expressed the ambition to connect the entire spectrum of social, political and economic energies, and to direct the conduct of all subjects, both private and public (see Mortati 2000 [1931]: 1940). The idea that politics has a certain primacy was a general characteristic of different twentieth-century experiences, from the Weimar Republic, to totalitarianism, to the democratic constitutions established after 1945.

Distinctively, however, the idea that politics has primacy in society reflected an attempt to transfer mediation between state and society onto a level of collective purposes and shared historical objectives. It is, therefore, no coincidence that after World War I references to the third way were not intended to describe a generic composition between individualism and the state's powers of (economic and social) intervention, between freedom and authority. Instead, these references began to express a varying attempt to realize an 'active concurrence' between the private and the public, and they endeavoured at once to bring about a correspondence between 'constitutional order' and 'the organizing principle of social elements' (Mortati 2000 [1931]: 73), and to sanction the full inclusion of the economy among the variables capable of determining the development of a given socio-political system. Previous social legislation (the liberal state's first massive act of infidelity to its classical promise of abstention) had remained reducible to a traditional idea of legal order. Such legislation had still permitted a glimpse of the contours of public intervention oriented toward rebalancing – through prohibitions and nullifications – the position of parties, and of capital and labour, thus confirming the eternal validity of formal contractual logic. Now, however, the reliability and utility of the distributive solutions autonomously produced by the market began to be contested in much more radical fashion. Moreover, the attention devoted to the problem of planning and management of the economy, even in the countries of Western Europe, testified in eloquent manner to the need to divest the economic dimension of social exchange of its self-referential quality.[3] This change of climate was also evidenced by the frequent references to the social function of property and, in general, to the functionalization of subjective rights, which were increasingly considered both as rights belonging to the individual and as rights capable of producing duties, in respect of the satisfaction of social or public interests.[4]

[3] For discussion of the widely circulating idea that these new regulative instruments should serve to 'curb the anarchic frenzy of capitalistic production' see Heller (quoted in Mannori and Sordi 2001: 456).

[4] In addition to the text of provision VII of the Labour Charter, it is necessary to refer to the provisions of the Weimar Constitution, the first genuinely 'twentieth-century' constitution. This constitution resulted from the attempt to provide adequate legal citizenship for parties and unions, and to establish a structural tie between private and public matters on the economic front by means of the functionalization of the most private of rights – property itself. 'Property brings obligations' states Art. 153 of the Weimar Constitution: 'its exercise must also be a service rendered to the common good.'

These concepts, circulating widely in the theoretical milieu of the early twentieth century, clearly assumed profoundly different meanings in different cases and in different theoretical articulations. This was because the selection of values employed to support a certain project of society was subject to variation, there were differences between the actors required to conceive the project, and the manner in which the guiding principles of the relation between state and society were reconstructed was variable. In general, however, legal theorists interested in promoting the nascent corporatistic order saw it as an opportunity, not only to reflect on trade union and production relations, but also, in more general terms, to provide an account of relations between the individual, state and social organizations; to concentrate attention on the function of political policy and to reflect on the relations between the different powers of the state; and, moreover, to enquire into the role given to policies that we would today call *welfare policies* or into the monopolistic characteristics of mature capitalism. Intellectual history, more than other sub-disciplines of history, assumes decisive importance, not only as a means to elucidate the different and, at times, opposed horizons that produced apparently comparable solutions, but also to demonstrate the role which, at the fall of fascism, was played by the enduring attachment to certain outdated images of society in interpreting the history of corporatism.

6.2 The doctrine of totalitarianism

In this section, we intend to shed light on a small number of aspects of the complex and variegated body of legal theory addressing questions of corporatistic order in interwar Italy. Firstly, we wish to highlight how the references to corporatism constituted a theoretical framework for concepts focusing on the idea of a new state: that is, of a state that was new because it was totalitarian, because it was required, in contrast to (what appeared to be) the indecisive character of old-style patterns of authoritarianism, to envelop all individual and social energies within its ranks. Of the most fundamental importance in this respect was the emergence and formation of a *third area of law*.

The doctrine of corporatism formed a composite front which branched out along various theoretical paths. For instance, Alfredo Rocco, a legal theorist with a traditional training, committed himself to devising a version of corporatism capable of subordinating the management of every form of social conflict and labour unrest to the decision-making powers of the state. In contrast, Sergio Panunzio and Giuseppe Bottai were intent on demonstrating the utility that a solid network of groups and associations, artfully manipulated by the new state, could acquire in creating the *new man* – a man who, even at the most fundamental level, was devoted to the regime's values. In addition, more idealist theorists, such as, to name but three, Giovanni Gentile, Arnaldo Volpicelli, and Ugo Spirito, were convinced that it was the duty of corporatism to realize an identification between state and individual, between the private and public domains. They claimed that it was only in this manner that a legal system could be protected from the disruptive demon of pluralism. Nonetheless, despite this considerable diversity of views, all formulations of totalitarian corporatism attributed a decisive role to so-called *intermediate bodies*: that is, to social and economic organizations positioned between the state and the individual, which they saw as establishing a *third area of law*. No longer viewed as threats, but rather as foundational resources of the new state, social, political and economic organizations were portrayed in corporatist theory as formidable *seminaria rei publicae*. If it was the case that the salvation of the state lay to a large degree in its proven capacities for organizing the society subject to its power, and if the antagonistic character of mass society found its own distinctive identity through its division into groups and subgroups, the state, on this account, also needed to avail itself of this omnipresent associative tendency in order to provide a foundation for its own power.

The emergence of the third area of the law presupposed a nuanced, balanced definition of statehood. In order for the party and the trade union (that is, the official union, necessarily described in the singular), together with the plethora of bodies summoned to forge the new fascist society and to co-ordinate the various associations (the workers, youth, women, etc.) which were expected to play a part in transforming the entire individual and social space, the state was obliged to pursue a sophisticated strategy of institutional engineering. First of all, it was necessary for the state to renounce any type of representative and participatory logic. That is to say, it was necessary for the state to avoid a situation in which different social organizations could act on the basis of a free and spontaneous aggregatory impulse, capable of conditioning and restricting the exercise of state power itself. At the same time, however, it was necessary for the state to mark out a distance between the new form of statehood and previous forms of administrative order and, in general, previous patterns of public control over social life. To avoid falling back into the errors of the liberal state, it was indispensable for the fascist state to replace the idea of supervision and 'external' control by the state with the new idea of a state presence capable of converting the related corporate bodies operating in society into 'productive auxiliaries of the state' (Bottai 1928: 398), or tools for the active and participatory cultivation of the new state. If the failure of the liberal state was perceived as to a large degree attributable to the insufficient consideration given to the social sphere and to the increasingly 'antagonistic' character of mass society, the corporatistic endeavour to sanction 'the state's nature and importance in all of individual and social life' (Volpicelli 1930: 211) could only be consolidated if a 'more subtle and discrete mission' was ascribed to the new organizations (Bottai 1949: 42). In brief, it was necessary for the state to find the path that would make it possible thoroughly to catalogue society in all its diverse social, political and economic organizations (the so-called corporatistic organizations). Yet it was also necessary for the state, at the same time, to avoid resorting (or rather, resorting too heavily) to the forcible recruitment of individuals into these organizations.

The contours of the new totalitarian state were most clearly traced in the writings of Alfredo Rocco. This is illuminated by the trade union law of 1926, which Rocco, over a long period of time, had designed, and which he ultimately drafted. This law represented, as already mentioned, the only entirely realized corporatistic charter. The content of this legislation, dedicated to the legal discipline of collective labour relations, is well known. It ensured the exclusive status of the recognized fascist union (recognition was given solely to fascist unions). It established collective bargaining with *erga omnes* effect. It provided for the institution of a new court (the magistracy of labour) with jurisdiction over collective labour disputes. It also foresaw the prohibition, under pain of penal persecution, of strikes and lock-outs.[5] While the contemporary interpretations of the law were primarily oriented, albeit from different points of view, toward underlining the classical conservative character of the state, this was not

[5] The law is no. 563 of 3 April 1926. Clause I provided for 'the legal recognition of unions and collective labour agreements' (Arts 1–12), but it only recognized fascist unions. Clause II regulated 'the magistracy of labour' (Arts 13–17). Clause III regulated 'shutdowns and strikes' (Arts 18–22). The law was followed by the executory regulations enacted on 1 July 1926. Rocco openly declared to the Senate, on the occasion of the law's presentation: 'We have no difficulty whatsoever in declaring this very moment that recognition will be given to Fascist unions' (Rocco 1926: 387). It was again Rocco, and again in Parliament, who declared how the Palazzo Vidoni Pact of 1925 was nothing other than the 'necessary logical antecedent' of the later union law of 1926 (Rocco 1925: 357).

the aim declared and pursued by Rocco himself, as the law's author. This law, which denied all autonomy to the interests of organized groups, positioned itself outside the traditional category of state legislation because it recognized both the existence and the specific value of these organized groups. A good part of contemporary legal science tended to avoid uncharted legal territory by attributing the collective legal dimension of society to one of the known areas – public or private – of law. Rocco, however, accentuated the *median dimension* or the third legal domain of socio-political reality, which he perceived as representing a central ingredient in the achievement of a 'total renewal of the idea of state' (Rocco 1921: 652).

What emerged from the text of Rocco's trade union legislation and from the parliamentary debates that accompanied its passage was that this was an ordinance claiming to possess a 'totalitarian and organic' nature (Rocco 1925: 368). This was due to the fact that it aimed, not only to subject the life of trade union associations to penetrating public control, but also to provide a system to govern trade union disputes and, in general, to regulate the entire associative life of organizations. In consequence, it comes as no surprise to learn that, under this law, many collective contracts were discussed and stipulated directly within the Ministry of Labour. In most cases of arbitration, in fact, it was the executive itself that referred the parties to the magistracy of labour. At the same time, the fact that the law provided opportunity for 'dialectical' conduct of disputes – contractual and procedural – represented an instrument that the state used to modulate, as required, the incisiveness of its intervention.[6] One need only consider the institution of the magistracy of labour, described as an 'authentic safety valve of the system' (Jocteau 1978: 56), which was inaugurated in 1926. The purpose of this institution was not to exploit the dependence of the magistracy of labour on the executive power in order exclusively to guarantee sentences in line with the policies of the state. In fact, the alignment between sentences and the will of the executive, which the legislator certainly pursued in establishing the magistracy of labour, was achieved through new and

[6] There was no aspect of the life of union organization that was not subjected to highly discretionary control by government authority. Government control covered legal recognition, which could be revoked at any time; approval of the by-laws and appointments/elections (with a consequent faculty of revocation) of secretaries and presidents; power to dissolve the union executive; annulment of acts and measures of any nature adopted by the associations and considered 'contrary to the essential ends of organisations'.

different modalities. On one hand, for instance, the decision not to conceal a trade union dispute, instituting a legal framework to make it visible and to regulate it, could be used to make the rhetoric of self-government and the autonomy of union organizations more credible, thus making the trade union laws of 1926 seem more acceptable. On the other hand, the contingency of judicial power brandished throughout hearings as a threat or a resource, enabled the state, in different ways in different cases, to decide whether and in what manner the dispute ought to be resolved, so preserving until the end of proceedings, until the sentence was handed down, the manoeuvrability of the social pawns subjected to its vigilance.

6.3 Social and individual law

Following this brief exposition, it can be observed that the attempt to give value to the third area of law did not produce a mere 'topographical' enrichment of the legal landscape: it did not merely add a further element – the law of social organizations – to the traditional dichotomy between private and public law. On the contrary, this third area of law proved capable of corroding the essential identity of the known extremes (the specifically private and public elements) of legal dynamics.

The third area of the law proved capable, first of all, of reformulating the identity of state power under public law. Whether it was focused on the new totalitarian conception of the state or on the attempt – as in the theorizations of non-totalitarian corporatism and in the Western conceptions of democracy – to combine participation and decision making, it imagined a state that appeared neither as a mere arbitrator in the interplay between social groups, nor as a power far removed from the expressions of social volition emerging 'from below': that is, from the lower strata of society. In addition, the third area of law was also capable of redefining the contours of private law. This was the case whether social organizations were seen as instruments to cultivate individuality – an individuality capable of combining the individual's freedom and responsibility – or whether they were seen as forming a sphere of society whose purpose was to demonstrate the uselessness and impracticability of the reference to rights and individual autonomy characterizing classical private law. The latter approach was a feature of the theoretical constructs of totalitarian corporatism. From this perspective, it was argued that 'the law does not trace the limits between individuals, but it organizes them in a system and a common task, and unifies them' (Volpicelli 1932: 88). The sole author of this unification was the state, called to act on society to remedy the 'lack of social content' of the modern state in general (Bottai 1930: 126). On this account, corporatism succeeded in presenting itself as an authentically totalitarian theoretical project, able to take hold of the individual, closing it within the ranks of the new state machine.

For this reason, under fascist government, social law, which remained a widely used expression, did not denote the law of social organizations. That is, it did not denote the law that these organizations could give to themselves in order to discipline their internal life and their relations with their external environment. Social law was, on the contrary, the expression used to indicate a process in which state power was expanded through society, a process that sought to relegate references to the rights and autonomy of the individual (and also of groups) to the redundant inheritance of the past. Central to corporate law was the perception of the state as the author of society, of the new society of organizations, and the perception of society as the conceptual genesis of the individual. Together, these concepts made it possible to construe the individual as a simple 'way of being of society' (Volpicelli 1932: 116), or as one of society's 'organic specifications' (Volpicelli 1930: 203). In this light, the individual could appear as an 'infinitesimal and transitory' element of the social game (Rocco 1938a [1914]: 43), and the classical ideal of singular freedom and autonomy was replaced by the new idea of 'organic development of the individual personality' (Rocco 1938b [1918]: 538). Social organizations were thus placed at the centre of the project in which all powers were reorganized in corporatistic fashion. Social organizations were required to fill the intermediate space between state and individual in order to make it possible to weld the individual to the state (Volpicelli 1930). In turn, this made it possible to bring about a condition in which the state provided organization for the individual personality, which alone guaranteed the realization of an active, participatory symbiosis, and not merely passive-transcriptive relation, between state and society.

The formation of a third area of the law had several important consequences, which will be briefly examined below. The first consequence was that the widespread reference to an organic and hierarchical structuring of social relations did not coincide with a celebration – typical of certain sectors of Catholic corporatism[7] – of the advantages of a legal system

[7] For an investigation into Catholic corporatism, see Vallauri (1971: 10–64) and Santomassimo (2006: 19). For the specific ties between the Christian social doctrine of a corporatistic sort and the fascist construction of an authoritarian political system, see Schiera (2005: 44–7).

capable of spontaneously producing and guaranteeing the harmonious coexistence of social actors, proceeding from the 'natural' inequalities among human beings. In organic corporatism, on the contrary, it became clear that the organism, the corporate whole, could only be the outcome of a process in which the legal system was constructed at the head of the new totalitarian state. Likewise, the references to hierarchy indicated the end of all (nineteenth-century) illusions regarding the legal system's capacity to produce itself in spontaneous fashion. Hierarchy indicated the theoretical design required to express and make possible an authentic *continuity* between state, social formations and individuals. That is to say, hierarchy acquired a specifically totalitarian significance in corporatistic doctrine because it did not solely describe a simple relation of superiority – of 'above' as distinct from 'below', of authority as distinct from autonomy. Instead, it was an instrument designed thoroughly to propagate a project of societal order formulated by the state. Hierarchy became, in short, the instrument used to promote and realize an *idem sentire* between leadership and rank and file, reflecting the principle that it was only under these conditions that the masses could be tied to the state, from the inside, in stable manner.

The second consequence of the third area of the law was that, in related theoretical contexts, it contained widespread references to the idea of the *city of producers*. This was a city that corporatism promised to build, which would (finally) move beyond the habitual class divisions, and which would organize social divisions around the distinction between active and passive citizens, based on their varying contribution to national production. Central to the third area of the law was thus an idea of the subject as *producer*. In most cases, the reference to the city of producers was an argumentative resource intended to affirm the state's new totalitarian face. To think of the subject as a producer was the only method for connecting no longer sustainable questions about rights with the features assumed by the new industrial society: as the state had to 'reach the individual [. . .] it did not look for the individual as the abstract political individual that the old liberalism took as an indifferent atom; it instead looked for the individual in the only way it could find it [. . .] as a specialized productive force' (Gentile 1982 [1927]: 275). The realization of an organic conception of the individual required, in consequence, an identification of the individual in the concreteness of its everyday position, which made it easier for the state to seize hold of the individual and close it in the cogs of the totalitarian machine. In consequence, it is not a coincidence that some of the most lucid and coherent advocates of the totalitarian construction of society argued that property and individual initiative were no longer concepts that described a boundary able to safeguard subjective autonomy, and which as such were capable of limiting and orienting the tenor of authoritarian interventions. Property and private initiative, on the contrary, tended to be perceived in developmentalist terms: that is, as the most appropriate instruments to stimulate individual productivity to the utmost, and thereby to celebrate the supremacy of the political world over the economy, so that the new total state obtained an important prop for its power (Stolzi 2007: 188).

A further consequence of the third area of law concerns the so-called social policies of fascism (and of many dictatorships in general). Viewed theoretically, these were an integral part of the emerging corporatistic machine and, for the most part, they developed outside that machine. Social policies were supposed to respond to two different and closely connected demands. Primarily, the constant reference to the necessity of providing economic gratification for the subordinate classes, combined with the idea that the fascist trade union, like the party and other social organizations, was an 'institution of propaganda' (Gentile 1982 [1927]: 274), to be used to promote adherence to the regime and to ensure that what Paolo Ungari poignantly termed 'the paradox of authority' (Ungari 1963: 112) was designed to secure and insulate the state against the theoretical implications of totalitarian corporatism. That is to say, fascist social policies obviated the possibility that the asserted supremacy of the totalitarian logic of the whole over the parts, of the organism over the organs, could give rise to an 'overturning' of 'middle-class rule into a unique form of communism' (Ungari 1963: 116). Indeed, the moment that fascism expressed a commitment to build a model of society intended to make the individual a transient and replaceable element of social interaction, and the moment that it legitimized dissent against the arguments traditionally used to justify the autonomy of private law and to identify private law with the law of middle-class society, it became quite difficult for fascism theoretically to articulate distinctive principles able to justify a retention of the traditional, and traditionally elitist, abstraction of 'social domination' (Costa 1976–77: 1066). The desire to abandon references to autonomy, rights and freedom, in short, made it difficult to reproduce the arguments that had permitted liberal thought to construe civil liberties and political freedoms as indissolubly connected, attributing the sanction of an accomplished legal subjectivity to a single part of society (the proprietary part). On this basis, in fact, it is no coincidence that some of the most dramatic corporatistic proposals – which were, not coincidentally, accused of Bolshevism – even admitted the possibility of an 'exchange of roles' between strong subjects and weak subjects of the economic game: between labour and capital. This was because the primary objective of an authentically totalitarian state was not so much the preservation of class differences as the potential for mobilizing the entire range of forces required by the production process (from the unskilled labourer to the business leader). Only in this manner could production appear to be a rationally organized reality, and as such capable of working for the power of the state (Stolzi 2007: 188–89).[8]

On one hand, therefore, the policy of allocating concessions, both economic and otherwise, to the subordinate classes served to ward off the prospect that social hierarchies might be overturned. On the other hand, however, these policies contributed to consolidating the state's totalitarian character, as they played an important role in increasing the consensus that the regime sought to obtain from the masses. The concern for material well-being played a decisive role in the corporate project and its endeavour to assimilate the masses into the state. However much we may underline the discrepancy between the lucidity and robustness of many theoretical versions of totalitarianism and the docility shown by the institutional procedures intended to interpret these visions and put them into practice, it is indubitable that fascist Italy (like National Socialist Germany) witnessed an exponential increase in the number of bodies and organizations for administering welfare. This increase also included the organization of leisure activities. This extended system of organizations, more than a simple second altar for the accomplished abolition of pluralism, constituted a central resource 'to reform society according to a certain plan' (Lanzillo 1980 [1932]: 746), and to realize and put into effect a process in which people were impelled to

[8] Despite this, no claim is made here that the alliance between fascism and capital did not play an important role in guaranteeing the regime's victory and progressive affirmation. A very recent book by Andrea Gagliardi (2010) – the only one, to our knowledge, that has addressed the history of corporatism from the viewpoint of its effective institutional success – underlines how the entrepreneurial class succeeded in utilizing its clumsy corporatistic scaffolding to promote policies favourable to its own interests. Eloquent proof in this sense is provided by the fact that the necessity to preserve the inequalities produced by the market stimulated diverse discursive strategies amongst theorists with a firmly totalitarian outlook. Take the obstinacy of Sergio Panunzio who argued that the corporatistic revolution needed to re-establish *ab imis* private law. He defended a one-sided notion of property, such that could not give rise to any obligation of conduct for the proprietor, continuing to express, *modo antiquo*, 'the full and totalitarian subjection of the thing to the person' (Panunzio 1938: 117). For analysis of this position, see Costa (1996).

assume an attitude of active and participatory devotion towards the state, which distinguished totalitarianism from government activism and from old-style dictatorships.

6.4 The end of fascist corporatism

At the fall of the fascist regime in Italy, most people found the argument that the regime's collapse marked '*the crisis of corporatism*' plausible (Cazzetta 1999: 594), and this argument formed the basis for imagining a new order (democratic or simply post-fascist). In reality, while legal science unanimously accepted the end of corporatism, attempts at reconstructing the reasons leading to the failure and/or break-up of the corporatistic order were once more shaped by divergent interpretations, and they reflected orientations in large part already expressed during the fascist era, or even before. It is not difficult to find interpretations of corporatism that run through time unaltered and connect the end of the nineteenth century, or the first decade of the twentieth century, to the years that followed World War II. In fact, the interpretations of the crisis of corporatism that reappeared after 1945 were divided into two camps. Some saw this crisis as an opportunity to re-define the parameters of legal order. Some saw this crisis as an opportunity to denounce the fact that corporatism had detached the law from the individualistic conception of order, which – they claimed – had been adequately formulated by the dogmatic categories employed in late nineteenth-century legal science (i.e. the study of pandects and the school of public law), which they viewed as constituting a definitive and indisputable achievement of legal culture. Depending on the point of view of the observer, corporatism either appeared to be a missed opportunity, irresponsibly soiled by the regime's indecisions, or it appeared to be an authoritarian excess: an impracticable *in re ipsa* hypothesis, inclined to subvert the sole and eternal conditions of legal order.

The earlier supporters of totalitarian corporatism, in particular, considered the collapse of corporatism a missed opportunity. They underlined how the indecisive actions of the fascist regime had prevented it from fulfilling corporatism's authentically totalitarian vocation. They argued that the regime had in the end diluted the innovative importance of corporatism into a mere proliferation of bodies and offices, which served only to bring to completion the bureaucratic excrescence of the Italian state (see Bottai 1952: 128). Moreover, they claimed that the fall of fascism could not, as if by magic, eradicate the demands that had led people to imagine a corporatistic reorganization of social, political and economic dynamics. This was exemplified by Giuseppe Bottai, who, after 1945, saw some preconditions of corporatism persisting in the new republic. He explained this as follows:

> [The] state, which the Right desires to be strong, cannot be strong or, in particular, remain strong except by identifying with the society of its time, as it is, with the precise forces that economic progress unleashes from concrete reality. And as this remains constant or moves toward the Left, towards a mass, collective economy, the state will not cease to be strong if it accepts this and makes it constitutionally its own. Indeed, it increases its strength hundredfold; it remains a state of the Right, with an economic and social structure of the Left.
>
> (Bottai 1949: 52)

Bottai concluded that if there were no definitive and central organization of parties, unions and enterprises in the new political order, the ghost of 'invisible government' – that is, of internal powers within the state capable of corroding its authority, caused by the state's inability to establish stable roots in society – would come back to life. This would condemn the state to certain death (Bottai 1952: 140).

The collapse of the corporatistic idea, however, was also considered a missed opportunity by the small number of legal theorists who, during the fascist era, attempted to propose an interpretation of corporatism, which, although hostile to the totalitarian perspective, sought to define the parameters for a new legal order. Such theorists hoped to see a legal order capable of combining the centrality assumed by collective bodies, the presence of a strong state, and lasting respect for individual rights and autonomy. This was a complex theoretical challenge, which, for the sake of brevity, cannot be examined here. It is sufficient to note here though that these interpretations of corporatism also harked back to quite different disciplinary and intellectual patterns. To refer only to the leading proponents of such theories, the idea of a non-totalitarian corporatism can, for instance, be traced to the theoretical objectives of Widar Cesarini Sforza. Sforza was a legal philosopher who saw corporatism as an institutional device to reproduce a liberal-elitist conception of society even in the twentieth-century climate, and to reproduce it by ascribing a central position to collective rights. He defined rights as institutions with a character that was 'more than private' and 'less than public' (Cesarini Sforza 1942 [1936]: 196), serving to overcome and reconcile the traditional dichotomy of authority and freedom. This line of reflection on corporatism can also be found in the thought of Enrico Finzi, an expert in civil law with a liberal training, who embraced the corporatistic cause. Finzi viewed corporatism as a means to reconstruct the relations between individuals, social groups and the state, so as to reconcile respect for individual freedoms and plans for a functionalization of private activities, in which the purely proprietary sense of subjective rights and property rights was abandoned. Finzi argued that rights, especially rights of property, needed to be viewed as objective rights, or as sources of duty and obligation towards the entire nation. This dimension of reflection on corporatism can also be found in the works of Lorenzo Mossa, the most unorthodox twentieth-century Italian specialist in commercial law. Mossa defined commercial law as an apparatus through which business, conceived as a unitary economic-legal reality, could reconcile the new logic of large-scale industrial production with a solidarist vision, capable of establishing the defence of subjectivity and individual rights in a manner that extended beyond simple proprietary ideals (Stolzi 2007: 359). The industrial enterprise had central status in Mossa's theory. He saw the enterprise as a solidaristic community, unifying rights of individuals with the exigencies of national industrial production, and so overcoming the purely private-legal models of rights in liberal individualism.

In the views of these legal theorists, the collapse of the corporatistic idea had been a failure for two different and related reasons. First, it had been a failure because the demands for renewal that had violently emerged following World War I were still relevant after the fall of the fascist regime. Second, it had been a failure because corporatism could have constituted an enormously beneficial opportunity for legal science as an academic discipline, as a result of which legal science might have assumed the status of an authentic planning vocation. It was perceived that, under corporatism, legal science was no longer expected to work solely on statutory law and to arrange its formulae in systematic form. On the contrary, it was given authority to contribute directly to imagining the future of legal orders and the changing relations between law, politics and economy, and so to provide important mediation and connections between the diverse dimensions of society. It was able to do this because it was most deeply concerned with the problem of order, which could only be comprehended if the relationships between individuals, both collective and public, politics, law and the economy, were approached in conjunction with one another.

Nevertheless, in the same way that they had been isolated in the twenty years between the wars, even after liberation, legal theorists representing such doctrines met with very little support. There were different reasons for this. In the case of Cesarini Sforza this was because his works expressed a very elaborate theoretical reconstruction, considered scarcely 'useable' at the level of concrete interpretative decisions. In Finzi's case this was because his works were the result of a few, very dense scientific interventions limited to the 1920s and 1930s. In the case of Mossa this was because his writings contained a wealth of intuitions, but were difficult to reduce to a unitary systematic picture. In any event, the work of these legal theorists did not occupy an outstanding place in the genealogy of their relative disciplines. They did not assume importance after World War II because their ideas were not in tune with the general trend toward revitalizing traditional distinctions (private/public, political/economical, individual/social) that characterized the dominant position of legal science in the 1940s and 1950s. Similarly, they also remained without great importance at a later stage, when, from the 1960s onwards, the meaning of these distinctions entered a crisis.

In this first instance, therefore, it can be observed that the abandonment of the corporatistic idea was contested, albeit from different viewpoints, by those who had made a specific investment in it, and who had attributed to it the capacity to produce a legal order adapted to the characteristics of the new twentieth-century reality. A closer look, however, reveals a slightly more surprising proximity between the majority position of the legal theorists who welcomed the end of corporatism with a liberating sigh of relief and the position of legal theorists who after the fall of fascism expressed regret at the loss of what they perceived as authentic corporatistic achievements. In the ranks of those who greeted the extinction of the corporatistic idea with relief, we can place many of the most influential names of twentieth-century Italian jurisprudence. These included, amongst public lawyers, Vittorio Emanuele Orlando, Oreste Ranelletti and Santi Romano. These also included, amongst private lawyers, Ludovico Barassi, Salvatore Pugliatti and Francesco Santoro Passarelli. These lawyers in fact formed a field of research which was marked by the greatest continuity through the twentieth century, and it survived the first fifty years of the century without substantial change. These lawyers emphasized the conviction that legal order could be produced only by means of a very strictly defined articulation between different domains and competences, between private and public spheres, between politics and law, and between fact and regulation. They viewed every principle, whether ideal or institutional, that sought to undermine the exactitude of these articulations as condemned to failure by virtue of the fact that it contested what they considered the natural and unchangeable parameters of legal order. Legal science, they claimed, had no choice but to work within established legal systems, and to force all claims of a different nature into compliance with known and established categories. Under fascism, some theorists had performed genuine acrobatics in the formulation of their arguments. This was evident, for example, in the fact that some tried to force the idea of the collective contract with *erga omnes* effect into the categories of a strictly individualist interpretation of the contractual phenomenon. This was also apparent in the fact that some attempted to avoid dismantling the traditionally authoritative appearance of property law. This was also seen in the fact that some denied constitutional status to parties and unions. After 1945, some lawyers deployed not dissimilar theoretical resources – as we shall see shortly – to contest the more distinctively twentieth-century aspects of the republican constitution (Stolzi 2007: 123, 237; Cazzetta 1999: 519).

Against this background, after 1945, interpretations of the interwar corporatistic experiment often became instrumental for attempts to reaffirm the centrality of traditional conceptions of the legal order. For experts in private law, corporatism became generically synonymous with authoritarian-dirigistic regulation. Private lawyers argued that corporatism had deserved stigmatization from the moment that it attempted to reinstate a conception of subjective law as absolute power of the will, such that it became incompatible with constraints of social finalization or a strictly privatistic-voluntarist idea of contracts. This applied in particular to the labour contract, which was, to a greater degree than other forms of contract, sensitive to the inequalities and imbalances produced by socio-economic competition (Cazzetta 1999: 606). Meanwhile, for experts in public law, corporatism often appeared synonymous with the unwarranted invasion of the state by society. The stigmatization of corporatism by public lawyers provided a basis for contesting those aspects of the republican constitution (popular sovereignty, the so-called programmatic rules, the role of parties and unions), which revised the modalities in which the relationship between state and society had traditionally been imagined.

However, similar views were represented amongst those who regretted the collapse of the corporatistic order. Emblematic in this regard were the opinions of Francesco Carnelutti, one of the major Italian legal theorists of the twentieth century. Although he worked within a theoretical model that was open to revision and self-criticism, Carnelutti always remained faithful to an individualistic conception of the legal order. More precisely expressed, he always remained faithful to the idea that the most essential sense of law was disclosed in a condition of social peace, and this peace was celebrated and realized each time a contract, the inter-subinfeuded agreement, was formed. He thus identified the contract as the only instrument capable of guaranteeing the peaceful coexistence of humanity. The responsibility of the state, therefore, was to stand watch and guarantee the peace consecrated each time a contract was entered. Or, in the case of conflict, its responsibility was to help parties reach the inter-subinfeuded agreement through the intervention of a third party: that is, of the judge, who was expected to render the judicial fulfilment of agreements between private parties possible. From this viewpoint, Carnelutti's main object of regret was the abrogation of the union law of 1926. He saw this law as a law 'whose origin contained principles that would honour any state and any legislation' (Carnelutti 1949: 249). For Carnelutti, this piece of legislation did not provide for a public-authoritarian regulation of union relations. Rather, it had served to immunize the legal order against the virus of the collective: that is, against the idea that there could be a third dimension of law, a collective dimension, capable of altering the habitual contours of private law and of law in general. In short, he argued that authoritarian intervention in the activities of unions served to consolidate the traditional identity of private and public law. It did not, as Rocco had projected, mark a consummation of the state's integral appropriation of society and individuals in a fashion which openly declared its own totalitarian character and considered union corporatism as 'one of the totalitarian necessities of the new order' (Ungari 1963: 114). It is easy to observe in the case of Carnelutti, too, that the pressure of a certain, traditional conception of society was principally responsible for conditioning – albeit in the spirit of 'regret' – his interpretation of the law of 1926 and of corporatism in general.

The danger implicit in all the interpretations of corporatism, which continued to express an unaltered faith in the nineteenth-century constructs of the legal order, is quite apparent. On one hand, they risked postdating the onset of the twentieth century to the end of World War II. On the other hand, they risked denying that a new historical period demanded institutional solutions different from those proper to the nineteenth century. In some cases, between the wars, this prevented these theories from adopting the clearly totalitarian – and not simply authoritarian – views typical of numerous theorizations of corporatism. Yet, after 1945, the tendency of legal science to pursue outdated images of legal order compromised the leading social and cultural role of legal science. In so doing, it made it impossible for many lawyers appropriately to experience the process of constitutional transition occurring at this time.

6.5 Democratic life and 'new corporatism'

On these grounds, it seems that the fall of fascism had greater importance in confirming the legitimacy of traditional conceptions of the legal order than in clearing the way for adequately modern legal-scientific responses. Under fascist rule, taking refuge in tradition, in traditional images of the legal order, could constitute – and it was considered in this way by many[9] – a strategic device to obstruct the authoritarian expansion of the legal space that fascism pursued. Once the regime fell, the complete rehabilitation of typically nineteenth-century images of the legal order coincided with Croce's interpretation of fascism as a parenthesis, an accidental, although perverted, deviation from the physiological line of development of the Italian socio-political system. We need to be clear here in noting that the ranks of those who advocated a return to tradition did not form the only theoretical camp. By necessity, we have only provided an outline of a reality that was quite complex. However, this was certainly a dominant camp at least until the mid-1950s, and it was a camp that also succeeded in gaining hegemonic status because, compared to those promoting more innovative responses, it could claim greater coherence for its views, and at the same time it could rely on what were already extensively tried and tested theoretical models (Cazzetta 1999: 585; Gregorio 2006: 888). It goes without saying that the many variations on the theme of the immutability of the legal order, characterized by the clear dichotomy between private and public law, inevitably influenced the new republican constitution of 1948. In particular, these ideas served to weaken the innovative importance of the constitution. They promoted, where possible, legal norms compatible with traditional images of legal order. Moreover, they refused to recognize the normative force and obligatory standing of those sections of the republican constitution which

[9] In this sense, see, for example, the well-known interpretation of Salvatore Pugliatti, the expert in civil law who 'divided' legal science under fascism into two large, wholly distinct categories. On one side, he saw the category of the apologists who were committed to the unwavering celebration of the virtues of fascism. On the other side, he identified the category – to which he declared that he himself belonged – of the formalists: those jurists who utilized the cult of forms and concepts to weaken the regime's reformist aims from the inside (Pugliatti 1950: 49–51).

did not simply reflect a neat division between private and public law, or between the political, the juridical and the economic spheres. They often explained this by stating that these parts had been drafted by politicians (or, in any event, by jurists foolishly inclined to confuse politics and law), and not by technicians of law (Gregorio 2006: 861). Overall, a neo-classical interpretation of the 1948 constitution was promoted, which sought to eradicate its dimensions derived from corporatistic ideas.

The distinctive features of the Italian constitution, similar to many post-World War II democratic constitutions, are well known. Simplifying to the utmost, we can say that the 1948 constitution expresses an attempt to define, *per relationem*, the identity of private, collective and public domains, and it attempts to see the articulations of a single relational context in these spheres. It is a constitution, in particular, that sees the relations between the different dimensions of society as obliged to project legal order into the future, focusing on a common life project whose fulfilment presupposes the contribution of all actors, both private and public. Indeed, it is this concept of social relations that, for example, led the constitution to attribute a role of primary importance to social and local organizations, which it considers as constitutive elements of the new democratic life, precisely because they are capable of contributing to defining the contours both of state authority and of subjective autonomy. Moreover, the idea of the relational character of political power led the constitution to imagine the state as a body expected to confront, and engage in dialogue with, various social groups, and (in addition to other prerogatives) to determine its own course of action in reference to this dialogue. Without ever reducing its status to the point of being a mere 'power among powers', the state imagined by the members of the post-war Constituent Assembly is a strong and present state. It is a state that possesses these characteristics precisely because it renounces all autocratic definitions of its power, and it is capable of consolidating its democratic identity through constant relations with individuals and groups. In short, it is a state that claims to obtain sure and solid legitimacy in the very moment that it proposes itself, not as the eternal antagonist of the individual and of society, but as the authoritative co-author of a project of society which incorporated various social interlocutors. Likewise, the relational conception of the state defines the contours of individual subjectivity as those of a protected individual, called to awareness of its responsibilities by the fact that it belongs at one and the same time both to the national community and to social groups. Moreover, the relational concept of the state is charged with responsibility for 'saving' social and local organizations from the risk of becoming the mouthpiece for dangerous particularisms or localisms.

The ambitious project underpinning the 1948 constitution was supported by the declared centrality of the person. It was sustained by a project that defined personal autonomy and dignity as guaranteed, not only by the indivisibility of civil, political and social rights, but also by the decisive centrality attributed to social rights. Under the constitution, social law and social rights began to advance hand in hand. At the same time, the vision of the Constituent Assembly was animated by the attempt to move beyond the idea of the reciprocal incompatibility between classes and rights. Social rights are defined as distinctively contemporary rights, but they are not simply added or, worse, juxtaposed, to traditional civil and political liberties. Under the constitution, the free subject is identified as the subject who is freed both from the fetters of despotism and from the fetters of need. Freedom is defined, not only as promoting uniform initial opportunities (so-called substantial equality), but also as supporting the individual through its entire existence, ensuring dignity and autonomy through all the adverse circumstances of life. On this basis, the guarantee of social rights constitutes the condition for the free and responsible exercise of equal civil and political rights. The concept of the subject as a 'social relation' in the constitution is intended to facilitate a reconciliation of the autonomy of the subject and its social ties with property and economic initiative, so that it remained possible to speak of public control of the economy. Moreover, the constitutional role assigned to social organizations (primarily parties and unions) constituted a decisive point of encounter between the private and public spheres, between society and the state, between politics and the economy.

The constitution, in short, is a constitution that gives valence to the areas of coexistence between different social dimensions and that – as we have already stated – defines this intersection, not as disruptive, but rather as an enriching moment of democratic reality. The constitution contains contours of a unitary design, whose coherent realization presupposed a concerted policy of constitutional implementation, capable of holding together the many and correlated aspects which it addressed. In this regard, however, we know that the constitution underwent a particularly troubled process of implementation, and the implications of its relational ideas never became reality. Piero Calamandrei said of it that it was 'more than an infanticide [...] it was an abortion' (Calamandrei 2004b [1955]: 135). It was, most particularly, the distinction, inaugurated by jurisprudence and consecrated by doctrine, between its preceptive (immediately practicable) provisions, and its programmatic provisions (provisions without a normative nature) that permitted a *sine die* postponement in the implementation of the new constitution.[10]

To be sure, the pro-constitution front progressively grew in numbers after 1948. This camp attracted prestigious figures, and it gave life to monographs – one important example was *La costituzione come norma giuridica* ('The constitution as legal norm') by Paolo Barile (1951) – that would eventually constitute authentic milestones in the history of Italian legal thought. Moreover, 1956 saw the first sentence handed down by the newly instituted Constitutional Court, and legal theorists began to view this organ of the state with interest and to entrust most of their hopes for the implementation of the constitution to this organ of the state. The constitution, though, could not live solely through the Constitutional Court. The organization of the constitution presupposed a 'political engine' (Gregorio 2006: 913): that is, it presupposed a system of parties capable of interpreting the sense of the new constitution and of guaranteeing the effective enactment of its provisions. Naturally, the constitution, like many others, was born in the shadow of a compromise between different constituent political forces. This compromise inevitably left unresolved the question of how its provisions should be enforced. This alone, however, need not have undermined the 'common respect' for the inspiring principles of the constitution itself (Calamandrei 2004a [1952]: 126).

Of particular note is the fact that, in the view of the members of the Constituent Assembly, the political parties were supposed to assume responsibility for the implementation of the constitution, which was conceived as a 'sort of politics on a grand scale, that was to unfold on a different and higher level than the mere majority political stance' (Fioravanti 1999: 877, 881). However, the disappointing reaction of the parties in this matter produced consequences of far-reaching importance. First, this contributed to a fundamental alteration of the physiognomy of the constitution. In principle, the constitution drew its value as a fundamental source of regulation from its markedly programmatic form: that is, from the fact that it proposed itself as the focus of a 'far-sighted' regulation, which was capable of looking into the distance and of conquering the future, overcoming the difficulties and divisions of

[10] See the pronouncement of the Corte di Cassazione (SSUU penali) on 7 February 1948.

the present. Yet the collapse of the relationship between 'politics and constitution' (Fioravanti 1999: 882), caused by the inability of the parties to fulfil its provisions, meant that the constitution was dangerously exposed to the risk that it would become near-sighted, incapable of assuming and preserving a strong regulatory role for the future, and thus destined to appear outmoded. This progressive erosion of the spirit of the constitution also meant that it tended to 'propose itself as a, in itself, founded norm, the expression of a sort of mandatory collective ethic'. This promoted an increasingly static concept of democracy, in which the purely normative functions of the constitution acquired greater importance that its implementation (Fioravanti 1999: 883).

Finally, from the 1970s onwards the growing inability of parties to implement the constitution and (at least in part) to conduct government as a shared undertaking has bolstered the perception that it is necessary to deploy instruments, either as collateral supplements or additional alternatives to parties and parliament, to manage and regulate social, political and economic dynamics. Therefore, it is no coincidence that the debate about the advisability of instituting so-called independent administrative authorities (similar to regulatory agencies in the UK) to oversee governmental administration has become widespread. Since the 1970s, the Italian government has been subject to independent regulation through a system of control by agencies designed to protect the most important interests of society (i.e. privacy, competition, market freedoms, and basic rights). Examples of these agencies are the Italian Securities and Exchange Commission (Consob), the Antitrust Agency (AGCM), and the Data Protection Agency. As a result, it is increasingly assumed that the existence of organizations possessing a certain independence of parliamentary political institutions is required to safeguard and address the relation between economy and society, in order to balance the force of the market through protective institutes. Because of this, moreover, it is no coincidence that neo-corporatism or corporate societies are also commonly discussed themes. In fact, neo-corporatism is discussed in a way that has two different, but complementary, meanings. On one hand, this term is used to designate, diagnostically, the growing oligopolistic segmentation of society (Rosanvallon 1984: 35) – of a society increasingly less capable of finding common seats of political representation. On the other hand, this term is used to examine the use of so-called concerted procedures: that is, 'neo-corporatistic' instruments to discipline the relations between government and unions. In both cases, neo-corporatism is discussed in order precisely to underline the insufficiency of party-parliamentary channels for preserving the relation between public and private, social and economic domains. In both cases, this discussion conjures the image of a very strong or a very weak state, which, depending on the hypothesis, appears either to be under siege or to be in collusion with various social groups. As a result, the state is seen as increasingly less 'naturally' capable of embodying the general interest.

The voices that have underlined the progressive oligopolistic fragmentation of contemporary societies are often characterized by a pessimistic-descriptive inflection – in the sense that they view these processes as reflecting a veritable 'crisis of the representations of the future' (Rosanvallon 1984: 31). However, the perspectives that profess to encounter an out-and-out difficulty in imagining a future of rules and shared values capable of bringing cohesion to the highly diverse and pluralistic components of socio-political coexistence – that is, reflections on concerted action and neo-corporatism – originated from the attempt to achieve a difficult but indispensable mediation between 'spontaneity and institution' (De Luca Tamajo 2008: 87), or between the autonomy of unions and the 'reaffirmed centrality of the role of the state' (Vardaro 1988: 20). In consequence, a situation has emerged in which, on one hand, the state remains charged with responsibility for embodying the general interest and promoting an interaction between social actors, which is considered as conforming to that interest. On the other hand, however, the idea has become widespread that access to the negotiating table should be voluntary for social actors, and, in any event, does not necessarily form an alternative to the use of methods of democratic conflict (primarily, the right to strike). This does not rehabilitate the rhetoric (so dear to the various corporatisms, from Catholic to fascist corporatism) of the harmonious collaboration of classes. Yet it does certainly lead to the attribution – as in the 'old' patterns of corporatism – of a central role to interactions between state, workers and employers in defining the balance of the entire socio-political and economic system.

This system of interaction between state, workers and employers is not generally observed solely as a means for resolving strictly contractual bargaining issues. On the contrary, it is also perceived as a technique for plotting the conditions of development and evolution for a certain sphere of production at a more global level. In consequence, any tripartite agreement between unions, industrialists and government is viewed, not simply as the signing of a truce, but rather as the identifying of a shared plan of development. At the centre of every neo-corporatistic option lies the decision to give valence to and, to a certain degree, to create areas of convergence or interdependence between interests. On this basis, it is perhaps not mistaken to observe that the wide interest in neo-corporate concerted action forms an important outcome of the Italian constitution. As we have discussed, this is a constitution characterized by a strongly programmatic design, oriented in particular toward entrusting the invention of the means and forms capable of realizing interactions between state, individuals and social formations, to the future. Somewhat speculatively, we might even claim that the idea of concerted action provided motivation for the plan to give trade unions a 'substantially' integrated role in the constitution. That is to say, this was a concept that has made it possible to accord to unions the central role that the Constituent Assembly had imagined for them, yet also to impute this role to them outside the forms provided for by the constitution itself. As is well known, Article 39 of the Italian constitution stipulates that the 'registration of unions in care of local or central [public] offices' constitutes a condition enabling unions to agree to collective contracts with *erga omnes* effect. Similarly, it is known that the requirement of registration has never been satisfied, due largely to the mistrust directed – in the wake of the fascist corporatism – towards the authoritarian appropriation of union life. At the same time, however, the 'decision that unions should have a position fully grounded in general law (whether this concerns the right of the union as an association, or the relations of unions with the State)' (Cazzetta 2007 [1996]: 322) has had the beneficial result that it has led to an affirmation of 'an inter-union order, as a particular, sectional order, distinct from that of the state, but capable of self-regulation' (Cazzetta 2007 [1996]: 322). As such, it has contributed to defining the identity of Italian democracy.

The position of unions under general law, therefore, developed in post-1945 Italy to form a 'model that lay outside the plan of the constitution but that was not against it', and it did not contradict the idea of social autonomy embraced by the constitution (Cazzetta 2007 [1996]: 322). The implications of this reconstruction, accompanied by the idea that collective autonomy could be portrayed as private, civil law autonomy, are quite evident. As soon as it was established that social groups were no longer capable of projecting their interests onto the level of the general order of the state (Cazzetta 2005: 338), it was difficult to prevent the return of legal ideals more or less strategically designed to identify labour law with the law of the individual labour contract (Cazzetta 2005: 338). In other words, labour law became identified with a law, which, even when it did not overtly favour the 'strong' private contracting party, tended to presuppose an elementary, simplified relational context. Such law was incapable of binding (or of binding with sufficient force) the state to the dictates of a constitution which was intended 'to oblige the republic to employ its regulatory resources' in order to elevate the position of the workers and other objects of social democracy (Cazzetta 2005: 339). As this is the case, the interest aroused by corporate concerted action also represented a means for acknowledging non-fulfilment of Article 39 without relegating unions exclusively to the sphere of civil law. In short, concerted action helped to reconcile the formal status of unions under general law with the public law significance of the functions which they performed. In so doing, it enabled unions to assure themselves that the state itself had a character that was not simply reducible to the varying 'contractual' strength of competitors and of lobbies, but was in fact capable of assuming tasks of mediation and, especially, of more complex and demanding planning. In a similar context, the attempt to institutionalize practices of concerted action – an attempt expressed by the so-called Ciampi–Giugni Protocol of 1993 – probably represented the (perhaps most extreme) endeavour to recreate, before the definitive collapse of these policies in 2002, a perception of the future that remained sensitive to the value and importance of collaboration and shared programmes.

The final legacy of corporatistic legal debates is perhaps visible in the fact that the most experienced exponents of legal science devoted to delineating the contours of the so-called social Europe insist today that it is necessary to incorporate social laws in the EU treaties. That is, these theorists argue that it is necessary for the sources of collective autonomy to be taken out of the fragile and mortifying category of *soft law*, and collective contracts need to be imputed binding status under EU law. What is at stake in this is not solely a question of transferring the solutions provided in many constitutions established in the years after World War II to the European level. On the contrary, the debate about European social law constitutes one of the means with which we can endeavour to imagine the concrete shape of a future that aspires to recreate the conditions for a stable (or more stable) relationship between economy and politics, between the market and protections, between private and public, between competition and regulation. The market has shown that it cannot guarantee even the 'stability of its own order' (Sordi 2003: 323). Moreover, we have seen how our capacity to safeguard many first-generation liberties – of which *privacy* might be cited as an example – necessarily depends on a complex system of regulation that, as such, presupposes a future dimension that still needs to be fully realized and to demonstrate its advantages. For these reasons, it is no coincidence that we now insist again on the correlation of social autonomy and rights. It is, in particular, no coincidence that we return to underline the importance of social autonomy and rights for planning an order that is new and is not solely designed to defend the existing order.

6.6 Conclusion

This discussion of corporatism – or corporatisms – provides a way of establishing a profile both of the persistent features and the discontinuities in Italian law and society in the twentieth century. The persistent features are the most obvious. Calls for corporatism have normally been used to address an 'eternal' problem of legal-political reflection (that is, the relation between the state and social forces), and to organize this problem in a context in which it was becoming more and more difficult to imagine society and state, the private and the public, law, economics and politics as autonomous, unconnected entities. From this point of view, corporatism constitutes a doorway that allows us to view the panorama of twentieth-century society and its main characteristics. On one hand, the twentieth century forced people to take account of mass society, or rather organized society, structured by the central role played by social organizations (parties, unions, companies), a role that made it essential to reconsider the limits both of private law and of public law. On the other hand, the state assumed a much more interventionist face in economic matters, and it became necessary to search for a balance between the new role of the state and respect for private property and individual economic initiative. There were many responses to this new panorama, both in terms of institutional organization and theoretical construction. The corporate order – the idea of a corporate restructuration of socio-political dynamics – was above all a key slogan of the fascist regime. In the discussion above, I tried to clarify ways in which the reference to corporatism represents one perspective through which we can bring into focus the total character of the fascist state and its attitudes as a force for socio-political control. However, I also tried to clarify how references to corporatism passed from fascism to the subsequent experience of democracy. In this respect, some discontinuities assumed relevance. The references to corporatism – or, more accurately, the corporate character of socio-economic interests – no longer served, as in the fascist era, to imply a way of organizing social, political and economic relations, which was designed to guarantee the triumph of general interests over particular or partial interests. Rather, the reference to the corporate character of Italian society served essentially to signal the inability of this society to liberate itself from the endemic precedence of the part over the whole, the particular over the general. However, from the 1980s onward, people began to speak of corporatism in a different way – this was primarily due to the reflections of labour lawyers. In particular, this term was used to describe so-called *procedures of reconciliation*: that is, agreements between government and unions that were intended to define present and future relations between them with regard to important productive sectors. In this case, it was hoped that it might be possible to find a point of mediation between opposing demands, and to create a plan to develop industrial and economic relations in a manner that reflected the general interests of the country. This was seen as a way of liberating these interests from the unprecedented primacy of partial interests and distinct sectors, and to bind them – through the presence of the state – to interests that could be classed as general. The era of reconciliation, however, was not long, and it was over by the beginning of the new millennium.

Of the many meanings of the term corporatism, the only one that has remained in current parlance refers to a process, seemingly uncontrollable, in which partial interests prevail over general interests and the interests of particular sectors prevail over interests with general status. From this perspective, we can say that we are still in the middle of the twentieth century, at least as far as the attempt to find instruments and solutions for establishing a balance between market and regulation, between individual autonomy and social autonomy, between old and new forms of political and economic citizenship, is concerned. Moreover, people began to talk of crisis – crises of law, of state, of parties, etc. – at the beginning of the twentieth century, and we still talk of this now. At a fundamental level, the reference to crisis is also just a way of reflecting on the enduring political/regulatory centrality of certain instruments in the attempt to identify new techniques for organizing the relation between individual, society and state.

Bibliography

Barile, Paolo (1951). *La costituzione come norma giuridica*. Firenze: Barbera.

Bottai, Giuseppe (1928). Discussion at the Senate (31 May 1928), in Giuseppe Bottai. *Esperienza corporative*. Roma: edizioni del diritto del lavoro, pp. 27–39.

(1930). 'Stato corporativo e democrazia', *Lo Stato* I: 126–30.
(1949). *Vent'anni e un giorno (24 luglio 1943)*. Cernusco sul Naviglio: Garzanti.
(1952). 'Verso il corporativismo democratico o verso una democrazia corporativa?', *Il diritto del lavoro* XXVI (3–4): 122–41.
Calamandrei, Piero (2004a [1952]). 'Incoscienza costituzionale', in Piero Calamandrei. *Costituzione e leggi di Antigone*. Firenze: Sansoni, pp. 123–34.
(2004b [1955]). 'La costituzione e le leggi per attuarla', in Piero Calamandrei. *Costituzione e leggi di Antigone*. Firenze: Sansoni, pp. 135–225.
Capograssi, Giuseppe (1959 [1922]). 'La nuova democrazia diretta', in Giuseppe Capograssi. *Opere*. Vol. I. Milano: Giuffrè, pp. 406–574.
Carnelutti, Francesco (1949). 'Stato democratico: Stato corporativo', in Alberto Canaletti Gaudenti and Saverio De Simone (eds). *Verso il corporativismo democratico*. Bari: Cacucci editore.
Cazzetta, Giovanni (1999). 'L'autonomia del diritto del lavoro nel dibattito giuridico tra fascismo e repubblica', *Quaderni fiorentini per la storia del pensiero giuridico moderno* 28: 511–629.
(2005). 'Il lavoro nella Costituzione di Costantino Mortati cinquant'anni dopo', in Giovanni Cazzetta. *Scienza giuridica e trasformazioni sociali*. Milano: Giuffrè, pp. 329–40.
(2007 [1996]). 'Il diritto del lavoro e l'insostenibile leggerezza delle origini', in Giovanni Cazzetta. *Scienza giuridica e trasformazioni sociali*. Milano: Giuffrè, pp. 291–328.
Cesarini Sforza, Widar (1929). 'Proprietà ed espropriazione', *Educazione fascista* III: 108–21.
(1942 [1936]). Preliminari sul diritto collettivo, in Widar Cesarini Sforza, *Il corporativismo come esperienza giuridica*, Milano: Giuffrè, pp. 189–207.
Costa, Pietro (1976–77). 'Widar Cesarini Sforza: "illusioni" e "certezze" della giurisprudenza', *Quaderni fiorentini per la storia del pensiero giuridico moderno* 5/6: 1031–95.
(1996). *La 'codificazione fascista', Osservazioni in margine ad un testo di S. Panunzio, Diritto privato* II: 569–90.
De Luca Tamajo, Raffaele (2008). 'Gli anni '70: dai fasti del garantismo al diritto del lavoro dell'emergenza', in Ichino Pietro (ed.). *Storia del diritto del lavoro nell'Italia repubblicana*. Milano: Giuffrè, pp. 79–162.
Fioravanti, Maurizio (1999). 'Costituzione e politica: bilancio di fine secolo', in Maurizio Fioravanti, *La scienza del diritto pubblico – dottrine dello Stato e della costituzione tra Otto e Novecento*. Milano: Giuffrè, II, pp. 871–88.
Gagliardi, Alessio (2010). *Il corporativismo fascista*. Roma-Bari: Laterza.
Gentile, Giovanni (1982 [1927]). 'Fascismo identità di stato e individuo', in Costanzo Casucci (ed.), *Il fascismo – antologia di scritti critici*. Bologna: Il Mulino, pp. 15–50.

Gregorio, Massimiliano (2006). 'Quale costituzione? Le interpretazioni della giuspubblicistica nell'immediato dopoguerra', *Quaderni fiorentini per la storia del pensiero giuridico moderno* 35: 849–913.

Jocteau, Gian Carlo (1978). *La magistratura e i conflitti di lavoro durante il fascismo – 1926/1934*. Milano: Feltrinelli.

Lanzillo, Agostino (1980 [1932]). 'Per una teoria dell'intervento dello Stato', in Francesco Malgeri (ed.). *Giuseppe Bottai e 'Critica fascista'*. Vol. I. S. Giovanni Valdarno: Landi editore, pp. 741–9.

Mannori, Luca and Bernardo Sordi (2001). *Storia del diritto amministrativo*. Roma – Bari: Laterza.

Mortati, Costantino (2000 [1931]). *L'ordinamento del governo nel diritto pubblico italiano*. Milano: Giuffrè (new print of original text).

Ornaghi, Lorenzo (1984). *Stato e corporazione – Storia di una dottrina nella crisi del sistema politico contemporaneo*. Milano: Giuffrè.

Panunzio, Sergio (1938). 'Prime osservazioni giuridiche sul concetto di proprietà nel regime fascista', in Confederazione fascista dei lavoratori dell'agricoltura (ed.). *La concezione fascista della proprietà privata*. Roma, pp. 109–27.

Pugliatti, Salvatore (1950). 'La giurisprudenza come scienza pratica', *Rivista italiana per le scienze giuridiche* IV: 47–71.

Rocco, Alfredo (1921). 'Programma politico nazionale', in Alfredo Rocco. *Scritti e discorsi politici*. Vol. II. Milano: Giuffrè, pp. 646–55.

(1925). 'Legge sulla disciplina giuridica dei rapporti collettivi di lavoro', Discussion at the Parliament (on 10 December 1925), in Alfredo Rocco. *La trasformazione dello Stato – dallo Stato liberale allo Stato fascista*. Roma: La voce anonima editrice, pp. 357–78.

(1926). 'Legge sulla disciplina giuridica dei rapporti collettivi di lavoro', speech pronounced in the Senate on 11 March 1926, in Alfredo Rocco. *La trasformazione dello Stato – dallo Stato liberale allo Stato fascista*. Roma: La voce anonima editrice, pp. 381–99.

(1938a [1914]). 'Economia liberale, economia socialista ed economia nazionale', in Alfredo Rocco. *Scritti e discorsi politici*. Vol. I. Milano: Giuffrè, pp. 30–44.

(1938b [1918]). 'Manifesto di <*Politica*>', in Alfredo Rocco. *Scritti e discorsi politici*. Vol. II. Milano: Giuffrè, pp. 536–42.

Rosanvallon, Pierre (1984). *Lo stato provvidenza tra liberalismo e socialismo*. Roma: Armando editore.

Santomassimo, Gian Pasquale (2006). *La terza via fascista – Il mito del corporativismo*. Roma: Carocci.

Schiera, Pierangelo (2005). 'Corporativismo: concetti storici', in Aldo Mazzacane, Alessandro Somma and Micheil Stolleis (eds). *Korporativismus in den südeuropäischen Diktaturen*. Frankfurt am Main: Vittorio Klostermann, pp. 35–48.

Sordi, Bernardo (2003). 'Ordine e disordine giuridico de mercato (in margine ad alcuni scritti di Tullio Ascarelli)', in *Ordo iuris – storia e forme dell'esperienza giuridica*. Milano: Giuffrè, pp. 319–60.

Stolzi, Irene (2007). *L'ordine corporativo – poteri organizzati e organizzazione del potere nella riflessione giuridica dell'Italia fascista*. Milano: Giuffrè.

Ungari, Paolo (1963). *Alfredo Rocco e l'ideologia giuridica del fascismo*. Brescia: Morcelliana.

Vallauri, Carlo (1971). *Le radici del corporativismo*. Roma: Bulzoni.

Vardaro, Gaetano (1988). 'Introduzione', in Gaetano Vardaro (ed.). *Diritto del lavoro e corporativismi in Europa: ieri e oggi*. Milano: Angeli, pp. 15–34.

Vassalli, Filippo (1960 [1918]). 'Della legislazione di guerra e dei nuovi confini del diritto privato', in Filippo Vassalli. *Studi giuridici*. Vol. II. Milano: Giuffrè, pp. 336–63.

Volpicelli, Arnaldo (1930). 'I fondamenti ideali del corporativismo', *Archivio di studi corporativi* I: 179–211.

(1932). 'Corporativismo e scienza del diritto – risposta al Prof. Cesarini Sforza', *Archivio di studi corporativi* III: 423–51.

7

Nazism and its legal aftermath: coming to terms with the past after World War II

DITLEV TAMM

7.1 Transitional justice

Law came to play a distinct role in the transition towards re-establishing democracy in Europe after the experiences of World War II. Today, we use the term transitional justice to describe this whole complex of statutes and court decisions directed against so-called collaborators, which marked the passage to a new era. However, transitional justice covers a much wider field. It refers to various ways in which justice can be achieved in a time of transition from repression to democracy, or from conflict to harmony. Criminal prosecutions may be an important part of this transition, but the concept of transitional justice includes Truth Commissions, as was the case in South Africa, and different kinds of economic compensation and reparation, or the re-establishing of institutions which have been discredited for their role in former repression. In addition, 'memorialization' – that is, keeping the memory of victims of repression or genocide – is also often mentioned as a means of transitional justice (Posner and Vermeule 2003). At the same time, amnesties or the express prohibition to dig up the past can be seen as belonging to the measures taken when it comes to transitional justice (Hack 2012). After World War II special attention was given in the countries formerly occupied by the Axis powers to the category of the '*collaborateur*', the collaborator, or in Nordic languages the '*landssviger*', or the betrayer of his country; many different national terms might be found referring to persons who during the war had acted in a way now seen as inadequate.[1] The positions of such persons ranked from leading politicians to those who had enlisted in the German army or performed service as guards protecting German property in an occupied country. On these grounds,

[1] The literature on the subject of collaboration and its different meanings is extensive. One of the first to define the issue was Hoffmann (1968).

these people had to be punished. The punishments can be seen simultaneously as an expression of a need for justice, as revenge, and as a necessary procedure in order to overcome the past and either return to democracy or constitute a new society.

The trials defined those citizens who had not sided with the majority of the population. The word collaborator was used to stigmatize a group of citizens and the ritual of the trial became an important part of the formation of post-war society in countries which had been occupied by Germany. During the war, compromises had to be made. In Denmark and in Vichy France official governments collaborated. This fact meant that after the war it could be difficult to identify and punish the collaborator. Some people had identified completely with the enemy; others had used the presence of the occupational forces to further their own totalitarian thinking; some had collaborated in order to avoid worse consequences. Some collaboration was intellectual; most collaboration consisted in some form of manual work, such as active military service, police service or simple labour in some unit attached to the occupational forces. The collaborator had many faces, but it took some time in post-war society before the collaborator could be re-integrated. The idea of the purge was to exclude the collaborator on legal grounds. Loss of civil rights by a collaborator was a common consequence of a judgment. The purge made a clear distinction between those who had been on the right side and those who had been on the wrong side, even if it had not been easy to find the right position during the occupation. This meant that post-war society in former occupied countries was marked by the existence of a group of people who were considered as former collaborators, and were thus located outside the national community of values. As time went on and the occupation receded into history, the reaction against the collaborators became less harsh. Yet, in many countries, collaborators continued to be collaborators, and they encountered great difficulties in finding positions in post-war society; even when they appeared to be re-integrated; having been a 'collaborator' was a fact that was not forgotten. The past and the interest in the past of certain individuals and the claim that justice should be done thus continued to shape the post-war period right up to the twenty-first century. In most countries, the collaborators formed a small group. The existence of a major group possessing shared values and a smaller group that had positioned itself as opponents of those values became an integrated factor in political life after 1945. Each country has its own story of transitional justice and the initiative to take action against collaborators could stem equally from a resistance movement, a new political elite, or foreign powers (Posner and Vermeule 2003). The past was forgotten at different speeds. Some people never forgave the collaborators, and others were selective in their forgiving, but it may be stated that generally the generation that grew up to live the war was marked by the fundamental idea that there was a clear distinction between those who were right and those who had been wrong, even if this scheme only partly covered the complicated web of collaboration and resistance.

7.2 Punishing collaboration in France and in the North

In the following, we will concentrate on transitional justice as it developed in Denmark and Norway, France, Belgium and the Netherlands. To be sure, the occupying powers themselves also had to undergo a purge, such as de-Nazification (*Entnazifizierung*) in Germany, or a rejection of fascism in Italy. However, what happened in the Western European countries considered here after the war may be seen as a closed experience in itself, which distinctively exemplifies how the law and trials became an integrated part of the transition. In this respect, it is significant to observe that, because many countries, not only in Europe but also – for example – South Africa and other areas, have experienced fundamental changes of government, the Western European experience can be seen today as just one of several ways in which such transition can take place. South Africa opted for the establishment of Truth Commissions instead of trials. In other places, transition has taken place without any reference to the law or by using the law to prevent investigation of the past. This has occurred in countries where a general amnesty or a prohibition on investigating the past has been issued. In this way, what happened after World War II in Western Europe can be seen today as just one within a spectrum of possibilities when it comes to the question of how to deal with the past. Western countries are countries with a long legal tradition and a long tradition of solving conflicts in courts. For a Western mind, it is natural to translate human behaviour into categories that can be penalized. The Third Reich was seen as an '*Unrechtsstaat*', a nation based on the opposite of the rule of law. It was, therefore, only too evident that acting in absence of law should be punished by the law in order to show how Western culture was based on the idea of law and justice. New crimes had to be invented in order to grasp what had happened. The category of crimes against humanity is an example that set a standard for the future development of Europe. The idea of what was acceptable in the state of war was changed, as was the idea that a country can do as it likes with its citizens or that a country can attack another at its own liking. New law was made and principles of prohibiting retroactive force had to give way to a new conception of justice that would not let atrocious crimes, which were not defined as such in law books, be unpunished on formal reasons. Courts saw themselves confronted with 'crimes' not known before. Doing justice under these circumstances was not always easy. Nonetheless, the coming to terms with the past had formative significance in post-war Europe. It is difficult to imagine European collaboration on the scale that has taken place since the 1950s without a Europe that had especially distanced itself from 'Nazism' as a negative concept covering totalitarianism, militarism and aggressive actions towards neighbours, racism and intolerance. The word 'purge' as a general denomination of the trials or other forms of exclusion of former 'Nazis' opened the door for democracy not only as the political foundation of the single European states that wanted to be accepted members of the European family but also as the pattern of political thinking that should be the foundation for European co-operation. Democracy became the ideal, and the opposite of the 'Nazism' that had led to destruction. As already said, there is no general formula for transitional justice. In a country such as Denmark it was probably the case that people expected more in terms of changes to the old system than actually occurred. However, it is also evident, especially when we consider the purge of the administrative system, that 'democratization' was a governing principle even if the country quickly returned to being a well-functioning democracy. To some degree, the real impact of the trials and the purge was seen only in the next generation, whose members had not lived through the experience of the German occupation, who had no living memory of Nazism, and who were brought up with the idea of democracy as the only acceptable political system, without any real alternative. In countries such as the Nordic countries, which historically had strong links to Germany and German culture, this also brought about a turn towards the Anglo-American world which was – rightly – seen as the guardian of democratic principles, whereas, in particular in Norway and Denmark, German occupation had left bad memories and complicated the re-establishment of political and cultural links with the new Federal Republic of Germany.

The trials of collaborators created a feeling of national coherence that may be considered in many cases exaggerated. The French myth of the Vichy government as the shield and the resistance movement as the sword (*'l'épée et le bouclier'*) was soon dismantled. But in Denmark, a similar idea of official policies as a shield for resistance persisted for a long time. Today in Denmark, for example, there is an awareness of how diverse the opinions and ideas of the future actually were that – either passively or actively – were united under a common 'resistance', and the myth of national unity which also lay behind the trials has been partly punctured. What probably requires greatest emphasis is the extent to which the national trials combined with the Nuremberg process against leading German war criminals led to a new understanding of the importance of courts as an expression of a European way of settling disputes and reaching reconciliation, based on the idea that nobody shall be punished without a right to defence. However, the idea of the significance of courts goes further, and it also became instrumental in the formation of the European Coal and Steel Community and of its successor, the European Union. Without Nuremberg, there would have been no Eichmann trial in Israel and perhaps no such profound writing on the importance of understanding and fighting against Nazism as a fundamental human condition as was the case with Hannah Arendt's foundational books on totalitarianism and the Eichmann case. From there, a line can be drawn to the International Criminal Court. Even in a time that oscillates between punishment and forgiveness, since World War II courts, to a still increasing degree, have been seen in Europe as the fundamental place to decide what is right and what is wrong.

Denmark and Norway are chosen as the main cases to present here as examples of ways in which the law had its part in the formation of a modern post-war Europe, but we will also digress to discuss France, Belgium and Holland in our endeavour to map the interesting confrontation of law and history that took place in the years following World War II. A general feature is that, as always in courts, the past had to be judged. However, the same human action that had been perpetrated during the war was judged under different circumstances after the war. Actions perpetrated at a point in time when the outcome of the war was unknown were not always appreciated in their full context. Another significant question that presents itself, when we consider the way in which transitional justice was carried out in the years immediately after 1945, has to do with the relation between what we can call legal truth and historical truth.[2] This issue becomes especially relevant when we compare the trials that took place immediately after 1944–1945 with

[2] On this interesting question, which can only be mentioned in passing here, see for example the essays in Wijffels (2001) and in Frei, van Laak and Stolleis (2000) and Jones, Östberg and Randeraad (2007).

those belated purges that took place in France in the 1980s and 1990s against German and French war criminals or former Vichy administrators accused of crimes against humanity. The scope changed from judging individuals for individual crimes into a general review of the past in a new light. Judges consider the facts brought before them in their relation to the law. A collaborator, in consequence, is a person who has committed the acts described in the law. The political context or the general understanding of the conditions that led to collaboration will in principle not be taken into consideration by a judge, unless this is expressly required by the law. Therefore, the way in which the historians, based on a 'thick' description of a case, will understand an individual case and the way the judge will judge according to legal facts may differ. Historians were not asked for their opinion as to the course of history when it came to the trials in the years immediately following the war. Collaboration was a crime to be judged according to statutes; it was not a part of a general history, which could be explained in historical terms. Later, however, and perhaps most distinctly in later French trials against German war criminals or French collaborators who had previously lived in impunity, historians were employed as expert witnesses in court, and their assessment of the past became evidence in such trials. Moreover, post-war history now came to play an important role. For instance, the French actions in Algeria were used as an example of how atrocities were not only found on the German side, and they were aptly used by the defence in such cases as a way of changing the perspective in which criminal acts committed during World War II should be judged. Most notable in this regard was the case of the 'Butcher of Lyon'. The trial of the German Gestapo officer Klaus Barbie, who was known for his part in the deportation of Jews and his cruelty when interrogating French resistance members, and who had been allowed to flee to South America, became a showcase for a new aggressive way of defending war criminals. Barbie was put on trial in 1987 in France after having been extradited from Bolivia. Barbie's advocate, Jacques Verger, made the headlines in the press by his comparisons between Barbie's acts and actions by French colonists during the Algerian war. Barbie himself even proclaimed his innocence.[3] What happened in courts long after the war thus really was a challenge to what Hannah Arendt in 1946 had written to Karl

[3] See on this case the inspiring essay by Finkelkraut (1992).

Jaspers: 'The Nazi crimes, it seems to me, explode the limits of the law; and that is precisely what constitute their monstrosity' (Arendt and Jasper 1992: 54).

A further example is the French case of Maurice Papon, who was tried as late as 1997 for his complicity, when acting as General Secretary of the Prefecture of the Gironde region, in crimes against humanity. This was due to his part in the organization of the deportation of French Jews during the Vichy regime.[4] The case raised questions both about the general responsibility of the Vichy regime for the fate of French Jews and concerning Papon's personal involvement. At a time when the outcome of the war was foreseeable, Papon had, to some degree, helped the resistance movement, and he had not only achieved high positions in post-war France but also avoided any kind of indictment during the purge after 1944. Papon was sentenced to ten years' imprisonment for his complicity in the deportations of 1,560 Jews, but he was not sentenced for complicity in murder. Papon was released after three years of prison, for health reasons. The indemnities that he was obliged to pay to the victims' families were partly covered by the French government, following a decision by the *Conseil d'Etat*, which ruled that his responsibility had been partly professional and partly personal. Parts of the procedure were challenged at the European Court of Human Rights, which in a ruling in 2002 considered some of the proceedings an infringement of the European Convention on Human Rights (Art. 6).

In the Papon case, historians were used as expert witnesses. Historians had previously participated in prominent cases, such as the Dreyfus case, the Auschwitz Trial and the Eichmann Trial, but the presence of historians in the Papon case gave rise to a specific debate as to the role of the historian in such cases. This was especially important, as a leading historian of Vichy France, Henry Rousso, refused to appear as a witness in a trial, as he considered the objectives of a court trial incompatible with his intellectual freedom when it came to the understanding of history (Rousso 2002: 4). The discussion gave rise to a clarification of the roles of the judge as the decision maker and the historian as the scientist who helps us to understand the past. Rousso maintained this position, whereas other historians saw it as a professional duty to share their view of the past with the public, not only in their writing but also assisting courts. This question of how historians should react to invitations

[4] See discussion of this trial in Golsan (2000).

to appear in court will not be followed up here (see Petrovics 2009). However, it is noteworthy that such forensic historiography was not used in the trials immediately following World War II. In later assessments of the purge conducted in these years, however, history and discussions regarding ways in which an alternative account of history might have influenced the cases have played an important role. This will be examined in the following.

7.3 Justice on trial?

The author of these lines has himself in some way experienced the change of focus in debate about transitional justice. A rather comprehensive study published in 1984 of how what was then talked of as the 'purge', or in Danish something corresponding to a 'legal reckoning' with Danish collaborators after World War II, is today a forerunner in what can be seen as an ongoing process of discussing the role of courts, of justice, punishment, forgiving and coming to terms with the past. The same applies to other publications on purges in France, Belgium and the Netherlands published at that time. What we then saw as a study of specific actions in a closed period of time proved to be a study of just one small piece of an issue that had parallels all over Europe, and a first step in a more complex compound of historical facts, which we now see as a transition to, and as part of, the formation of modern Europe. In 1984, we were still in many ways inclined to see this whole complex of action against collaborators in a broad sense as part of the history of World War II. Or – expressed in different words – we looked back and not forward. One of the questions raised at that time had to do with the relative 'justice' of court trials that were conducted at a time when the general view of what had happened – the context – had changed. Could the courts in a climate of exhilaration caused by 'victory' and recriminations against collaborators judge the past in an unbiased manner? The question was whether, and in what way, the context of the war and the conditions during the occupation in the period 1940–1945 could and should be taken into account. As already mentioned, the trials after World War II were part of the creation of a new pattern of legal thinking that led to the formation of a new legal foundation for Europe. New crimes and the new and more important position of the court as the place to judge the past were evident results of this new thinking. The concept of transitional justice, which did not exist at the time of the post-war trials, has placed these trials in a new perspective. We know much more about the war today and scholarly investigation has added immensely to our understanding of what actually happened at a time which could only partly be understood by those who were living through it. Our idea of the history of these years has changed from the years immediately after the war and until today, and a judge who today should hear a case related to war-time will necessarily have another perspective than the judges of the post-war years. We tend to see what happened just after World War II in a new light when we look back today. Those questions about legitimacy that were discussed at that time are not necessarily relevant today. The Nuremberg procedure or the Eichmann trial in Israel may not be seen today, as was actually the case, as questionable examples of the 'victor's justice'. Instead, they can be viewed as necessary steps towards creating a new world order, in which certain atrocities would not be forgotten but brought to justice on an international scale. Most particularly, in the time after the collapse of Communist regimes in 1989 contemporary historical narratives have been reshaped, public memory has been recovered, official attitudes towards the past have been changed and the past, like other sectors of human life, has been 'judicialized'.

Seen in a general perspective, the Nuremberg trial and the many trials of war criminals in other courts inspired by or dependent on the Nuremberg military court stand as landmarks in the formation of a new vision of the law which defines law as a means to construct a world devoid of crimes such as genocide or attacks on other states. The example of Nuremberg was especially important as regards war criminals but it may serve also as an illustration of the will and necessity in countries occupied by the Axis powers to deal with the past in the form of trials against those who had been on the wrong side. What we are talking about is thus a more general phenomenon which became much more dominant after World War II than it had been earlier. After World War I, trials had also been conducted against war criminals, and Germany had been supposed to carry out such trials. On the whole, however, this attempt to make certain persons accountable for having acted against the rules of war proved unsuccessful. The trials were few, and sentences were lenient. The idea that a country could try its own nationals for war crimes was discredited by this process. In a new Europe, to be created after World War II, which dreamed of a future without internal wars and based on a common will to prosper in consonance and not dissonance, the law and the effective enforcement of the law as a deterrent for future attempts to act as the Axis powers had done assumed symbolic importance, and underlined the refusal to tolerate inhuman ways of treating either soldiers or civilians. In this way, the law looked back and looked forward at the same time. Punishing the past was a necessary step in the making of a new Europe.

7.4 Case studies: Denmark and Norway

Denmark and Norway will be my main examples of how transitional justice was carried through after World War II. I will note differences between these countries and the situation in Belgium, the Netherlands and France. Basically, however, we can see the 'purge' in these countries as a common phenomenon, albeit one showing local variations.

'The purpose of the trial is to render Justice, and nothing else…' Hannah Arendt said in a famous quote in her book on the Eichmann trial (Arendt 1963: 254). The courts are not there to decide questions about history. Often history has to be modelled in a certain shape in order for the lawyers to make their decision. History can take the form of excuses. An important excuse in Danish cases after World War II was that the defendant conceived the situation in a way different from the now accepted description in the law. Danish nationals who had volunteered as soldiers in the German army thus put forward as an excuse that they had believed that the Danish government had shown tolerance for military enlisting. To compete with the language of the law, however, it was necessary to construct this belief to the effect that enlisting soldiers had been following a 'guideline' set out by the government; the courts were not inclined to go that far, even if this belief had some foundation in fact.[5] The 'excuse' is an important figure in the understanding of the relation between law and history. When excuses regarding how the situation actually was or was conceived are not heard history is left out. The judges do not judge 'the past'. Rather, they judge individuals according to the law.

In the following, we will analyse the way in which transitional justice, at a moment when this concept was still unknown, took place in the Nordic countries, especially the Kingdoms of Denmark and Norway in the years that followed World War II. German occupation and even Nazism took different shapes in the Nordic countries during World War II. Denmark and Norway were both occupied by Germany, however, in different ways. Sweden was neutral but had to give concessions to the

[5] See, for discussion in English, Tamm (2011).

Germans as regards passage of troops through Sweden, whereas Finland was at war with Russia and at certain times allied with Germany.

To illustrate the legal complexity of the Danish situation during the German occupation the following incident told by Alf Ross, a well-known Danish jurist and expert on international law and jurisprudence, may be illustrative.[6] The incident happened shortly after 29 August 1943. This date was decisive in the history of the occupation. Up to that date, the Danish government had still functioned. However, confronted with a number of German demands, including, for example, the demand that the death penalty should be introduced for members of the Danish resistance judged by Danish courts, the government chose to demit office, and no new government was nominated. Shortly after the dismissal of the government, the Germans rounded up Danish officers and others. Alf Ross tells how he received a telephone call at home from a Danish officer who had been arrested by German troops as part of this round-up. The Danish officer, as well as the German commander, did not know how to define the case in terms of international law. Was Denmark actually at war with Germany? Was the Danish officer to be treated as a prisoner of war? The two officers involved agreed to make a telephone call to the Danish expert in international law. He replied that neither of the two countries had expressed intentions to engage in deliberate warfare. Consequently, a status of war had not been established and one might, at most, refer to the situation as one involving a 'risk of war'. However, one may also say that Denmark had merely reverted to a policy of strict neutrality. It is implicit in this story that Danish courts also functioned and, as part of their work, were required to punish members of the Danish resistance according to legislation made by the Danish Parliament in an attempt to preserve Danish jurisdiction over Danish citizens avoiding German war tribunals. This meant that Danish courts, including the Supreme Court, acted against the resistance as part of official Danish policies. The Norwegian Supreme Court already in 1940 had resigned, unwilling to be a tool in a system of Nazi government headed by Vidkun Quisling.

These differences in the situation with which the different Nordic countries were confronted cannot be fully explained here. They must, however, be taken into account in order to understand differences in

[6] Alf Ross was a professor of law at the University of Copenhagen, until 1969. Among his major works is Ross (1959), which has been translated into several languages.

transitional justice in the Nordic countries and they are also reflected in differences as regards what happened after 1945.

The Danish case is complicated. After the German occupation of Denmark from 1940 to 1945, historians have been confronted with a series of difficult questions, which were all linked to the fact that, apart from a few hours on 9 April 1940, there had not been any visible warfare between Denmark and Germany: What had been the general attitude towards collaboration during the occupation? Was the punishment meted out reasonably proportionate to the acts of collaboration? To what degree should the fact that the Danish government had not confronted the Germans directly but had followed a so-called policy of negotiation until 1943 affect the legal outcome of the purges? What was the legal basis for prosecuting the collaborators? In whose interests did the proceedings take place? Who exerted most influence on the form and content of the trials?

Different kinds of collaboration are found (see Rings 1979), and it is too simplistic to consider collaboration merely as being supportive of Nazism, as was often the case immediately after World War II. Even if we see World War II as a deeply ideological war and an all-out struggle against National Socialism, its philosophy and its methods, there remain different shades of guilt. At the top of the scale we find the type of collaboration which involves a direct identification with the interests of the occupying power. Leading Danish Nazis, those who became members of the German police force and Nazi terror organizations like the SS or other types of 'armed collaboration', fall into this group (Tamm 1984). At a different level, a 'conditional' collaboration occurs when persons do not necessarily identify themselves with the ultimate aims of the enemy but exploit the presence of the occupiers for their own political purposes, as was the case with certain anti-parliamentary groups, who, disgusted by the impotence of parliamentary government, took advantage of the enemy with the purpose of achieving changes in government by undemocratic means.

What we can call a 'neutral' collaboration, consisted of adapting oneself to the situation, accepting the presence of the enemy in the country, and acting according to this fact. This was what happened in Denmark, and it was reflected politically in what we have coined 'the policy of negotiation', which in the years 1940–1943 was carried out by the government and especially the leading politician, Erik Scavenius.[7] According to this policy,

[7] For an account of his views, see the defence in the biographical book Scavenius (1948).

if saboteurs were to be punished, it was better for them to be punished by Danish courts than by enemy martial courts. If military airports had to be built, it was better that it be done by Danish labour than by imported foreign labour. Given the need of the country to be governed, it was seen as preferable that it be done by the country's own government, even if this made concessions necessary. On 4 July 1940, Stauning, the then Prime Minister, speaking in Parliament on German–Danish relations, stated that the issue was to ensure implementation of co-operation with the Germans within the limits imposed by international law. There are no strict boundaries between this kind of neutral collaboration and a fourth category: that is, collaboration or co-operation as a *tactical weapon*. In this policy, an appearance of co-operation can be given, but the real purpose of apparent collaboration is to provide cover for resistance. The major difference between Vichy and Denmark during the war can be perceived if we observe the collaboration of the Vichy government as gradually taking the form of identification with the German cause, whereas in Denmark official collaboration remained neutral.

Needless to say, there was a close interrelation between the Danish trials of collaborators after the occupation and the history of the period. As a result, a vital question is precisely whether the trial of collaborators can be seen as a corollary of the policy pursued during the occupation, or whether the purges can be seen as a break with these policies, which can actually be viewed as a consequence of Danish foreign policy in the 1930s. Denmark wanted to preserve complete neutrality, hoping in this way to avoid the occupation, which ultimately took place on 9 April 1940. Against the most powerful European military power, there was not much the authorities could do in the situation except to accept occupation as an established fact. Actual warfare took place only in the border area, Copenhagen was taken by a surprise attack, and after a few hours all warfare ceased. The German government presented the Danish government with a memorandum in which it was guaranteed that Germany would not take steps aiming at an infringement on the territorial integrity or political independence of the Kingdom of Denmark. The German 'Memorandum', and the fact that it was accepted by Denmark, gave the German occupation of Denmark its own legal character. Germany guaranteed that German military authorities would not undermine the jurisdiction of the Danish police force.[8] The Danish government, the

[8] A broad presentation of the general history of Danish policy during the Occupation is found in Nissen (1973).

Parliament, the public administration and the courts continued to function. Diplomatic relations between Denmark and Germany were maintained between the foreign ministries of each country. Contact between Denmark and Germany was maintained at the level of the Ministries of Foreign Affairs, and, in contrast to the situation in Norway, where there had been active resistance to the occupation, no military administration or *Reichskommissar* was appointed (see Nissen 1973; Thomsen 1971; Rosengren 1982).

The construction of such an *occupatio sui generis* raised the problem whether Denmark actually was at war with Germany. This became crucial for discussion concerning the legitimacy of the trials after the war. If Denmark had not been at war with Germany after 9 April 1940, collaboration that did not involve crimes according to ordinary penal law would only be punishable if new laws were given retroactive force.[9] During the period from 9 April 1940 until the end of August 1943, which was known as the period of 'co-operation' or 'negotiation', the Danish government still held state authority, and one of its goals was to preserve as much as possible of the Danish jurisdiction over Danish citizens, even at the cost of making certain concessions to the occupying power. This policy of compromise gradually led to a series of dilemmas. As an effect of Operation Barbarossa, the German invasion of Soviet Russia on 22 June 1941, German authorities demanded the internment of leading Danish Communists. This task was to be carried out by ordinary Danish police. At the end of August 1941, approximately 120 Communists had been detained, and a specific act had been issued by the Parliament prohibiting Communist activities and authorizing the arrest of leading Communists. The Danish press, under censorship, endorsed this move. The Communists, joined by broad segments outside the party, regarded this act to be unconstitutional, but it was upheld by the Supreme Court on the grounds of national emergency. However, these arrests were heatedly debated after the liberation, when the Soviet Union and Communist participation in the resistance movement was – correctly – seen as determinant factors in the struggle against fascism.

[9] See on this question Tamm (1984: esp. 737). Under the Danish Penal Code it was a condition for declaring collaboration with the enemy liable for punishment that the actions punishable took place during war or at a time of imminent risk of war. If one wanted *not to* define the situation as war and had doubts about the concept 'risk of war', it would be necessary to adopt new legislation with retroactive force. The provisions of the Danish Penal Code on treason presupposed a situation of *de facto* war, or a chance of outbreak of war, not only the 'risk of war'.

Another consequence of the German attack on the Soviet Union was the establishment of a Danish military unit, the so-called *Freikorps Dänemark*, which was organized as a Danish unit under Danish command within the German Waffen SS. The *Freikorps* was not established as an official Danish initiative, but, notably, the Danish government did not oppose open recruitment to the *Freikorps*, and gave leave for two Danish officers to take charge of it. Moreover, in a letter issued by the Ministry of Defence in June 1941, the Danish government allowed Danish officers to join German forces on the Eastern front.[10] A communication issued by the Ministry of Defence in June 1941 explicitly stressed that Danish officers who volunteered would maintain their position and rank in the official Danish Army. This promise was not kept after the occupation. After the war, the ambiguous official Danish attitude towards recruitment of Danes as German soldiers was a matter for particular discussion, but the courts did not accept this ambiguity as an excuse.

In July 1940, Erik Scavenius (1877–1962) was appointed Minister of Foreign Affairs as part of the government changes. From November 1942, he was Prime Minister. During the occupation and afterwards, Erik Scavenius was seen as the personification of a policy of no resistance and neutrality, the reasons for which were forgotten after the war. After the war, Scavenius himself did not hesitate in acknowledging and defending his responsibility for this policy, which he saw as the only possible solution to save the country. He believed in his policy as the only realistic way to deal with the Germans, and he consequently pursued this until the government was dissolved in August 1943. His position during the occupation is still debated. However, it is recognized today that his politics in general were realistic and to the benefit of the country. In November 1942, the German Ambassador to Denmark was replaced by a so-called German *Reichsbevollmächtigter* (German Imperial plenipotentiary), Dr Werner Best,[11] whose main endeavour was to continue the 'policy of negotiation'. This policy was seen as advantageous to both sides; for the Germans it brought the benefit that it minimized the need for an extensive German civil administration and additional military presence in the country.

[10] I have discussed this in more detail in Tamm (1984).

[11] See in general the biography by Herbert (1996). In Rosengren (1982), the policy of Dr Werner Best is dealt with at length. Best wrote an apologetic description of his policy in Matlok (1988).

In contrast to Norway, normal Danish authorities remained in charge of the country's public administration. There did exist a party of National Socialists in Denmark, the DNSAP (*Danmarks National-Socialistiske Arbejderparti*), headed by Fritz Clausen, a medical doctor. However, in parliamentary elections, the party never obtained more than 2 per cent of the total vote. From the German side, thus, there was no real interest in substituting the legal government by one composed by the DNSAP. Only for a short period during the autumn of 1940 was there a chance that the DNSAP might be able to form a government. However, this possibility was discarded. It was in fact the case that the Danish Nazis and their political ambitions were let down by the German occupiers (see Poulson 1970).

Several smaller Nazi parties were formed in Denmark in the 1930s. Only the DNSAP was represented in the *Folketing* (Parliament). At its peak, the party numbered around 39,000 members. The party had not been politically disloyal, and it did not act as a fifth column helping the German occupation, even if single members of the party did help or later enlisted as soldiers in the German army, or, as was more usual, the Waffen SS. Even the leading Danish Nazis were taken by surprise by the German occupation, but they soon launched a collaboration policy, in which they tried to use the German occupation as a means to gain power.[12] The party itself at the outset was not tainted with collaboration. Even some Danish officers joined the Nazi party after 9 April 1940, frustrated by the official Danish defence policy, which they considered responsible for the German occupation. These officers believed at that time in the strong nationalist appeal of the Danish Nazis. Most of them soon left the party when the DNSAP turned towards the Germans.

The role of the Nazi party constitutes a major difference between Denmark and Norway. In Norway, the party acquired a political role, and its members were collectively punished after the war. Nobody was punished in Denmark after the war on the sole grounds that they had been a member of the DNSAP. Some fifty party leaders received sentences from one to fifteen years of imprisonment for their responsibility for the collaborationist policy of the party – even if this policy was not successful. Ordinary DNSAP members were only prosecuted for other acts of collaboration, for example voluntary service in the German army, denunciation or direct economic collaboration. Out of about 39,000 Danish Nazis about 10 per cent were prosecuted.

[12] Djursaa (1981) has given a very broad presentation of the Danish Nazi party in her two-volume publication.

Of 13,500 collaborators sentenced, thus about 4,000 or some 30 per cent were members of the DNSAP.

A characteristic of the Danish occupation was that the public sector was not restructured due to German demands. No single civil servant was appointed or discharged on German orders. Denmark's civil service was left untouched (see Tamm 1984). Even members of the DNSAP in public service did not profit from their party membership through preferential treatment. However, after the liberation civil servants who had been members of the DNSAP were purged on the grounds of their membership alone. Their oath to the *Führer* of the DNSAP was considered incompatible with their obligation towards the Danish Constitution.

On 29 August 1943, the Danish government ceased to function. Germany had demanded that judicial steps be taken against an increase in the acts of sabotage against German military forces. The introduction of capital punishment was demanded, a demand to which the Danish government refused to submit. From August 1943 until the end of the war, governmental authority in Denmark was exercised by a non-political body consisting of undersecretaries of the state. An official Danish government did not come into being, and it was now evident that the relation to Germany had entered into a different phase.[13] At the same time, the resistance movement organized itself by establishing a national council, which publicly proclaimed its existence and published an outline programme for what was to happen when Denmark could once again be considered free. A draft bill sketching the procedure and the penal law necessary for punishing collaborators was set up by lawyers attached to the resistance movement in the autumn of 1944 and was finished just before liberation in May 1945. This draft was based on the principle that any penal action should be in conformity with traditional Danish ideas of justice and be implemented respecting the 'rule of law'. Originally capital punishment was not foreseen, but in the light of German actions in the later part of the occupation the attitude on this point changed (Tamm 1984: 675). The principle that no one should be punished merely for political reasons was also stated at an early date. The final draft for legislation on collaboration was a compromise between the resistance movement and the politicians, who agreed on the text of an act to be submitted for adoption by the Danish Parliament

[13] The main work on this is Hæstrup (1966–71).

in May 1945. The final act introduced the death penalty for certain acts of collaboration, and it had retroactive force back to 9 April 1940 (Tamm 1984: 115).

This result was determined by the actual political conditions. The resistance movement was popular, and the official Danish policy during the occupation, which aimed at saving the country from damage through 'negotiations' with the occupying powers, was practically forgotten. For the sake of the continuity of the system the politicians gave in and accepted legislation with retroactive force that was not in accordance with this official policy. Thus the starting day for collaboration was fixed at 9 April 1940, at a time when the government was functioning, and not, as the politicians wanted, at 23 August, when no government was active. This meant that in principle the politics of the government or persons who had acted within what they saw as government politics could also be judged. The position of the politicians was pragmatic and was explained as an act necessary for democracy to be reinstated. Democracy was rescued; the politicians themselves, however, were not taken to task. Members of the government during the occupation were not put to justice for their politics. A Commission appointed by the Parliament, and whose membership included politicians, was set up to investigate whether there was any reason to bring any former cabinet member before the special court, which, according to the Danish Constitution, is the designated forum for cases against cabinet ministers for their official acts. This Commission only ended its work in 1951 and no cabinet member was put on trial. The difference in the treatment of ordinary collaboration and the non-liability of the politicians was a point highly criticized by those contemporaries who took part in the debate as to how 'justice' was made during the purge. While the French resistance movement refused to recognize the legality of the Vichy government, the situation was different in Denmark.[14] The Danish resistance movement wanted the official policies of the governments during the time of occupation to be regarded as a mere political liability. It was therefore for the voters to decide whether they wanted to retain the politicians who had been involved in a policy of co-operation with the Germans during the occupation. During the occupation, Danish courts and Danish police had played a major role in implementing official policy. An extensive series of acts were adopted involving severe reactions against anyone harming the occupying power,

[14] A comprehensive discussion of the French case is given by Rousso (1990). A condensed version is found in Henke and Woller (1991).

particularly acts of espionage, sabotage and 'undermining morale' (*Zersetzung*). Such actions were severely punished by official Danish courts. This legislation was meant as a means to keep Danish jurisdiction vis-à-vis Danish citizens. The role of the judges during the war led the resistance movement to object to the ordinary courts being entrusted with the task of carrying through the purge after the war. Instead of this, the resistance movement wanted to create specific courts, in deciding the composition of which the movement should have an influence. The politicians, however, succeeded in upholding the authority of the ordinary judiciary, despite the grievances from the freedom fighters. As a result, the ordinary Danish courts, which had carried out their duties under the policy of negotiation during the occupation, were subsequently to sentence collaborators, who might have acted corresponding to government admonitions during the time of occupation. The continuity of Danish state authority was maintained, but obviously the task meant that the courts were confronted with a moral dilemma. Persons who had informed the Danish police of illegal activity could refer to the fact that Prime Minister Buhl in 1942 had encouraged them to do so. From the records of the considerations in the courts, it appears that the judges were not at ease in convicting people who voluntarily had given information according to laws which now were regarded as illegal, but not at the time when the act had taken place (Tamm 1984: 283).

In the end approximately 13,500 people were sentenced to jail during the judicial purge, out of a population of about four and a half million. Some 3,500 received sentences of imprisonment for more than four years, while the remaining 10,000 were imprisoned for less than four years. Seventy-eight received capital punishment, and out of the seventy-eight sentences, forty-six were actually executed for homicide, torture or denouncing activities of the resistance movement. About 7,500 persons were sentenced for joining the German forces and some 2,000 persons for having served with German security forces, the SS, or some other branch of the German police. Another 1,100 persons were sentenced for some kind of economic collaboration.

A special act was issued against such public servants who had been members of a Nazi party or in some way or other had demonstrated what was denominated 'national indignity', corresponding to the French concept of '*indignité nationale*'. Such public servants were to be dismissed or subject to other disciplinary forms of punishment. A special disciplinary court was set up to treat such cases. Some six hundred public servants were dismissed, and even fewer were subject to other sanctions.

Most of the public servants dismissed had held positions in public services, such as state railways, the postal service or the police. About half of the dismissals were in cases of Nazi membership. The other half were dismissed in cases of national indignity. Generally, however, Danish administration had been kept free of infiltration by the Nazis. The public servants dismissed as members of a Nazi party had not profited from their membership in their jobs. The general principle of the purge was the 'democratization' of public service. However, the number of people purged was so small and the reason for the sanctions often so unimportant that the purge cannot be considered to have been of importance in this respect.[15] Many private organizations had their own committees, who worked on similar lines to the disciplinary courts for the civil service. The results of these purges often seemed disappointing to a public that expected a much more profound purge, based on exaggerated ideas of real Nazi involvement.

As mentioned, the resistance movement in its draft for the post-war purges had not aimed at punishing the politicians responsible for the official policies. Instead, a so-called parliamentary commission was established to investigate whether there was any reason to take criminal action. Only in 1955, ten years after the end of the occupation, did the Danish Parliament, after much debate, reach the conclusion that no politician was to be held liable (Tamm 1984: 283).

The border set up between Denmark and Germany in 1920 had the consequence that a German minority within Denmark faced a special problem of loyalty after the occupation in 1940, as the leaders of the German minority typically took the German side and actively supported German warfare, hoping thus for a revision of the border. The minority hoped for a reunification with Germany. Many volunteered for active military service – often under pressure from the leadership – and many served in special units set up to fight in case of an Allied invasion.[16]

[15] There were very few examples of grave forms of collaboration. As a result, many small fish were caught, and during the difficult process of defining 'un-nationality' one sometimes got the feeling that some outsiders in an office could easily come before the court because of hatred among their colleagues, rather than for explicit collaboration (Tamm 1984: 535–45).

[16] The leaders of the German minority organized a *Zeitfriwilligendienst* (voluntary service) amounting to 1,700 members, which should be used as guards on the occasion of an invasion. They also organized a *Selbstschutz* (self-defence) with 500 members, which was primarily aimed at protecting vital factories against sabotage. Both groups wore uniforms and were trained with weapons. In the courts membership of such groups was regarded as

German policy during the war, however, did not support the minority. The leaders of the German minority saw themselves in a difficult position, as they tried in vain to influence the German leaders to change policy and try to win support for their position. After the war, the minority leaders were subject to heavy punishment.

In the end, roughly 3,000 persons or about 25 per cent of the male adult population of the German minority were punished for some act of collaboration.[17] The sentences of imprisonment were generally shorter than sentences for the same type of offences committed by ordinary Danish citizens.[18] Generally the problem of the German minority had to be seen as a question of cohabitation after the war. The resistance movement had even gone as far as to demand the expulsion of the German minority members when found guilty of collaboration. In the end, however, a compromise was launched which included criminal punishments on a less harsh level. Even today complaints are still heard that members of the German minority were too harshly treated.

The purge in Denmark can be divided into two phases. There was a first phase, in which rather harsh sentences were carried out, and there was a second phase, in which some of the consequences of the more severe judgments were mitigated. Even if the law had prescribed four years of prison as minimum, the average term was less than two years of imprisonment. Only some 3,000 of those convicted were sentenced to four years of imprisonment or more. As early as 1948, the authorities started reducing sentences and a practice evolved of reducing the sentences to half the time. Those who had been sentenced to longer prison terms even had their punishments further reduced. From 1947,

collaboration, even if it was held that the German minority in this way tried to avoid voluntary recruitment to the Waffen SS of young male Germans, which meant they would have been sent to the Eastern Front.

[17] In total, 2,958 of the German minority were punished by Danish courts. Among them 2,150 were punished for volunteering for some form of German military service: 1,121 as *Zeitfreiwillige*, 901 for service in the Waffen SS or the Wehrmacht and 128 as members of *Selbstschutz*. Fifty-two people were punished for German police service, and thirty-one for various kinds of *informing*/denunciation (Tamm 1984: 408–31).

[18] The most serious sentence was given to the leader of the German minority, Jens Møller, and his second-in-command, Peter Larsen. Both were given sentences of fifteen years in prison, which were later reduced to twelve years. The leader of the *Selbstschutz*, O.F. Korset, and the Kreitsleiter in Haderslev, D. Clausen, both received custodial sentences of twelve years, which were later reduced to nine years. The other eleven leaders received custodial sentences of between five to ten years. In 1950 the leader, Peter Møller, was given amnesty, and by that time all the others had been set free (Tamm 1984: 430–1).

the government also commuted death sentences to life imprisonment. In 1960, the last of these prisoners was released. Thus the purge was over, but the debate as to how this was performed continues to play a major role in Denmark.

7.5 Transitional justice compared

The trial of collaborators in Denmark is often compared with the situation in Norway. Some similarities are obvious, but there are also important differences, especially regarding the legal foundation of the purge. Norway had taken up arms against the German invaders as early as 9 April 1940, and, although later members of the Norwegian Nazi party were to deny it, there was no doubt that during the occupation Norway and Germany were *de facto* at war. In June 1940, the Norwegian government fled to London where legislation in the form of emergency decrees was enacted. This legislation was to serve as the legal basis for the trial of Norwegian collaborators. While there was doubt as to whether Denmark was at war with Germany, the Norwegian position was clear, at least for the majority of the population. One constitutional issue did, however, raise certain problems. Unlike the Danish Constitution, the Norwegian Constitution contained a prohibition against retroactive laws. This problem, however, was seen as partly solved or overcome through the emergency decrees issued in London.[19]

In Norway, as in Denmark, collaborators were indicted by ordinary courts. This posed no moral problem in Norway, whereas certain questions emerged in Denmark due to the fact that Danish courts had supported the official policy of collaboration during the occupation. After the war, the same courts had to impose punishment for actions which might conceivably be seen as an expression of collaboration in a manner that was similar to their war-time co-operation. However, no judge saw a moral dilemma to such an extent that he wanted to desist from taking part in the purge. In Norway, with a population at the time of approximately three million, 46,000 people were prosecuted, including 26,000 members of the Quisling party. Eighteen thousand people were

[19] A broad summary of the Norwegian Trials is given in Andenæs (1979). On retroactive law see Andenæs (1979: 91). A general overview of the entire results of the trials against the collaborators in Norway is found in (1962) *Om Landsvikoppgjøret* ('On the Trial of the traitors'), Oslo. This comprehensive publication was published by the Department of Justice and intended as an overall report to the Norwegian Storting (Parliament).

sentenced to imprisonment. This figure may be compared to the Danish figure of 13,500 people who were sentenced to imprisonment. Prosecution in Norway was stricter than in Denmark, but it rested on a more clear-cut foundation. This could also be seen from the way in which the trials proceeded. In Norway, the trial of Quisling was of special importance. His execution as early as October 1945 was the high water-mark of the purges of collaborators. Denmark had no similar court decision providing a precedent and establishing, from the very outset, principles of fundamental responsibility. The initial cases of prosecution in Denmark dealt with smaller offenders. Their offences consisted in having been recruited to the German forces as ordinary soldiers or as guards at Danish airports, etc. The outcomes of the first verdicts in court resulted in such cases in heavy sentences.

In Norway, all 100,000 members of the Nazi party, the *Nasjonal Samling*, were collectively sentenced to fines and required to pay damages for the estimated wrongs done by the party during the Quisling government. In Denmark, membership of a Nazi party per se was not considered criminal. In Norway a German *Reichskommissariat* had been established, and Vidkun Quisling had been allowed to form a National Socialist government supervised by the German *Reichskommissar*. The Nazi party in Norway thus played a much more central political role than in Denmark.

Both in Denmark and in Norway German war criminals were tried and convicted. The majority of the seventy-seven people tried in Denmark were former members of the German security forces. The leading case was conducted against the former German plenipotentiary, Dr Werner Best, whose case was heard together with cases against the local SS-*Führer*, the Commander of German police and the head of the German army in Denmark. The case against Best and its outcome have been subsequently subject to extensive dispute. The decisive element in the case for the prosecution was his responsibility for the action against Danish Jews in October 1943, and the harsher course in the second part of the Danish occupation, involving assassinations, the '*Nacht und Nebelaktion*', in which other civilian citizens were murdered as retaliation for actions of the resistance, and extensive material destruction in acts of deterrence or revenge. More than 200 such actions were included in the indictment. Two special actions were likewise included: the action in October 1943 against Danish Jews, and the action in September 1944 against the Danish police, which was dissolved on 19 September 1944, whereupon approximately 2,000 Danish police officers were sent to German concentration camps (Tamm 1984: 634).

As far as the action against the Jews was concerned, the situation was particularly nebulous. What carried particular weight in the case against Dr Best was the fact that in September 1943 he had cabled the German Foreign Ministry, pointing out that it was necessary to carry out such an action, but at the same time referring to a number of difficulties. Dr Best maintained that he dispatched this telegram at a time when it was known to him that German authorities had already decided on the action. Hence he could only influence the timing of their action. In the first-instance, Best was sentenced to death. However, the High Court, upon hearing the case, found that a warning that was decisive for the rescue of the Jews had stemmed from Best. As a result of this warning, it had been possible in advance to notify approximately 7,000 of the 7,500 Danish Jews, and to ensure that most of them could be transported to Sweden. In the High Court, Best was not held liable for the action against the Jews, and his punishment was reduced to five years' imprisonment. The Supreme Court sentenced him to twelve years in prison. He was discharged as early as 1951, and at the end of 1953 the last of the German war criminals were sent to Germany.[20] In Norway, eighty-two war criminals were tried and, unlike Denmark where in the end no war criminal was sentenced to death, in Norway thirteen war criminals of the sixteen that were sentenced to death were actually executed.

In the Netherlands, trials took place before special courts established for that particular purpose. As in Norway, a series of orders issued by the Dutch government in exile constituted the basis of the trials. The judicial system included two types of courts, partly mixed civilian and partly military. Both were in charge of actual criminal prosecution of the collaborators, but there also existed certain so-called tribunals which could impose other sanctions. Approximately 14,000 were sentenced to imprisonment by the military and civil courts. About one-half of the prosecuted received more than five years of imprisonment; 152 received capital punishment, and thirty-nine were executed. The penalties were harsher than in the Nordic countries. Thus the sanction for joining the German forces was imprisonment for between ten and fifteen years. The so-called tribunals might impose such sanctions as confinement for one to two years, loss of civil rights, and confiscation of money and property. About 37,000 persons, among whom were a great many members of the Dutch National Socialist

[20] For German readers I also refer to Tamm (1983).

Party (NSB), were sentenced by these tribunals (see Belifante 1978). Belgian collaborators on the other hand were sentenced under the ordinary Penal Code, as was the case with most Norwegian collaborators. Belgium used military courts as well. Fifty-three thousand persons were prosecuted, 31,000 of them for German war service. Capital punishment was imposed upon 1,200 persons, of whom 250 were actually executed (Huyse and Dhondt 1991).

France has particular relevance in a comparison with the Danish purges. The existence of a 'free zone', with Vichy as its capital under the leadership of Marshal Pétain, made the situation in France reminiscent of the situation during the Danish occupation and the policy of collaboration. Only France and Denmark had their own non-Nazi government while under German occupation. A major difference between Denmark and France is, however, that the French Vichy government had linked its fate closely to a final German victory. From the time Pierre Laval became Prime Minister, most notably, the French government went much further than the Danish government in its efforts of collaboration. The deportation and killing of the French Jews, contrasted with the Danish action of rescue, illustrates this difference. As long as Denmark had an official Danish government, there was no question of taking any measure against the 7,500 Danish Jews, whereas the French government initiated a deportation of Jews on its own initiative.[21]

The first step in Denmark toward drafting the legislation directed towards the prosecution of collaborators was taken by the resistance movement and its highest authority, the Freedom Council, which had been established in the fall of 1943. The same happened in France: The demand came from the resistance movement, the Free French, under the leadership of General de Gaulle. The fundamental starting point came with the non-recognition of the armistice of June 1940, and the non-recognition of the Vichy regime. In the opinion of the French resistance movement, France had actually been at war with Germany all the time during World War II. This concept was parallel to the position of the Danish Freedom movement. In France, the idea behind the trials was to settle the account with actual collaborators, and at the same time the resistance wanted to make sure that the Vichy regime was delegitimized as such. In this respect, the result in Denmark was different, as only criminal

[21] See further details in Marrus and Paxton (1981).

liability was prosecuted, whereas political co-operation was omitted, or decided on a different level.

In France, the purge was carried out by special courts. The so-called *cours de justice* sentenced 2,640 persons to capital punishment; 13,000 were sentenced to hard labour; and, finally, 30,000 to imprisonment. Minor cases of *indignité nationale* came before co-called *tribunaux*, and in 49,000 such cases the defendant lost his civil rights. Furthermore, a so-called *Haute Cour de Justice* was established for the purpose of trying politicians. The court passed fifty-five judgments, including five cases of capital punishment, among others for Laval and Pétain. In considering these numbers, it must be taken into account that a large number of French collaborators had been summarily executed without trial. Figures ranging from about 4,000 to 40,000 have been mentioned to calculate the number of such victims. In France, as in Belgium, the relative number of capital punishments was considerably higher than in Denmark, the Netherlands or Norway. This must be seen in connection with the fact that in those two countries capital punishment in the criminal code had not been abolished.

A comparison of the way in which transitional justice is carried out reveals certain common features, which were also relevant for Denmark and Norway after World War II. In such situations, time is scarce, and demands for something to happen are loud, and so a purge has to be carried out more quickly than is provided for under normal criminal procedure. A characteristic of transitional justice, at least as it was implemented after World War II, was that resources were scarce, especially in view of the overwhelming case load that suddenly had to be dealt with by police, prosecution and courts. As a means to facilitate the cases, often guarantees such as the treatment of certain cases before a jury were cancelled and the assistance of lay judges was reduced. This was also the case in the two Nordic countries. The legal foundation of the purge may be questionable, as was specifically the case in Denmark, where it entailed the introduction of retroactive force and the death penalty, which had been abolished since 1930. The attitude towards Nazism as a political phenomenon was different in the two countries. In Denmark, Nazism and collaboration might be confused, but basically Nazism in itself was not punished, although it was stigmatized in other ways, such as through dismissal from public service or from membership of private associations. In Norway, by contrast, the members of the official Norwegian Nazi party were all considered responsible for damage to the Norwegian state. In both countries the criminal actions and other actions of purge were aimed at satisfying a claim for some kind of justice. Transitional justice is a kind of justice of its own. The transition in an orderly way may prevail over a narrow concept of justice. In both Denmark and Norway justice was done but the discussion as to whether justice was real justice has continued.

Bibliography

Andenæs, Johannes (1979). *Det vanskelige oppgjøret.* Oslo: Tanum-Norli.

Arendt, Hannah (1963). *Eichmann in Jerusalem. A Report on the Banality of Evil.* New York, NY: The Viking Press.

Arendt, Hannah and Karl Jaspers (1992). *Hannah Arendt and Karl Jaspers correspondence 1926–1969.* New York, NY: Harcourt Brace Jovanovich.

Belifante, A.D. (1978). *In plaats van bijltjesdag. De geschiedenis van de bijzondere rechtspleging na de Tweede Wereldoorlog.* Assen: Van Gorcum.

Djursaa, Malene (1981). *DNSAP. Danske Nazister 1930–45.* Copenhagen: Gyldendal.

Finkelkraut, Alain (1992). *Remembering in Vain.* New York, NY: Columbia University Press.

Frei, Norbert, Dirk van Laak and Micahel Stolleis (2000). *Geschichte vor Gericht. Historiker, Richter und di Suche nach Gerechtigkeit.* Munich: C.H. Beck.

Golsan, Richard (2000). *The Papon Affair.* New York, NY and London: Routledge.

Hack, Peter (2012). 'Transitional Justice and the Rule of Law – East European Examples'. Available via legalresearchnetwork.eu.

Hæstrup, Jørgen (1966). *. . .Til landets bedste. Hovedtræk af departementschefstyrets virke 1943–45.* Copenhagen: Gyldendal.

Henke, Klaus-Dietmar and Hans Woller (eds) (1991). *Politische Säuberung in Europa.* Munich: Deutscher Taschenbuch Verlag.

Herbert, Ulrich (1996). *Best: Biographische Studien über Radikalismus, Weltanschauung und Vernunft, 1903–1989.* Bonn: Dietz Verlag.

Hoffmann, Stanley (1968). 'Collaborationism in France during World War II', *The Journal of Modern History* 40(3): 375–95.

Huyse, Luc and Steven Dhondt (1991). *Onverwerkt verleden: Collaboratie en repressie in België, 1942–52.* Leuven: Kritak.

Jones, Harriet, Kjell Östberg and Nico Randeraad (eds) (2007). *Contemporary History on Trial: Europe since 1989 and the Role of the Expert Historian.* Manchester: Manchester University Press.

Marrus, Michael R. and Robert O. Paxton (1981). *Vichy, France and the Jews.* New York, NY: Basic Books.

Matlok, Siegfried (1988). *Dänemark in Hitlers Hand. Der Bericht des Reichsbevollmächtigten Werner Best über seine Bestazungspolitik in Dänemark.* Husum: Husum Verlag.

Nissen, Henrik (1973). *1940. Studier i forhandlingspolitikken og samarbejdspolitikken.* Copenhagen: Gyldendal.

Norway, Department of Justice (1962). *Om Landssvikoppgjøret.* A report to the Norwegian Storting (Parliament).

Petrovics, Vlademir (2009). *Historians as Expert Witnesses in the Age of Extremes* (dissertation). Budapest. Available at: www.etd.ceu.hu/2009/hphpev01.pdf.

Posner, Eric A. and Adrian Vermeule (2003). 'Transitional Justice as Ordinary Justice', *Chicago Public Law and Legal Theory Working Paper* 40.

Poulsen, Henning (1970). *Besættelsesmagten og de danske nazister.* Copenhagen: Gyldendal.

Rings, Werner (1979). *Kollaboration und Widerstand. Europa im Krieg 1939–1945.* Germany: Ex-Libris-Verlag.

Rosengren, Bjørn (1982). *Dr. Werner og tysk besættelsespolitik i Danmark 1943–1945.* Odense: Odense Universitetsforlag

Ross, Alf (1959). *On Law and Justice.* Berkeley, CA: University of California Press.

Rousso, Henry (1990). *Le syndrom de Vichy de 1944 à nos jours.* Paris: Seuil.

(2002). *The Haunting Past.* Philadelphia, PA: University of Pennsylvania Press.

Scavenius, Eric (1948). *Forhandlingspolitikken under besættelsen.* Copenhagen: Hasselbalch.

Tamm, Ditlev (1983). 'Kollaboration und Strafrechtliche Ahndung in Dänemark nach dem Zweiten Weltkrieg', *Zeitschrift für Neuere Rechtsgeschichte* 44–73.

(1984). *Retsoppgøret efter Besættelsen.* Copenhagen: Jurist-og Økonomforbundets Forlag.

(2011). 'Phases of Collaboration, Shades of Guilt: Coping with the Tangled Web of Collaboration in Post-war Denmark', in Ditlev Tamm. *The History of Danish Law. Selected Articles and Bibliography.* Copenhagen: DJØF Publishing.

Thomsen, Erich (1971). *Deutsche Besatzungspolitik in Dänemark 1940–1945.* Bertelsmann Universitätsverlag.

Wijffels, Alain (ed.) (2001). *History in Court.* Leiden: Ius Deco Publications.

8

Between socialism and liberalism: law, emancipation and Solidarność

JACEK KURCZEWSKI

This chapter addresses the legal aspects of political conflict in Polish society during the time when it was subject to the control of the Soviet Union, or, more accurately, of the international Communist movement, based in the Soviet Union, as it developed after the October Revolution in Russia, and gained influence, not only in Europe but in the whole world in the years 1917–1998. This chapter describes the process of the third modernization of Poland in the twentieth century. The first era of modernization started in 1918, with the re-establishment of the national Polish state, which in the 1930s descended into semi-authoritarian rule. The policies of this state aimed at industrialization, but they ended abruptly following the attack of Nazi and Soviet neighbours in 1939. The second era of modernization was organized by the victorious Soviet Union through the new Polish Communist Party state, which accelerated the industrialization and urbanization of Polish society. The authoritarian Constitution of 1935 and totalitarian Constitution of 1952 provided for the normative legalization of the new system, although unwritten or unpublicized rules were part of the real Constitution of the country. After the limitation of political rights in the 1930s came the elimination of political rights in the 1940s. Against these currents, the process of liberalization commencing in 1956 marked the beginning of the first stage in the third modernization of Poland, which placed increasing emphasis on individual freedom. The second stage of this process was the direct confrontation between the Communist Party state and students in 1968, between the Communist Party and workers in 1970 and 1976, and between the Communist Party and intellectuals almost constantly until the strikes of the summer of 1980 and the emergence of the only independent mass social organization in the Communist system – Solidarność. This chapter discusses the legal form which the movement took and the normative contents of its action, pointing to the lasting effects upon the official legal system until it ended in 1989, and it examines the legacy of the movement in the post-1989 so-called Third Polish Republic. The chapter places its focus on the main processes and effects of the movement, and in so doing it attempts to provide a more general analysis of the place of law in these transformations.[1]

The post-war history of Europe is generally influenced by three distinct waves of democratization. The first was the democratization of those countries where, until the end of World War II, totalitarian and authoritarian regimes were in force. The de-Nazification of West Germany and Austria, the de-Vichyization of the French Republic, and the de-fascisization of Italy were the major cases, accompanied by a series of regime changes in the collaborating satellite countries. Regime change in these instances was exogenous, although only in some of these countries was an occupation necessary to bring about democratization. More commonly, a military alliance sufficed. The Western Allies, committed to democracy, arrived and abolished non-democratic governments, placing potential opponents under military control, while the Soviet Red Army in most cases prepared the ground for the Communist Party dictatorship.

The second wave of democratization concerned the authoritarian regimes in Portugal, Spain, and Greece. All three transitions are similar in that they were endogenous, although the external sanctions against the Greek junta were also a powerful agent for change. The old regimes were in two cases linked to personal rule and a biological end was the solution. Despite the expectations of the enemies of these regimes, the United States and their democratic allies were not interested in open intervention in their internal arrangements. Like today's undemocratic Islamic regimes that support American global and regional policy, the Iberian authoritarian regimes were reliable allies of the West during the Cold War. The risk of the Left coming to power after a collapse of the authoritarian regime (a risk almost fatal in Italy, less so in France, and equally dangerous in Greece) was perhaps too great to allow for the introduction of democracy by force in these peripheral countries. So, at the expense of the delayed emancipation of the populations in question, these regimes continued until the armed machinery of personal rule imploded upon the death of a particular authority (or, in the case

[1] For a more detailed sociological and political history of Polish official law one may look for instance in Fuszara (2013 in print); here some more abstract points repeatedly told in my earlier publications (especially Kurczewski 1993 and Kurczewski and Sullivan 2002) are illustrated with historical events.

of Greece, the symbolic death of the army that allowed for the catastrophic developments in Cyprus).

The third wave was the democratization of state-Socialist countries. The label given to these countries is as controversial as the democratization process itself. Except for the Soviet Union, those post-1945 states ruled by Communist parties were first called 'people's democracies'. Little by little they were reclassified as 'Socialist states', first Czechoslovakia, then Romania, each adopting it as its official name, until the whole bloc eventually took on the name of 'Socialist states'. Mainland China, to this day, is still defined as the 'People's Republic'. These 'people's democracies' were placed in opposition to 'bourgeois democracies' with free elections, political pluralism, and a decisive position on parliamentary representation. In contrast to the 'democracy for the capitalists', 'people's democracies' were ruled by the vanguard of the working class: that is, the hierarchically organized Communist Party (though, in practice, by its ruling elite) and its subordinate allies, if it allowed for the existence of any such groups. Elections were limited to those political actors already in power, allowing for no legal institutionalized opposition, while the Parliament functioned, at best, as the consultative body.

In section 8.1, I describe the political system that had developed east of Elbe, which was arranged as the 'vanguard' political organization subjugating to itself the political structure and monopoly of power and using it to put all economic life, and all social life in general, under its control. The model developed in the Soviet Union was imposed as binding for all Communist countries, and even if, as was the case in Yugoslavia or Albania, national sovereignty had been successfully defended, the monopoly of the Communist Party rule was universal with its consequences as to the totalitarian transformation of law and administration of justice. Using the Polish case, section 8.2 examines the evidence of a permanent pressure from the 'bottom' of the public sphere, however limited, towards the 'liberalization' and civic rights, once the direct terror under Joseph Stalin ended with his death in 1953. Section 8.3 describes the little-known history of Solidarność's struggle for rule of law and human rights during the short but decisive period of its legal existence (summer 1980 to 13 December 1981), in which it formed the first successful social movement against the Communist regime in history. Section 8.4 explains the 'success' of the movement, as the withdrawal of recognition of Solidarność did not stop the process of partial transformation of the regime and administration of justice in the direction of a 'legal state', which was achieved politically at the Round Table negotiations in June 1989 that opened the way for the construction of the liberal-democratic republic. In section 8.5, I describe the strong emphasis on the rights that gave particular colour to the evolving new democracy and made the transformation progressive and emancipatory and not just retroactive and conservatory despite an abrupt return to the capitalist economy and parliamentary democracy.

8.1 The Communist dual state

World War II ended with liberation and democratization of Western Europe and the imposition of Communist totalitarian rule in the Eastern half. That was the price paid for the elimination of the German National Socialist regime with its racial holocaust policies and nationalist imperialism. It should be recalled, however, that the Iron Curtain did not divide the followers of Communism from their opponents. The role of the Soviet Union and Red Army under Stalin following victory over the Nazis reinforced the already present political trends all over Europe. Neutralized through the 1939 Molotov–Ribbentrop Treaty, Communists were mobilized against Nazis when Hitler attacked the Soviet Union in 1941, and only then did they take an active, often leading, role in the anti-Fascist Resistance movement in the Balkans, Greece, Italy, and France. Poland fought a war on two fronts after the German–Soviet invasion in September 1939. On the eastern side, there was anti-Soviet resistance active in Poland, the Baltic countries, and Ukraine until the 1950s. But the military delineation agreed by the Western Allies and Stalin held until the end of the Cold War. The West had not helped the Berlin workers in 1955, the Poznań workers in 1956, the Hungarian uprising in 1956, nor the democratic transformation of Czechoslovakia in 1968, and Stalin had not sent troops to help Greek Communists in the late 1940s. In the West, the practical reality of Communism was known only from the positive or negative images projected by parties in international and national political debate. East of the Elbe, the Communist system, which, independently of the wishes of the population, was in existence for almost fifty years, was considered by most as a distinct variety of political, economic, and social life, with its own faults and merits.

But what was the inner rationale of this system? Following Marxist theory, primary consideration was given to the economic base of social life. Scientific positivism led to the abolition of the market and the assumption of control of the economy by the state as a basic part of the rational governance of society. Since the failure of the plan for a great world revolution in 1920 on battlefields in Poland, the policy promoted by Lenin and later by Stalin was above all an economic policy, aiming at the accelerated modernization of the former Russian empire. The American model of mass industrialization was followed as the planned state policy, and the dream of leaving the United States behind in industrial development remained the goal of post-Stalinist Communist Party leaders for decades. Brutal state coercion was seen as a necessary instrument for achieving the goal, and the forced labour system was at the base of Soviet modernization. The reward was the abolition of the private ownership of the means of production (land included) and resulting disappearance of the (previous) class structure as promised by the Marxist utopia. The system had its own stratification and its own rationality. The permanent inventing of class enemies and relaxation of all standards of justice were neither an ideological aberration nor an expression of psychopathological tendencies of individuals, but the guarantee of the permanent influx into the Gulag barracks of an army of unpaid manpower, which helped to transform Russia into one of the most developed superpowers and to defend it against direct military threat from abroad.

The economic need for unpaid labour that helped to fulfil the *pyatiletkas* (the five-year plans for economic development, starting with Stalin's Five Year Plan 1928–1932) explains the doctrine of the Soviet system of law and justice. On the one hand there was terror, which atomizes and pacifies the population. Exemplary shootings and show trials served to document that nobody was exempted from the regime of cruelty. What looked from the outside like sadistic political cannibalism had its teaching value. Commissars of the political police accused of treason and sentenced to death one after another provided at once the certainty that nobody is safe and the sense of justice that even the top rulers were subject to the same treatment as the 'class enemy' of the lowest rank. Over the decades, the Socialist system of law and justice proved its effectiveness in keeping members of the population resigned to their unpredictable fate and in providing an obedient forced labour force. But this force, in addition to child labour, was used, not for the frivolous pleasure of the rulers, but in order to achieve the never-ending goal of accelerated modernization, epitomized by the iron and steel works of Magnitogorsk, opened in 1931, *Byelomor kanal*, opened in 1933, the Kolyma M56 'Highway of Bones' into the gold, platinum, and uranium mines built between 1932 and 1953, and the test of a nuclear bomb (codename First Lightning) on 29 August 1949 at Semipalatinsk.

As for law and justice in the Communist system, it led a double life. The concept of 'legality', more exactly 'Socialist legality', was from time to time extolled to the extreme as the necessary medicine against the 'abuses' committed by the zealots of the system. It is interesting that even when the system was first created the idea of revolutionary justice as the expression of the legal intuition of working masses (the doctrine formulated by M. Reisner, the only follower of Leon Petrażycki to remain on the side of the Bolsheviks after the Revolution) was attacked by Lenin, who defended the principle of formal legality (i.e. positive written official law). It is hard today to imagine this, but even Stalin's rise to dictatorial power was narrated as a return to order. The role of A. Vyshinsky, whom Stalin nominated as General Prosecutor, was precisely to combine the instrumentality of Soviet law with its positive formalism, which he did by publishing theoretical statements running contrary to his own practice, as exemplified by the fact that he proclaimed his notorious principle 'confession of the accused is the queen of evidence' despite stating otherwise in his monograph *Theory of Judicial Proofs in Soviet Justice* (Vaksberg 1990). He praised Stalin for inventing the doctrine that under revolutionary conditions if the law does not fit existing needs the law has to be either amended or put aside, and he glorified Stalin's use of the extraordinary measures and so-called 'Ural-Siberian way' (Vyshinsky 1952). He constructed the notion of the new 'Socialist legality' in service of the new regime, which he contrasted with the old 'bourgeois legality' (Vyshinsky 1948), thus developing the doctrine of the Red Terror proclaimed in the heyday of the Bolshevik Revolution in 1917, and consolidating it for the subsequent decades of the Communist system.[2] But the formality of Soviet law already demanded by Lenin was, in my view, strengthened when Stalin decided to further modernization and industrialization based upon the principle of 'economic calculus' and contractual relations between the units of the state economy against the opponents who advised the full elimination of civil law and the administrative direct planning regime. But whenever the circumstances

[2] Excerpt from an interview with Felix Dzerzhinsky published in *Novaia Zhizn* on 14 July 1917. 'We stand for organized terror – this should be frankly admitted. Terror is an absolute necessity during times of revolution. Our aim is to fight against the enemies of the Soviet Government and of the new order of life. We judge quickly. In most cases only a day passes between the apprehension of the criminal and his sentence. When confronted with evidence criminals in almost every case confess; and what argument can have greater weight than a criminal's own confession.' www.worldfuturefund.org/wffmaster/Reading/Quotes/leninkeyquotes.htm accessed 14 September 2013.

demanded direct rule was applied (Nowicki and Łunc 1960 [1954]: 20–42) and the contracts were by no means 'bourgeois' free contracts, but government-controlled as the General Terms of Supply and administratively issued Plan set limits to the terms which might be included in contracts governing, 'broadly or narrowly, such questions as: what kinds of enterprises shall buy and sell what kinds of goods; how much shall be bought and sold during the year; what prices shall be paid' (Berman 1947: 213). '[T]he restoration of the ancient principle that contracts must be kept has not meant the rejection of the revolutionary doctrine that plans must be followed. The two-contracts and plans bear a polar relation to each other' (Berman 1947: 225).

The Communist government imposed in Poland by the Soviet military administration in the aftermath of World War II gradually overturned and subverted the pre-war system of justice for its own purposes. In the late 1940s, many pre-war laws were simply ruled null and void by the courts. The Communist Party openly gave directives to the courts on matters of judicial policy and conduct. Legal periodicals discussed speeches by Communist politicians and established the ways in which the courts ought to apply them. Those speeches and interpretive Articles were discussed at judicial conferences. Government administration issued orders for the enforcement of the resolutions passed by the Party that became *extra legem* sources of the law, following the principles of 'people's legality' and the 'social interpretation' of statutes. The independence of the judiciary and security of judicial tenure were destroyed by a variety of methods. One was the creation of special tribunals, including military ones, which tried certain types of cases, notably 'offences against public security and public order' and 'offences against the economic interests of the state'. The entire proceedings and identity of courts that freely used the death penalty remained secret.

The Judiciary Act of 1950 codified the various informal practices previously applied by the Communist administration. Judges were obliged by law to show political bias as 'revolutionary constructors of a Socialist society'. On the other hand, the Minister of Justice was empowered to waive all legal and educational criteria in appointing judges to their offices. Although the later 1952 Constitution made provision for the popular election of judges, no legislation or administrative action implemented it, which meant that judicial office, except the Supreme Court named by the Council of State, remained a gift of the Minister of Justice. Protection of judicial tenure, revocable only upon legal conviction, was set aside. The Minister could remove, demote, or transfer judges as easily as any other state bureaucrats. Judicial salaries, which were in any case rather low, enjoyed no statutory protection against government manipulation.

Of 3,109 judges appointed before 1939, over 30 per cent were exterminated or died during the war. Of the remainder, the Communists hired more than half (1,346) almost immediately on taking power, and, by February 1946, the Minister of Justice qualified new ones from the security forces, political military apparatus, and so on to serve on a 'temporary' basis, after an expedited and ideologically loaded training in the basics of law. A decree of 14 March 1945 annulled the pre-war ban on political party membership of the judges. Article 82.1 of the law amending the law on courts of 20 July 1950 listed as the first requirement of the judge that he or she '(1) must warrant the proper execution of duties of a judge in People's Poland' leaving the assessment of the said propriety to the Minister of Justice. Moreover, paragraph 2 of this Article granted the Minister the right in individual cases to nominate persons as judges who had not completed a legal education(!) (Ziemba 1997). Another way of subordinating the judiciary to control by the Party was through the rapid introduction of selected lay assessors. Prior to the war, in Polish procedure lay assessors were involved only as jurors in criminal proceedings, or in special labour or commercial tribunals when appointed by private associations. In 1950, in all courts, lay assessors were introduced with the same powers as a judge, so decisions could be made by a majority of two lay assessors against the professional judge. Officially elected by the local council, the assessors were in practice selected by the Communist five-person Board of the Council from among people felt to be useful by the Party. In this case, together with age, the 'safeguarding the proper execution of the duty' was the decisive requirement, and it made it possible to introduce politically reliable people as lay assessors controlling the professional judges.

One should take into consideration that all these changes occurred within the context of the legally unrestricted terror which, from 1944 onwards, was organized by the Communist Party under the direct control of Soviet KGB experts and under supervision from Moscow, while the Red Army was present in military bases on Polish territory until 1992. There was no freedom of the press and no procedure against the administration except expressions of grievances to the upper levels of the administrative hierarchy or to the Communist Procuracy Office. Various uniformed or secret internal policing forces were in control of the prisons but under no judicial control at all, and practised torture at will. To this day, the number of victims of the post-war decade of Stalinism has not been established, due to the secrecy of arrests, imprisonments, executions, and burials. Stalin's death in 1953 slowed down the vortex of terror that was finally officially condemned in 1956.

One of the key factors in the Communist administration was the development of the special type of public prosecution called *Prokuratura* both in Russian and in Polish.[3] The procuracy operated independently of administrative supervision – in this it was, together with the political police, the only institution independent of the administration – and it had broadly defined functions, ranging from supervision over every government action and involvement in every stage of the judicial process to the investigation of grievances by citizens dissatisfied with the administration. Not surprisingly, in the common lore of Communist societies, the procurator served as the symbolic figure of the Last Judgement, and in colloquial wisdom the omnipotence of the procuracy was recorded, while court, judiciary, and defence attorneys appeared as second-rank auxiliary elements of justice. In the courtroom, the procurator functioned as a prosecuting attorney, with greatly expanded powers. Procurators were empowered to detain, arrest, conduct pre-trial investigations, determine cause, indict, initiate trial, transfer a case, release the accused, recommend sentences, appeal decisions, and supervise detention. If the procurator decided that a civil case involved state interests, he might enter the case. If at any stage of the judicial process the procurator became convinced of the innocence of the accused, he was able to inform the judiciary that the case had been halted. The interest of the state was the ultimate reference point for a procurator; his duty to defend the citizens' interests was understood as also being the state interest, and therefore, in practice, he worked in the state's interest. The key to understanding the role of the procuracy in the Socialist system lies, in turn, in the hierarchical organization of this all-powerful institution. At the top was the Procurator General named by the Council of State, who nominated his deputies, among whom the most important was the Chief Military Procurator. The procuracy was divided into several departments, such as military, general supervision, bureau of investigation, supervision of penal institutions, criminal and civil supervision, criminological research, statistics, finance, and administration. The same structure was repeated in the lower ranks of the nation-wide

[3] In describing the *Prokuratura* and the Supreme Court I follow the characterization given in McCrea, Piano and Klein (1984).

centralized organization, which, due to its structural similarity and patterns of close co-operation, crossed national boundaries in a way similar to the international alliance of the Communist parties of the Soviet bloc. Lenin, who in 1922 re-established the absolutist institution introduced by Peter the Great in 1722 in order to control the bureaucracy, placed great stress on the role of the procuracy as the arm of the Party.

When faced with the uncontrolled and omnipotent procurator the judge seems really a pale figure. The occupational dependency of the procurator outweighs in that context the constitutionally acknowledged independence of the judge in court. The procurator is the explicitly political element in the structure of the proceedings and represents the will of the Communist Party state. The judge is, of course, independent but: (1) is limited by statute; (2) has only one out of three votes in the final verdict; (3) depends upon superiors for material advances. The case is allotted to a judge, not on a random basis, but by a knowledgeable president of the court. Political convictions will thus be taken into account, as well as the degree of personal integrity. A decision that is against the opinion of the directly political *Prokuratura* will be appealed to the upper court, and subject to the same process of selection in case something went wrong at an earlier point in the procedure. By this process we arrive at the Supreme Court.

As Western experts used to warn, the Supreme Court in People's Poland, just like in any other Communist country, should not be mistaken for its homonym in the United States. The Supreme Court was divided into four panels – civil, labour and social welfare, criminal, and military affairs – and it was presided over by a chairman and vice-chairman. Members were appointed for five-year terms by the Council of State. The Supreme Court had no power of judicial review over legislative or executive actions; it exercised supervision over the judiciary, reviewing cases emanating from the district and regional courts. It also served as the court of cassation in cases of extraordinary appeal when a protest was brought by the Procurator General or the Minister of Justice. One should keep in mind that the decision in all those cases was valid for the particular case only, though was cited as of auxiliary interpretive value in later cases. The Polish legal system, based upon the continental principles of Roman law, does not operate on the principle of judicial review and judicial precedent. Here, the important role of the Supreme Court was, however, to issue general instructions, interpretations of laws, and applications that were legally binding. In this way, the Supreme

Court was quasi-legislative, since those general instructions carried the force of law and were frequently used to instruct the courts as to how relevant legislation should be interpreted and applied. Through its power to issue binding practice, it served as an arm of the Ministry of Justice, supervising the actions of all courts. The role of the Supreme Court was thus openly political, and it followed the main principles of the Communist Party state with its centralization and hierarchical subordination. It was not political in the American sense, as the Supreme Court was not empowered to rule on the constitutionality of executive and legislative acts. As both the Minister of Justice and the General Procurator had privileged access to the Supreme Court through extraordinary appellation, the Supreme Court was a co-operative element in the context of this branch of justice.

The Communist system in its organizational aspect has been characterized by a duality that corresponds to the ambiguity of its normative aspect. The official law textbooks did not mention the directives and instructions issued by Party officials as the source of law, but the Constitution, since the 1976 amendments, acknowledged in the preamble 'the leading role' of the Party. The organization of society is dual: first, there is the open state; then there is the Party, confined to its members but ruling the whole state as its instrument of power. This duality makes it impossible to trace responsibility for political decisions. Not surprisingly, the Tribunal of State when re-established in 1982 could not discuss the constitutional responsibility of the most responsible person of all (that is, the former First Secretary of the Communist Party), but only of his subordinates such as the former Prime Minister and members of the Cabinet. Such obsessive duality may be explained as a deliberate attempt to eliminate individual and institutional responsibility, and is evidenced in the administration of justice as such. First, there is the duality of justice, 'political' and 'mundane', the former applied by the courts in trials of a political character where accusation is based upon vague statements in special laws, and the latter applied by the civil chapters of the courts and by criminal chapters in cases of a conventional criminal character (petty theft, burglary etc.). Secondly, there is the duality of the 'common courts' and the 'military courts' and other special courts that were given jurisdiction over civilians in a large range of cases vaguely defined as concerning – for instance – state security. Thirdly, there is the duality of the 'profane' Ministry of Justice that embraces the judiciary from the bottom up to the Supreme Court, and the 'sacred' and secret procuracy that is above the 'secular' administration. In a sense the latter division is corroborated by the official information on salaries of those two sectors published in the 1990 *Statistical Yearbook for 1989*, the last year of the old system (*Mały Rocznik Statystyczny* 1990: 58). According to that source, there were in Poland altogether 5,530 professional judges (69,400 assessor judges) and 4,286 prosecutors. The average monthly income of the lower- and middle-level prosecutors was 416,000 złotys; of the judiciary, 392,203 złotys; in the General Procuracy 660,775 złotys; and in the Supreme Court, 589,991 złotys. Those figures show the difference in the social status between the two professions.

In its most extreme expression, the administration of justice, and thus the duality, can be summarized in three main points (see further Kurczewski 1993: 83–8):

1. The existence of a parallel system of special courts in two basic forms: (a) the military justice empowered to judge civilians in crimes affecting the national defence and 'the stability of state'; (b) the petty justice administered to punish misdemeanours by an administrative body empowered to use the light criminal sanctions and vaguely defined law.
2. Factual political subordination of presidents of the courts nominated from among the Party members and subject to Communist Party discipline, allocating the cases according to criteria of political expediency.
3. The independence of Prokuratura from the Ministry of Justice and its direct subordination to the highest Party-state ruling centre.

The secondary role of the judiciary in this Party-state system run by First Secretaries with no constitutional accountability is the direct consequence of the secondary role of the state as an instrument of the power of the Communist Party. As final illustration of this duality (and duplicity) it should be added that for decades in People's Poland two criminal codes were in force simultaneously. First, there was the 'normal' Criminal Code in force since 1 September 1932 (with amendments) and second the decree on crimes especially dangerous in the time of the reconstruction of the state issued on 13 June 1946 and referred to officially also as the 'Small Criminal Code'. This code was supposedly designed to help to reconstruct public order and state structure after the war, and it remained in force for thirty-four years of peace until some of its provisions were transferred into the new, unified Criminal Code of 19 April 1969. This code:

> expanded the pre-war criminal code by adding provisions on espionage, sabotage, and illegal possession of weapons. Both the decree and a number of other regulations were designed with a specific purpose in mind: the so-called 'overcoming of difficulties in the period of state reconstruction'. Provisions of this type, which tended to carry extremely punitive criminal sanctions, were later found flagrant and excessive. Moreover, they were easy to use in trials of political opponents, which were typically held before military courts (Fuszara 2013: 166).

Notably, Article 22 of the Small Criminal Code placed under sanction the 'dissemination of false information that could endanger the essential interests of the State or degrade the dignity of its bodies': that is, the information not provided by the censored state's media, but again most typically coming from the Western or dissident media.

8.2 Permanent pressure for reforms

The so-called 'thaw' of de-stalinization meant more a practical change, a mass release of political prisoners from prisons and labour camps and a sudden end to the idolatrous cult of Stalin and his local (national) followers, than a change in the substance of law and doctrine. Shortly after Stalin's death, on 27 March 1953, an amnesty was promulgated in the USSR, followed by another on 17 September 1955. But the first truly important step was the abolition, on 1 September 1953, of the Special Commission of the Ministry of Internal Affairs by a decree of the Presidium of the Supreme Soviet. The Special Commission was instituted on 10 July 1934, by the Central Executive Committee's decree, 'On the Creation of an All-Union People's Commissariat of Internal Affairs', and it was given authority to 'pronounce, by administrative order, sentences of banishment, exile, imprisonment in corrective labor camps up to a period of five years, and deportation beyond the borders of the U.S.S.R.'. Empowered to apply extrajudicial measures, the Commission replaced the court board and the extraordinary three-man tribunals of the GPU (State Political Administration), and its liquidation must doubtless be understood as part of the general policy of downgrading the secret police initiated soon after Stalin's death. Branded as 'an extralegal body used very frequently by Beria and his gang to deal summarily with innocent persons', its demise was hailed as of 'great significance in strengthening Socialist legality' (Ginsburgs 1957).

The depth of change varied in different countries. In Hungary, the liberalization led in 1956 to military intervention by the Soviet Union and resulting bloodshed followed by open terror. In Poland, Soviet military intervention was stopped after new Communist leaders convinced Soviet comrades of their loyalty to the cause at the expense of some deviations from the overall course of 'socialism building'. In other countries no major change seemed to happen. These national differences should be seen in the context of general détente and improvement of standards of sovereignty. The Soviet pressure on the politically independent Yugoslav Communist leaders was relaxed, while generally Soviet relations with satellites became more equal as their independence benefited from the conflict opening up between two major Communist superpowers – the Soviet Union and the People's Republic of China.

In Poland, the death of Beria and afterwards of Stalin's pupil, Bolesław Bierut, created space for the freeing of Communist Party politicians imprisoned under Stalin's rule and of masses of non-Communist political prisoners as well. Only a few security officials, notorious for institutionalizing torture, were tried by courts, but more were dismissed, and the political police was reorganized. The call for 'Socialist legality' was introduced here as well. The official manifesto of the Communist-led National Front issued on 14 December 1956 included a commitment to 'legality' [in Polish: *praworządność*], safeguarded by the independence of the courts, to the harmonization of all laws with the Constitution and control over legality of administrative actions' (Mażewski 2010: 230). The leading Marxist law professor Stanisław Ehrlich wrote the pamphlet on 'Legality' (Ehrlich 1956), in which two elements were stressed: (1) respect for legal form and (2) Socialist contents of the form, secured by its accordance with social reality. Ehrlich also advocated the strengthening of the role of Parliament (*Sejm*) in the Polish political system. One should recall that during the height of the liberalization in 1956–1957 far more radical demands were formulated by lawyers themselves and by the satellite Democratic Party of professionals and small private entrepreneurs, which had been preserved in order formally to demonstrate the political pluralism of Communist Poland, together with the United Agrarian Party and the post-fascist and pro-Communist 'socially progressive Catholic movement' (PAX). The Democrats urged the reintroduction of the presidency and the creation of a Tribunal of State, which remained in their manifesto until 1958. Some urged for re-establishment of a Constitutional Tribunal, and many supported rule by the Parliament, although the slogan of free elections soon yielded to the election of individual candidates from the one list presented jointly by the Communist Party and the satellite organizations mentioned above, which remained a distinguishing feature of the electoral system in Communist Poland until 1989. It is noteworthy that, in contrast to the Soviet Union, in the so-called people's democracies (Poland, East Germany, Czechoslovakia, Hungary, Rumania, and Bulgaria) Stalin allowed the existence of licensed satellite parties under the hegemony of local Communist parties. In 1981, at the twelfth Congress of the Democratic Party, demands for a Tribunal of State, a Constitutional Tribunal, an Ombudsman, and a second House in Parliament were presented.

In the first instance, the two important novelties instituted after the 'thaw' were: (1) The Supreme Audit Office (NIK), and (2) The Administrative Procedure Code of 14 July 1960. The Supreme Audit Office was created after national independence had been regained in 1919, and within the frame of the 1921 Constitution it became independent of the executive power and responsible to Parliament (*Sejm*) only. This autonomy was abolished during the period of most intense Stalinism, but it was revived in 1957 as part of the move to strengthen parliamentary control of the government. In 1976, when the Communists were amending the Constitution and the structure of the state they once more made sure that NIK was subject to executive control. Ultimately, they renounced that centralizing impulse after the strikes in summer 1980 and the signing of the agreements with the emerging Solidarność movement. As for the Administrative Procedure, it had been considered a major achievement as it regulated strictly the relations between the overwhelmingly powerful administration and individual clients, although for decades there was no judicial review of administrative decisions; this remained the case almost until the end of the period, when on 30 January 1980 the Supreme Administrative Court (like NIK active in interwar Poland) was re-established. The weakness of this court, however, lay in its competence, as it had to decide on the fulfilment of the procedural form and not on the merits of cases brought before it. Nonetheless, for the first time, individual citizens of a Communist state acquired access to judicial mechanisms in action against the administration in civil matters (although not including military and related matters).

8.3 1980–1981 – peaceful revolution of Solidarność

In Poland, the dissident movement, which was made possible and encouraged by the Helsinki Accords, sparked the creation of Solidarność in 1980, which was the first independent trade union recognized by Communist authorities.

There were three major points in Solidarność rhetoric and action in 1980–1981 that mark the important contribution of the mass political trade union to the European *acquis commune*, widely understood as the common experience and legacy. These points were:

1. A call for formalistic justice based upon black-letter law that is transparent to both sides, rulers and the ruled, who may read it aloud and compare readings.
2. A recognition of certain natural rights understood as preceding the officially proclaimed rights in laws.
3. A call for the creation of rules above the rulers, and that the rule of law should be understood as the external bounds to local sovereignty as exemplified by the Helsinki rules.

In contrast to this, the normative discourse of the authorities was centred on propaganda and planning. The official language in the Communist countries used the descriptive mood. An example of this was the statement 'Poland is a country of social justice' to express the assumption that the fundamental normative postulate 'Poland should be a country of social justice' had been already implemented in social practice. The key to resistance is in deciphering the 'ought' as still far from what 'is'. 'Propagandists and planners use this language to create the appearance of description. (...) The rebellious worker rejects appearances and instead says that "Poland should be a country of social justice" and puts such a demand on the list' (Kurczewski 1993: 142). Sociologically, the demands written down during the strikes of December 1970 (see Laba 1986; Kaczyńska and Chmiel 1998), which met with bloody pacification by the Communist army and police, are of the utmost interest as the intensity of contacts between workers and educated advisors was then negligible. When I conducted comparative analysis of these demands (Kurczewski 1993: 155), I realized that despite the common stereotype, as early as December 1970 strikers were demanding the establishment of free trade unions. Therefore, the project to create 'Solidarity, an Independent and Self-Governing Trade Union', was already present at that point. The first open bloody mass-scale confrontation between the ordinary people and Communist authorities took place in Poznań in June 1956. From that point on, the need to 'reform' trade unions was discussed intermittently within the ruling circles as well as amongst the workers. The forgotten outcome of the liberalization of the regime in 1956 was the introduction of 'workers' self-management' in factories, which was soon diluted to the tripartite scheme of factory organization:

that is, comprising the Communist Party organization, the trade union organization, and workers' self-management, in which scheme the latter were put under the control of the former. This needs to be explained: Each public organization, institution and enterprise was in the Communist system an area where ruling Communist Party cells had to be established from amongst the Party members. Following the Leninist model of so-called centralized democracy all cells were obliged to follow the commands from the top of the Party, and the individual members (judges, workers, professors, managers, etc.) were obliged to follow Party discipline under threat of expulsion or other Party sanctions. This gave the Party direct control of the enterprise, independently of the trade unions, whose leadership also had to be approved by the Party. The workers' self-management, being the only body directly elected by the workers (and other employees) was thus put in the minority position if it dared to enter in the conflict with managers nominated by the Party-controlled state. This model led to the development of the complex type of self-management structures in Yugoslavia. Its geopolitical heresy, however, undermined the possible exchange of ideas between Yugoslav and Polish self-management activists and theorists. Interestingly, we do not encounter the demand for workers' self-management among workers' demands of 1970–1971 and 1980. This is most likely the result of a lesson learned from the dramatic failure of the workers' self-management movement which spontaneously developed throughout Poland in 1956 and then was first pacified, and later completely marginalized, by Communist authorities, who for tactical reasons liberated it anew after introducing martial law in December 1981.

It is necessary to remind that the brutal pacification of workers' protests against price increases on 25 June 1976 and the unjust verdicts which followed sparked off the emergence of the KOR (Committee of Defence of Workers[4]) whose direct function was monitoring the trials of the protesters as to the possible breaches of the procedural rules of justice.

[4] The first public statement signed on 23 September 1976 by Jerzy Andrzejewski, Stanisław Barańczak, Ludwik Cohn, Jacek Kuroń, Edward Lipiński, Jan Józef Lipski, Antoni Macierewicz, Piotr Naimski, Antoni Pajdak, Józef Rybicki, Aniela Steinsbergowa, Adam Szczypiorski, Rev. Jan Zieja and Wojciech Ziembiński supported directly the 'right to strike, right to express freely one's opinions and right to assembly and demonstrations' pointing that workers cannot count of help of trade unions playing the 'deplorable role' (*Apel do społeczeństwa i władz PRL* 1976). Independently on 23 February 1978 r. in Katowice Kazimierz Świtoń, Roman Kściuczek, Władysław Sulecki, Ignacy Pines and Tadeusz Kicki established the first Committee of Free Trade Unions in Communist Poland.

In this way, the independent public monitoring of the administration of justice was introduced without Party-state recognition and stayed until 1980.

Political life for the eighteen months after the signing of the Gdansk, Szczecin, and Jastrzębie agreements between the government (however, always including members of the Central Committee of the Communist Party) and Inter-Enterprise Striking Committees, ending the strikes begun in the Gdansk Shipyard, was based upon those agreements serving as a kind of constitutional law redefining the relationship between authorities and citizens. This was in itself the first and most revolutionary element subverting the doctrinal dogmas of the Communist Party state, in particular the Leninist concept of the Party as political vanguard of the working people. In the name of this dogma, securing the monopoly of power in the hands of the Communist Party elite, the Kronstadt rebellion had been crushed as early as 1921,[5] and the same had happened to all attempts of popular movements and organizations to gain emancipation.

[5] The rebels' demands, from free elections through trade union and assemblies' freedom to food rationing, known as 'Pyetropavlovsk's Resolution' of 28 February 1921, sound familiar to any student of Polish and Central European history: '(1) Immediate new elections to the Soviets; the present Soviets no longer express the wishes of the workers and peasants. The new elections should be held by secret ballot, and should be preceded by free electoral propaganda for all workers and peasants before the elections. (2) Freedom of speech and of the press for workers and peasants, for the Anarchists, and for the Left Socialist parties. (3) The right of assembly, and freedom for trade union and peasant associations. (4) The organisation, at the latest on 10 March 1921, of a Conference of non-Party workers, soldiers and sailors of Petrograd, Kronstadt and the Petrograd District. (5) The liberation of all political prisoners of the Socialist parties, and of all imprisoned workers and peasants, soldiers and sailors belonging to working class and peasant organisations. (6) The election of a commission to look into the dossiers of all those detained in prisons and concentration camps. (7) The abolition of all political sections in the armed forces; no political party should have privileges for the propagation of its ideas, or receive State subsidies to this end. In place of the political section, various cultural groups should be set up, deriving resources from the State. (8) The immediate abolition of the militia detachments set up between towns and countryside. (9) The equalisation of rations for all workers, except those engaged in dangerous or unhealthy jobs. (10) The abolition of Party combat detachments in all military groups; the abolition of Party guards in factories and enterprises. If guards are required, they should be nominated, taking into account the views of the workers. (11) The granting to the peasants of freedom of action on their own soil, and of the right to own cattle, provided they look after them themselves and do not employ hired labour. (12) We request that all military units and officer trainee groups associate themselves with this resolution. (13) We demand that the Press give proper publicity to this resolution. (14) We demand the institution of mobile workers' control groups. (15) We demand that handicraft production be authorised, provided it does not utilise wage labour.'

The second element consisted in the demand that the Party was to surrender to the need to negotiate a binding compromise with the strikers, and to agree to the establishment of an independent public power: that is, the independent and self-governing trade union Solidarność.

The post-1956 Communist order had in fact also changed in comparison with the Stalinist era, partly because the Catholic Church was recognized. Despite some rumours, Stalin's plans for making the schismatic Catholic Church independent of the Holy See in Rome and dependent on the state had not materialized in Europe, unlike in the People's Republic of China. The Polish Primate had been freed from internment, where he had spent some years, limited access to dissemination of strictly religious literature was given, and freedom of recruitment for the clergy and religious orders was permitted. The public involvement of the Church was nevertheless prohibited in practice, and the sermons recorded by the political police infesting clergy with its informers remained the practice until 1989. But Primate Stefan Wyszyński remained the only alternative public authority despite periods of neglect and explosions of aggression on the part of the First Secretary of the Party, Władysław Gomułka. But the Church was independent, as it remained dependent on the Vatican and the Pope. With the Gdansk Agreements, a mass organization acting wholly on Polish soil was to be recognized as independent. In the days that followed the signing of the Gdansk Agreements Party-supervised courts were reluctant to recognize the new public body unless the leaders agreed to respect the constitutional order, placing emphasis on the paragraph in the 1976 preamble that, in face of protests from independent intellectuals, proclaimed among other points that: 'The basis of public power in Poland today lies in the alliance of the working class with the working peasantry. The foremost role in this alliance belongs to the working class as the leading class of the people' while Article 3(1) stated explicitly that: 'The leading political force of society in the building of socialism is the Polish United Workers' Party' (Constitution 152/76; see Szawlowski and Szawlowski 1980). The Gdansk Agreements were signed by government representatives under the explicit condition that strikers would recognize the 'leading role of the Communist Party', which they vehemently did, and the insertion of that constitutional clause into the union's rules was seen as a step too far, so a new compromise was achieved by adding to the registered charter of Solidarność an annex including the part of the Gdansk Agreements that included, among other points, the above-mentioned recognition of the constitutional clause. The charter in turn included paragraph 4, declaring that 'The union is independent of state administration bodies and political organizations' (Statut NSZZ Solidarność 1980).

As I attempted at that time to sum up the quickly developing reality, I arrived at the conclusion that the implementation of the Gdansk Agreements, the new trade union's Charter and the continuing leading role of the Communist Party meant that 'the new shape of public life in Poland is the process of a dynamic balance between two forces: the authorities and the union, both respectively attracting weaker organizations and social groups'. In writing this, I tried to point to the need for 'defining the best institutional environment that would preserve this dynamic balance established six months ago' (Kurczewski 2010 [1981]: 47). Up to that point, I noted, the mediatory role in this institutionalized conflict had been played by the Church, by the Communist Party, by the *Sejm*, and by the Supreme Court. However, only the Church was successful, although evidently it could not act in that manner in the public sphere forever. Thus, I argued, 'in the future public relations in Poland will be based on the law, legality meaning the "rule of law"' (Kurczewski 2010 [1981]: 50). This, however, necessitated a thoroughgoing process of reform, due to:

1. the lack of legitimacy of the law-creating bodies as the political system was imposed on Poland against the will of the majority;
2. the fact that the unification of the machinery of power led to the 'belittling of the role of judiciary, to the questioning of its independence, and the collapse of the rule of law' as 'the rulers were no longer subject to the law' (Kurczewski 2010 [1981]: 51); and
3. the magnitude of the gap between the 'law' and citizens' beliefs.

As a result of this, I raised the question whether a single-Party democracy was possible, and I argued that 'a necessary condition, that is, the emergence of the strong independent social power, is fulfilled by "Solidarity"'. In addition, however, I stated that 'the acceptance of the 'leadership role of the Communist Party in the state' does not contradict the demand that all the forces in the state, 'leadership' or not, ought to be subject to the law. Pointing to the role of the Supreme Court as a possible example, I explained that 'it is in the ideal of the "rule of law" as an impersonal power over the authorities and society that I perceive the doctrinal solution to our problems, while its practical solution is to be seen in the struggle of independent social forces with the "leading" force to shape the regulations in an appropriate way' (Kurczewski 2010 [1981]: 52). The main point in my 1981 argument is that even the acknowledged 'leadership' of the Party would be subject to judicial review. This was small doctrinal legitimation of the practical pressures placed by Solidarność on the Communist government in issues of law and justice. The special delegation of the National Committee of Solidarność headed by Zbigniew Bujak, President of the Mazowsze (that means also Warsaw) Regional Chapter of the Union, including myself and three independent lawyers,[6] began talks with Professor Jerzy Bafia, Minister of Justice, on 25 and 30 April 1981. These talks continued on 4 May, but they stalled after a few months. In the meantime the independent pressure group of experts called Seminar 'Doświadczenie i Przyszłość' (Experience and Future), organized by liberals in the Communist Party semi-officially even before the summer 1980 in order to promote reforms in the system, prepared the lengthy memorandum titled 'Law, Legality and Legal Safeguards', which was presented publicly on 5 August 1981. This included a lengthy chapter on 'Rights and civil liberties' apart from plans for territorial self-government, humanization of criminal law, independence of the judiciary, etc. (DiP 1981). On 20 August 1981, we met with Professor Sylwester Zawadzki, the new Minister of Justice, and afterwards we had to issue the communiqué that the 'Ministry of Justice still had not presented a draft of the complex reform of judiciary, *prokuratura* and law enforcement agencies' (Kurczewski 2003: 20). We were unofficially informed by our interlocutors from the Ministry of Justice that further negotiations on the issue were terminated. Ominously, the General Prosecutor's Office had not dared to respond to our initial queries. Law and justice were not in the negotiating arena, if there was any negotiating arena left at all. But there was a growing movement for political change and for the transformation of Communist law and the administration of justice into a system based on the 'rule of law'. Lawyers were becoming more courageous each day, the nation-wide forum met to discuss the necessary changes, lawyers' corporations also launched such slogans and the 'Experience and Future' semi-legal seminar criticized by the future Communist Prime Minister, Mieczysław Rakowski, considered as the foremost 'liberal' in the Party, also prepared a lengthy list of necessary reforms. The First Congress of Solidarność, which met in

[6] Zbigniew Bujak, Chair of Mazowsze Region, worker, after 1989 parliamentarian and Head of Customs; Aleksander Karczewski, Chair of Kujawy Region, chemist, forced to emigrate in 1984; Aleksander Herzog, prosecutor; Adam Strzembosz, judge, President of Supreme Court after 1989; Jacek Kurczewski and Jan Olszewski, lawyer defending in political trials, Prime Minister after 1989.

Gdansk Oliwa in the autumn of 1981, specifically addressed the subject of human rights and law reform. The First Congress of Solidarność included the following, as Thesis 23, in its final resolution:

> [The] legal system must guarantee basic civic freedoms, respect principles of equality of all citizens and all institutions of public life before the law.
>
> This requires:
>
> Implementing principles and decisions of international conventions, especially international covenants of rights, ratified by Poland. We see the safeguarding of it in the ratification by the Polish People's Republic of the Optional Protocol of the International Covenant of Civic and Political Rights, that foresees international control of implementation of the Covenant.
>
> Clear formulation in the Constitution of the principle of equality of citizens, also independent of their beliefs, political views, and organizational affiliation.
>
> Subordination of all elements of public life, including the political and social organizations, to law. It is therefore necessary to change the constitutional regulations referring to the legal status of these organizations and unequivocal clarification of their legal relationship with the Sejm [Polish House of Deputies] and other agencies of administration.
>
> Setting up of an independent Constitutional Tribunal (or the equivalent Chamber of the Supreme Court), the task of which shall be to judge the constitutionality of legal statutes and the legality of legal decisions of lower rank. The concordance of national law with the ratified conventions and International Covenants of Rights should also be reviewed.
>
> Amendment of the law on assemblies, associations and passports (law on passports should include right to choose freely residence abroad and right to return to Poland). Decisions restricting civic freedoms should be subject to the judicial control.
>
> Introducing the full transparency of public life, one of the conditions of which is the access of citizens to the documents of administration. Restrictions on transparency of public life and access to documents should be clearly set forth by the statute.
>
> (Solidarność 1981; see also Ash 1984: 216–43; Paczkowski and Byrne 2007).

Thesis 23, which contains Solidarność's clear demand for constitutional change, was well understood by Communist politicians as a threat and intrusion into the core of their political domain – from which the reluctantly legalized trade union, Solidarność, was intended to keep its distance. Though cryptic, the language of Thesis 23 expresses Solidarność's objective of curtailing the unconstitutional power of both the Communist Party and its satellite 'political and social organizations', as well as that of the ministry of interior and the 'administrative agencies' of the secret police. In addition, Solidarność made a direct demand for genuine political representation that was counter-effective in the short term, provoking the besieged Party leaders to introduce martial law, but which has since proved to be the most prophetic and consequential of the trade union's efforts.[7] In Thesis 24, Solidarność demanded that 'Courts must be independent, and prosecution subject to social control', and in Thesis 25 it demanded that no one 'should be persecuted for beliefs or forced to act against the conscience'.

The demands made by Solidarność were remarkable for their time and place; that Solidarność could exist at all was also remarkable, and it was only made possible because of indigenous conditions and the tide of rising expectations that was released by the Helsinki Agreement. On the other hand, the contents seem trivial from the 'normal modern European' perspective. No new project was offered but the project of the democratic legal state which already served as the standard for Western Europe and which became the standard in all parts of Eastern Europe that joined the European Union. This is what I call the 'Third Modernization' of this part of Europe, bringing it back to the overall European liberal-democratic standard worked out after World War II, but initiated much earlier. In any event, in the latter part of the twentieth century human rights ceased to be the pursuit of idealistic goals by a handful of volunteers, but took on normative strength, becoming a body of law with its own market, its own professional specialization, and its own institutions. One may even cynically observe that it also became a new business for lawyers and a new rhetorical device for politicians. Whatever suspicions we might justifiably entertain, however, human rights law must be taken as a serious step into a new way of thinking about individual and collective relations. Thus, it is appropriate to point to some features of human rights law that seem to be singularly important.

[7] In Thesis 22, Solidarność demanded that genuine representation should exist at the highest national level: 'We shall strive for recovery of the supreme power of the country by the Sejm, as well as to that the changed electoral law will reestablish its widely acknowledged representative character by allowing all political parties, social organizations and groups of citizens the nomination of candidates' in elections (Solidarność 1981). This demand was construed by the Communist Party as a declaration of civil war and was used by General Jaruzelski to justify the imposition of martial law on 13 December 1981 (Davies 1986: 16–25).

Table 8.1: *Individual versus social world four directions of rights*

	Public arena	Private arena
	Rights against the polity	Rights against the collectives
Positive rights to receive	IV. Social rights	I. Participation rights
Protective rights to be tolerated	III. Political rights	II. Civil rights

Theoretically, the emancipation debate might be summarized by Table 8.1.

Although fitting historically developing categories into a fourfold table may seem to stretch them too far, this exercise provides some insight into the logic of the historical and social process. Privatization as emancipation covers liberation both from state control and from control by other collectivities. The contradiction of the emancipation process is that it also allows other (private) collectivities to try to assert themselves at the expense of individual freedom. The privatization of the body is the assertion of the individual right over family and other obligations, while the privatization of property is the assertion of individual independence from the claims of others, whether as a polity or as individuals, and the privatization of *anima* reasserts the political freedoms (freedom of expression) of the individual. The civil rights of the individual include both the freedom to establish or join collectivities, such as families, associations, political parties, and other corporate entities, at the will of the contracting partners, and also the freedom to withdraw from those collectivities according to one's own choice.

Positive claims against private collectivities constitute another set of 'social rights'. Although these claims are most often linked to voluntary participation in economic enterprise, they also include such things as the right to be nurtured and cared for by parents. Social rights make sense when they are understood as the right to benefit from the community in which one belongs and in which one participates. In addition to social rights against private enterprise, one may posit participation rights against the polity. In a democracy, this nexus between the citizen and the polity is fundamental. The central problem rests in the fact that one cannot discuss the scheme without assuming some basic right that constitutes the scheme. These rights in fact should be called civic rights: the right to constitute the civil, private sphere, and the right to participate in the polity, at least in the sense of having certain rights against it. On the other hand, individual freedom consists of freedom both from the communities and from the polity. Thus, a more inclusive scheme should take into account all three of these perspectives at one time. This formulation does not exclude conflict. On the contrary, it points to the possible major areas of conflict between rights in society. Janoski has moved to greater elaboration of his theory of rights since the position he articulated in 1990 (Janoski 1998), but his later work has continued to use the basic fourfold scheme he introduced then, and, as modified, it remains a useful mechanism for investigating these issues.

Social citizenship is a broad category – a bundle of rights that belong to the citizen in a particular society and accord to each citizen a status of equality with others in the society. It is usually linked with state citizenship, but that is not necessarily the case. Civil society is composed of the citizens who enjoy the full rights of social citizenship, although a more limited definition is also possible. While the contents of citizenship are changing, the core remains stable. On the other hand, the social rights that are enshrined in abundance in Marxist constitutions have not provided those societies with an adequate basis for the development of civil society as such. The security of life and property, privacy, freedom of expression, and association seem basic, even if they may sometimes be traded for the security of dependence. If the key element of citizenship is independence (similar to the sovereignty of the community at the collective level), civil or legal rights necessarily are fundamental to such citizenship. But with its development, other rights – political, social, and participatory – are an important, though not a necessary, element. The political process in civil society involves debate on the scope of social citizenship and the rights to be included in it.

8.4 Reaction and progress under martial law

Although at least some of the Communist Polish politicians may have wanted the new liberal Socialist arrangements put in place in 1981 to remain, the pressure from the Soviet and other 'brotherly' parties was too hard to withstand, especially with the economy deteriorating and economic support from abroad more and more needed. Living conditions became harsh, there was little food, other basic items were not available, and prospects for winter 1981–1982 were grim. Some Solidarność activists were pressing for a full attack on Communist rule, while most people in the army and police were against Solidarność. On the night of 12 December 1981, General Jaruzelski ordered the armed forces to take over the ruling functions in the country and proclaimed martial law. The legality of the motion was dubious; it was first executed and later legalized not without individual dissent in the ruling institutions. Martial law was in itself an institutional innovation in the Communist world. Never before had the army taken power, and never before had such a sudden political change been given legal form. One of the basic assumptions of the Communist political doctrine was that the army was just one more executive branch of the Communist Party dictatorship, an instrument of power and not an independent actor. Jaruzelski combined army functions with functions of the Party and the state. In itself, this was not new, as Stalin himself set the precedent for this, but Jaruzelski was a professional officer in charge of the army and his new ruling body, called WRON (Military Council of National Salvation) – nicknamed *wrona* i.e. 'crow' or simply 'junta' by the opposition – was composed of generals as well. That had a positive propaganda effect in Poland as well as in the West. For most Poles, the army was the only institution of the Polish Communist state which they respected, while the unusual assumption of power by Communist generals produced a rather positive response, as the patriotic intentions of the junta also gained recognition.

8.4.1 The delayed effects of Solidarność (1982–1988)

The effect of Solidarność action at the beginning of the 1980s and subsequently is seen in the public legal structures that evolved in Poland, not only, as is commonly assumed, after 1989, but also earlier, as a result of political pressure exerted by the union. This included the establishment of the elements of the so-called Socialist legal state, predating the democratic legal state institutionalized after the Round Table talks and semi-free elections of 1989. Among the institutions of this first generation, one should mention the Law on Censorship and the introduction of substantive judicial control of administration; the setting up of the Constitutional Tribunal and the Ombudsperson; finally, the primacy of Parliament that led the regime to transition. One of the first tasks of independent lawyers (and a sociologist of law) after the signing of the Gdansk Agreement was the drafting of a regulation on preventive censorship. This exploited as much as possible point 3 of the twenty-one demands agreed in Lenin's Shipyard before the government could provide its own draft of what was agreed in the Shipyard. As expected, the reluctant government was only saying that it was preparing the draft while we succeeded in moving first by quickly drafting an independent, so-called 'social draft' that was then approved by Solidarność's authorities and negotiated with the government as a compromise solution. The achievement may now seem morally rather dubious, but, once again, it was revolutionary in those days. For the first time in a Communist country, censorship was exposed publicly and subject to legislative regulation. One of the major controversial points in the drafting was the demand that interventions by the censors should be made visible by a definite marked spot in the text (that is, by a break in the sentence with brackets and punctuation showing where the censors had intervened: (. . .)), and there should be a reference to the Articles of the Law on Censorship pointing to the fact and scope of the intervention. With the exception of the publications of the union intended only (!) for 'internal circulation' amongst its almost ten million members, which were removed at the time, first, of the 'freezing' and then the de-legalization of Solidarność from December 1981, all other provisions of the 1981 Law on Censorship remained valid. This applies too to an apparently minor detail, which was in fact of great import: the new law introduced for the first time the right of appeal regarding censorship decisions to the Supreme Administrative Court, which was then obliged to decide on the merits of the case, so taking an active role in controlling the administration. Once censorship was simply abolished in 1989, full judicial review of the administrative decisions remained and developed fully.

The Ombudsman was introduced to Poland in the final collapse of Communist rule, after the re-establishment of the Supreme Administrative Court (1980) and the Tribunal of State (1982) dealing with the impeachment procedure and constitutional accountability of the government, and the establishment of the Constitutional Tribunal in 1985.[8] Nevertheless, it should be stressed that, like all these institutions, the introduction of the Ombudsman had already been demanded in 1981 by representatives of Solidarność in negotiations over justice and law. Once introduced, the institution served as an important check on the government and administration. It was M.F. Rakowski, the Communist Prime Minister, who introduced the notion of the Socialist *Rechtsstaat*, directly referring to its Prussian proto-model. The Constitutional Tribunal was designed to interpret the existing Constitution, uphold the notion that the constitutional principles are not directly justiciable,

[8] The full history and sociological analysis of the functioning of the Ombudsman's office in the years 1987–1996 can be found in Arcimowicz (2003).

while the Supreme Administrative Court was supposed to review only the procedure and not the substance of the cases brought before it by disappointed citizenry.

Despite some criticism on the part of the Polish anti-Communist opposition over the first (1988–1989) phase of Professor Ewa Łętowska's tenure as Ombudsman, the assessment of her activities by the civil rights advocates in general was positive. In the difficult conditions of the final stage of Communist rule, almost everything was political, and certainly, she defended the individual, even if not necessarily the delegalized trade unions and parties. Thus, for instance, in case RPO 40893/89/I she invoked Article 17 of the Covenant on Civil and Political Rights (recognizing the protection of privacy) in order successfully to intervene against the customary practice of the police to order hotels to provide them with the guest lists. Article 19 of the Covenant (safeguarding the right to one's own opinions) was also successfully invoked to settle the case of a teacher who had challenged the legality of another duty, customary under the Communist regime, to attend May Day celebrations (RPO 1553/89/I). One should note in this context that not long beforehand the reference to the same Covenant was made only as lip service, either by the official advocates of the regime or in underground pronouncements of the Helsinki Committee for the Defence of Human Rights and similar bodies.

8.5 Round Table 1989 and human rights as a vehicle of transformation into liberal democracy

Let me repeat here the main points formulated earlier (Kurczewski and Sullivan 2002). First, the law of human rights is transnational; in fact, human rights law has developed so as to place restraints on the actions of individual states, with respect both to their own citizens and to others. However sceptical one may be as to the effectiveness of this control, one need only recall the reluctance of Communist countries to accept the human rights law provisions of the Helsinki Accords – a reluctance that proved wholly justified in retrospect (at least from the viewpoint of their ruling elites), as the linkage between international monitoring processes and gradual de-communization became clear. Human rights law thus became a mechanism for facilitating the development of a legal order capable of keeping pace with the globalization of social relations.

Second, the nature of human rights law is such that it imposes affirmative duties on the state and other political organizations. Instead of the old regime of self-imposed limitations on the authority of the state, as in the *Rechtsstaat*, the state is now considered under the rights regime to be one of the many organizations that is placed on a par with the society of individuals, who are entitled to its services. No longer does the state dwell entirely in the splendid isolation of absolute sovereignty.

Third, an important aspect of human rights law is its aspirational character. Human rights law mandates that each state implements minimum standards, but the notion of a minimum dialectically entails as well the notion of something more demanding than the minimum – that is, the possible expansion of rights to which people are entitled. Classical notions of morality of duties and morality of aspirations, as developed by Lon L. Fuller (1969) in relation to the law in general, seem directly relevant to human rights law.[9] There is growing support for the idea that an international – or hopefully, supranational – force should be used to bring an abusing state back in line with minimum expectations. At the same time, there is no global consensus about the degree and quality of rights that should be extended by any state beyond the minimum. In this way (as we observe when we consider the extension of civil and political rights into social and economic rights), human rights law becomes a new, developmental type of law. As a matter of fact, devices such as human rights world maps created by organizations like Amnesty International can be seen both as politically efficient instruments for encouraging politicians to foster this development and as measuring rods for ascertaining their degree of definition and development.

Fourth, and philosophically most intriguing, the development of human rights law has affirmed the possibility of a dialectical reformulation of the normative order. Although there were some original acts of violence involved – witness the Nuremberg and Tokyo trials – most of the history of human rights law was made through boring hours of debate in which participants formally agreed to subscribe to some common standards, even if the participants may have contemplated deviating from those standards in some respects in the future. This

[9] Fuller believes the 'morality of aspiration' to be best exemplified in Greek philosophy. He writes that '[i]t is the morality of the Good Life, of excellence, of the highest realization of human powers' (Fuller 1969). When a person fails to achieve that excellence and is found wanting, she is 'condemned for failure, not for being recreant to duty; for shortcoming, not for wrongdoing'. *Ibid.* On the other hand, '[w]here the morality of aspiration starts at the top of human achievement, the morality of duty starts at the bottom … [laying] down the basic rules without which an ordered society is impossible, or without which an ordered society directed towards specific goals must fail of its mark'. *Ibid.* at 5–6.

process of collective discovery and creation of standards to be applied by common agreement seems to be both the essence of the new body of law and the defining characteristic which most clearly distinguishes it from the traditional authoritarian positivism of Behemoth-like state legal systems. Despite criticism of the notion and philosophy of rights advanced by the American Left throughout the 1970s, the fall of Communism, as an historical event, strengthened overall confidence in the discourse of human rights law. Within this discourse we can also reconstruct the original, moral meaning of crime to provide legislators with the conviction necessary to take their task seriously and criminologists with a renewed sense of mission.

Fifth, and by virtue of the features we have previously identified, human rights law has achieved a paramount importance in the contemporary legal order. It now serves as a reference point to judge the validity of national legislation and judicial practice. Its real test in the future, however, may well concern its ability to control the supranational economic organizational links that may with time become more of a threat to the rights of individuals than the actions of nation states. Nonetheless, human rights law has already changed the meaning we give to the rule of law. If we speak of the *Rechtsstaat*, we fall victim to using an antiquated notion perpetuated in the usage of the European Union; the *Rechtsstaat* of today is in fact bound by the requirements of international human rights law, which serve as a pattern against which the particular laws and practices of nations are judged. If so understood, the Rules of Law and Justice are co-extensive.

The effect of Solidarność was the resurrection of rights in Polish public discourse, and that continued even through the martial law period when Communists tried to suppress the union's activity, despite allowing other bodies, such as the Catholic Church, which had previously been marginalized or repressed, an independent associational life. The experiment in pluralism without Solidarność failed, and as early as 1988 the idea of an at least partial re-establishment of Solidarność re-appeared within the ruling nucleus of the Communist Party-junta government. In 1989, the negotiations, which had started in secret, came out in public at the Round Table and led to the contract that after the 4 June elections soon resulted in the peaceful disintegration of the Communist ancient regime.

Two institutions still bear witness to the significance of human rights law – one constitutional, and the second based in civil society. The first is the Ombudsman, whose role was much more important in the democratic emancipation in Poland than in other ex-Communist countries. The Ombudsman still plays an important role today, and is politically independent and armed with the legislative initiative as well as the right to apply directly to the Constitutional Court.

A German student of its activities decided that:

> the Polish ombudsman was a factor conducive to creating a new culture of fundamental rights and law (. . .) The way the ombudsman did it, having at her disposal only the brief text of the Constitution, where civil rights have been regulated most superficially, was to adduce the general principles of law borrowed from the Western doctrine of human rights (. . .) The ombudsman addressed her pronouncement, complaints, and opinions to the courts, Constitutional Tribunal, and administrative agencies. She also widely informed the press about her actions and their rationale. By doing this, the Polish ombudsman led to the consolidation of the belief that human rights have to be known and included in the work of courts, tribunals, and the administration; and that citizens may invoke those rights when seeking protection. That human rights more and more perceptibly shape the thinking and actions of the Polish establishment today, is largely due to the efforts of the Polish ombudsman.
>
> (Jaster 1994: 113–14, 144–5, citation after Łętowska 1995: 65)

A further institution is the Helsinki Committee, which – again in contrast to most ex-Communist countries – survived the transformation and continues, with its practical apparatus the Helsinki Foundation, to serve as an independent monitoring body for citizens, and which not only states its evaluation of controversial practices that trespass human rights but is also invited by official bodies to monitor the practice of implementation of law in this respect. It is not an accident that the beginning of its history coincided with thorough underground research on, and then preparation, publication, and dissemination of a report on, abuses of human rights under martial law in Poland, which was presented in 1983 to delegates at the Madrid Review Conference in the framework of the Conference for Security and Co-operation in Europe by the Committee initiated by dissident philologist and editor Stefan Starczewski in autumn 1982 (Nowicki 2013). This time Solidarność, first suspended, then delegalized by the Communist authorities, was itself the victim of Party-state abuses. But the 1980–1981 period was sufficient for the emergence and 'normalization' of the issue of human rights, and it became a focus of attention for people who otherwise would not have met to undertake such collective investigation.

Both institutions lost importance in the second decade of democracy in Poland. This may be understood, not only as result of the maturation of the democratic legal state, but also, or – some would say – to a still greater degree because of, the development of the transnational system for the protection of rights that includes not only the Council of Europe but also the European Union and its jurisdiction.

The degree to which international human rights were used instrumentally in Poland in order to provide a legitimate basis for emancipatory action remains a matter of dispute. However, the whole history of Solidarność is an illustration of this mechanism. On the other hand, one should be cautious when extending this human rights philosophy to the legal culture of the democratic Poland as it emerged from Solidarność. Yet, the role of the Constitutional Tribunal, as in other post-Communist countries, assumed paramount importance in shaping the further process of the development of the rule of law in the country. The same applies to the complex and lengthy Constitution-making process that ended only in 1997, involving not only the Parliament, with its political composition changing from election to election, but – and this is again unusual – Solidarność, which was allowed to participate in the process from outside Parliament due to its civic constitutional draft initiative. This was the last appearance of Solidarność as an independent actor on the law-making stage, even if the trade union remains *primus inter pares* as one of the many unions participating in the collective bargaining process at local and national level and in lobbying in the national legislature. With the passage of time, however, there is a tendency to show decreasing concern for safeguards for individual rights, a fact which unexpectedly results from pressures coming from the United States and the European Union. There are many examples of comparatively lower standards in countries with established democracies that often justify the lowering of standards for reasons of administrative expediency. But this is another story to be told.

8.6 Conclusion

Communism was – in contrast to Fascism and National Socialism – a long experience of first Eastern Europe, then also in Central-Eastern and South-Eastern Europe. It began as an elitist project of forced, accelerated modernization. However, after decades of industrialization, it lost its legitimacy even in the eyes of its totalitarian managers. The state socialism went economically bankrupt and so too did its political superstructure as the promise of taking over the capitalist economic development was compromised on the global scale. Even in the 1930s the Soviet state economy was forced to adapt the structure of civil law to secure the functioning of an economy then expanding due to cheap and compulsory labour. The political enslavement of the society was relatively easy though, based on organized state terror on the one side and the enthusiasm of the rapidly advancing masses on the other. The expansion of the Communist system was made not through voluntary imitation but through the military expansion after World War II. The Soviet model had to function within the different circumstances of the Central-Eastern societies that had already experienced a democratic political system, even if weak by contemporary standards. Russia had never been a constitutional monarchy; its elected Parliament functioned only from 1906 and the republican democracy functioned only a few months before the Bolshevik takeover on 7 November 1917, while most of the newly Communist societies had a much longer experience of parliamentary politics and constitutional regime, however limited, in the former German Empire, Austro-Hungarian monarchy, Rumania, Bulgaria and Serbia and in the new Central-European States (Estonia, Latvia, Lithuania, Poland, Czechoslovakia, Hungary, and Yugoslavia) between World War I and World War II.

This applies also to the recognition of political and civil rights. The Polish case shows that with society remembering the capitalist development, each time there was more room for the attempt to catch at the basic direction of the development from bureaucratic liberal state towards democratic liberal state and recognition of individual rights as its basis was attempted. It is my thesis that the preceding experience of political activity at the borders of occupying powers undergoing modernization at different paces through the nineteenth century (Austria, Prussia, and Russia) combined with the memory of the Golden Polish-Lithuanian Commonwealth (*Res Publica*) of nobility, comprising about 10 per cent of the population and enjoying freedom of expression and of faith, immunity against royal power, and the right to elect a monarch as well as other officials, including the judiciary, formed a dense substratum through which the strong sense of individual rights function (see Kurczewski 1993, 2007). In more general terms this supports the view that *á la longue durée* the legal culture and the intuitive-living law (Podgórecki 1991; cf. Kurczewski 2013: 87), which is part of this culture as objectified in the cultural products as models of action passed from generation to generation, determined the strength of the resistance against the authoritative-totalitarian regime and the ways of abandoning it. Like other Central European countries, Poland was gradually forced to move very far towards the Leninist/Stalinist system developed in the Soviet Union but, as in the Paretian model of equilibrium, its institutions swung back again once more freedom of action was allowed for the professionals, intellectuals, workers, and other groups. The partial continuation of the 'bourgeois' legal order, in fact impossible without the legal professionals and law-educated people, helped to secure this apparent inertia or, better, resistance by inertia. The unofficial culture of rights had come back to the fore in the mid-1970s after the recognition of the human rights basket by the Soviet bloc in Helsinki and was step-by-step implemented by the dissident activists as well as by the grievant masses (Kurczewski 1993). In 1989, the country had reverted neither to the Polish parliamentary republic of 1921, nor to the semi-presidential system with an authoritarian tint that developed after 1935, but to the liberal-democratic standards of the 1980s. The official isolation of the Communist bloc was just a thin institutional cover that was easily corrected the day after the omnipotent Party lost its power over the state. But the social reasons that were behind the anti-systemic movements of the nineteenth and twentieth centuries, dissatisfaction with the redistribution of economic growth within the society, had remained unsolved. This is the paradox of 'Solidarity'. It helped to destroy Communism, proving its promises were false. It resurrected the political citizenship, but it still has not led to the full emancipation of social citizenship. Unless it is just a dream.

Bibliography

Arcimowicz, Jolanta (2003). *Rzecznik praw obywatelskich*. Warsaw: Trio.

Ash, Timothy Garton (1984). *The Polish Revolution: Solidarity, 1980–82*. New York, NY: Scribner.

Berman, Harold J. (1947). 'Commercial Contracts in Soviet Law', *California Law Review* 35(2): 191–234.

Davies, Norman (1986). *Heart of Europe: A Short History of Poland*. Oxford: Oxford University Press.

Ehrlich, Stanisław (1956). *Praworządność*. Warsaw: Sejm, Biblioteka Po Prostu 5, KiW.

Fuller, Lon L. (1969). *The Morality of Law – revised edition*. New Haven, CT: Yale University Press.

Fuszara, Małgorzata (2013). 'Law, Politics and Justice', *Societas/Communitas* 1(15), in print.

Ginsburgs, George, (1957). '"Socialist Legality" in the U.S.S.R. since the XXth Party Congress', *The American Journal of Comparative Law* 6(4): 546–59.

Janoski, Thomas (1998). *Citizenship and Civil Society: A Framework of Rights and Obligations in Liberal, Traditional, and Social Democratic Regimes.* Cambridge: Cambridge University Press.

Jaster, Georg (1994). *Der polnische Beauftragte für Bürgerrechte: eine Institution zum Schutz der Grundrechte im Übergang vom realen Sozialismus zum bürgerlichen Rechtsstaat.* Baden-Baden: Nomos.

Kaczyńska, Elzbieta and Beata Chmiel (1998). *Postulaty 1970–71 i 1980.* Warsaw: NOW.

Kurczewski, Jacek (1993). *Resurrection of Rights in Poland.* Oxford: Oxford University Press.

(2003). 'Przedmowa', in Jolanta Arcimowicz. *Rzecznik praw obywatelskich.* Warsaw: Trio, pp. 9–22.

(2007). 'Prawem i lewem. Kultura prawna społeczeństwa polskiego po komuniźmie', *Studia Socjologiczne* 2: 33–60.

(2010 [1981]). 'Solidarity, State and Law', in Jacek Kurczewski and Joanna Kurczewska. *Conflict and 'Solidarność' 1980/1981*, Warsaw: Instytut Lecha Wałęsy, pp. 47–54.

(2013). 'Adam Podgórecki's Empirical Theory of Law', *Societas/Communitas* 15: 79–95.

Kurczewski, Jacek and Barry Sullivan (2002). 'The Bill of Rights and the Emerging Democracies', *Law and Contemporary Problems* 65(2): 251–94.

Laba, Roman (1986). 'Worker Roots of Solidarity', *Problems of Communism* July: 47–67.

Łętowska, Ewa (1995). *Po co ludziom konstytucja?* Warsaw: ABC.

Mażewski, Lech (2010). 'Dyskusja na temat reform ustroju Polskiej Rzeczypospolitej Ludowej w latach 1956–1957', *Czasopismo prawno-historyczne,* LXII (1): 225–42.

McCrea, Barbara P., Jack C. Piano and George Klein (1984). *The Soviet and East European Political Dictionary.* Santa Barbara, CA: ABC-CLIO.

Nowicki (Novicky), Ivan and Łazar Łunc (L'unc) (1960 [1954]). *Kurs radzieckiego prawa cywilnego.* Warsaw: KiW.

Nowicki, Marek Antoni (2013). '"Raport madrycki" o stanie wojennym' *HR. Helsinska Fundacja Praw Człowieka. Kwartalnik o prawach człowieka* 2(6): 3–7.

Paczkowski, Andrzej and Malcolm Byrne (2007). *From Solidarity to Martial Law: The Polish Crisis of 1980–1981: A Documentary History.* Budapest: Central European University Press.

Podgórecki, Adam (1991). *A Sociologial Theory of Law.* Milan: Giuffrè

Vaksberg, Arkady (1990). *Stalin's Prosecutor: The Life of Andrei Vyshinsky.* New York, NY: Grove Weidenfeld.

Vyshinsky, Andrei Y. (ed.) (1948). *The Law of the Soviet State.* New York, NY: Macmillan.

(1952). *Zagadnienia teorii państwa i prawa A.J. Wyszyńskiego*, Biblioteka Zrzeszenia Prawników Polskich.

Ziemba, Zdzisław A. (1997). *Prawo przeciwko społeczeństwu*. Warsaw: ISNS University of Warsaw.

Documents

Apel do społeczeństwa i władz PRL (1976) available at www.kor30.sws.org.pl/kor_2doc.htm accessed 6 January 2014.

DiP (1981). Ciemniewski, Jerzy, Jan Górski, Jacek Kurczewski, Jerzy Stembrowicz and Janina Zakrzewska (eds). DiP (Doświadczenie i Przyszłość) Report '*Prawo, praworzadność i gwarancje prawne*' mimeographed, Warsaw.

Mały Rocznik Statystyczny 1990 (1990). Warsaw: GUS.

Solidarność (1981). 'Oświadczenie "SOLIDARNOŚĆ"', *I Krajowy Zjazd Delegatow NSZZ, Uchwała Programowa z Aneksem* [Program Declaration with Appendix]. Gdansk, 1981.

Statut NSZZ Solidarność 1980.

Szawlowski, Hanna and Richard Szawlowski (trans.) (1980). 'Constitution of the Polish People's Republic', in William B. Simons (ed.). *The Constitutions of the Communist World*. Aalphen an den Rijn: Sijthoff & Noordhoff.

PART III

Law and the supranational reinvention of Europe

9

International human rights and the transformation of European society: from 'Free Europe' to the Europe of human rights

MIKAEL RASK MADSEN

One of the most salient societal evolutions of the post-World War II era is the rise of international and European human rights as important institutional and normative features of modern society (Bobbio 1995; Henkin 1990; Madsen and Verschraegen 2013a). In no place has this transformation been greater, and perhaps more surprising, than in Western Europe. As Europe emerged from the ashes of World War II, the need for a new socio-political master-plan that could both impede a resurgence of the totalitarian ills of the Fascism, Nazism and Communism that had dominated the Continent's immediate past, and supply a vision for a stable democratic society was much in need (see Moravcsik 2000: 226). Fuelled by Cold War tensions, international human rights to a large extent embodied precisely that utopia for the many politicians and lawyers involved in European restructuring in the immediate years following the end of World War II (Madsen 2010). However, in the course of the subsequent decades, human rights became considerably more than simply a politico-legal master-plan of 'Free Europe'. International human rights became, in many ways, indispensable to modern complex societies in the West, that is, international human rights became fundamentally *societal*. As a result, issues as different as the protection of social benefits and the operation of the judiciary were eventually influenced by European human rights. This 'rights revolution', to use the term coined by Charles Epp in his seminal analysis of the Anglo-American post-war society (Epp 1998), has changed European society in profound ways by transforming not only the crucial interface between individuals and state but also the ways in which the human being is perceived in society at large.

In this light, it is perhaps surprising that human rights are still mainly debated in more classic liberal terms in philosophy, politics and law. Currently, there is a new, mainly historical, literature that seeks to explain the emergence of international human rights as a key dimension of post-war international law and politics.[1] The focus of this literature is the politics of human rights and how it explains the largely unforeseen success of international human rights. Other social scientists, anthropologists in particular, have debated the cultural foundations of human rights, typically arguing against modernist and often Westernized interpretations of international human rights (see for example Riles 2006; Wilson 1997). Philosophers and lawyers, debating in each of their respective camps, have focused on the moral and legal foundations of human rights. What all these studies nevertheless have in common is the fact that they only pay scant attention to the connection between human rights and society (for details see Madsen 2011c: 265–71).

Exceptions to this trend are few but important. Classical sociologists – notably Karl Marx, Max Weber and Émile Durkheim – all examined human rights. However, they all also exhibited an unease with the concept, which they found either normative and ideological or abstracted and speculative (Madsen and Verschraegen 2013a: 2). While classical sociologists strictly rejected ideas of universal human rights for these reasons, they were keen on exploring the roles of law and morality in relation to the development of particular structures of contemporary society (Madsen and Verschraegen 2013a: 2; Verschraegen 2002: 259). Instead of viewing human rights as pre-social, individual or simply liberal (serving mainly as protections against coercive state power), early sociologists went in the opposite direction and focused on ways in which questions concerning human rights were above all questions about the capacity of state and society to realize those rights as part of realizing modern society. For these reasons, many subsequent sociological studies focused to a large extent on citizenship, as this functioned as a sociologically satisfying substitute for the loaded notion of human rights (Turner 1993; Somers and Roberts 2008). Recent years have seen a renewal of genuine attempts at a sociological reading of human rights.[2] These works generally reject the idea of viewing society through the lens of an analysis of state and citizenship, and instead examine the broader transnational and societal embeddedness of human rights as a way of making intelligible the force of human rights in today's society. They thereby offer a genuinely sociological reading of human rights which is

[1] See Moyn (2010); Morsink (1999); Lauren (2003); Hoffmann (2011).

[2] See, for example, Turner (2006); Joas (2013); Madsen (2010); Gideon *et al.* (2001); Verschraegen (2002); Sjoberg *et al.* (2001).

significantly different from what is found in the existing literature of law, political science and history.

While this chapter is informed by this scholarship, my objective here is not to debate the possible virtues of a sociology of human rights when compared to other approaches.[3] I take as my starting-point the presumption that human rights are deeply embedded in the fabric of society for the broad reasons stated above (see also further below). Moreover, my assertion is that the force of human rights in contemporary Europe is the product both of long-term processes of European societal transformation and of more specific legal, political and cultural events that have influenced the specific characteristics of what we have come to understand as human rights. My focus is on contemporary society, and particularly the effect of the Europeanization of human rights since the end of World War II: that is, this chapter discusses how European human rights went from being the strategic instrument of 'Free Europe' to becoming deeply embedded in contemporary European society.

Theoretically, this chapter is broadly anchored in the sociology of Pierre Bourdieu (1980) and particularly the sociology of law and the internationalization of law which can be derived from Bourdieu's work.[4] The analysis is thus centred on the emergence and transformation of what can be termed the *field of human rights*: a symbolic space in which human rights are being contested by a host of agents seeking to further their respective notions of human rights. This field is by no means autonomous or closed (Madsen 2011c: 263). On the contrary, it has broad homologies with other social fields – in particular it imports conflicts between liberalism and socialism from the field of politics, conflicts regarding the place of the individual in the operation of modern law from the legal field, as well as other conflicts from other social fields. Yet, it is also a specific microcosm of these many conflicts that are articulated and, importantly, transformed through human rights, and over time it has resonance for both law and politics, with widespread consequences not only for these specific social fields but also society more generally. This chapter proceeds in the following way.[5] I first provide a brief analysis of how human rights

[3] See instead Madsen and Verschraegen (2013b); Somers and Roberts (2008); Turner (1993); Madsen (2011c).

[4] Bourdieu (1987); Dezalay and Madsen (2009; 2012).

[5] This chapter builds on a series of previous publications on a range of issues related to the rise of post-1945 international human rights but framed in a different more historical sociological fashion for this analysis. When relating to findings from previous

are historically embedded in society through an outline of key sociological works on human rights. In the subsequent two sections, I turn to the international and European reinvention of human rights in the post-war period as a new form of law and politics and how it was gradually institutionalized and juridified in Europe. Following this, I examine how human rights – via the international domain – gradually move beyond the horizon of post-1945 politics and begin to link with key societal developments. In a fifth section, I analyse the relative force of human rights in contemporary European society.

9.1 The historical-societal embeddedness of human rights

Human rights were by no means invented following World War II, and the place of human rights in the emergence of modern society and the modern state is obviously relevant for understanding how human rights subsequently – through its international reinvention – came to influence the structure of contemporary European society. Sociologies of human rights generally take a starting-point in the analysis of the emergence of modern society and its associated problems of specialization, declining trust, technicalization, market-making etc., which can be derived from classical sociology (in particular Weber 1980 [1921]; Durkheim 1893). Basically, with the advent of modernity, the centralization of power by the (sovereign, bureaucratic) state and the growing penetration of the (capitalist) market intruded upon the social order of more local 'traditional' communities. These new forces disrupted and even radically transformed traditional systems of mutual support and obligation (for example the support of the extended family) and thereby left large numbers of separate families and individuals to face a growing range of unbuffered economic and political threats to their interests and dignity. At the same time, the erosion of traditional moral orders, growing social and geographical mobility, mass literacy, and the emergence of mass education created more and new options for individuals. Generally, the idea and concept of individual and, in theory, inalienable rights emerge at this point as a reaction to these new threats and possibilities. Individual basic rights provide the conceptual and institutional tools to help protect individuals from the increasingly invasive powers of state, market, etc. and to guarantee them free and equal inclusion in new social institutions and systems, which provide them

publications, I refer to these. This research was funded by the Danish National Research Foundation, Grant no. DNRF105.

with the means – both material and symbolic (health, education, work, minimum income, democratic participation, etc.) – for the construction of their life-projects.[6]

Gert Verschraegen has probably provided the most direct attempt at a theoretical sociological understanding of how human rights and modern society are intrinsically linked (Verschraegen 2002). Drawing on Niklas Luhmann's early work on basic rights (Luhmann 1974), Verschraegen advances the idea that the centrality of human rights in modern society is largely a result of the overarching social process of functional differentiation. This process is potentially disruptive and even destructive to society as also emphasized by early sociologists (Weber 1980 [1921]; Durkheim 1893). Yet, human rights, according to Verschraegen, provide the means for both ensuring the functional differentiation of society's subsystems and of maintaining stability and the protection of individuals. While rejecting any attempt at a normative or philosophical grounding of human rights, Verschraegen convincingly shows how modern human rights essentially become a 'social institution with a specific function', and a function fundamental not only to upholding but also generating modern society (Verschraegen 2002: 262). In a subsequent work, using a more Weberian as well as more empirical perspective, Verschraegen and Madsen have argued that human rights in contemporary complex societies therefore assume a key role in the reproduction of practically all main societal institutions, including citizenship, civil society, education, health, the family, the police and even the market (Madsen and Verschraegen 2013a: 7). In other words, human rights become not only increasingly legally and politically pervasive in contemporary complex societies but also fundamental institutions both for and of society. We return to this point below.

Also using a Luhmannian starting-point, Chris Thornhill analyses the sociology of constitutions as a means for explaining how the modern state and modern rights emerge (Thornhill 2011). Thornhill's analysis is pertinent here as he very clearly demonstrates how modern state power necessitates the invention of public law and human rights. In his analysis, this is essentially a process of transferring power from the private to the public sphere, the culmination of which is the creation of the modern constitutional state. Using a historical-sociological approach, he shows how early constitutional arrangements, following the American and French Revolutions, fell short of realizing this potential. This is due

[6] This paragraph is derived from a previous publication. For the full argument please see Madsen and Verschraegen (2013b: 7–8).

to the fact that power in part remains with the pre-revolutionary political classes (aristocrats, merchant elites, etc.) and that the modern state therefore does not effectively establish itself until into the twentieth century (see also Thornhill, Chapter 2 in this book). Rights – and human rights in particular – are crucial instruments in this process of making power increasingly public and abstract (Thornhill 2013: 39–42). Early constitutional democracies seem to use rights mainly to limit state power but they do so in a process in which the state increases its abstract public power over the citizens (compare Bourdieu 2012: 521–4). State power is thus always limited yet in a process of expansion. It is exactly in this conjunction that human rights become fundamental instruments for ordering society.

A very different sociological reading of how rights become embedded in the making of modern society is found in Hans Joas' recent work on the genealogy of human rights (Joas 2013). His starting-point is markedly different than the more structural analyses found in Verschraegen, Thornhill and Madsen. Instead of explaining the structural transformation of society as a background to human rights, Joas instead argues that the centrality of the human person in modern society is the product of a significant cultural shift that occurred in the course of the nineteenth century. According to Joas, this process of increasing and centralizing the value of the human leads effectively to a new sacredness of the person which is closely tied up to the emergence of the idea of human rights. Albeit the religious connotations, the notion is non-religious: Joas examines instead a series of key socio-political and legal developments spurring this process, including the development of modern punishment, the abolition of slavery and the codification of human rights in the Universal Declaration of Human Rights (UDHR). Moreover, he examines the intellectual backgrounds to this process. The key point made by Joas, drawing on Weber, Durkheim and Parsons, is that it is this process which makes human rights thinkable in the first place. Of course, making human rights possible and thinkable is not the same as making human rights effective. Joas' analysis does not directly deal with this problem but is instead centred on the introduction of a particular value which gains a very particular importance in modern society and its organization, at least at the discursive level.

Another sociologist, Bryan Turner, goes in a more normative direction in his work on human rights and vulnerability (Turner 2006). Based in the tradition of human rights and citizenship, yet also seeking to understand the global codification of human rights, Turner follows up on one of Joas' earlier analyses, in which he claims that the conflict between national sovereignty and universal human rights has become perhaps the most central value conflict of contemporary society (Joas 2003: 23). But whereas Joas seeks what he terms an affirmative genealogy of human rights – as opposed to 'a destructive history of origins' in a Nietzschean sense (Joas 2013: 3) – Turner goes one step further and seeks to realize the potential of human rights against the background of an analysis of human vulnerability, mass violence and the very institutions assumed to protect human beings via human rights. The starting-point of his analysis is that the human body is frail and it needs collective arrangements for its protection. But because of the 'institutional precariousness' of the institutions protecting human rights in contemporary society (see Beck *et al.* 1994), Turner's analysis becomes a more normative endeavour that seeks to develop frameworks for the realization of human rights and not a historically founded analysis of human rights and society.

What these very different sociological interpretations have in common is the centrality and salience they attach to human rights in modern society and its construction. They also all, directly or indirectly, relate to a now relatively established sociological narrative, which observes the emergence of modern society as a process of restructuring and reordering as outlined above. The cited studies of course vary in the extent to which they place emphasis, respectively, on agency, on institutions, or on social structure for explaining the place of human rights. Yet, they all concur in the observation that it is because of the emergence of modern society that human rights start to assume concrete form and symbolic power: that is, human rights are essentially societal. In some of these accounts, fundamental rights become a form of institutional device to uphold protection not only for the individual, but also for the social order of modern societies (Verschraegen, Thornhill and Madsen). In other accounts, the construction (Joas) or affirmation (Turner) of the underlying notion of the human person is the focal point of analysis. In what follows, I emphasize the structural and institutional level using an overarching Bourdieusian framework which focuses on the locations in which human rights are practised. However, using this framework I also consider how the category itself is being transformed through these broader processes.

9.2 The re-birth of human rights as international norms

In relation to these preliminary sociological observations on the historical-societal embeddedness of human rights, I raise basic questions in the subsequent sections: What happened to human rights following their internationalization in the aftermath of World War II? Did human rights simply emerge, once again, as responses to new threats and possibilities as with the advent of modernity – or was there something uniquely new about post-1945 human rights? In other words, this basic question raises a larger question concerning the role of more fundamental sociological processes of change underlying 'the re-birth' of human rights in the post-war era: that is, it raises the question of how post-1945 international human rights were the result both of long-term processes of European societal transformation and of more specific legal, political and cultural events. There is, of course, no doubt that human rights were under enormous pressure during World War II because of both authoritarian politics and security politics. However, the more structural role of human rights as an institutional device for ordering and upholding modern society was not as such suspended by the war (Madsen 2010). Moreover, the new international – and European – dimension of human rights cannot simply be viewed as an isolated international diplomatic phenomenon because of the pre-existing historical-societal embeddedness of human rights. What I will argue in the following is that although human rights came to influence international affairs, perhaps their most significant impact in the European context was manifest in the ways in which they also contributed to a transformation of national society. They were initially ingrained in some of the most important social restructuring of the post-war period, especially those social processes triggered by both the Cold War and decolonization. Subsequently, human rights also increasingly became more directly a part of the restructuring of national society in a complex transnational process of constructing a contemporary Europe of human rights. While the latter is the subject of a subsequent section, in this section I will first analyse the reinvention of human rights in the post-war era and particularly as it pertains to Europe. To highlight both the geopolitical and national societal dimension of this transformation, I generally emphasize the role of France and the United Kingdom (UK).

The standard narrative of the post-war human rights revolution normally begins with the 1948 UDHR and its negotiation and adoption. Those who take this as a starting-point, however, tend to overlook the fact that the internationalization and Europeanization of human rights as a norm and institution-building process after World War II was first and foremost the product of competitive international projections of national traditions in areas ranging from established civil and political rights to novel rights deriving from the welfare state projects common to much of Europe as well as elsewhere during the period. Thus, the actual starting-point for the emergence of European human rights in many ways lies in conditions that pre-existed the internationalization of human rights. A striking illustration of this crucial correlation is the role played by France and the UK in both the internationalization and the Europeanization of human rights. Key players in both regards, they generally projected two relatively different visions and traditions of human rights onto the international and European realms, both presenting themselves as the pioneers of human rights.

In very simple terms, the main difference between France and the UK with regard to human rights is found in their socio-political and legal conditions in which rights were produced, and in the resulting place of human rights between law and politics. In France, human rights had long played an important political role, shaped by the almost mythological status of the French Revolution and the subsequent Dreyfus Affair and its resulting social movements for human rights, notably the pioneering *Ligue des droits de l'Homme* (Agrikoliansky 2002). In the immediate post-1945 period, human rights remained politically important but hardly took centre-stage in the many attempts to resurrect French society and grandeur after the Vichy collaboration and the general humiliation resulting from the German occupation. In fact, human rights had a mainly declaratory role in the preamble of the Fourth Republic's Constitution (1946) in the form of a list of great prior achievements in the area and a proclamation of the new social and economic rights (Lochak 2002: 28). Comparatively, in the UK human rights and particularly civil rights were the product of a more general societal development which had largely been delegated to the 'closed circuit' of the legal system dominated by an Oxbridge network of judges in collaboration with Parliament. This constellation had over a long period produced and found expression in a complex set of documents, principles and unwritten 'conventions', including Magna Carta (1215), the Bill of Rights (1689) and the Habeas Corpus Acts (1640 and 1679), which together formed the basis for the protection of civil rights and liberties in the UK. While human rights had relatively higher legal status in the UK, they were less politically central to public discourse on the transformation of the post-war state.

These relative differences in conception and practices of human rights first played out at the level of the United Nations (UN), where the clash between proposals for an international *declaration of human rights* or an international *bill of rights* were tabled by France and the UK respectively (Madsen 2004a: 60–1). The vision for an international declaration, eventually termed the Universal Declaration, was the preferred option for a number of reasons at the UN (for details, see Simpson 2004: 391, 461;

Morsink 1999). However, France was quick to project this as a diplomatic victory, as well as evidence of its key place as *le pays des droits de l'Homme*, and even as an example of its universal duty in terms of *la mission civilisatrice* (Pateyron 1998; Winter and Prost 2013). In practice, political elites in both societies were playing a double game as they were keen to make sure that the post-war internationalization of human rights was not to determine their post-war colonial restructuring. In other words, in the scheme of sociological analysis suggested above, human rights had a central position for these late-imperial European powers on two very different levels. This was the case domestically because they acted as foundational societal institutions. This was the case internationally because they acted as mainly rhetorical devices – to justify the highly flexible *mission civilisatrice* of the French Empire and the more pragmatic notion of markets and constrained liberty of the British Empire. In a more sociological sense, both states agreed that the sacred individual was European – whether it could be transplanted abroad was more of an open question and one on which the two imperial models seemingly differed. However, regardless of these differences, as well as the pressure resulting from the anti-colonial lobby of the United States (US) and the Soviet Union, there was French and British consensus that these two levels were not to be confounded by international human rights measures. It was thus to a large extent mission accomplished at the UN when it was decided that the UN's prime objective was peace – human rights were somewhat secondary. The simultaneous eruption of Cold War politics right at the heart of the UN Human Rights Commission acted only further to ensure that it would take some thirty years before the UDHR was turned into something resembling a binding document.

European human rights were a different matter. While the notion of international human rights as an ordering device for the future of international society was very far from being accomplished at the UN, partly because of the double game of the European imperial powers and partly because of the oppositional Cold War politics of the new superpowers in the area, European human rights from their initial stage were tied up with a broader project: European integration. Among the many Europeanists who assembled at the decisive Congress for Europe in The Hague in 1948 the distinction between Europe of the market and Europe of human rights was not overly important. In 1949, when negotiations regarding the European Convention on Human Rights (ECHR) began to gain momentum, many of the key players still envisaged that European human rights, in the words of Pierre-Henri Teitgen, one of the key negotiators, would form part of a broader 'generalisation of social democracy' (as cited in Merrills and Robertson 2001: 8). Moreover, the Convention was viewed by its main proponents as the Court not only for protecting human rights but also for integrating Europe more generally. Above all, the ECHR, as sustained by the European Court of Human Rights (ECtHR), was meant to produce a common conscience for all of (Western) Europe (Bates 2010: 44–76). Notwithstanding these efforts, European integration was to be divided between market integration under the Coal and Steel Community (later the European Economic Community (EEC)) and human rights integration under the Council of Europe. Importantly, this was not a *fait accompli* when the ECHR was drafted in the late 1940s. In the early 1950s, the idea of a common European Constitution was indeed tabled with the goal of unifying the field of European law (Cohen 2007; Cohen and Madsen 2007; De Burca 2011). What was initially a French-sponsored project, however, eventually failed because French ratification became increasingly difficult as the Gaullists denounced it as surrendering sovereignty to West Germany. Other factors also acted greatly to obstruct the project, in particular a change in priority of US interests caused by the outbreak of the Korean War and, importantly, the death of Stalin, which made the project somewhat less urgent in the larger scheme of Cold War politics. Effectively, Europe was institutionally split between human rights and the market, and the two different paths of European integration would not start to converge until the 1990s (Madsen 2013). For these reasons, the ECHR was to be the backdrop of a distinct and quite separate process of Europeanization.

9.3 The complex diplomacy of institutionalizing European human rights

As argued elsewhere, regardless of its obvious place in the process of engagement with the immediate past, the European Convention had been drafted primarily as a Cold War instrument (see for example Madsen 2007). While the 1948 UDHR had been presented as a utopia for all mankind, a vision enjoying a brief momentum in the aftermath of Allied victory among lawyers, intellectuals and some statesmen, such rhetoric was supplanted by an unequivocally Westernized vocabulary of 'liberty and democracy' in the Treaties establishing the Council of Europe and its associated human rights system. The founding fathers, from the aforementioned Pierre-Henri Teitgen to Sir Maxwell Fyfe of the UK, a former prosecutor at the Nuremberg trials, had, in many ways, anticipated the crucial shift from the Utopia to the Cold War of human rights that occurred during the late 1940s. The European Convention obviously perpetuated the idea – developed first by the UN – that human rights could be secured through international law. That said, the rapid drafting of the ECHR reflected above all a growing fear of, on the one hand, the rising power of the national Communist parties, and, on the other, Soviet imperial expansionism into Western Europe.

A closer consideration of the drafting of the ECHR suggests that the negotiating parties were indeed not afraid of using the high prose of democracy and liberty. Yet, the document lacked a dimension of legal obligation on the member states. It was virtually a 'Convention à la carte' (Madsen 2011a); that is to say, the most central clauses, particularly those concerning the jurisdiction of the Court and individual petition, were in fact made optional in the original Convention. Thus, signing the document did not necessarily imply a surrender of sovereignty to an uncertain supranational legal body. On the contrary, it involved subscribing to a political agenda of growing importance: that of ensuring a free and democratic Europe in an increasingly hostile geopolitical environment. For these reasons, the initial process of turning the ECHR into a real legal and operative system revolved around the need to convince the member states of the Council of Europe to actually accept the jurisdiction of the Court and the right to individual petition. On the legal-institutional level, this resulted in the development of a conspicuous 'legal diplomacy' at the Court, a situation in which the actual jurisprudential developments had to be carefully balanced with diplomatic considerations vis-à-vis the member states in order to satisfy the twin objectives of, on the one hand, ensuring further institutional support, and, on the other hand, maintaining at least formally the institution's role as the guardian of human rights in Europe (Madsen 2011b).

Formally, for the Convention to be effective, ten member states had to ratify it. While this was achieved by 1952 with its ratification by Britain, the Federal Republic of Germany and a series of smaller states, the real challenge consisted in the need to make individual petition and the Court operational. The clause on individual petition stipulated that six states had to accept before it was made effective. This was achieved by 1955, which meant that the procedure was made effective in the Federal Republic of Germany and a number of smaller countries (Sweden, Ireland, Denmark, Iceland and Belgium). However, for the Court to start operating, eight countries had to accept, which did not happen until 1958, by which time seven smaller states (Ireland, Denmark, the Netherlands, Belgium,

Luxembourg, Austria and Iceland) and the Federal Republic of Germany had accepted its jurisdiction. What is striking is the absence of the three major European powers of France, the UK and Italy. As concerns France and the UK, their absence was by and large due to problems encountered in their colonies, where a growing number of activists were seeking self-determination, in part because of human rights abuses perpetrated by French and British colonial administrators. However, the fact that probably the two most important European states were absent in Strasbourg only put further pressure on the nascent Strasbourg institutions. As a result, both the Commission and the Court were forced to make it their main objective to convince precisely these two states of both the relevance and reasonableness of their workings and jurisprudence and, thus, that they should impose on themselves a set of checks-and-balances of a very real nature.

The fact that the UK, unlike, for example, France, had ratified the Convention meant that the European system as reflected in the European Commission on Human Rights was authorized to receive inter-state complaints against the UK, notwithstanding that the UK had not accepted the clauses on individual petition and the jurisdiction of the Court. It was, however, deemed very unlikely in the British Foreign Office that this backdoor entrance to the European system would pose a problem. This would turn out to be completely wrong. In May 1956, Greece chose precisely to launch an inter-state complaint against the UK for its neglect of human rights in Cyprus, which at the time was a colonial holding of the UK. The fact that Cyprus was under the jurisdiction of the European Convention was due to a symbolic decision made in the 1950s to extend the reach of the Convention to most of the British Empire. The Foreign Office had basically played a double game of conveying a message to the colonies that they would benefit from the protection offered by the Convention, yet assuming that they could never use these options due to limited access to the Strasbourg institutions. As noted by A.W.B. Simpson, it was probably not an accident that the notification of the extension took place the exact same day that the Central African Federation came into force (Simpson 2004: 838–9). Put differently, it was the increasingly collision-prone high politics of decolonization and maintaining imperial grandeur that prompted the decision.

Clearly, bringing colonial conflicts to the heart of Strasbourg was not welcomed – particularly because this was the very first case before the European human rights system. The distinguished international lawyer

Henri Rolin, counsel for the prosecution in *Greece v. United Kingdom* appl. no. 176/56 (1956 and 1958), made this very clear in his opening speech before the European Commission: 'I am the first to admit the paradox – and personally I regret it – that by a chance of fate the first government to be brought to the bar by another government is the UK, which governs a country which surely, more than any other in Europe, has always shown concern for human rights' (Simpson 2004: 322). The point was hard to miss: European human rights were the inalienable rights of the free and civilized world and this should not be confused with some temporary problems with colonial insurrections. The outcome of this case was, if anything, telling of the system. As it became more and more evident during the proceedings that the UK had indeed breached the Convention, the matter was eventually solved by recourse to diplomacy. The case was closed with a friendly settlement – the 1959 Zurich and London agreements settlement on Cyprus – which also meant the end of the British Empire in Cyprus.

From the point of view of the European human rights system, this was probably a convenient solution as it evaded the need to pronounce violations, but it was also able to convey the message that it was diplomatically sound. Nonetheless, shortly afterwards, the diplomatic skills of the Strasbourg institutions were once again tested as yet another key case, the *Lawless* case (*Lawless v. Ireland*, appl. no. 332/57 (1960)), was submitted to the Court as its very first case. This case concerned the use of detention without trial in Ireland as a response to IRA insurgency. The European Commission, as well as the European Court, both found that this was not in compliance with Article 5 of the Convention. Yet, the case did not ultimately lead to a judgment against the Irish government, as the Court interpreted Article 15 with respect to emergency situations in such a way that the Irish government was entitled to apply these measures since the 'life of the nation' was threatened. Once again the European system arrived at a conclusion which placated the member states and underlined that it was receptive to the complexities of interior politics. And it was exactly against a background of common perceptions of sound judgment – or perhaps more accurately of a well-developed sense of 'legal diplomacy' (Madsen 2011a: 78–9) – that the UK, in 1966, chose to accept the optional clauses regarding individual petition and the jurisdiction of the Court. In the early 1970s, the UK's decision to pursue full integration in the European Union (EU) was followed by a number of other countries, although this only occurred after some very significant geopolitical transformations with regard to human rights.

9.4 Beyond post-war global restructuring: from empire to European integration

The initial phase of European human rights addressed above is probably best described as a prolonged negotiation regarding the ECHR and its institutional organization. It is also an important historical backdrop for understanding the subsequent developments in the jurisprudence of the ECtHR, in which the Court in a series of landmark decisions set in motion a very significant change, both in law and in the discourse on human rights. Not only did the European Court in 1978, in sharp contrast to the above-mentioned *Lawless* case, come to the conclusion that the emergency interrogation measures used in Northern Ireland by the British security forces could not be justified by evoking emergency arguments (*Ireland v. the United Kingdom*, appl. no. 5310/71 (1978)), it also accorded to the European Convention the character of '[...] a living instrument ... [which] must be interpreted in the light of present-day conditions ... standards in the ... members states' (para. 31, *Tyrer v. the United Kingdom*, appl. no. 5856/72 (1978)). To make things absolutely clear, a year later in 1979, the Court established in the *Airey* case (*Airey v. Ireland*, appl. No. 6289/73 (1979)) that '[t]he Convention is intended to guarantee not rights that are theoretical or illusory but rights that are practical and effective' (para. 24). This suddenly more progressive or, according to some, aggressive doctrine can obviously not be explained simply as the fruit of the gradual legitimization of the Court in the eyes of the member states described above; nor can it be explained as the outcome of new judges being appointed to the bench.[7] While these factors are necessary conditions for the change, the transformation – or metamorphosis – of the Court at this time is in some ways linked most particularly to important changes in the geopolitical context of human rights in Europe and in the very project of European integration.

The Court generally benefited from the fact that the Cold War of human rights was ebbing out and that the major European powers had succumbed to the idea of 'Empire lost' – France even ratified the Convention in 1974. Due to these two closely related processes, European imperial societies were no longer the object of criticism *par excellence* of human rights activists. In Western Europe, throughout the 1970s, most human rights activism was directed against non-democratic regimes outside the

[7] Particularly as the judges during the 1970s sociologically greatly resembled the judges of the 1960s. See Madsen (2011b: 55–6).

jurisdiction of European human rights: the Greek Colonels, Franco's Spain and Portugal under Salazar.[8] In fact, in the optic of 1970s human rights activism, the real perpetrators of human rights abuses were to a large extent geographically found outside Western Europe: in Latin America, South Africa and Eastern Europe. During the same period, Western Europe sought alongside the US to introduce human rights more expressly in foreign policies, most famously in the Helsinki Final Act of 1975, which triggered and eventually legitimized a series of Watch groups, including Human Rights Watch and Charter 77, as well as other Helsinki Watch committees. Intra-European developments further added to this development. If Greece, Portugal and Spain had been the trouble spots of Western Europe in the first part of the 1970s, the situation was being reversed by the second part of the decade. In 1974, 1976 and 1977 respectively, they became integrated into the ECHR protection system, and, as already suggested, the initially reluctant Western European member states had all at this point changed tack on the issue of institutional support to the ECtHR, thereby making it – at last – fully operational.

These important developments in the ECtHR were also part of a distinct process of Europeanization, both in terms of integrating European society and of building European law. By the mid-1970s, it is striking that all member states of the EEC were now also full members of the ECHR system.[9] In fact, the change in commitment to the ECtHR happened to take place at the precise moment the EEC undertook its first enlargement, when Denmark, Ireland, and the UK entered the Community.[10] In the early 1970s, however, the most significant EEC-related development with respect to human rights was taking place under the auspices of the European Court of Justice (ECJ). After an initial battle in the mid-1960s, over the supremacy and direct effect of EC law (the seminal rulings in *van Gend en Loos* and *Costa v. ENEL*[11]), the ECJ began developing EC law in terms of the fundamental rights they derived from a set of unwritten general principles of Community law in the 1970s. It would take the ECJ about a decade to carefully craft a doctrine of fundamental rights. In the initial cases *Stauder*[12] and *Internationale*

[8] Greece had withdrawn from the European system from 1970 to 1975, whilst Portugal and Spain only joined the system in 1977 and 1978, respectively.

[9] With the exception of France, which only accepted individual petition in 1981.

[10] Norway did not join the EEC at this occasion following a 'no vote' at a referendum. Greece joined in 1981, while Spain and Portugal joined in 1986.

[11] 26/62 *van Gend en Loos* (1963) ECR 1 and 28/62–30/62 *Costa* (1954–64) ECR 395.

[12] 29/69 *Stauder* (1969).

Handelsgesellschaft,[13] the ECJ underlined the importance of fundamental rights to the EC legal order. And, in the strikingly well-timed *Nold* decision of 1974,[14] it went a step further. While predating the long awaited *Solange I*[15] decision of the German *Bundesverfassungsgericht* by some two weeks, yet eagerly awaiting French ratification of the ECHR, eleven days later it pronounced that it intended to take inspiration particularly from the ECHR and not only the constitutional rights of the member states (Scheeck 2005). Moreover, in 1975 the ECJ explicitly cited individual articles of the ECHR for the first time in the *Rutili* case[16] and again in 1979 in the *Hauer* case.[17]

What can be observed in this process is a general orientation towards human rights in the two European courts, so that they began to take human rights seriously as real legal entitlements and thus law. But it went further than that. The ECJ did not only add to the overall human rights momentum of the time; its judgments on fundamental rights and freedoms also underlined another crucial development of great importance for the ECtHR, namely that human rights had regard, not only to gross violations, but also to the more mundane entitlements of ordinary citizens under European law. In a similar way, the ECtHR cases of *Tyrer* and *Airey* concerning issues related to corporal punishment and the access to divorce also raised the question of human rights in respect to the evolving societal fabric of Europe: that is to say, dynamic interpretation was not simply teleological interpretation with respect to the *telos* of the ECHR, but in respect to European society and its evolution more generally. While the ECJ could rely on the notion of an 'ever closer Union', the ECtHR distilled its notion of 'present-day conditions' to legitimize progressive European law. In both cases, the courts not only found a common driving force in a general notion of European integration, they also took advantage of the geopolitical transformations of international human rights in the context of détente to improve their position. In so doing, they managed to put themselves on par with general social developments in Europe – and in some cases probably to be ahead of general societal evolution.

These developments marked European human rights to a considerable degree in the following decades. The ECtHR, building on its landmark

[13] 11/70 *Internationale Handelsgesellschaft v. Einfuhr- und Vorratsstelle für Getreide und Futtermittel case* (1970).

[14] 4/73 *Nold* (1974).

[15] BVerfGE 37, 271 2 BvL 52/71 *Solange I-Beschluß*.

[16] 36/75 *Rutili* (1975).

[17] 44/79 *Hauer* (1979).

decisions of the late 1970s, further consolidated its position and basically became the *de facto* supreme court of human rights in Europe. Although the decisions of the 1980s and early 1990s may not have changed human rights law as radically as the decisions of the late 1970s, the ECtHR nevertheless expanded significantly both in reach and productivity during this period. In the 1970s, the ECtHR had only judged a few cases each year but already by the mid-1980s the number was steadily climbing and by the early 1990s it had reached a rate of some eighty cases per year (Greer 2006). The institutional and legal organization changed in equal fashion, first with Protocols 6–10 in the period 1983–1992, and then most drastically with the complete overhaul of the system as a result of Protocol 11 (Harmsen 2001, 2011). The latter established a new and permanent ECtHR, which by 2000 issued close to 900 judgments a year, concerning an ever larger number of member states. And these numbers would only climb even further as the impact of Eastern European enlargement made a clear mark on the case-load (Christoffersen and Madsen 2013). Although the parallel evolution of the ECJ is perhaps not quite as striking, at least numerically, the ECJ also expanded both legally and institutionally during the same period.[18] The ECJ effectively developed a catalogue of EC/EU rights which gradually played an increasingly central role, not only in the increasingly dense legal order of the EU, but also in the very idea of European citizenship. In fact, by the late 1990s, as a result of the complex reorganization of Europe following the upheavals in Eastern Europe and its spill-overs on Western Europe, the EU sought to affirm itself as an organization founded in the respect for human rights and the rule of law (Madsen 2013: 155–8; Manners 2002). While the Europe of human rights was thus effectively implemented at the inter- and supranational level in both the EU and the Council of Europe by the late 1990s, the real penetration of human rights in Europe came through the deep embeddedness of these institutional revolutions in European society. This process of national – indeed transnational – integration is the subject of the following section.

9.5 The force of human rights in post-Cold War European society

This analysis has thus far highlighted how human rights were gradually crafted at the international level as part of the transformation of

[18] On the institutional level, the ECJ was most notably reformed and divided into a two-level jurisdiction with the introduction of the Court of First Instance (now General Court) in the late 1980s.

European society and its external and internal interfaces. In this regard the institutionalization of the ECtHR provides a tangible empirical object, which has emblematic importance for explaining in depth how these processes unfolded. As argued, it was initially marked by the politics of the Cold War and decolonization, which effectively turned the Court into a complex forum for negotiating the broader transformation of European society from its imperial past into a unified legal and political order. Moreover, the subsequent breakthrough of the ECtHR in the late 1970s was equally emblematic of new socio-legal and political transformations within European society and its place in the world. The combined effects of the significant socio-cultural changes of European societies in the 1970s and the geopolitical reorientation of the larger international cause of human rights once again changed the structural position of the ECtHR, so that it became the bridgehead for European integration as a progressive endeavour under law. During the periods addressed above, however, the actual field of human rights in terms of agency was surprisingly limited and involved only a relatively small number of agents who early on invested in the subject-area. In the bigger picture of the evolution of human rights in Europe, the real 'breakthrough' of human rights, evidenced in the massive expansion of human rights discourse in society, was not to be found until the 1990s after the end of the Cold War. Empirically, it is in practice difficult to precisely identify this process as it included an ever growing number of agents and institutions, all turning to human rights as a way of furthering their agendas, which ranged from patients' rights to penal reform. In other words, the process of sacralisation – or sanctification – of the person identified by Joas in his analysis of modern society seems to have taken an even stronger hold in Europe during the 1990s, and at this time it acquired a new and significant legal component and, as a result, increased social and political sanctity; that is to say, the symbolic force of human rights gained a new pervasive power in society, reaching far beyond the human rights field itself. In this last section I will briefly sketch out this change, and in particular consider how it impacted those European societies that had long seen themselves as the exporters of human rights, but which now found themselves increasingly under pressure to increase rights protection. A case in point here is the UK.

Striking examples of these deep transformations are the processes through which the ECHR was incorporated into national law in different European societies. While this was viewed as mainly a legal matter in most European countries and therefore executed by a closed legal-political network, the case of the UK differs in this regard. In the UK the progress towards the passing of the 1998 Human Rights Act is highly illustrative of the ways in which the new force of human rights came to have an impact on society at large and even challenge the classic configuration of law and politics in Britain.[19] The beginning of this process can be dated back to the 1970s. In particular, the legal problems emerging from the handling of the crisis in Northern Ireland and the subsequent high-profile miscarriage of justice cases – most notoriously the 'Birmingham Six', 'Guildford Four' and the 'Maguire Seven' – gave human rights issues elevated standing on the socio-political agenda. On its own, the crisis in Northern Ireland had already given rise to a civil rights movement in the 1970s, but beyond these particular practices, radical lawyers in Britain showed surprisingly little interest in the concept on the home front (Madsen 2010: 151–80). Civil rights did, however, assume prominence occasionally as a means to further political goals and challenge the state's at times '. . .cack-handed attempts to punish some [of the] excesses of the Sixties' (Robertson 1999: xi). This challenge – a mixture of political and social practices with a common foothold in the events of the late 1960s and early 1970s – was never to be the locus of the transformation of civil rights and human rights in the UK, even though many of its key players would later become key human rights activists.

It was not until the 1980s that a real human rights counter-strategy started to take shape. This movement took its starting-point in a variety of causes marking the period: first the miscarriages of justice, Thatcher's attack on trade unions in the early 1980s, the Miners' Strike in 1984, the government's attempts to limit public protests, and finally the Poll Tax legislation (1989–1990). The offensive against the trade unions was viewed by many as a declaration of war against the Socialist legal establishments in and around the Labour Party. Also fuelling this counter-strategy, examples of a criminal justice system increasingly experiencing problems in handling new social problems were seen in the context of the racial riots in places such as Brixton in South London and the Toxteth suburb of Liverpool in the early 1980s. All in all, this fragmented, cause- and case-oriented movement sought to use civil liberties and European human rights law as a means to expose the alleged arbitrariness of the Tory government's actions concerning basic freedoms, including the fundamental rights to protest, to

[19] For a comparison between France and the UK in this respect, see Madsen (2004b). The outline of the politics of human rights in the UK during the 1980s and 1990s is largely derived from this publication.

assemble in public places and to participate in the democratic political process. In the legal field, developments in the area had already begun in the 1970s, pioneered by a series of lawyers, unsurprisingly many of whom were closely linked to the central organizations that had marked the post-war period, such as the National Council for Civil Liberties, Justice and Amnesty International (Madsen 2004b). Further, the British acceptance of individual petition to the ECHR in the late 1960s had an impact on the legal system, helping to push a general advancement of human rights within the British legal field beginning in the 1980s.

The gradually increased importance of the ECHR in legal practices in the UK eventually received political attention at the highest level and particularly during the 1980s. As a surprising development, the UK became one of the most frequent customers before the Court in Strasbourg during the period. And politically, as one legal advisor of the Foreign Office during the Thatcher era recalls in an interview (Int. 111. 8 May 2001), the continuous acceptance of 'the right to individual petition came up as a real question'.[20] But typical of the conservative accommodationist internationalism of the 1980s, the formal response was that 'the UK was not to pull out, but the Court to pull back' (Int. 111. no. 1, 8 May 2001). The development of human rights law in the Court accelerated in the mid-1970s, as did the frequency of dissent by the English judge Sir Gerald Fitzmaurice, a former legal advisor of the Foreign Office and at the ECHR from 1974 to 1980. The legal orthodoxy arising from schooling in public international law, both academically and professionally, was also reflected in the legal and social outlook of Fitzmaurice's successor in Strasbourg, Sir Vincent Evans. Sir Vincent Evans, however, entered the Court when the jurisprudence of the Court had taken a more progressive course, so that it defined its main goal as to provide up-to-date human rights protection through a dynamic interpretive style, calling for reluctance among the judges who represented the more sceptical countries. Generally, the original dominance of the Foreign Office in the field of human rights declined and the strongest local agents – in particular the Home Office – became increasingly involved in finding a solution to what was now referred to as the 'ECHR problem'. Indeed, the progressive expansion of the ECHR implied a change in the national perception of the ECHR from being purely international to becoming a matter between domestically oriented institutions and the

[20] The 1966 decision to accept the jurisdiction of the European Court and Commission only ran for a renewable period of three years until the incorporation into British law of the ECHR by the 1998 Human Rights Act.

gradually more autonomous Strasbourg Court. In practice, although disagreement was expressed at the political level, the British response was to put in place administrative procedures, screening all new legislation in regard to ECHR standards. Perhaps unintentionally, this effectively allowed the Europeanization of human rights law to gain priority over national laws and legal projects.

In light of the overriding institutional aspects of the transformations caused by the ECHR, it might seem surprising that the idea of advocating the full incorporation of the ECHR into British domestic law developed into a more popular movement. It is only when taking into consideration the series of events in the area of civil rights outlined above that this development can be explained as a strategy of challenging government and state practices by trying to transplant a series of norms that had already shown their potential as points of reference beyond state control in, for example, South America. Towards the late 1980s, some of the civil society organizations, which were influenced or founded by an avant-garde of progressive human rights lawyers of the post-war period, became key advocates of the incorporation of the ECHR into UK law (Madsen 2004b; 2005). This was to some extent marked by a clash between the older generations, who emphasized the idea of a bill of rights for legal reasons, and a younger generation of socially aware lawyers and social scientists, who sought to make human rights a question of culture, even of popular culture, as well as a new societal ethos. The new generation had matured politically in the 1980s, during what was perceived as the very long 'presidency' of Mrs Thatcher. The battles with Thatcherism, alongside the defeatism of the Labour Party, had given them a collective memory of, on the one hand, the questionable protection of civil rights in the UK, and on the other hand, the limits of representative democracy. As one key player recalls: 'There was no other way to challenge the Government than through constitutional changes' (Int. 95, no. 1, 5 March 2001). Human rights were back in the core debate of society and political weaponry for challenging the government – just as the Tories for a brief moment in the 1970s had sought a new bill of rights as a way of challenging the then Labour government (Int. 95, no. 1, 5 March 2001).[21] Yet throughout the 1980s, the response to the idea of a bill of rights from across the political spectrum remained that such an instrument would delegate an unreasonable power to judges beyond Parliamentary control.

[21] Similar attempts at instrumentalizing human rights were pursued in French politics in the 1970s. See for example Agrikoliansky (2003).

Basically, both the Tory and Labour parties regarded it as if not an undemocratic measure, then an un-British measure in conflict with the widespread idea of the 'supremacy of Parliament'.

After Labour's 1987 election defeat, this movement realized that new measures were needed more than ever before. In this climate, Charter88 was founded as a pressure group for constitutional reform with a bill of rights on the agenda as one of ten suggestions for constitutional change. Rapidly, the group collected thousands of signatures and a row of high-profile agents, including Law Lords, lawyers and academics – even a few celebrities joined the effort (Klug 2000: 158). The time was literally *right*, and as the name of the organization suggested with its slight reference to the famous Charter 77, it was part of the global human rights movement which at the same time was celebrating some of its greatest triumphs. In 1989, the National Council for Civil Liberties re-launched itself as 'Liberty – a Human Rights Organization', and JUSTICE also jumped on the human rights bandwagon. One milestone in the campaign was Liberty's publication of 'A People's Charter' in 1991 (Klug 2000). This publication contained an indiscreet appeal to the Labour party, 'a solution that fitted Labour's concerns' in the words of one of the activists (Int. 95, no. 1, 5 March 2001). In the same year, the Institute for Public Policy Research (IPPR), a think-tank close to the Labour party, published an outline of a new bill of rights. The Labour party, too, internally debated a human rights agenda, and the heads of the leading non-governmental organizations (NGOs) were invited to join some of these discussions behind the scenes. This led to the eventual inclusion of the incorporation of the ECHR into British law as a policy of the Labour party.[22]

New Labour's approval of a human rights policy that included the incorporation of the ECHR into British law became a political turning-point for the movement. In parallel to the political bargaining, the key NGOs – Liberty, Charter88 and JUSTICE – had pursued a popular outreach campaign which was designed to maintain the momentum, as well as more practically to seek a realization of their notion of 'human rights culture'. Once again, Tory practices provided a good opportunity for popular rebellion. This time, the most fashionable of the protests concerned the (human) right to organize techno raves. By mobilizing this

[22] Even if Tony Blair and Jack Straw were to become the formal political architects of the Human Rights Act, a great deal of the work was prepared by the Scottish lawyer and Labour leader John Smith (Klug 2000: 161).

young environment, Liberty attracted significant attention to themselves and their projects. Also, Charter88 followed this paradigm of human rights as culture, and they initiated teaching campaigns aimed at British society at large (Int. 87, no. 1, 27 February 2001). Spending £4.5 million on the training of judges alone and launching a highly visible £1 million publicity campaign concerning the Human Rights Act, the new Labour government sought to present itself as a protagonist of the new idea of human rights culture. And, at the heart of the legal system, due to an unparalleled interest and investment in this new area of practice, solicitors, barristers and academics added to the 'symbolic boom' that followed the Human Rights Act when it came into full force on 2 November 2000. Primarily concentrated in a handful of chambers and solicitor's firms, the disciples of the British post-war pioneers of human rights generally took the lead in this growing business. Favoured through their access to and familiarity with the media, they were able to communicate information about this new area of legal practice widely to the public, thus adding to the booming interest.

9.6 Conclusion

The recent history of human rights in the UK does not, however, end at the turn of the new millennium, at the height of the cultural human rights movements. Significant changes have occurred in the subsequent period that have generally challenged human rights in Britain. Strikingly, the current Tory government has on several occasions voiced the idea of changing the Human Rights Act or even altogether abolishing it. Indeed, this idea had already been floated by Tony Blair himself. Home Secretary Theresa May has gone as far as suggesting the UK leave the ECHR. The background for the new hard line against the ECHR in the UK is shaped mainly by developments in counter-terrorism and immigration over the last decade, where the ECtHR has been perceived as a legal barrier to the expulsion of terrorists or unwanted asylum seekers. This reflects new societal anxieties linked to multiculturalism and the so-called war on terror that do not sit well with the idea of every person being equally sacred. I will not analyse this development here, but simply point to the underlying conflict between international human rights norms and national sovereignty illustrated by this clash: this is what Joas has termed the most fundamental conflict of values of contemporary society (Joas 2003). Moreover, although the UK, together with Russia, has been the most outspoken critic of the ECHR system, it would be a mistake to assume that they stand alone. As a matter of fact, the recent Brighton Declaration (2012), the first change to the ECHR system since 1950 that has explicitly sought to curtail its power, was at the end of the day agreed on by all forty-seven member states of the ECHR system (Christoffersen and Madsen 2013). This relative backlash against the ECHR is above all a firm reminder that, although human rights in many ways are perceived as the ultimate modernist expression of the centrality – even sacredness (Joas 2013) – of the human being, in their current incarnation, in which they are neither entirely international nor national and neither entirely legal nor solely ideational, they remain above all a contested concept, which nevertheless is a highly central dynamic in the evolution of contemporary society in its many and overlapping fields of practice. Human rights might appear to be 'the last utopia' (Moyn 2010) or even the 'last great narrative of post-modernity' (Lindgren Alves 2000). Yet, such general analysis risks overlooking the extent to which they have become an integral part of the changing fabric of society and how this itself produces new conflicts over new social problems such as immigration, terrorism, etc.

Following the line of inquiry adopted in this analysis, human rights are above all a contested notion, and the contest over human rights produces effects far beyond its immediate field of action. In other words, although the idea of human rights is linked to a certain centrality of the person as argued by Joas, this centrality is in practice highly contingent on how human rights are embedded in the transformation of society and its institutions. While my analysis of the dynamic process of human rights in some ways agrees with the notion of the double vulnerability of human rights that Turner suggests in his more normative analysis – claiming that human rights are vulnerable as a product of both the vulnerability of the human being and the institutions protecting human beings through human rights – the more structural historical-sociological approach to human rights used in this analysis reveals that this fragility of human rights is in important ways societally cemented. As is argued by other structural sociologists, notably Gert Verschraegen (Verschraegen 2002; Madsen and Verschraegen 2013a), human rights are crucial institutional devices for the creation of modern society. They enable individuals in complex abstract societies but, as also pointed out by a number of other chapters in this book, processes of modernity are not automated. Put differently, the sacredness of the person is not an ongoing process of sacralisation. The case of the rise and fall of human rights as part of a cultural movement in the UK above all underlines this fragility of human rights in the face of social crises caused by war, demographic change, etc. It would, of course, be highly surprising if this were not the case, especially if we consider the previous failures of human rights, for example in the aftermath of the French Revolution, in the 1930s and during World War II. From a critical sociological perspective, it is apparent that human rights are, simultaneously, a key institution of modern society and an institution permanently in conflict with other forces in society – perhaps most particularly the never-quite-balanced constellation of abstract power and individualism as witnessed in the many totalitarian tendencies in Europe during the twentieth century. Therefore, although European human rights in many ways have been a surprising legal and political success, this should not be confused with a fundamental resolution of the most basic paradox of modern society: the unhinged interface of the increasingly individualized individual in an increasingly abstract and enlarged state.

Bibliography

Agrikoliansky, Éric (2002). *La Ligue française des droits de l'homme et du citoyen depuis 1945: Sociologie d'un engagement civique*. Paris: L'Harmattan.

(2003). 'La gauche, le libéralisme politique et les droits de l'homme', in Jean-Jacques Becker and Gilles Candar (eds). *Histoire des gauches en France*. Paris: La Découverte, pp. 525–42.

Bates, Ed (2010). *The Evolution of the European Convention on Human Rights: From Its Inception to the Creation of a Permanent Court of Human Rights*. Oxford: Oxford University Press.

Beck, Ulrich, Anthony Giddens and Scott Lash (1994). *Reflexive Modernization: Politics, Tradition and Aesthetics in the Modern Social Order*. Cambridge: Polity Press.

Bobbio, Norberto (1995). *The Age of Rights*. Cambridge: Polity Press.

Bourdieu, Pierre (1980). *Le sens pratique*. Paris: Minuit.

(1987). 'The Force of Law: Toward a Sociology of the Juridical Field', *The Hastings Law Journal* 38: 805–53.

(2012). *Sur l'État: Cours au Collège de France*. Paris: Seuil.

Christoffersen, Jonas and Mikael R. Madsen (2013). 'Postscript: Understanding the Past, Present and Future of the European Court of Human Rights', in Jonas Christoffersen and Mikael R. Madsen (eds). *The European Court of Human Rights between Law and Politics*, 2nd edition. Oxford: Oxford University Press, pp. 230–49.

Cohen, Antonin (2007). 'Constitutionalism without Constitution: Transnational Elites between Political Mobilization and Legal Expertise in the Making of a Constitution for Europe (1940s–1960s)', *Law & Social Inquiry* 32: 109–35.

Cohen, Antonin and Mikael R. Madsen (2007). 'Cold War Law: Legal Entrepreneurs and the Emergence of a European Legal Field (1945–1965)', in Volkmar Gessner and David Nelken (eds). *European Ways of Law: Towards a European Sociology of Law*. Oxford: Hart Publishing, pp. 175–202.

De Burca, Grainne (2011). 'The Road Not Taken: The European Union as a Global Human Rights Actor', *The American Journal of International Law* 105: 649–93.

Dezalay, Yves and Mikael R. Madsen (2009). 'Espaces de pouvoir nationaux, espaces de pouvoir internationaux', in Antonin Cohen, Bernard Lacroix and Phillippe Riutort (eds). *Nouveau manuel de science politique*. Paris: La Découverte, pp. 681–93.

(2012). 'The Force of Law and Lawyers: Pierre Bourdieu and the Reflexive Sociology of Law', *Annual Review of Law and Social Science* 8: 433–52.

Durkheim, Émile (1893). *De la division du travail social: Étude sur l'organisation des sociétés supérieures*. Paris: Alcan.

Epp, Charles (1998). *The Rights Revolution: Lawyers, Activists and Supreme Courts in Comparative Perspective*. Chicago, IL: University of Chicago Press.

Gideon, Sjoberg, Elizabeth A. Gill and Norma Williams (2001). 'A Sociology of Human Rights', *Social Problems* 48: 11–47.

Greer, Steven (2006). *The European Convention on Human Rights: Achievements, Problems and Prospects*. Cambridge: Cambridge University Press.

Harmsen, Robert (2001). 'The European Convention on Human Rights after Enlargement', *The International Journal of Human Rights* 5: 18–43.

(2011). 'The Reform of the Convention System: Institutional Restructuring and the (Geo-)Politics of Human Rights', in Jonas Christoffersen and Mikael R. Madsen (eds). *The European Court of Human Rights between Law and Politics*. Oxford: Oxford University Press, pp. 119–43.

Henkin, Louis (1990). *The Age of Rights*. New York, NY: Columbia University Press.

Hoffmann, Stefan Ludwig (2011). *Human Rights in the Twentieth Century: A Critical History*. Cambridge: Cambridge University Press.

Joas, Hans (2003). *War and Modernity: Studies in the History of Violence in the 20th Century*. Cambridge: Polity Press.

(2013). *The Sacredness of the Person: A New Genealogy of Human Rights*. Washington DC: Georgetown University Press.

Klug, Francesca (2000). *Values for a Godless Age: The Story of the United Kingdom's New Bill of Rights*. London: Penguin.

Lauren, Gordon (2003). *The Evolution of International Human Rights: Visions Seen*. Philadelphia, PA: University of Pennsylvania Press.

Lindgren Alves, José A. (2000). 'The Declaration of Human Rights in Postmodernity', *Human Rights Quarterly* 22: 478–500.

Lochak, Danièle (2002). *Les droits de l'homme*. Paris: La Découverte.

Luhmann, Niklas (1974). *Grundrechte als Institution: ein Beitrag zur politischen Soziologie*. Berlin: Duncker & Humblot.

Madsen, Mikael R. (2004a). '"Make Law, Not War": les "sociétés impériales" confrontées à l'institutionnalisation internationale des droits de l'Homme', *Actes de la recherche en sciences sociales* 97–106.

(2004b). 'France, the UK and "Boomerang" of the Internationalization of Human Rights (1945–2000)', in Simon Halliday and Patrick Schmidt (eds). *Human Rights Brought Home: Socio-Legal Perspectives on Human Rights in the National Context*. Oxford: Hart Publishing, pp. 57–86.

(2005). 'L'Emergence d'un champ des droits de l'homme dans les pays européens: enjeux professionnels et stratégies d'Etat au carrefour du droit et de la politique (France, Grande-Bretagne et pays scandinaves, 1945–2000)'. Doctoral Thesis in Sociology. Paris: l'École des hautes études en sciences sociales.

(2007). 'From Cold War Instrument to Supreme European Court: The European Court of Human Rights at the Crossroads of International and National Law and Politics', *Law & Social Inquiry* 32: 137–59.

(2010). *La genèse de l'Europe des droits de l'homme: Enjeux juridiques et stratégies d'Etat (France, Grande-Bretagne et pays scandinaves, 1945–1970)*. Strasbourg: Presses universitaires de Strasbourg.

(2011a). 'Legal Diplomacy – Law, Politics and the Genesis of Postwar European Human Rights', in Stefan Ludwig Hoffmann (ed.). *Human Rights in the Twentieth Century: A Critical History*. Cambridge: Cambridge University Press, pp. 62–81.

(2011b). 'The Protracted Institutionalisation of the Strasbourg Court: From Legal Diplomacy to Integrationist Jurisprudence', in Mikael R. Madsen and Jonas Christoffersen (eds). *The European Court of Human Rights between Law and Politics*. Oxford: Oxford University Press, pp. 43–60.

(2011c). 'Reflexivity and the Construction of the International Object: The Case of Human Rights', *International Political Sociology* 5: 259–75.

(2013). 'Human Rights and European Integration: From Institutional Divide to Convergent Practice', in Niilo Kauppi (ed.). *A Political Sociology of Transnational Europe*. Colchester: ECPR Press, pp. 147–59.

Madsen, Mikael R. and Yves Dezalay (2002). 'The Power of the Legal Field: Pierre Bourdieu and the Law', in Reza Banakar and Max Travers (eds). *An Introduction to Law and Social Theory*. Oxford: Hart Publishing, pp. 189–204.

Madsen, Mikael R. and Gert Verschraegen (2013a). 'Making Human Rights Intelligible: An Introduction to Sociology of Human Rights', in Mikael R. Madsen and Gert Verschraegen (eds). *Making Human Rights Intelligible: Towards a Sociology of Human Rights*. Oxford: Hart, pp. 1–22.

(eds) (2013b). *Making Human Rights Intelligible: Towards a Sociology of Human Rights*. Oxford: Hart Publishing.

Manners, Ian (2002). 'Normative Power Europe: A Contradiction in Terms?', *Journal of Common Market Studies* 40: 235–58.

Merrills, John G. and Arthur H. Robertson (2001). *Human Rights in Europe: A Study of the European Convention on Human Rights*. Manchester: Manchester University Press.

Moravcsik, Andrew (2000). 'The Origins of Human Rights Regimes: Democratic Delegation in Postwar Europe', *International Organization* 54: 217–52.

Morsink, Johannes (1999). *The Universal Declaration of Human Rights: Origins, Drafting and Intent*. Philadelphia, PA: University of Pennsylvania Press.

Moyn, Samuel (2010). *The Last Utopia: Human Rights in History*. Cambridge: Belknap Press.

Pateyron, Éric (1998). *La contribution française à la rédaction de la Déclaration universelle des droits de l'homme*. Paris: La Documentation française.

Riles, Annelise (2006). 'Anthropology, Human Rights, and Legal Knowledge: Culture in the Iron Cage', *American Anthropologist* 108: 52–65.

Robertson, Geoffrey (1999). *The Justice Game*. London: Vintage.

Scheeck, Laurent (2005). 'The Relationship between the European Courts and Integration through Human Rights', *Zeitschrift für ausländisches öffentliches Recht und Völkerrecht* 65: 837–85.

Simpson, Alfred W.B. (2004). *Human Rights and the End of Empire: Britain and the Genesis of the European Convention*. Oxford: Oxford University Press.

Sjoberg, Gideon, Elizabeth A. Gill and Norma Williams (2001). 'A Sociology of Human Rights', *Social Problems* 48: 11–47.

Somers, Margaret R. and Christopher N.J. Roberts (2008). 'Toward a New Sociology of Rights: A Genealogy of "Buried Bodies" of Citizenship and Human Rights', *Annual Review of Law and Social Science* 4: 385–425.

Thornhill, Chris (2011). *A Sociology of Constitutions: Constitutions and State Legitimacy in Historical-Sociological Perspective*. Cambridge: Cambridge University Press.

(2013). 'State Building, Constitutional Rights and the Social Construction of Norms: Outline for a Sociology of Constitutions', in Mikael R. Madsen and Gert Verschraegen (eds). *Making Human Rights Intelligible: Towards a Sociology of Human Rights*. Oxford: Hart Publishing, pp. 25–59.

Turner, Bryan S. (1993). 'Outline of a Theory of Human Rights', *Sociology* 27: 489–512.

(2006). *Vulnerability and Human Rights*. Philadelphia, PA: Pennsylvania University Press.

Verschraegen, Gert (2002). 'Human Rights and Modern Society: A Sociological Analysis from the Perspective of Systems Theory', *Journal of Law and Society* 29: 258–81.

Weber, Max (1980 [1921]). *Wirtschaft und Gesellschaft. Grundriss der verstehenden Soziologie*, 5th edition. Tübingen: Mohr.

Wilson, Richard A. (1997). 'Human Rights, Culture and Context: An Introduction', in Richard A. Wilson (ed.). *Human Rights, Culture and Context: Anthropological Perspectives*. London: Pluto Press.

Winter, Jay and Antoine Prost (2013). *René Cassin and Human Rights – from the Great War to the Universal Declaration*. Cambridge: Cambridge University Press.

10

Lawyers and the transformations of the fields of state power: osmosis, hysteresis and *aggiornamento*

YVES DEZALAY AND BRYANT G. GARTH

The recent book by Antoine Vauchez, *L'union par le droit* (2013), emphasizes the dramatic legal changes that came with the development of the European Community. He focuses especially on how the legal categories of community law were able to break with 'national constitutional traditions'. The establishment of the European Community – what Walter Halstein termed a 'new political animal' – is portrayed by Vauchez as a 'coup of symbolic force' that made 'imperative the construction of new intellectual equipment' (2013: 120). Further, as Vauchez shows, the success of this political and doctrinal rupture came from a new organization for the production of legal doctrine – FIDE (*Fédération Internationale pour le Droit Européen*) – under the aegis of institutional legal leaders and structured around a small core of pioneers of European law. The pioneers were able to accumulate a variety of positions – bureaucratic, diplomatic, political, judicial, and academic – and to mobilize a range of resources for their project, ranging from organizational and financial resources to the media and learned resources (Vauchez 2013).

The invention of a new legal paradigm for Europe was therefore accompanied by a challenge to the different national models and hierarchical divisions of labour of legal work. Those national models within European states were structured around a double opposition and professional distance – seen in the distinction between justice and politics and in the separation between practitioners and the producers of pure law. The high status of those identified with pure law was represented by the grand professors on the Continent and by the elite barristers in the United Kingdom (UK) (Dezalay 1992). Europe confounded these models and hierarchies.

This revolution in Europe, as noted, drew especially on the networks connected to FIDE, deemed a 'private army of the European Community' which supplied an entire 'legal arsenal' (Vauchez 2013: 139). But at the same time, as Vauchez also shows, the revolution resulted from a transplantation of the model of legal practice from the United States (US). The key to the transplantation was the beginning of a European corporate Bar in Brussels, which served multinational businesses and focused especially on the construction of a new Competition Law for Europe. These 'young Turks' were well placed to play the role of 'transatlantic courtiers' drawing on US connections to go with their own social capital. As Vauchez notes, they were the inheritors of diverse political and legal dynasties in Belgium and the relatives or protégés of Belgian 'grand masters of European and international law' (2013: 106). And they often brought a double career as practitioners and law professors.

Above all, these European corporate lawyers drew on strong cosmopolitan resources. Typically educated at Harvard, they worked at prestigious US law firms, in particular Cleary Gottlieb, where one of the founders, George Ball, was the lawyer and friend of European founder Jean Monnet. These 'turbulent inheritors' were able to create a 'territorial enclave' in Brussels despite the hostility of the Belgian Bar, which denounced a purported violation of the laws that controlled the organization of legal professions and practice (Vauchez 2013: 104).

The European construction depicted by Vauchez represents a coup of symbolic force in the political and state order, and it was accomplished through a 'mini palace revolution' in the hierarchy of legal elites and a transplantation of the US model of business law. The question is how to explain the process of transformation in Europe. Most commentators are content to describe the developments with labels such as juridification, justicialization, legalization, or a return to law. But these conclusory labels neglect the internal dynamics that produce important readjustments within legal orders in relation to transformations in the field of state power.

In the introduction to his first book on law and revolution, Harold Berman wrote: 'The Western legal tradition has been transformed (...) by six great revolutions' (Berman 1983: 18). Berman's own research covered three of these revolutions: first, the Gregorian reforms (Berman 1983), next the Lutheran reforms and finally the English revolution (Berman 2003). But his initial project was also to treat the American, French, and Russian revolutions as well. His bold ambition raises the question of whether the same *problématique* that Berman developed for the revolutions he identified would help to explain other transformations that are at the same time legal and political. The principal heuristic merit of Berman's *problématique* is that it facilitates an analysis of the processes both of rupture and recomposition that occur at the same time in the field of state power and in the field of legal representations and practice. The processes occur through alliances and converging strategies that shake up and realign boundaries between the two universes. Modernist leaders and reformers construct new modes of government by relying on a small group of producers of learned law whom they then make their influential advisors. The scholars furnish them not only with legitimate arms to fight to gain power but also with collaborators predisposed to participate in the new governance regime.

This general process helps explain the transformation of Europe. Berman limited his research to revolutions that were both political and religious. But the same *problématique* can more generally be extended to regime transformations such as from a monarchy to a republic or through the process of decolonization. It also helps to clarify major political reorientations, such as the arrival of the New Deal or the welfare state, or the retreat from those developments in favour of the 'neo-liberal revolution'. And it not only helps to understand the legal transformation that Vauchez examines at the European level and within European states, but it further helps to explain the impacts of deregulation and internationalization of markets in Europe – reinforced through profound transformations in the relationships among law, markets, and states.

In each of these moments, whatever the intensity and violence of the political-ideological breaks, transformations within the legal order were part of the recomposition of scholarly learning, legal practice, and the governance of the state. The *problématique* developed by Berman retains its heuristic strength in these situations, and may usefully be expanded to cover them. The approach provides analytical tools to explain how, and precisely through what internal dynamic, these successful readjustments operate, and how they are also able to preserve the relative autonomy of the legal field with respect to the holders of political power. That autonomy, as shown famously by Kantorowicz and others (see, for example, Thompson 1975), is the basis of the social credibility of legal institutions and the reason that the law may both serve political leaders and make their power more legitimate.

It is necessary, however, to inquire more deeply into details that complicate that basic insight. If the process of change involves converging political and legal strategies successfully working a kind of osmosis between the two spaces, leading to the emergence of new legal hierarchies conforming to the interests of the new holders of power, it is still important to explain why the two sides of law and state power diverge sufficiently such that new strategic alliances potentially come into play. The question is how reformers and political opponents of the status quo get together with 'young Turks' of law who themselves are ready to risk their capital of legal authority by questioning established legal hierarchies consolidated out of prior configurations of the field of state power.

In order to help resolve this puzzle, we focus our particular analysis here on the producers of learned law and how the alliances are formed between dominated or new groups of the legal scholarly subfield and the modernist leaders and reformers seeking to gain power and legitimacy in the field of state power. The producers, while putting their doctrinal expertise in the service of these new regimes, also deploy political resources to invest in the reproduction of legal learning. They contribute not only to reshape legal scholarly representations that then conform to the new dominant ideologies, but also their over-investment in legal science serves to legitimize the innovations as part of the existing tradition of legal science – now skilfully reinterpreted. Despite being quite politically marked, therefore, the new legal discourse is assimilated into the discourse and tradition of pure law and its universal and almost timeless pretensions.

This outcome is not inconsistent with a process where new producers of legal doctrine, disposed to take the risk of strategies looking toward a new political regime, initially oppose not only the hierarchies of the legal field but also its doxa of independence with respect to the holders of political power. Despite the seeming vehemence of the challenge, the new group's approach stems from dominated professional and social positions along with a habitus that values legal science as the apex of this field of practice. Contradictions are inherent in their status of dominant–dominated in their professional subfield and explain the mix of hysteresis and *aggiornamento* that is the rule for these successful 'legal-political revolutions'.

The *problématique* developed by Berman goes well with Bourdieu's sociology of fields and in particular can be matched fruitfully with Bourdieu's lectures from the early 1990s, recently published with the title of *Sur l'État* (Bourdieu 2012). Sociological tools applied to state transitions help to clarify the internal fights between different factions of jurists opposing each other at the core of the legal field while mobilizing the resources of the state. In particular, this sociological approach permits an analysis of why new generations of learned jurists are predisposed to put their legal skills in the service of new political projects or reformers who present an opportunity for the jurists to re-actualize the law and at the same time revalorise their positions in the legal field.

These hypotheses are consistent with the Berman approach, which emphasizes that the legal 'revolutions' represent strategies of transition and conversion. Looking to promote the political upheavals, dominated factions of jurists put their legal competence in the service of new political leaders in order to inscribe the political break within the traditions of legal legitimacy. The legitimation of these '*coups d'état*' is accomplished by means of learned investments that serve to build up the value of legal capital and the credibility of law. The work of reinterpretation of the doctrinal corpus helps to facilitate the political transition but also the reconversion of the hierarchies of law around the new governance regimes. The construction of this *problématique* is consistent with the theory of fields and specifically the legal field.

10.1 Legal fields as historically connected and interstitial spaces

We thus far have described the changes in Europe and suggested that tools from Berman's approach to history and Bourdieu's sociology offer promise for examining the complex processes of legal and political change that produce, as stated, both hysteresis and *aggiornamento*. Drawing further on Bourdieu's analyses in his course, *Sur l'État* (Bourdieu 2012), we can suggest national differences and similarities through a comparative social history of legal fields. Two fundamental axioms structure the legal fields:

1. The embeddedness of legal fields in the fields of national power. The opposing strategies and alliances between different fractions of professionals are played out simultaneously in terms of legal capital, social capital, and political or state resources that groups are able to mobilize. Legal fields are structured as crossroads – spaces that permit and at the same time favour strategies of a double game played by an elite of notables of the law, as counsellors to the Prince (or merchant princes), legislators, politicians, or high functionaries of the state.
2. The reproduction of legal learning and the hierarchy of professional competences as one of the components of the reproduction and legitimation of social elites, through the holders of governmental expertise, homologized and guaranteed by the institutions of national states and claiming a governing knowledge of universal validity. The contradictions tied to this double logic of reproduction of legal capital – through scholarly paths that are more or less selective and meritocratic, but also through inherited capital transmitted

> through family lineage (including through the mechanism of the biases built into processes of apprenticeship or co-optation) – are a permanent source of tensions and internal conflicts which serve as one of the engines of the transformation of the legal field.

These contradictions are also inherent in the legal field as a result of the double genesis of the field, which combines at the same time the rationality of the law and state justice, but also the authority of traditional leaders – communal, religious, or feudal – that exercise de facto a legal justice with respect to the groups under their responsibility. As Martines (1968) shows with respect to the genesis of the legal profession in medieval Italy, the development of a state justice that is rationalized and professionalized comes at the expense of feudal justice, which it helps to disqualify as archaic and biased. Nevertheless, this competition is accomplished through a hybridization brought about by strategies of reconversion. Martines also explains the cost and the cultural barriers which reserved access to the new law faculties to the descendants of old feudal lines, who gained control of this law and justice.

This new '*noblesse de robe*', in Bourdieu's terms, is able through this process to combine a capital of traditional authority with learned legitimacy and a delegation of state power. Legal capital is inscribed in the modes of reproduction of social hierarchies, which helps both to renovate them and to render them more legitimate. As Berman showed, the common law is an example of this hybridization, mixing royal justice and feudal justice. Taking advantage of the weakness of the royal bureaucracy, leading feudal groups profited from royal writs by imposing themselves as justices of the peace of the new common law. This process continues through the permanent tension between codification and custom, judges, and mediators – notably apparent at the time of the colonial transplantation of imperial justice (Dezalay and Garth 2010).

The contradictions are exacerbated by the fact that the faculties and schools of law are strictly connected with the reproduction of the ruling classes and modes of governance. The ruling elite, the churches, the state, and multinationals have always sustained and financed faculties of government in order to be able to select and educate their collaborators and successors. This way, paradoxically, their grip on politics – or the world of business – is built in part on the learned processes upon which the autonomy of this professional field resides.

This discussion, even if in summary form, of the axioms we presented shows that a sociology of the legal field must be deployed simultaneously on a plurality of national fields and spaces, but also on interstitial spaces between these different universes. Obviously this is particularly essential for Europe, with clear connections between the national and transnational. It is necessary also to add an historical dimension essential to an understanding of the transformation of these fields, both for the internal logic and the fact of interactions between different spaces. This analysis can be made more economical, in fact, both in terms of synchrony and diachrony, through research at a number of sites, because agents possessing a diversity of capital, which permits them to circulate and intervene in multiple spaces, are also the persons who occupy the dominant positions in each of the spaces.

The ubiquity of this mobility of elites contradicts the facade of autonomy constructed by each of these spaces through an ensemble of institutions, of learning and of norms, even of specific habituses. It is therefore vital to be able to follow the trajectories of these influential agents, since they provide insight into how these fields continually interact while maintaining the relative autonomy essential to their internal operation and their social credibility. In order to illustrate the heuristic relevance of this theoretical approach, we will briefly present the case of the Legal Realists and the New Deal, which illustrates perfectly the play of strategic alliances that proceeds in Europe as well.

It is helpful to start with a statement that the legal historian R.C. van Caenegem used as a chapter title in one of his books: 'Law professors serve the powers that be' (van Caenegem 1987: 155). He emphasized that, contrary to the professional ideology of jurists, which insists on a separation between law and politics, 'law is politics under another guise'. The paradox is that this formula, borrowed from the Legal Realists, applies particularly well to the strategy of the dominated academics who contested for power in their own professional field while putting their scholarly learning in the service of the political project of the New Deal.

Ronen Shamir's examination of 'The Revolt of Academics: Legal Realists and the New Deal' (1995), demonstrates brilliantly the relevance of these hypotheses to the relationships between the subfield of learned law and US legal and political fields. Shamir begins by emphasizing the 'dual marginality' of the young generation of law professors who became identified with Legal Realism. They were relegated to the role of 'adjuncts' to the elite of legal practitioners and judges. Law professors were charged mainly with engaging in the work of legal classification: 'Academics were the librarians, Judges the authors' (Shamir 1995: 139). They taught the law on the basis only of appellate cases, and, '[i]n stark contrast with the vivid intellectual activity in the emerging social sciences', their scholarly approach made them unable to be 'fully integrated – either institutionally or intellectually – into the rest of the academic world' (1995: 140).

The revolt of the Legal Realists can therefore be examined as a 'collective mobility project' resting on a 'two tiered assault on the established legal order' (Shamir 1995: 141): 'questioning the field's established hierarchies (...) (by) comprehensive challenge of judicial supremacy on the one hand and the privileged position of the bar's elite on the other' (1995: 147).[1] The first effort was to question the learned representations that were the basis of the authority of the courts: '[t]o dethrone the King' (1995: 143), they demonstrated the chaotic, indeterminate, inconsistent, and above all unpredictable nature of judicial decisions. By undermining the certainty of judicial pronouncements, they looked toward 'legitimating alternative sources of law' (1995: 145) as well as 'promoting different strategies of uncertainty reduction' drawing on the 'social scientific foundation for the study of judicial decisions' – a 'real science' to challenge 'legal science' (1995: 149).[2]

Simultaneously, the Legal Realists attacked the monopoly of the case method in legal education, which they saw as promoting one-dimensional deductive analyses that 'over-emphasized and canonized appellate court decisions' (Shamir 1995: 146). In order to remedy this problem, they called for the study of law 'in context' facilitated by 'closer relationships with the social sciences', which they sought to bring into the law schools. And by bringing social scientists into their terrain, they benefited not only by fostering the image of an 'intellectual vanguard', but also reaffirmed their own authority as the 'final arbiters of the law'. This success came also from the fact that the Legal Realists became the 'architects of the new social order' thanks to the privileged relationships that they formed in the field of state power.

The alliance formed with new and intellectually prestigious academic disciplines that lacked the personal and political capital associated with the law helped to reposition the Legal Realists in the legal and governmental fields. The scientific investment was accompanied by a moral stance as well. They condemned lawyers who enacted the role of 'obsequious servant of business, tainted with the morals and manners of the market place' (Shamir 1995: 148). They thus offered their services

[1] More precisely, 'Challenging the privileged bond between appellate courts and the bar's elite' (Shamir 1995: 148).

[2] 'Theirs was a true science.'

to the politics and bureaucracy of the New Deal as experts in 'socially informed law' through 'enlightened legislation' designed to resolve problems that were 'too complex, too difficult to be handled by the average judge' (1995: 150).

The great success of this project came from the context of economic and political crisis that permitted the law professors 'to escape their dual marginality. (. . .) The New Deal opened an entirely new market of legal services, that of the legal expert in the new governmental agencies, and, in the same act opened the doors of the law schools to the social sciences' (Shamir 1995: 152). Nevertheless, this success came with a corresponding change in their approach: '[t]he alliance with Roosevelt's administration led the realists away from a critical discourse towards an operational one' (1995: 156). In order to play the role of 'responsible social-legal planner', they had to contribute to reinforcing the credibility of the law, constructing again the myth of a doubly legitimate law, both from the point of view of the new social sciences and a new political morality consistent with the ideals of the regulatory and welfare state.

Another excellent national example of this process comes from Guillaume Sacriste in his book *La République des constitutionnalistes* (2011). He shows how the leaders of the French Republic in the late nineteenth century favoured the promotion of a young group of professors of constitutional law. The academic group, in return, consolidated the legitimacy of the new regime through their scholarly production and set the framework for new generations of jurists predisposed to serve the new institutions of the state. These examples from France and the US suggest that the double game combining doctrinal innovations and political reform goes beyond the 'revolutionary' contexts examined by Berman – providing a more general motor for the parallel recomposition of legal and political fields.

From the point of view of a division of labour in the legal field, these alliances between academics and politicians appear somewhat paradoxical. Law professors, in addition to their teaching duties, are charged with maintaining the appearance of 'pure law' consistent with the neutrality central to legitimacy of the legal field. The paradox in fact reveals the heteronomy of the subfield of learned law, which has boundaries that are ever changing and porous with respect to legal practice and the fields of state power.

The play of these two relationships is connected. As shown by the examples from Shamir and Sacriste, the new arrivals in the doctrinal or scholarly field, whose position in the legal hierarchy is relatively low, whether dominated by grand law professors, high court judges, Queen's counsel, or partners of large law firms, are inclined to build alliances with reformers in the political field who are also in a relatively dominated position. In this triangular relationship, the new academic arrivals are predisposed to put themselves in the service of new state leaders because marginality in their own subfield leads them to look for allies who can promote career success. And the relative marginality may come from many sources. The primarily Jewish background of the Legal Realists was likely a key component of the story in the US, and for the Third Republic the relative marginalization came from specialization in constitutional law, a branch of law that was not highly valued in France.

This system of triangular relationships operated in two ways. First, it permitted the academics to seek the support of political protectors in order to make up for their marginal position within the hierarchy of practitioners. Second, the ultimate success of the strategies of *aggiornamento* came when the academics became intermediaries connecting the new political order to legal practice. This way, even though the young Turks of legal doctrine were highly critical initially of the orthodoxies of the doctrinal field, they were careful not to cut themselves off from the institutions at the top of the existing legal hierarchy. Indeed, their capital of learning and legal authority was the principal asset that they aspired to offer to their protectors in the political field. The new leaders invested in the legal careers of their protégés in order to acquire legal capital favourable to their politics and their interests.

This investment in the institutions for the production of learned law, therefore, does not garner rewards unless the investment is recognized and homologized by the ensemble of the legal field, as much by the academic hierarchy as by the legal practitioners. The success of the strategy of *aggiornamento* is then dependent on the realization of particular advantages to the field as a whole: the re-actualization of doctrinal representations conforming to the new political order, and at the same time the opening of new markets of legal practice stemming from proximity to the new rules of governance.

10.2 The courtiers of law: strategies of a double game in and between fields of power

In *L'union par le droit* (2013), Antoine Vauchez, as noted above, explains the significant influence of legal professionals on the European scene by the fact that they were very early able to occupy the position of intermediaries both between national spaces and between the multiple networks of interests, political and economic, around which numerous and diverse constructions of Europe took place. Their ability to serve as preeminent mediators within fields of state power – made possible by the project to build Europe – was relatively unique in the period of a relative decline for law and lawyers in the national welfare states after World War II. There was a return to power, which parallels earlier European returns to the sources of the power of law, in particular in the thirteenth and fourteenth centuries when the birth of the state was accompanied by a reinvention of Roman law. The modern European experience parallels and, of course, builds on the earlier European construction of states and law.

The construction of the powerful city states in Italy at the beginning of the Renaissance involved the affirmation of legal and political autonomy at the expense of older feudal, imperial, and religious jurisdictions (Martines 1968). But the old jurisdictions continued to exist and to confront each other and the city states, at all levels – commercial, military, territorial – and the management of those confrontations added a powerful international dimension to the construction of state law. The multiple turf battles between and among overlapping and competing state institutions provided one of the principal markets for the legal experts who could interpret texts in order to justify the pretensions of one or another side, serving also as arbitrator or consultant in proceedings before powerful groups or authorities (including, for example, the Council of the Seigneurie of Florence or the Papal Courts).[3]

Contrary to the depiction of international law – and the internationalization of legal practices – as developments that followed the construction of nation states with diplomatic practices evolving into principles to tame power relationships, Martines shows that the patricians of law drew on their cosmopolitan capital to gain their positions at the top of the new '*noblesse d'état*'. Elite jurists positioned themselves very early as courtiers of the international in the name of universal principles of learned law valid for civil law as well as canon law. In fact, if we look deeper at the process, we see that the success of the learned capital was at the same time inseparable from investments in cosmopolitan capital. These jurists acquired their cosmopolitan capital through trips that they took at a very young age as well as the long years spent in the prominent universities

[3] '[O]verlapping jurisdictions (are the) source of many conflicts (and) legal knowledge (represents) a useful weapon on both sides' (Martines 1968: 251).

such as Bologna, where they met their counterparts from other cities. They took advantage of numerous opportunities to grow their international capital – whether in legal practice or in the service of the state.

A practice that assisted them was that certain judicial activities were reserved to foreign judges. This tradition, which goes back to the model of the Roman Empire, was justified in the name of a concern for impartiality. Judges coming from city states not involved in a dispute were considered more neutral than their local counterparts for the purpose of deciding disputes, preventing adverse parties from mobilizing extended family and clientelist networks that would extend to legal practitioners and judges.

This imperial holdover helped build cosmopolitan connections and experience, but in fact it represented but a small part of the international market for legal expertise responding to the demands of the new states. The mix of relational and learned capital acquired by the offspring of old patrician families furnished useful instruments to the new holders of power of the city states to manage confrontations between rival cities nourished by competition between commercial powers and by their own power ambitions. The resort to these legal diplomats limited recourse to military resources that risked disrupting the prosperity of these merchant economies.

As Martines showed, these courtiers in international legal relations fulfilled many functions: negotiating and drafting treaties, drafting legal opinions where there were potential differences of interpretation, offering the services of arbitrator in order to avoid the resort to force or to settle a dispute between rival cities. Finally, for the ambassadors to Rome, these jurists also fulfilled a double function: to advise and negotiate the numerous fiscal and jurisdictional relationships between the religious and state authorities; and then also to handle judicial proceedings involving important individuals before the Papacy.

The legal field in the world Martines depicts was constructed around the circulation of individuals and learned and relational resources between state spaces – or more precisely between different levels of state institutions found inside and outside the boundaries of the city states. They included local communal, religious, or feudal enclaves, which maintained a certain autonomy, especially jurisdictional, up to learned and religious institutions with influence or authority in a kind of interstate market involving legal expertise with legitimacy across borders and with access reserved to the descendants of the great patrician families – those able to take full advantage of a learned capital claiming to be universal through combination with cosmopolitan relational capital.

This trans-frontier dimension seen in early European legal history supports a clarification of the analysis developed by Kantorowicz (1997). The reliance on multiple sites to construct cosmopolitan capital enabled legal elites to succeed in playing on two essential scales. They constructed their professional autonomy and credibility, but they also put their expertise in the service of the new holders of state power – which then allowed the acquisition of the capital of political notoriety and influence vital to continuing professional success. The descendants of aristocratic and patrician families, therefore, played a particular role in the construction of the modern state because they could rely on family resources that permitted them to connect themselves to trans-frontier power through networks situated above – but also within – the city states.

Since the role of international courtier was central to the genesis of the European legal field, it is necessary to examine the relationship to institutionalization and normalization within the group of nation states. Our hypothesis is that the role of international courtier is not just a key to the genesis of states, but that it continues to play a vital role that is still restricted to an influential and selective fraction of the legal elite. That role was quite evident in the story of law and the European Community.

This line of analysis can be furthered by drawing on Bourdieu in his course, *Sur l'État* (Bourdieu 2012), mentioned above. Bourdieu suggests a parallel genesis of law and state associated with great religious transformations in which jurists served as conduits between successive versions of the field of state power (2012: 528). This hypothesis fits perfectly with the themes developed by Berman and enriched considerably by the work of historians such as Brundage. It clarifies the internal fights between different groups of jurists contending within the legal field and in the field of state power.

Even if the contending fractions differed according to their legal status and their legal functions, they were also strongly implicated in political fights where the holders of power – whether royal, religious, feudal, or communal – faced each other by mobilizing resources of legal expertise and legitimacy. As a counterpart, these state strategies are also at the centre of the opposition between different fractions of the clerks differentiated at the same time by their more or less close proximity to royal or religious power, but also by their modes of recruitment and learned education, determined in large part by their origins and social position.

In his lectures examining the genesis of the field of state power, Bourdieu proposed a general scheme of analysis structured around three groups of jurists. This analysis facilitates an understanding both of national developments and Europe. The first is the category of jurists of the state, characterized by their role in the construction of more or less authoritarian states and constituting a kind of bureaucratic layer with respect to the king or ruler. They contrast with another jurist fraction of the '*noblesse de robe*', characterized by the role of justice officials organized around high court jurisdictions. The British model inspired the ideology and objectives of this group. In the case of France the relevant group organized around a specific institution, the Parliament of Paris, which drew on delegated power from the king to affirm a certain degree of autonomy in checking royal power. The third category is what Bourdieu termed the 'low legal clergy', 'making themselves the spokespersons for collective interests, the popular will according to the trans-historic alliance between the "proletarian intelligentsia," as Max Weber suggested, and popular classes' (Bourdieu 2012: 515).

This categorization is, of course, very general and shifts in important ways with transformations in the political field. But the general classifications are helpful to delineate the basic national hierarchies. Bourdieu thus noted that the French Revolution disrupted the existing French hierarchy in favour of the third category, and then the French advocates imposed a homologous conception of the nation state as the only legitimate form of the modern state. Along with achieving state power, furthermore, the new group was able to appropriate 'a quasi-monopoly on the specific profits associated with this institution' (Bourdieu 2012: 544).

As we have explained in more detail elsewhere (Dezalay and Garth 2010; 2013), Great Britain provides an example of a different evolution. It involved the elimination of the royal jurists – analogous to the first of Bourdieu's categories – in favour of a new group, the barristers, who succeeded through the civil war in gaining a monopoly over the high courts. They drew on their privileged ties with the gentry and the merchant bourgeoisie – from which they came and whose interests they represented in Parliament. Another contrasting experience is represented by the German legal field, characterized by the embedding of jurists in the different levels within the field of political power which coexisted or developed out of the complex state configuration growing out of the German Holy Roman Empire (Whaley 2011).

Before going deeper into these examples, we wish to emphasize the particular merit of this *problématique*. It provides a fluid conception of legal fields as multi-dimensional spaces with shifting relationships and positions (Bourdieu 2012: 518). It facilitates a focus on how the positions of the holders of legal capital are quite mobile, with jurists able to play between different spaces and to modify their strategies and the positions they take in relation to opportunities available – within various spaces – in different historical and political contexts.

This conception of the legal field as fluid and shifting while maintaining a kind of crossroads position[4] – between religion, state, community, etc. – is quite rich. It introduces the possibility of analysing not only the role of jurists as courtiers and diplomats between different fields of power, but also strategies in periods of transition that link together different political regimes which succeed each other in national histories. This same paradigm also takes into account the diversity of connections between law and state in different national spaces (Bourdieu 2012: 556). More generally, this approach helps to explain and demonstrate the paradox formulated by Kantorowicz: the clerks of the law affirm their autonomy with respect to power at the same time as they put their expertise in the service of power. As shown by numerous works of history (Martines 1968; Brundage 2008; Whaley 2011) consistent with this theoretical approach, the relative mobility of jurists – for example, between different royal courts or principalities and the hierarchies of the church – is the best guarantee of their autonomy in the sense that it permits them to break from holders of power who are too heavy-handed or undertake activities that threaten the clerks' credibility.

The embedding of the legal fields within national fields of power is combined therefore with a relative mobility of legal professionals who can circulate not only among different national spaces on the basis of their expertise and claim to universality, but can also undertake strategic reconversions in the process of political transitions while serving as providers of continuity between successive regimes.

As Berman showed in *Law and Revolution* (1983), these revolutionary changes, which may be religious or political, are also opportunities for a fraction of legal elites to promote an updating or *aggiornamento* in the production of legal doctrine, getting themselves in phase with the political objectives of new ruling groups seeking allies and privileged collaborators. This way, as Berman indicates, law professors made an alliance with theologians and protestant leaders in order to construct a new

[4] This conception was developed earlier by Christophe Charle in 1989 in a short programmatic note where he observed that legal professions served as 'professional crossroads where social capital is converted more easily into other diverse forms of capital: economic, intellectual, political' (119).

political-legal order – which served in large part also to reintegrate the Roman and even canon law that formed the basis of their authority.

The diachronic and synchronic dimensions combine to provide an image of law professors operating a kind of ferry between regimes – as courtier, diplomat, mediator, arbitrator – reshaping the model of excellence and mechanisms of influence by drawing on legal capital strengthened in fights for state power or in battles between states. In order to be able to disentangle the strategies of double agent that are employed here, it is useful to draw again on the comparative sociology of legal fields, which brings into focus the connected history of national political spaces.

In his course on the genesis of legal capital and the state, Bourdieu examined the competitive struggles between religious power and royal power. 'The jurists, at bottom, helped themselves to the resources from the church and used them to make the state against the church (. . .) The state was constructed on the model of the church, but against it' (Bourdieu 2012: 526). The lines of analysis, since developed brilliantly by Brundage, show the complexity of the strategies played by learned jurists simultaneously in the religious hierarchy as well as royal bureaucracies.

In what Brundage described as a (very expensive) 'managerial revolution' (2008: 274) the acquisition of legal learning became the elite path to riches and the accumulation of power and influence for the younger sons of the nobility for whom their learning represented a reconversion and valorisation of their relational capital (2008: 267). This promotion was all the more rapid because the status of jurist permitted them to play on several registers, including counsellor to the king and to princes, but also within the Catholic Church hierarchy. In order to develop and reward potential advisors, in fact, powerful protectors often used their influence to distribute ecclesiastical positions to the graduates. That was the case, according to Brundage, for a third of the Germans bishops at one point.[5] This double game was not only quite profitable, but also allowed a strategy of prudence, offering possibilities of withdrawal when conflicts put advisors at risk as well. The success of this strategy is exemplified by

[5] An example of these double careers cited by Brundage is the trajectory of Arundel (Brundage 2008: 392): this younger son of an earl was successively Chancellor of England and Archbishop of Canterbury and had numerous protégés who also accumulated numerous high bureaucratic posts – Treasurer of England, Chief Justice, Constable of Bordeaux – as well as ecclesiastical ones – Papal Chaplain, Auditor Apostolic Camera, Archbishop of England.

the fact that the learned managers succeeded in gaining key positions within the entourage of the princes as well as in the church, dominating the Curiates at the end of the thirteenth century and then the Papacy (2008: 132).

It is useful then to enlarge the formula developed by Bourdieu. Certainly, the jurists constructed the state with the learning and resources of the church. But the inverse was also true. They also mobilized the capital of relationships and resources of the state in order to consolidate the symbolic power of the Catholic institutions while growing their secular power and their material riches. Managing the fights between different fields of power represented not only an imperative for survival but also the basis of their prosperity. In this respect, it is interesting to examine how the strategies of a double game renovated each other in following very similar structural logics.

As Berman shows, the Lutheran revolution was a reaction against the abuses facilitated by the double game of religious authority and royal power. Nevertheless, it followed in large part the same model. The revolution was developed and was consolidated on the basis of an alliance between scholars – theologians or jurists – and leaders – princes, bishops, and merchants. At the core of the emergent governing alliance, legal elites – judges, professors, and counsellors – enjoyed relative autonomy thanks to university degrees recognized throughout the empire. This autonomy and prestige permitted them to circulate between the different courts and to play at the same time the essential role of courtier, diplomat, or mediator among the different competing powers (Berman 2003: 66).

Within this legal hierarchy the professors occupied a privileged position. This position came both from their proximity to the different holders of power that they advised but also from their doctrinal authority, which they put to use when consulted by high courts in cases involving important questions of law (*Aktenversendung*). These opinions were both lucrative and prestigious. They showed and reaffirmed the collective authority of the professoriate over the field of legal practice, and more generally over the interpretation and redefinition of legal norms.

In fact, the grand professors were not content to demonstrate their mastery of principles and codifications of Roman or canon law. Their historical learning allowed them to claim the mantle of the best-placed interpreters of the ensemble of customs and collective norms that came out of the Germanic tradition. According to van Caenegem (1987: 156),

Carl von Savigny, one of the founders of the historical school, 'claimed that jurists were best placed to know the historic law of the people'. In Savigny's words, a 'naturally evolved and ever developing law of the people' is preferable to a codified law, since it is 'expounded by aristocratic and learned jurists, the natural leaders of the nation' (1987: 91).

The revolution from above launched by the Prussian monarchy and the bureaucratic restructuring of the German empire under Bismarck (Rueschemeyer 1997: 151) did not fundamentally challenge the basis of articulation between the legal field and the political field that emerges from Berman's work. On the contrary, the bureaucratic relaunch of law was supported by an alliance with the professors and thus the reinvestment both in legal learning and in more meritocratic lines of recruitment.

The proximity between the hierarchies of law and the places of power led to a logic of connivance. As Rueschemeyer wrote (1997: 147–8), in order to serve the interests of the landed aristocracy and the merchant class, legal and judicial expertise tended to be mixed with the ensemble of government, including the aristocratic and merchant elites – at the risk of weakening the credibility of institutions of government appearing only as tools of the instruments of political power.

In this context, the offensive of the Prussian bureaucracy, which took place through a massive purge of the Bar (more than 60 per cent), permitted it to consolidate royal power at the expense of the feudal aristocracy, but also to restore the authority of judicial institutions while rationalizing and imposing on them a more meritocratic and rigorous recruitment. This way, '[t]he new order represented an authoritarian rule by professional, highly educated administrators which was based on compromises with the nobility and concessions to the aspiring bourgeoisie, especially the educated bourgeoisie. (. . .) While traditional privileges were de facto retained, education became "now the official mainspring of privilege"' (Rueschemeyer 1997: 151–2).

10.3 *Noblesse de robe* and diploma of the bourgeoisie: the contradictions of a meritocracy of inheritors

One of the main heuristics of a sociology of the reproduction of legal fields is that it offers lines of analysis to explain the structural contradictions that characterize the subfield of the faculties and schools of law. The faculties and schools of law play an essential role in the periodic resurgence of these strategies of political-legal *aggiornamento*, exemplified in our accounts of the Legal Realists in the US and by the constitutionalists in France. That role draws on the fact that aristocratic or notable groups having a stranglehold on the dominant positions in the legal field tend to look to transmit those positions to their descendants, thereby bypassing the scholarly lines – and also the agents – of reproduction in favour of their own criteria of excellence.

A hypothesis formulated by Bourdieu helps to better understand the evolution of legal fields by addressing structural contradictions inherent in the reproduction of legal capital. Bourdieu develops the idea that legal capital is at the same time inherited and acquired through scholarly achievement. Legal capital on one side represents a kind of cultural capital defined in opposition to aristocratic or royal capital. It valorises individual scholarly expertise in relation to the inherited privileges of family lineage. It offers a diploma against the title of nobility. Nevertheless, Bourdieu notes, this depiction is in fact a matter of a false opposition, since the doctors of law also want to be recognized as a *noblesse de robe*. The representatives of the judicial hierarchy in France, for example, while managing positions bought from the king, defended the principle of dynastic reproduction against the idea of meritocratic promotion (Bourdieu 2012: 510).

As mentioned briefly above, a claim of the status of nobility was part of the process of erecting barriers to entry – both financial and cultural – that reserved access to the most prestigious schools of law to the offspring of aristocratic families who could rely on the support of their families or powerful civil or religious protectors – notably through the granting of stipends and later clerical positions (Brundage 2008: 121). Martines (1968) also shows how this mobilization of family capital is not at all inconsistent with scholarly investment. The first stage in the most successful careers passed through diplomatic tasks that permitted the accumulation of relational capital diversified among the various holders of state power – the princes of the church, monarchs, or *Condottiere*. And there, too, the support of a great name was indispensable to be recognized and received; and the importance of financial support should also not be neglected given sumptuary investments that were not always reimbursed but went along with the missions.

This conversion of the social capital of family lineage into learned legal capital opened the door to state careers not only in the period of the Renaissance and the genesis of the state. Karady described a process that was quite similar in Hungary before World War II (Karady 1991; see also Rueschemeyer 1997 for the faculties of law in Germany in the period after that war). This process of converting cultural capital into state capital through investment in legal learning was also exported by the colonial societies, as we have shown for Latin America and Asia (Dezalay and Garth 2002; 2010). In the case of Brazil, Miceli (1983) has shown that the construction by Vargas of the institutions of the modern Brazilian state – in opposition to a more patrimonial and clientelistic state – was fed by the reconversion of the descendants of old families from the oligarchy of the Northeast, who were then on the decline, into new notables of the state and politics, thanks to the legitimacy of their diplomas in law.

This strong complementarity between family heritage and the legal diploma – which Bourdieu (2012) termed 'the diploma of the bourgeoisie' – was not inconsistent with the continuing existence of tensions between the two types of resources. More precisely, the tensions were between different fractions of jurists who sought to valorise one or the other according to which one favoured their side. And there were also many intermediate positions between the two poles representing, on one side, the inheritors of the *noblesse de robe*, and, on the other, new arrivals seeking to gain recognition for their learned expertise, their personal merits, their leadership abilities, or their oratorical skills. Nevertheless, since the representatives of the *noblesse de robe* in general occupy the dominant positions within the hierarchy of the legal field, they also tend to hold the institutional resources that allow them to prevail in setting the criteria for success. They tend to favour modes of production privileging cultural capital and family origins at the expense of too rigorous scholarly selection – selection entirely based on individual intellectual merit.[6]

This structural contradiction therefore provides the starting point for a process involving the relative devalorisation of learned capital – and a corresponding marginalization of the most intellectual fraction of the legal field, which can become a source of obsolescence, even of decline. This process so far has not been documented as such by legal historians, and the likely reason for this omission is simply that these legal histories, as Bourdieu notes, are written mainly by and for jurists and, therefore, tend to provide mainly 'internal history, a history without agents'. Nevertheless, one can find a number of indications of this general tendency toward the obsolescence of learned legal capital.

[6] Cf. this remark cited by A.J. Arnaud about a prominent French high court judge, a child of one of Napoleon's peers. '*Il n'y a pas de meilleure garantie d'une bonne justice qu'un grand nom.*'

The most flagrant example is doubtless the evolution of the Inns of Court in Great Britain, which lost all their intellectual functions at the time of the triumph of the barristers. The barristers imposed a recruitment process entirely through co-optation and apprenticeship – directed toward social origins and political strategies. The political victory of Parliament and the barristers who served the groups from which they themselves came – the gentry and bourgeois commercial interests – provoked at the same time a weakening of the royal bureaucracy and the academic learning associated with Roman law that had provided its members' education.

The Inns of Court have not escaped from the lingering impact of this traditional disqualification of academic learning. They long served as finishing schools for the descendants of the gentry. Barristers learned some skills in legal practice, enabling them to manage their jurisdictional domains and fulfil the function of justice of the peace in local conflicts. And provincial elites becoming barristers were able, therefore, to acquire a cultural and relational capital which permitted them to represent their interests effectively in the political fights between Parliament and the monarchy.

But the general political and professional victory of the Bar also signalled the beginning of a long decline, and the near elimination of the professors and schools of law continues to have an impact today on the British legal field. It was only at the end of the eighteenth century that the first chairs of law were created at the prestigious English universities, notably Oxford and Cambridge. And it was only after World War II that the first law departments began to operate in the new universities such as Warwick.

This process of marginalization and obsolescence of the institutions for the reproduction of learned law is much less prominent in the continental legal fields, where, as Weber noted, the 'law of professors' reigned, but one observes nevertheless similar tendencies. In particular, one analogue is the tendency of the faculties of law on the Continent to become places for the reproduction of a doctrine that is mainly exegetic, dominated by 'guardians of the temple of the texts' – seeking to minimize any jurisprudential evolution by refusing to take into account any new social realities. As Bourdieu remarked in his conclusion to his article on 'The Force of Law' (1987), the dominated of the field, made up often of the new arrivals, take up the position of investing in the renovation of legal science, including by borrowing from relatively new disciplines such as the social sciences in order to gain recognition for themselves and new social interests for which they seek to become spokespersons within the legal field. But the traditional faculties on the Continent have resisted these influences.

10.4 Marginalization and obsolescence in the institutions of the reproduction of learned law

On the Continent, Germany is the only exception to a general tendency toward the weakening or even decline in the position of the faculties of law in national legal fields. This exception is explained by the Lutheran revolution and the internal fights of the German empire, noted above, which helped to maintain the prestige and influence of the faculties as competing and complementary places of intellectual and cultural production. In a context of fragmented powers weakened by religious and political conflicts, the faculties of law possessed a strong symbolic authority by serving as a crossroads and melting pot between different regimes and the elites who confronted them. Still, as noted above, there were indications even in Germany of a relative decline in the value of scholarly capital with respect to family capital (Dahrendorf 1969; for Hungary see Karady 1991).

In France, the decline was far sharper, precipitated especially by the transformation of the high judicial positions into ones that could be bought and sold and passed on through inheritance. This eighteenth-century development greatly weakened the control of the faculties of law over the reproduction of professionals. The decline was accelerated further by the impacts that this venality had on the practice of law and therefore on the criteria of excellence of the Bar. Excluded from the traditional legal markets by the high prices, the new entrants were stimulated to develop new practices looking toward the role of tribune – inside and outside the courts – at the expense of the traditional legal learning taught within the faculties of law.

10.5 A virtue out of poverty and an ethic of disinterestedness as a strategy of reconversion

Bell (1994: 70) points out that the French Bar was a 'nursery of dignities' and the means of access to positions of power in and around the state. At least, this was the situation before the venality of legal positions constrained the less rich fraction of the Bar to find other means of valorising their expertise – professional, scholarly, and civic investments.

This was the beginning of the professional valorisation identified with and promoted by d'Aguesseau – making the defence of the public and the citizen the new sources of prestige,[7] which developed in conjunction with flourishing presses also fuelled by the Jansenist affair. 'Young barristers saw participation in these causes célèbres as a quick way to make names for themselves (. . .) God has put the Church of Christ itself amongst your clients.' Lacking the ability to obtain state positions, the French advocates reconverted into pamphleteers, first in the service of bourgeois Jansenists and then the Enlightenment bourgeoisie more generally. 'Thus the career of barrister suddenly began to seem attractive not only to upwardly-mobile bourgeois and would be Jansenist priests, but also to would be philosophers' (Bell 1994: 83).

This new opportunity helped change the recruitment into the French Bar toward a different professional profile. Linguet, for example, one of the well-known representatives of this new generation, entered the profession after failing as a writer, stating that he would rather be a 'rich cook than a poor and unknown savant' (Bell 1994: 84). In contrast to the earlier generation that sought to be 'high priests of the law' and validate their technical skill, their legal science, and their political wisdom, the new arrivals valued rhetorical and theatrical skills that allowed them to speak effectively for various causes.[8] They valued 'genius, a good voice and the art of touching hearts'.[9] Nevertheless, even if this new approach to practice was dressed up in the language of civic virtue and lack of concern with money, the profits were not insignificant: 'barristers' careers reached new peaks as a result of the public's endless taste for sensational causes célèbres' (1994: 84).

This conversion from dignitaries serving the constitutional monarchy into tribunes for the public corresponded to an enlargement in the recruitment into the Bar. Reforms promoted by Maupeou abolished the

[7] Bell 1994: 73. 'Given that barristers could no longer aspire to high office, or hope to influence royal policy, the late XVIIth also saw the publication of a flurry of works aimed at providing the bar with new professional ideals.'

[8] Relevant skills included setting the stage for the performance. 'In one particularly sensational trial, in which a family of bourgeois money lenders sued an aristocratic client, Linguet, appearing for the defendant, employed a clique of 300 noblemen to hiss and jeer the opposing counsel and strode through the Palais with a bodyguard of 60 nobles' (Bell 1994: 93).

[9] The older generation therefore tended to take their distance from training that in their opinion was 'useless, pedantic, promoting a stultifying and unworthy style in oratory and legal writing and stifling the careers of most promising advocates' (Bell 1994: 94).

monopoly of the organized Bar and opened the profession to all law graduates. This strategy also permitted them to short-circuit legal jurisdictions while obliging them to take into account public opinion – which they helped to construct thanks to their monopoly control of the market for political pamphlets free of royal censorship.[10] Factums describing particular arguments were diffused by the thousands. 'Factums take the place of judicial rulings and direct those of the judge' (Voltaire, cited in Bell 1994: 131); 'your judges will be, even without realizing the fact, compelled or restrained by the Public, by the most widely spread opinion. It is thus the Public we must instruct, convince and win over' (Simon Benguet quoted in Bell 1994: 85).

The strategy of conversion into tribunes of the public and political causes permitted this group to dominate the emerging market of political representation even if it meant sacrificing the organization of the Bar. This attitude explains the paradox of revolutionary assemblies dominated by advocates acting to abolish the Bar. After the revolutionary turmoil passed, to be sure, Napoleon restored the professional structures while restraining their autonomy. But the strategy of advocate-politician and champion of public opinion was sufficiently profitable that it reappeared when the political circumstances allowed it.[11] Young advocates from the urban middle classes built fame in the courts and through the media by denouncing governmental abuses of power. The need to maintain credibility through this strategy of mobilization of legal resources in the political field did impose limitations in terms of investments in business law, which meant business lawyers occupied only the margins of the legal field. But political profits, as noted above, were not trivial, even if they had to await the arrival of the '*république des avocats*' representing the consecration of this strategy of the advocate as notable professional of the political field.

The strict connection between law and politics helped to continue to marginalize the production of legal learning that characterized the eighteenth century. In a recent book calling for the modernization of the teaching of law, Christophe Jamin, the founding director of the faculty of law at Sciences Po, wrote: 'We know that the old faculties of the Ancien Régime were nearly abandoned at the time the Revolutionaries

[10] 'In a single movement, lawyers both constituted the public and claimed to be its representatives' (Karpik 2000: 114).

[11] In Karpik's words (Karpik 2000: 116): 'Such a choice was not irreversible; it turned out to be too fortunate to be renounced.'

suppressed them in 1793: the professors barely gave their lessons and the students no longer attended in mass. Better to learn the law at the office of a practitioner than to go and follow, in Latin, the vague teachings of Roman law and canon law, with lessons on French law being almost negligible' (Jamin 2012: 34).

The faculties of law were re-established by the Napoleonic reforms, but their professors were limited to the function, in Jamin's terms, of 'repeaters of the imperial catechism about the codes' (Jamin 2012: 36), and they were quite reticent with respect to new disciplines, such as history and political economy. In order to illustrate the intellectual poverty of this manner of teaching, Jamin quotes Flaubert, who referred to his years of studying the law as evoking 'huge amounts of boredom' (2012: 39).

In order to better situate the professional context and clarify its internal criticisms, we can rely again on the historical research by Sacriste on the genesis of *La République des constitutionnalistes* (2011), which covers the period 1870–1914. He described the faculties of law as essentially professional schools. This characterization especially applied to provincial faculties, who responded to the demands of local practitioners seeking to assure the reproduction of highly segmented regional legal worlds in which the professors were themselves highly involved. They were therefore much closer to the pole of legal practice than to the intellectual pole. 'The production of written works – articles, notes on jurisprudence, treatises or manuals – did not constitute a valued criterion of professional excellence' (2011: 48). And they spent much of their time and resources in their legal offices, 'pleading most often themselves or providing written opinions for the benefit of the local bourgeoisie' (2011: 48).

The domination of the civil law professors from the faculties of law was directly linked to their integration into these parochial legal worlds, which they served to reproduce while educating the inheritors of the local notables of the bench and Bar in the rules established by the Civil Code. With teaching activity dominated by the exegesis of texts, all form of innovation was, if not excluded, at least marginalized – a fortiori any reference to new ideological currents or new disciplines such as sociology or other social sciences that emerged in new intellectual circles close to the reformist milieu, such as the school of '*Sciences Morales et Politiques*'.

This situation makes it easier to understand why the young Turks of the faculties of law, with learned expertise that went unrecognized – both by the hierarchy of professors of civil law as well as by the notables of the Bar – were inclined to form an alliance with emerging political leaders. This alliance offered positions and a career that could valorise their capital of legal authority. The success of these promotional strategies came from the ability to put forward a new scientific legitimacy that conformed to the university's new model of academic excellence encouraged by the new political leaders. In this manner the partisans of these reforms in legal education were also able to bring scientific value where the actual production of scientific value had been lacking (Sacriste 2011: 121).

The European stories, including that of Great Britain, point to a relative decline in the value of scholarly capital in favour of the scholarship dominated by the exegesis of civil codes, by conservative and relatively static scholarship, by the elevation of the role of dinners at the Inns of Court over any pretensions of learned activity, all of which was consistent with the relatively higher value of family capital as opposed to learned legal capital. In such settings, despite dramatic exceptions such as the rise of the constitutional law scholars, there were no ongoing mechanisms to keep law and legal discourse abreast of new political interests, new disciplinary approaches, and new political regimes. The role of law and lawyers in the fields of political power correspondingly declined, as many commentators noted in the post-World War II period. More recently, the relative inability of the law faculties to produce new representations fitting the interests of globalized markets has led to further challenges that we will discuss below.

Vauchez's story of the reshuffling of legal hierarchies that took place through the development of the European Community provides a notable counterpoint to this story of relative decline and a lack of hospitality to innovation and change. The changes that took place with the development of the transnational level, as we have seen, fit the historical analyses of Berman and even accounts of the earlier development of city states. Our suggestion here, however, is that the European national legal fields, however the hierarchies were unsettled with the rise of Europe, are still relatively slow to facilitate the kind of scholarly entrepreneurship and political alliance that leads to regime change – but also strengthened legal credibility.

10.6 Law schools in the US, scholarly production, and regime changes

In contrast to the great difficulty that faculties of law in Europe have had in retooling to serve new governing regimes and constellations of interest, the law schools in the US present a more open and adaptable structure. The development of the corporate law firm – described as the Cravath model – late in the nineteenth century coincided with the triumph of the Harvard case method and the model of elite law schools producing graduates to work at the corporate law firms. The corporate law firms, in turn, grounded their legitimacy not only on their close connection to the elite law schools – cemented through philanthropy and alumni networks – but also on the investment by leading partners in government service and more generally in good governance. As we have written elsewhere (Dezalay and Garth 2010), the firms prospered, gained a distance from their corporate law firms in order to serve them better, and made the rules – along with the philanthropic foundations that they helped to create – that helped bring order and legitimacy to the world in which their clients could thrive.

Until the Great Depression of the 1930s, the doctrinal scholarship produced by law professors largely in the form of treatises sufficed to give the law schools a prominent role – even if secondary to the leading practitioners and judges – in maintaining the position of law in the governance of the state and the economy. The Depression, as noted above, unsettled the hierarchies, and indeed the corporate Bar was extremely hostile to New Deal measures strengthening the power of the state over the economy. The collective mobility project of law professors at the elite law schools, which Shamir detailed in his book (Shamir 1995), centred on an alliance with New Dealers and the new disciplines gaining strength on the campus, especially social science and economics, and the scholarly banner of Legal Realism to challenge the formalism of the earlier generation of academics.

The result was not only a new status for law professors but also Washington law firms serving clients in relation to the new state regulations and bureaucracies. The law schools continued to draw on the rest of the university while maintaining a central position in the production of representations geared to the increasingly activist state that accompanied the civil rights revolution (Kabaservice 2004; Garth and Sterling 1998). By the beginning of the 1970s, with the development of public interest law by the Ford Foundation in particular, elite law schools were well aligned with the relatively activist US state.

The Reagan coalition, which came to power with the mission of countering the welfare state and deregulating business, was closely aligned with Chicago neo-liberal economics, but the coalition began with relatively little presence in the law schools. There was a small number of 'law and economics' scholars, centred in Chicago, and supported by the Olin Foundation, a conservative foundation seeking self-consciously to build a conservative economics presence in law faculties; and they assisted the new government in changing antitrust policy in favour of allowing more mergers and acquisitions and in deregulating the economy (Eisner 1991). But the elite schools at the time were dominated by scholars of a generation tied to the more activist state.

Reagan's Attorney General, Edwin Meese, who had served Reagan during his California governorship and who later became a University of San Diego law professor before joining the Reagan presidential administration, joined with a relatively small number of law professors and law students in the early 1980s to create the Federalist Society (Southworth 2008). The agenda was to build a conservative presence, especially in the elite law schools, and to produce people and ideas that would serve to implement the Reagan agenda behind a strong cadre of lawyers and academics. The Federalist Society was extremely successful in nurturing new and reinvented doctrines that worked perfectly with the Reagan and later Bush agendas, including one in constitutional law termed 'originalism', designed to guide the Supreme Court away from expanding constitutional rights to disadvantaged groups. Indeed, Reagan appointed leading proponents of the doctrine, including Antonin Scalia, to the US Supreme Court. Similarly, doctrines developed with respect to Executive Power became the legal source for the George W. Bush administration's War on Terror, including the justifications for torture and the confinement of prisoners indefinitely to Guantanamo (Hollis-Bruskey 2011; 2012; 2013). The success of this movement in transforming the legal doctrines used by the government, the Supreme Court, and academia more generally, was quite remarkable. One further indicator is that the same process led to the creation and transformation of a new brand of elite public interest law firms, modelled on the ones serving the more activist state agenda and occupying precisely the same space, but serving conservative causes.

The ability of the large cadre of law professors in the US, building ties through corporate law firms, politics, and foundations, to produce a constant stream of legal scholarship aiming to serve potential governing regimes, allows the US legal field to shift relatively quickly in response to successive political and economic 'revolutions'. This ability is also reflected in the doctrines and norms that operate in the transnational governance mechanisms that have become so significant since the 1990s and the end of the Cold War.

The combination of hegemonic power and this constant production helps to explain why the legal architecture of the European Community is linked most closely to US-based academics, Eric Stein and Joseph Weiler, and why the World Trade Organization is especially linked to US legal academics such as Robert Hudec and John Jackson. There are numerous examples of the ability of US legal academics to produce representations, and it is notable that the production also continues apace in the human rights and public interest law fields, seeking to temper the impacts of economic globalization (see, for example, Cummings and Trubek 2009). In the global competition among professions, competing 'empires', and governing expertise, among other things, this scholarly production of new and competing representations provides a relative advantage to the US legal field in global competition.

10.7 Potential academic counterattacks in Europe

The European Community, as Vauchez and others point out, reshaped professional hierarchies with the European national legal fields. The position of corporate lawyers, as one notable example, became stronger. Similarly the scholarly influence of legal scholarship beyond the exegesis of codes and incorporating interdisciplinary perspectives has also increased. But, as noted, European corporate law firms have relied less on national legal education and more on programmes of study abroad, especially in the US, to train the growing cadre of corporate practitioners; and interdisciplinary legal theories, such as those promoted by the US scholars cited above, have played a major role in European debates and changes. In assessing the ability of European legal fields to compete and shift with major national and transnational power shifts, one key variable will be whether the quite conservative systems of legal education become more open to interdisciplinary scholarship and more entrepreneurial.

Christoph Jamin's critical examination of French legal education, discussed above, represents part of a new effort to push a leading national legal academy to find a place in a new national and also global regime. The purpose of his book was to justify the creation in 2009 of a law school within Sciences Po, long at the top of the hierarchy in producing French political and economic leaders. Making an argument in favour of interdisciplinary scholarship and education, more selective admission, full-time professors, English language instruction, and a rejection of the formalism associated with the exegesis of civil codes, Sciences Po has sought to challenge the traditional faculties of law represented especially by Paris I and Paris II. The traditional law faculties have criticized the two-year curriculum at Sciences Po as insufficient to train real French lawyers versed in the Civil Code, and they have also instituted some reforms seeking to provide a special track to hold onto the best students. The Sciences Po law school, and others that are also outside the traditional faculties, are also consistent with the shifting hierarchy within the legal profession that recognizes the major role and prestige of corporate law firms serving transnational businesses. The legal establishment best represented by the faculties of law remains, but Sciences Po has resources – including strong ties to the media and the state – to play effectively in the French field of state power. This national battle is part of transnational competition as well.

Inspired in part by the US law and economics movement, the first private German faculty of law, Bucerius law school, located in Hamburg, is also positioned to serve the corporate law market. There is also a new faculty of law connected to the EBS in Wiesbaden. Again there is a greater emphasis in these schools on interdisciplinary research and teaching, facility in English, selective admissions, and opportunities for experience abroad to gain cosmopolitan skills and expertise. The Bucerius law school does not represent the same kind of player in the field of state power that Sciences Po represents, but it too is taking advantage of the slowness of the German educational establishment to move into and retool for the space created by the new global order.

There are other examples of new and reformed law schools and faculties of law adopting similar strategies because of the slowness of traditional faculties to move and a new market logic that now makes it easier to produce competitors to the traditional faculties of law. Within the UK, faculties of law such as Oxford and Cambridge, which have topped the hierarchy of legal education but not occupied the same kind of position that law schools have in the US, also seek to embrace reform and gain a stronger position at home as well.

The working hypothesis, based on the general analyses of this chapter, is that a key to understanding this phenomenon of the globalization of legal education – now well evident in Europe – is to understand how individual examples are properly also characterized as local initiatives to take advantage of and contribute to new state political and economic regimes – also within emerging transnational orders. In each case, the reformist rhetoric draws on the US model of legal education – full-time faculties, scholarly production that draws on interdisciplinary connections, and selective admission standards. One argument that is made to promote the new school or reform is that it will facilitate more success in global competition. The conservative and backward-looking approach dependent on exegesis of national codes will be replaced by a more dynamic and less formal approach. But it would be a mistake to expect that these efforts to challenge the existing hierarchies in national legal education will in fact topple those hierarchies and replace them with the highly entrepreneurial, relatively flexible and adaptable US model.

The approach we have provided here, based on Berman as supplemented by Bourdieu's sociology, provides tools to see how these national examples relate to the position of law and lawyers in the changing field of state power. The result even of these relatively successful revolutions or regime changes is likely to be a strengthening and rebuilding of the credibility of the law and the hierarchies within the legal field.

10.8 Conclusion

The success story of Europe as reviving in some sense the role of law and lawyers within European nations invites closer inquiry into the processes that account for that change. Drawing on Berman's linking of law and revolution and Bourdieu's comparative analyses of law in the field of state power, we note that the European story – involving cosmopolitan legal elites occupying multiple positions at various levels of governance, a self-conscious production of European legal scholarship and institutions organized to promote that scholarship, and new corporate law firms with lawyers able to link multinational businesses and emerging European structures – is an example of a process of change and adaptation that is seen more generally. It is especially easy to see in studies of the legal field in the US, in part because of a relative openness to processes of regime change through relationships among politics, corporate law, and legal education.

In addition, this sociological and historical approach provides tools for examining the national legal fields that help to make up and are in part changed by the development of legal Europe. The national comparisons show different hierarchical structures but similarities in the relative decline of the national positions of law and lawyers in the twentieth century. Legal education as part of this relative decline came to involve a focus more on the reproduction of social capital than meritocratic investment in scholarly legitimacy.

Finally, we mention efforts underway to reform legal education in Europe to move more toward the more entrepreneurial and less formal US system, suggesting that what might be expected from the sociological and historical examples in the chapter is a new cycle of national processes of change which both challenge the existing hierarchies and facilitate change that from a longer perspective can be seen to reaffirm those hierarchies.

Bibliography

Bell, David A. (1994). *Lawyers and Citizens: The Making of a Political Elite in Old Regime France*. Oxford: Oxford University Press.

Berman, Harold J. (1983). *Law and Revolution: The Formation of the Western Legal Tradition*. Cambridge, MA: Harvard University Press.

(2003). *Law and Revolution II: The Impact of the Protestant Reformations on the Western Legal Tradition*. Cambridge, MA: Belknap Press of Harvard University Press.

Bourdieu, Pierre (1987). 'The Force of Law: Toward a Sociology of the Juridical Field', *Hastings Law Review* 38: 805–52.

(2012). *Sur l'État: Cours au Collège de France (1989–1992)*. Paris: Seuil.

Brundage, James (2008). *The Medieval Origins of the Legal Profession*. Chicago, IL: University of Chicago Press.

Christophe, Charle (1989). 'Pour une histoire sociale des professions juridiques à l'époque contemporaine. Notes pour une recherche', *Actes de la recherche en sciences sociales* 76–7: 117–19.

Cummings, Scott and Louise Trubek (2009). 'Globalizing Public Interest Law', *UCLA Journal of International Law and Foreign Affairs* 13: 1–53.

Dahrendorf, Ralf (1969). 'Law Faculties and the German Upper Class', in W. Aubert (ed.). *Sociology of Law*. Harmondsworth: Penguin, pp. 294–309.

Dezalay, Yves (1992). *Marchands de droit. La restructuration de l'ordre juridique international par les multinationales du droit*. Paris: Fayard.

Dezalay, Yves and Bryant G. Garth (2002). *The Internationalization of Palace Wars*. Chicago, IL: University of Chicago Press.

(2010). *Asian Legal Revivals: Lawyers in the Shadow of Empires*. Chicago, IL: University of Chicago Press.

(2013). 'Elite European Lawyers? The Common Market as New Golden Age or Missed Opportunity', in Niilo Kauppi and Mikael R. Madsen (eds). *Transnational Power Elites: The European Complex in the Global Field of Power*. Milton Park: Routledge.

Eisner, Marc (1991). *Antitrust and the Triumph of Economics: Institutions, Expertise, and Policy Change*. Chapel Hill, NC: University of North Carolina Press.

Garth, Bryant and Joyce Sterling (1998). 'From Legal Realism to Law and Society: Reshaping Law for the Last Stages of the Social Activist State', *Law and Society Review* 32: 409–72.

Hollis-Bruskey, Amanda (2011). 'Support Structures and Constitutional Change', *Law and Social Inquiry* 36(2): 516–36.

(2012). 'Helping Ideas Have Consequences: Political and Intellectual Investment in the Unitary Executive Theory, 1981–2000', *Denver University Law Review* 89(1): 197–244.

(2013). 'It's the Network: The Federalist Society as a Supplier of Intellectual Capital for the Supreme Court', *Studies in Law, Politics, and Society* 61: 137–78.

Jamin, Christoph (2012). *La cuisine du droit. L'école de droit de Science Po: une expérience française*. Paris: Lextenso.

Kabaservice, Geoffrey (2004). *The Guardians: Kingman Brewster, His Circle, and the Rise of the Liberal Establishment*. New York, NY: Henry Holt.

Kantorowicz, Ernst H. (1997). *The King's Two Bodies: A Study in Medieval Political Theology*. Princeton, NJ: Princeton University Press.

Karady, Victor (1991). 'Une nation de juristes', *Actes de la Recherche en Sciences Sociales* 90: 106–15.

Karpik, Lucian (2000). *French Lawyers: A Study in Collective Action 1274–1994*. Oxford: Oxford University Press.

Martines, Lauro (1968). *Lawyers and Statecraft in Renaissance Florence*. Princeton, NJ: Princeton University Press.

Miceli, Sergio (1983). *Les intellectuels et le pouvoir au Brésil*. Paris: A.M. Metaille.

Rueschemeyer, Dietrich (1997). 'State, Capitalism and the Organization of Legal Counsel: Examining an Extreme Case – the Prussian Bar, 1700–1914', in Terence C. Halliday and Guillaume Sacriste (eds). *La république des constitutionnalistes*. Paris: Sciences Po.

Sacriste, Guillaume (2011). *La République des constitutionnalistes: Professeurs de droit et légitimation de l'État en France (1870-1914)*. Paris: Sciences-Po.

Shamir, Ronen (1995). *Managing Legal Uncertainty: Elite Lawyers in the New Deal*. Durham, NC: Duke University Press.

Southworth, Ann (2008). *Lawyers of the Right: Professionalizing the Conservative Coalition*. Chicago, IL: University of Chicago Press.

Thompson, Edward Palmer (1975). *Whigs and Hunters*. London: Allen Lane.

van Caenegem, Raoul Charles (1987). *Judges, Legislators and Professors*. Cambridge: Cambridge University Press.

Vauchez, Antoine (2013). *L'union par le droit*. Paris: Sciences Po.

Whaley, Joachim (2011). *Germany and the Holy Roman Empire (1493–1806)*. Vols I and II. Oxford: Oxford University Press.

11

Europe in crisis – an evolutionary genealogy

HAUKE BRUNKHORST

This chapter sets out a blueprint for a critical theory of constitutional evolution, and it shows how this can be applied to the legal evolution of the European Union (EU).[1] The crucial point in this theory is the distinction between two kinds of evolutionary change. The first kind of evolutionary change is the *gradual and incremental adaption* of a specific constitutional regime. Gradual adaption leads to the progressive *constitutionalization* of society through the structural coupling of law and other social systems. In this process, functional imperatives and social class formations act as the mechanisms of selection (of 'natural selection' in the classical Darwinian theory of organic evolution). The second kind of evolutionary change is *rapid, catalytic or revolutionary change*, which leads, not to an improvement of the adaptive capacities of the society, but to a new system of *normative constraints*, which shapes and limits the ongoing adaptive process, and opens up new paths for social and legal evolution (this corresponds to the principles of 'speciation' and 'punctuation' in the neo-Darwinian theory of evolution). This theory is then applied to the case of the EU. As in other instances, we can also distinguish in this case between an act of revolutionary foundation and a successive and incremental process of functional constitutionalization. Our reconstruction of the main stages of the European constitutional evolution leads us to the thesis that the process of constitutionalization and integration, which possesses an ultimately technocratic character, is accompanied by a latent crisis of legitimization. This is the critical, *genealogical* aspect of the evolutionary analysis offered here, and it ultimately provides a basis for a diagnosis of the present crisis of the Union.

In section 11.1 of this chapter, I will give a brief outline of my theoretical framework, which is founded in evolutionary theory. I will argue that constitutions form *evolutionary universals* or evolutionary advances.

[1] I am very much obliged to Chris Thornhill for his remarks on the chapter, and for polishing my German English, and I have to thank Mikael Rask Madsen for important queries.

In section 11.2, I will draw a distinction between *revolutionary* and *gradual* (or 'evolutionary') change within the process of social evolution. Then, in section 11.3, I will give some examples of *sequences* of revolutionary and evolutionary change in constitutional history. In section 11.4, I will propose the thesis that, although the foundation of the EU in 1951 (European Coal and Steel Community) was a very limited act of unification, it was nevertheless an example of a *revolutionary founding act*. In the last two sections, I will reconstruct the *evolutionary development* of the European constitution and demonstrate that the evolution of European constitutional law poses structural problems of legitimization, which are likely to become manifest in a serious and existential *crisis of legitimization*.

11.1 Evolutionary advances

My first thesis is that, if observed from a sociological point of view, the *constitution is an evolutionary universal*.[2] Procedures for constitutional normalization exist in all societies, and they are commonly used to solve functional problems that are caused by the production of a growing multitude of legal norms, which become increasingly confusing, fragmented and inconsistent. This usually leads to an elementary process of constitutionalization, which, as a minimum, consists in classification, codification, corpus formation (as in the *corpus iuris*), or hierarchical organization of norms. Of particular importance in this is the need to resolve collisions between the self-referentially closed social systems of politics and law by structural coupling of the two systems through law (see Luhmann 1990).

Once invented, constitutions are copied or re-invented again and again in very different ways, and in nearly all kinds of societal community. If constitutions are evolutionary universals, then the original and essential *concept* of the constitution is broader than that of the *constitution of the nation state*. In consequence, this concept is able to accommodate other constitutional formations such as *inter-, trans- and supranational public law constitutions* on the one side, and *societal civil law constitutions* on the other side. Understood as an evolutionary universal, the concept of the constitution can be used to bridge the *dualism of national and international*

[2] On the concept of evolutionary universals see Parsons (1964). For the application of this to constitutional evolution see Luhmann (1990). There is not that much difference here between Parsons and Luhmann, Luhmann merely tries to avoid any teleological misunderstanding that could be associated with the word 'universal'.

law as well as the *dualism of state and society*. Notably, both dualisms were (epistemologically) constitutive for German statist (or monarchical) constitutionalism of the nineteenth century (*Staatsrechtslehre*).[3]

The referential openness of the evolutionary concept of a constitution is due to the fact that evolutionary universals (Parsons) or evolutionary advances (Luhmann) contain multiple evolutionary inventions (see Parsons 1964; Luhmann 1997: 505). Paradigmatic for evolutionary universals are the invention of the eye or the brain. There is great diversity amongst brains. Every species has a distinct brain. There are brains of rats, sparrows, men, dogs, ticks, cockroaches, apes or sharks. They are as different as the eyes of different species (those of the eagle from those of the bat) or other evolutionary universals in biology as well as in sociology. Social universals of evolution are bureaucracy, kinship, religion, constitutions, stratification, urbanization and others. In these instances, there is a huge variety of forms. Modern German bureaucracy is as different from old Egyptian bureaucracy as the eye of the eagle is different from the eye of the dog. Both paganism and monotheism are realizations of the evolutionary universal of religion. Both Flensburg and Hong Kong reflect an evolutionary advance of urbanization. This argument can be applied *ad infinitum*.

In analogy to this, there are different societal communities with a wide range of constitutions. Flensburg University has a constitution. China has a constitution and Germany has a different one. But Bavaria, Texas, Goa and New York taxi drivers also have a constitution, and there are even constitutional amendment procedures for scientific journals such as *Constellations*. The first time that an international organization referred to its statutes *as* a constitution was the International Labour Organization (ILO) in its foundational treaty of 1919. Alternatively, the EU *has* a constitution even though the Lisbon Treaty is not called a 'constitution' (because of the failure of its *Constitutional Treaty* in 2005). The Charter of the United Nations is a constitution that is binding for all states and individual human beings (as we can see from the listed terrorists as well as from the existence of international human rights regimes). Furthermore, newspapers, commercial enterprises, and chess clubs have documents called 'constitutions', and in Germany there exists a law that includes the constitution of industrial companies (*Betriebsverfassungsgesetz*) as a law under the German Basic Law. Europe has a plurality of constitutions, and this plurality is not in any way a European peculiarity

[3] In the first third of the twentieth century both forms of dualism were sharply criticized as features of bourgeois legal theory by Hans Kelsen. See chapter 11 in Brunkhorst (2012).

or *Sonderweg*. In the first instance, Europe has a constitution 'in the sense of the co-existence of transnational and national constitutions'. Second, it has a constitution in the sense that it contains a variety of functionally specialized constitutions, constitutionalizing the economic, legal, political, social relations and security system of the EU (Tuori 2010: 3). From an evolutionary point of view, it is pointless to argue that there are *true, real* or *substantial* constitutions, which can be strictly distinguished from *false, unreal* or *accidental* constitutions. This opposition has been one of the fundamental doctrines of the German science of constitutional law (*Staatsrechtslehre*) since Paul Laband. The distinction between substantial and accidental constitutions is just as pointless as the assertion that the eagle has a true, substantial or real eye, that the half-blind dog or the nearly blind bat have only accidental or unreal eyes, or that the pinnacle of creation, the human being, has the real brain, and all other animals such as cockroaches have brains that are not truly real.

Constitutions usually consist in a circular relation between two provisions or conditions. That is, they express a circular relation between a number of *subjective rights* (which need not be human or civic rights, but can also be privileges), and a set *principles of checks and balances* ('rules to make rules'). The thesis that I wish to propose here is that both these conditions *constitute* (in the sense of Searle's 'constitutive rules') the *constituent power* in which a constitution is founded. The constituent power, on this account, is, first, 'permanent',[4] and, second, it is *always already* both *constituent* and *constituted power*.[5] The constituent power is always already (in the sense of Heidegger's transcendental perfect: *immer schon*) constituted by the above provisions. This is because, first, the constituent power is permanent, and, second, because (and in particular *if* it is permanently *enacted*) it makes no sense to draw a *categorical distinction* between the first (but not primordial!) act of a specific constituent power ('We the People') and later acts of the same power which interpret, concretize, change or renew the constitution (an example is Basic Law Article 146). The first act of making a constitution (say the French Constitution of 1791) is not primordial because there already existed a constituent power before 1789. This *legally* institutionalized power was changed by a legal act (it is of no significance whether this occurred in conformity, or not in conformity, with

[4] See the argument in Böckenförde (1986).

[5] The idea of the norm-free *pouvoir constituant* existing as an entity prior to the law (and prior to subjective rights) is a myth. For an empirical and historical account, see Thornhill (2011). For a conceptual account, see Maus (1992: 148, 176).

the existing legal rules) in June 1789 when the Estates-General declared themselves to be the representatives of the Third Estate that *is* the Nation. This was an act that could not be performed anywhere else but *within* the legal body of the Estates-General (using its positive, changeable rules to make rules, be it in accordance with the existing law or not). Second, there is no classical case (France, America) in which constituent power was performed that does not include an idea of equal rights (no matter whether their reference was restricted to select groups, i.e. to those with white coloured skin, self-employment, etc.). Historically, both things – rights and constituent power – were not even distinguished (see Thornhill, Chapter 2 in this book). For example, when Germany received its first democratic constitution in 1919 the constitutional lawyer Richard Thoma asked why it needed a list of subjective rights if Germany had a constitution that was *democratic*. Thoma, a former lawyer of the German Empire, still thought about democracy in terms based in the tradition of the eighteenth century. His argument was that a constitutional *monarchy* was deeply in need of a legally valid list of rights, which defend the people from the executive power of monarchy, which was in fact the constituent power. But why, he asked, should the people defend themselves from themselves once *they* had become the constituent power?

The two conditions outlined above are necessary but not sufficient conditions for a constitution, and it is a myth that there are necessary *and* sufficient conditions of a *true* constitution. From an evolutionary point of view, there is only family resemblance between different constitutions. Even if there exist great and *crucial differences* between different kinds of constitution, there is no such thing as a *categorical difference* between the *real* constitution of the nation state and the *unreal* constitutions of Europe or the constitution of the *New York Times*. In other words, there are *no unbridgeable dualisms* but only *continua of differences* (Brandom 2000: 856, 864–6).

11.2 Revolutionary and evolutionary change

The second thesis that I wish to propose is that constitutions are, not only evolutionary advances, but also *revolutionary* advances. That is, constitutions are revolutionary advances if they can claim they have some bearing on *progress in the embodiment of freedom and equality*. Revolutionary advances are normative advances. Great legal and constitutional revolutions (and all great revolutions are legal revolutions) such as the papal revolution of the eleventh century, the Protestant revolutions of the sixteenth and seventeenth centuries, the constitutional revolutions of the eighteenth century, or the social world revolutions of the twentieth century, consisted in comprehensive and massive legal and constitutional change, which *cannot be explained by gradual adaption* and *social structural selection alone*. Revolutionary change occurs far too rapidly to adapt gradually to its environment. In contrast, successful revolutionary change experiments with radically unmatched social inventions, which are at the limit of adaptive processes. On this account, social evolution, at least in modern societies, is marked by an alternation between short periods of abrupt, catalytic, or *revolutionary change* and longer periods of equilibration, during which no change, or only gradual and incremental succession or *evolutionary change*, occurs, or which may even show signs of regressive transformation. Yet both kinds of change, whether rapid or gradual, are *examples of evolution*. Everything is evolution. In consequence, revolution is also a kind of evolution. In this respect, we can re-visit the old political and constitutional distinction between *revolutionary* or *power-founding constitutions*, and *evolutionary* or *power-limiting constitutions*, which has been discussed in political theory and constitutional law since Kant and Sieyès, Burke and Hegel (Maus 1994; Möllers 2003: 1; Fossum and Menéndez 2011: 35). But we need to ensure that this distinction is integrated completely into the categorical framework of a *theory of social evolution*. Here again, we need to overcome the dualistic principle that there exist two exclusive types or categories, and replace this dualism with the concept of an *evolutionary continuum*, marked by an alteration between gradual change *and* rapid change.

To conclude, social evolution strongly resembles the pattern of rapid and catalytic change by *punctuational bursts* and *punctuated equilibria*, which characterizes organic evolution.[6] Punctual bursts engender a new species by effecting rapid change in the basic design of an animal species (speciation, hybridization).[7] In analogy to punctuated equilibria in organic evolution, the *great legal revolutions* are the triggers of the evolution of society that we describe as 'modern'. Legal and constitutional revolutionary change cannot be explained by the improvement of adaption (that was the mistake

[6] There is a similar distinction, like that in biology between punctuated equilibria and gradual change by natural selection, in the meta-science (or philosophy) of science. This is the famous distinction made by Thomas Kuhn between revolutionary and normal science (1967). See also Lakatos (1977).

[7] On the neo-Darwinist theory of punctuated equilibria see Gould and Lewontin (1979); Eldredge and Gould (1972); Mayr (1992); Gould (1978); Gould (2002); Gersick (1991); Kubon-Gilke and Schlicht (1998: 68).

of orthodox Marxism, which reduced revolutions and revolutionary class-struggle to the function of the midwife of the unleashing of the growth of productive forces). On the contrary, revolutions are loaded with *negativity*: with maladjustment, deviance and non-conformism. Revolutions destroy the old basic design or the material and formal constitution of society (Marx speaks in this respect of the *Gliederung* of society, by which he means the structure or organization of society), and they invent from scratch a new material and formal constitutional design for society This new design or *new model of constitutional organization* does not improve society. Instead, it directs and constrains the adaptive evolutionary progress of society. It does this, not physically (as in the case of organisms), but *normatively*. It makes certain actions and certain kinds of evolutionary progress *illegal* and *wrong*. In consequence, the results of revolutionary change can be defined as *constitutional systems of normative constraints*.

Revolutionary constitutions engender within societal reality an additional reality that subordinates societal reality to normative prescriptions (see Möllers 2010). These constitutions *constrain arbitrary adaption* and certain kinds of evolutionary experiments (for example, experiments with concentration camps), and by constraining arbitrary adaption they *direct* social evolution on a new course. In disclosing a realm of new evolutionary possibilities, they close others. To exemplify this, for instance, we can consider how the legally institutionalized corporative freedom of the church in the twelfth century constrained the adaptive power of the worldly empires and kingdoms, and the legally organized separation of the sacred and the profane placed a prohibition on sacred kingdoms as well as theocracy. Analogously, we can observe how the rise of the democratic constitutional laws of checks and balances (America 1787–89; France 1789, 1791, 1793) subject the adaptive capacities of executive power to normative constraint by binding it to legislation. It opened up a new evolutionary path of democratic (and constitutional) experimentalism (which can – and in fact did – lead to the new formation, maintenance and growth of executive power within and beyond the constitution, as we will see in the case of the EU). As a further example, we can cite the constitutional principle of equal human dignity (1948), which erects normative constraints against the use of torture, against evolutionary experiments with slavery and concentration camps, and against economic expropriation and totalitarian rule (even if that were to lead to the evolutionary success of the neo-liberal world economy, or for instance of the Chinese model of modern capitalism).

11.3 Constitutional evolution

The third thesis that I wish to propose is that revolutionary constitutionalization is usually followed by *incremental, gradual and successive constitutional evolution*. What the German lawyer Hans Peter Ipsen has called the European *Wandelverfassung* (meaning, a progressively shifting or incrementally founded constitution) is a description that can be used to characterize constitutions at a high level of generalization. In evolutionary terms, all constitutions are shifting constitutions – *Wandelverfassungen*. This thesis suggests that constitutional evolution typically follows a two-stage pattern. The catalytic moment of revolution usually makes possible a process of gradual incremental constitutional evolution, and this is normally *carried out in functionally differentiated steps*. Incremental constitutional evolution consists in an evolutionary process marked by the *successive step-by-step constitutionalization of distinct functional spheres*.[8] These spheres are constitutionalized gradually, in the following fashion. First, they are constitutionalized by small legal *variations* and small constitutional changes (everyday juridical puzzle solving in a growing number of cases, conventional doctrinal interpretation and commentary, ordinary legislative procedures and concretization of legal norms). Then they are directed by the two *selective* mechanisms: that is, *social class* structure and *functional* imperatives. These spheres are ultimately *re-stabilized* by systemic formation (reflexive closure through the formation of a hegemonic academic discourse (*herrschende Meinung*)).[9]

On this basis, all constitutions are reliant on the *pre-existing framework*, which has been established by the great legal revolutions (Taylor 2007: 274). In 1815, after the French Revolution, and under its new conceptual framework, *formal and written constitutionalization became unavoidable*. Even the reactionary hereditary monarchy of the French restoration had to be re-introduced *as* a constitutional regime *under* the law of the *Charte Constitutionelle* (Sellin 2001). It was no coincidence that, as in 1789, 1795 and 1799, Sieyès acted again as one of the founding fathers of the *Charte Constitutionelle*, which meant that he was forced to leave the country just after Napoleon's final defeat. The young Marx offered the following

[8] I am generalizing here an idea that Tuori has suggested for the reconstruction of the European constitutionalization process, briefly mentioned earlier in the text. For a functional differentiation in constitutional theory, see additionally the essays in Tuori and Sankari (2010); Fischer-Lescano and Teubner (2006).

[9] Uwe Wesel gives a sound short description of the evolutionary formation of the hegemonic opinion in the legal system (1984: 189).

brilliant interpretation of the world-historical meaning of the national revolution in France, which lasted from 1789 to 1815, and of the revolution in England led in 1648 by Cromwell:

> The revolutions of 1648 and 1789 were not English and French revolutions, they were revolutions in the European fashion [*Revolutionen Europäischen Stils*]. They did not represent the victory of a particular social class over the old political system; they proclaimed the political system of the new European society. The bourgeoisie was victorious in these revolutions, but the victory of the bourgeoisie was at that time the victory of a new social order, the victory of bourgeois ownership over feudal ownership, of nationality over provincialism, of competition over the guild, of partitioning [of the land] over primogeniture, of the rule of the landowner over the domination of the owner by the land, of enlightenment over superstition, of the family over the family name, of industry over heroic idleness, of bourgeois law over medieval privileges. [. . .] These revolutions reflected the needs of the world at that time rather than the needs of those parts of the world where they occurred, that is, England and France. [. . .] The French bourgeoisie of 1789, when it confronted monarchy and aristocracy, the representatives of the old society, was [. . .] a class speaking for the whole of modern society (Marx 1973: 107–9).

Marx was right, even if he did not go far enough and still retained a Eurocentric perspective. He did not even mention the American Revolution, let alone Haiti and other places where revolutions occurred all over the world. As has recently been demonstrated in the historiographical literature, the entire global legal and political order was re-founded and constituted anew in the decades following the constitutional revolutions of the late eighteenth century. This was a fact which contributed greatly to the formation of *one modern world society*. The new political, legal, economic and cultural world order consisted from the beginning in the *invention and co-evolution* of a new national *as well as* a new international order of powers. It was also based in the dense and momentous intersection and interpenetration of national *and* international law, and, more generally, of processes of nationalization *and* internationalization (or globalization).[10]

[10] It is a big mistake to accept Carl Schmitt's thesis that the Westfalian order of *jus gentium* lasted from 1648 to the threshold of the twenty-first century. This order only lasted until the French and American Revolutions and was replaced by the nineteenth-century balance of power and international law, which itself ended with the Great Russian Revolution and the entry of the US into the war in 1917, and was replaced by a new legal world order. Parsons is an exception to the repression of globalization and even global constitutionalization (see Parsons 1961). For a recent alternative approach in political and legal theory, see Thornhill (2011). For historical analysis, see Conrad (2008).

As a result, even if the incremental process of *constitutionalization* that followed the *constitutional revolutionary foundations* (in a very small number of countries) was perceived by liberals and defeated revolutionaries as the triumph of the counter-revolution and the so-called restoration, at a more fundamental historical level incremental constitutionalization was the triumph, not of the counter-revolutionary restoration, but, despite its complete military defeat, of the French Revolution in the sphere of the *objective spirit* of the emerging world society. The advances brought forth by the revolution assumed an *inchoate* status even in the motherlands of the revolution. The revolution successfully constituted a new political and legal regime during the long transformation from the eighteenth to the nineteenth century. But only the subsequent process of gradual and successive step-by-step evolution succeeded in *transforming the inchoate original constitution into an increasingly complete, increasingly comprehensive and increasingly normative and effective constitutional order.*

After the outbreak of the revolution in France the first constitutional step that assumed normative (or normatively effective) status and proved enduring for a longer period of time was the *security and military constitution* arising from the revolutionary wars. This was then followed by the *legal constitution* of the Napoleonic Civil Code early in the nineteenth century. This constitutional advance was immediately generalized on the European level as a long-term effect of Napoleon's short-term revolutionary imperialism. The first steps in the process were accomplished by the revolution, and Hegel recognized that this was an immutable progress. But Hegel did not recognize that there were many further steps to come. In this respect, his philosophy of history fell back behind the evolutionary level of thinking that had already been attained by Kant. A long period of constitutional evolution only began after the revolution, and it led to a further great revolutionary transformation only one hundred years later. In France the security and legal constitution – after a couple of attempts – was followed by a lasting *political constitution*, established at the advent of the bourgeois democratic republic in 1871. Yet, only the radical democratization of the bourgeois republic at a much later stage (and after the next period of world-revolutionary transformation) led to the present *social-welfare constitution* of post-bourgeois mass democracy.

The German Confederation and the process of constitutional evolution in Germany might be cited as a further example of incremental constitutionalization. The legal *model* for the German Confederation was the Confederation of the Rhine (*Rheinbund*), founded in revolutionary fashion by Napoleon in 1806 (Luther 2011). The officially restorative German Confederation was thus a direct *product of the power-founding constitutions of the French Revolution*. As a first step, Germany was constitutionalized under Prussian hegemony by means of the *military constitution* of the German Confederation, established during the Congress of Vienna. This was followed by the *economic constitution* of the Tax Union and Customs Union (*Zollunion*). It was finally supplemented with a self-referential *legal constitution* after the foundation of the German Reich: that is, with the power-limiting constitutional text implemented by Bismarck in 1871. In the course of the late nineteenth century intense class struggles, the alarming growth of the Social Democratic Party, and a steady process of juridification driven by the courts (expressed in the evolution of German administrative law (*Verwaltungsrecht*)) led to a successive transformation of the constitution of the Reich into an increasingly *political constitution*. This constitution was only established anew after World War I, following the resultant revolutionary abolition of the monarchy.

The evolution of American constitutional law was not so different from these cases, even if it was, at its inception, founded in revolutionary fashion and was never replaced through a counter-revolutionary regime. In US-American history we see first the *political constitution* that was invented by revolution. Initially, however, the working constitution of the United States (US) was not much more than a foreign policy constitution (and a military constitution) whose primary function was to defend the democratic advances of the single American states against external enemies. A short time later, as the judgments of the Marshall Court neatly illustrate, this was flanked by the institution of an *economic constitution*, founded in principles of possessive individualism, which assumed functional primacy. This was evident in *Fletcher v. Peck* (1810); *Martin's v. Hunter's Lessee* (1816); *Dartmouth College v. Woodward* (1819); it was reinforced a hundred years later by the same court in *Lochner v. New York* (1905), and endured until the New Deal of the 1930s. After the end of the American Civil War, the federal economic constitution was accompanied by a strong *legal-state constitution*, which had a federal character, and under which for the first time *direct effect* of federal law was guaranteed. It was only much later that the federal *social and security constitution* developed, which transformed bourgeois democracy into social mass democracy and completed the constitutional evolution of the US, which increasingly became a conclusively national state after World War II.

11.4 Revolutionary foundation of Europe

The fourth thesis that I wish to propose is that Europe too has a *revolutionary constitution*, which is currently inchoate (as are all revolutionary constitutions in the time of their invention). The constitutional evolution of the EU is not an exception to the broader evolutionary pattern.[11] In fact, the EU has a *revolutionary foundation*. It has a revolutionary foundation first in the *historical* sense that the foundation of the EU is one of the consequences of the world-revolutionary transformations of the years between 1917 (that is, the Russian Revolution and the American entry into World War I) and 1949 (that is, the end of the Chinese Revolution) (see Hobsbawm 1994). Moreover, it has a revolutionary foundation, second, in the sense that it enacts the constituent power of the peoples that founded the Union (Fossum and Menéndez 2011).

Regarding the origins of the European constitution in world-revolutionary transformations, the European Communities founded in 1951, and expanded in 1957, developed (together with its newly constituted founding member states) as *a consequence of the massive revolutionary change* that occurred after the equilibrium of the long nineteenth century during the catastrophic decades between 1917 and 1949. If we include the finally successful struggle for liberation from colonialism, apartheid and Soviet-Russian imperialism during the 1960s and the 1980s, then the period can be viewed as having lasted until 1989. But during the years between 1951 and 1989, *the institutional foundations of a new world order* that framed the struggles of the colonized peoples for liberation, the conflicts regarding apartheid and the dismantling of the Soviet Union were already in place (see Parsons 1961).

The new pre-existing legal and political framework instituted at this time constituted 'the entire world as a social system' (Parsons 1961: 120). The constitutional system of the world ('constitutional' at least in material, sociological and evolutionary terms) consisted in a completely new *global order of world law* together with a growing and enduring system of new *inter-, trans- and supranational political, economic, cultural and legal organizations and institutions* (including an ever denser network of border-traversing private associations, global commercial relations

[11] Speaking about the European Communities and the European Union and its different names in the course of history I use European Union as a term that covers all the different European Communities: i.e. it includes the Union of the past and the present single European Union together.

and private–public partnerships).[12] These organizations no longer simply *complement* more classical functions of the state: in fact, they act as substitutes for these functions (just one striking example of this is the present role of the International Monetary Fund) (Albert 2005: 229). Furthermore, under the umbrella of the United Nations (UN), the ILO and other international organizations the *process of decolonization* was finalized. The *struggle of the colonized peoples for liberation* was finally successful, and colonialism (although not imperial hegemony) was abolished once and for all (Osterhammel 2009a). Finally, a system of inter- and transnational private and public courts emerged that, together with the world public and the system of international institutions, performs and secures the *structural coupling of world politics and world law*.[13] There remain of course 'elements of sheer power' in world society (as well as in its national segments). But what is categorically *new* since, at the latest, the end of World War II is the fact that we can also see 'elements of genuine *leadership*' and the beginning of a differentiation between *government and opposition* on the global level, and 'leadership in this sense exists only when there is a political support for the position, backed by interests other than the most elementary security and subject to an accepted (i.e. institutionalized) normative order' (Parsons 1961: 125).[14] To be sure, the national state still plays a constitutive role in the dissonant concerts of world society, and the state plays an important role not lastly as the only power that is able to *enforce binding decisions*. But the state has itself been deeply transformed by its own globalization. The now completely *globalized system of national states* (there is no longer a square metre of any continental landmass that is not at least nominally part of a state territory) was in fact made possible by, and increasingly depends on, the co-evolution of the *systems of world law* and *world and regional politics*. These inter-, trans- and supranational systems absorb a constantly increasing number of important elements of *legislative competence*. They constantly replace state legislation, which is partly backed by, and partly in growing conflict with, a world public and

[12] See Parsons (1961). For a more formal but also more contentious approach relying on the UN Charter, see Fassbender (2009); Brunkhorst (2005; 2012).

[13] On these points separately, Bogdandy and Venzke (2009). On the emergence of a world public since the last decades of the nineteenth century, see Osterhammel (2009b: 1012, 1023). For the middle part of the twentieth century, see the remarks in Parsons (1961: 126); Chimni (2004).

[14] On the global differentiation of elements of government and opposition see chapter 8 in Brunkhorst (2012).

a *world societal community of world citizens*, or at least bearers of *international human rights* (including social-welfare rights sustained more or less adequately by international and national welfarism).[15] Finally, the globalization of the national state relied both on the (in a macro-phenomenological sense 'constitutive') existence of a *fully fledged world culture* and on a new *world economy*, which disembedded itself from the grip of state power during the last thirty years of neo-liberal globalization (Meyer 2005; Streek 2005; 2010; Crouch 2011). The whole process of the formation of a new global constitutional order, after all, was strongly reinforced by the partly already existing, partly newly engendered system of *continental regimes* that now reaches all around the world: from India, China, Brazil and the US to the EU.[16]

It was within this already existing framework of the new world order that the Council of Europe, which preceded the European Communities, was founded in 1949. First, at an institutional level, the Council of Europe invented a new *dual structure* in which representatives of governments *and* national parliamentarians worked together in a common parliamentary assembly. Second, in addition the Council implemented a new *regional regime of human rights* that was later followed by similar regimes in other world regions. Whereas the instrument for the enforcement of the Council's European Convention for the Protection of Human Rights and Fundamental Freedoms, the European Court of Human Rights, was established by representatives of governments acting as the High Contracting Parties of an international treaty (Article 19 of the Convention), the judges were elected through the parliamentary assembly 'by a majority of votes' (Article 22 para. 1 of the Convention) – even if the

[15] See Kreide (2008; 2009). On the antecedence of international welfarism see Leisering (2007).

[16] The revolutionary change from the late 1940s on was preceded by one hundred years of world-wide class struggles: that is, by the formation of the powerful workers' movement in the late nineteenth century, accompanied by other world-wide mass movements such as the women's movement or the diverse peace movements; by the Great Russian and the Chinese Revolutions; by series of successful and unsuccessful smaller legal revolutions in other countries (including Austria and Germany after World War I); by the two world wars that were at least partly revolutionary in character and followed revolutionary (and counter-revolutionary) goals (for the good as well as for the bad); by massive and revolutionary legal reforms such as the New Deal; by the world-wide struggle against colonization that led in the 1950s and 1960s to an almost complete decolonization of the world and the global spread of the model of the national state; by struggles between, social classes, peoples and states for (or against) a complete new foundation of international law and the international community beginning immediately at the end of World War I.

crucial decision in that regard is taken by the member states who provide a shortlist of candidates.[17] Yet, the new dual structure of international institutions was revolutionary in itself. It was subsequently copied by the European Communities, NATO and the OECD, and other organizations in all world regions. The EU, in particular, has radicalized and further developed the dual structure by *bridging*, and even *levelling out*, the former gap between national and international law. Indeed, it has established a *dual structure of citizenship*, which was anticipated by other confederations and federations from the late eighteenth century onward (Schönberger 2005; Forsythe 1981), but which in its radical form is *unique* (it shows a remote resemblance only to the constitutions of Switzerland and the US). *As individual bearers of subjective rights*, Europeans are at the same time *European citizens* and *citizens of their respective national states*, endowed with *fully fledged negative, active and positive rights* at both levels of citizenship (including the relevant *representative bodies* of decision making that are necessary for the use of these rights) (Habermas 2011).

Regarding the origins of the European constitution in a distinct form of constituent power, the revolutionary foundation of the EU can be traced back to the *constituent power* of the peoples of the founding members of the EU in 1951 and 1957. The European constituent power thus first primarily consisted, and now still consists, in a *synthetic constitutionalism*, which is drawn from a synthesis of the constitutional powers of the founding peoples. The democratic legitimacy of the EU was originally derived from the *synthetic constitutional moments* taking place in 1951 and 1957.[18]

This can be seen in the following ways. First, all constitutions of the founding members of 1951 provided new *revolutionary foundations* to support the use of power by a political and legal community. This power did not exist before or during the time of the Nazi occupation. Rebels, guerrillas and exiled politicians became heads and members of government. They risked their lives, not solely as patriots, but as democrats or socialists, who had struggled for certain rights and universal constitutional principles (Osterhammel and Petersson 2007: 85; Hobsbawm 1994: 185). New powers, in some cases new countries (such as West

[17] I have to thank Mikael Madsen for clarification in this matter.

[18] Fossum and Menéndez (2011: 3, 43, 77, 92, 126, 174, 180, 215). For earlier but conceptually less clear attempts with similar emphasis, see Häberle (1991: 261; 2009: 111); Pernice (2010). See recently, Voßkuhle (2010).

Germany) were constituted, and new constitutions were written. Second, these new (or revised) constitutions *opened themselves* for the first time in history to *international law*. All founding members of the European Communities designed their newly constituted states as *open states* – open for the incorporation of international law and international co-operation (an important example of this is, in the German Basic Law (*Grundgesetz*), the obligatory *Völkerrechtsfreundlichkeit* [openness to international law] established in Article 24(1) (Wahl 2003; Di Fabio 1988)). Third, the new constitutions declared the *strong commitment of their respective peoples to the project of European unification*, which was to be realized in the near future (Preamble in combination with Article 24(1) of the German Basic Law). All founding members of the European Communities bound themselves to the constitutional project of European unification, which then, from 1951 onwards, became constitutive for all European constitutional (or quasi-constitutional) treaties (Fossum and Menéndez 2011: 175). The only instance of a constitution of a founding member that made no declaration about Europe, the Constitution of Luxembourg, is of itself a revealing case. In this case the Luxembourg *Conseil d'État* decided in 1952 that the Constitution implicitly committed the representatives of the people to join the European Coal and Steel Community, and to strive for further European unification.[19]

In consequence, it can be concluded that, from the outset, the EU was not founded as an international association of states. On the contrary, it was founded as a *community of peoples* who legitimated the project of European unification *directly* and *democratically* through their combined, but still national, constitutional powers (represented later in the Council of the EU and the European Council). At the same time and with the same founding act, these peoples, acting plurally, constituted a single *European citizenship*, embodying *new rights for the European citizen*, which were different from the rights of the citizens of the respective member states (represented later by the European Parliament). These remained implicit for the first decades, but the European Court of Justice

[19] It is argued that, even if the constitution of Luxembourg did not contain anything vaguely resembling a proto-European clause, the *Conseil d'État* constructed its fundamental law along very similar lines. When reviewing the constitutionality of the Treaty establishing the Coal and Steel Community, the *Conseil* affirmed that Luxembourg not only could, but should, renounce certain sovereign powers if the public good so required (Fossum and Menéndez 2011). See the Report on the 1952 judgment of the *Conseil d'État*.

(ECJ) made them explicit in *van Gend en Loos* and *Costa* in 1963 and 1964. The community of European citizens as a whole thus now constitutes a second and independent 'subject of legitimization'.[20]

It was this process of revolutionary foundation that opened the path for the following *evolutionary constitutionalization* of Europe.

11.5 Gradual change and functional stages

The fifth thesis that I wish to propose is that the revolutionary foundation of Europe was followed by a process of *incremental evolutionary constitutionalization*. This was based in a sequence of *functional developmental stages*, which were accompanied by successive steps in the *legal implementation of equal freedom*. Even if the *functional constitutionalization* of Europe was formally accomplished through treaty changes, politics often only performed the rearguard function of codification. In many cases, it was the courts, both transnational *and* national, that conducted the process of constitutionalization: indeed, the courts had often done most of the work before the politicians played a part. It seems that Kelsen's evolutionary speculation that in (relatively) decentralized legal states the courts act as the leading evolutionary system is true (Kelsen 1944; Fischer-Lescano 2004). The concrete formation, implementation, re-foundation and revision of the Treaties of Paris and Rome were conducted, not by the political leaders of Europe, but rather by the *judges* and the *individual European citizens*, who initiated an endless stream of *single actions of legal communication*. It is not elites, but the masses who drive forward evolution (and in this case as in others these 'masses' are not necessarily the masses of ordinary people, but the masses of ordinary communicative actions of higher and in particular lower courts). The 'invisible constitution' of Europe (Wiener 2008) was primarily the effect of *thousands and thousands of individual legal actions selected by innumerable decisions of lower courts*. The successive interpenetration of the national with the transnational system of courts was stabilized by the *reflexive closure of the European legal system* through the *incremental formation* of

[20] On the double legitimization of the EU by the community of peoples of the member states and the people of the European Union see Habermas (2011). For a striking comparison with the development of the US founded by a similar kind of 'double sovereignty' (which still is a technical term of constitutional law in the US), see Schönberger (2005). See also Forsythe (1981). Augustín Menéndez has made an important contribution to that thesis, comparing in a case study the implementation of federal taxes in the US and the EU, demonstrating the striking parallels (2003).

a hegemonic legal discourse in the growing branch of European law and European legal studies and scholarship (Buckel and Oberndorfer 2009).

The *gradual adaption* of national to European law and European to national law was conditioned by three factors. It was determined, first, by the increasing *number of legal cases* in which European norms had to be applied. Second, it was determined by selective development expressed both at a social level (through emerging hegemonic structures, and transnational class formation) and at a structural level through functional differentiation. It was determined, third, by the growing hegemonic opinion (*herrschende Meinung*) of European legal science. In the course of this evolutionary development national law finally became European law, and European became national law. A common European constitutional order, defined as an order of overlapping and even interpenetrating national, inter- (Council of Europe) and transnational (EU) orders, emerged in the European world region (Hitzel-Cassagnes 2012: 160; Schwarze 2000; Cooper 2011).

To construct a usable categorical framework for the analysis of Europe's evolutionary constitutionalization, it is necessary to deploy a perspective combining a focus on both *judicial (and political) incrementalism* and *functional differentiation*. Judicial incrementalism provides a mechanism for communicative *variation*. Functional differentiation, *together with the formation of a new political and economic ruling class*, which for the first time in history is genuinely *transnational* (as is its entourage of highly paid global journalists, talk show actors and subservient experts, such as professors of economics from the Deutsche Bank), provides a sufficient *selective structure* for the transformation of judicial variation into European constitutional law. In turn, this is *re-stabilized* by the expanding *system* of the common European constitutional order, which has been made possible by the reflexive closure of the dominant legal discourse (*herrschende Meinung*). The adaptive evolutionary process follows a step-by-step trajectory of functional differentiation, in which different social systems have assumed a constitution enabling them to provide services for other systems, to stabilize their identity as differentiated systems, and to fulfil a function for society in its entirety. Our theoretical framework, in short, construes the development of European constitutional law as a process combining communicative variation in judicial practices and the selective differentiation in legal structures. Following this model, the demand for legal norms (variation) is steered by powerful imperatives and dynamics of functional differentiation (selection), and these processes act, step-by-step, to create a constitutional order in differentiated spheres of social exchange – primarily, economy, law and politics. This model allows us to reconstruct the different stages in the formation of a European constitution.

11.5.1 Stage 1: The Economic Constitution

First, the Treaties of Paris and Rome created a common economy on a supranational basis. This step engendered immediately the need for *services* provided by a European legal system. The solution of this *systemic problem* resulted in the emergence of the *European Economic Constitution*. The Economic Constitution consisted in the *structural coupling of European law and economy*.[21] It developed autonomous organs, in particular the ECJ and the Commission. As a constitutional court the ECJ was the guardian of Europe's Economic Constitution and its competition law.[22] The Commission was designed in particular as a transnational antitrust authority, implementing competition law. The prevailing schema of legitimization (*social integration*) at this stage of constitutional formation was, not *democratic input-legitimization*, but *technocratic output-legitimization*: that is, the 'promise of economic prosperity' (Tuori 2010: 16). Output-legitimization reduces legitimization to the politically neutralized acquisition of the allegiance of the masses (*Massenloyalität*). It was as useful for Roosevelt as it was for Stalin or Hitler, and it has remained of use for the legitimization of all political forms of government since the old Assyrian Empire. The structural coupling of law and economy is effective as long as it can satisfy (if we accept and apply the AGIL scheme devised by Parsons) the *adaptive function* of the respective society (*system integration*).[23] The fulfilment of this adaptive function opened the evolutionary path of the European Communities for the expansion and autopoietic closure of the common market.

The original idea behind the Economic Constitution stemmed from the doctrines associated with *ordo-liberalism*, a movement originally established

[21] An important cultural push in the direction of an economic constitution came from the specific cultural background of German ordo-liberalism. This School invented and introduced the category of the economic constitution (*Wirtschaftsverfassung*) in German public-legal discourse.

[22] On the role of the supreme court of a polity as the guardian of the constitution see Kelsen (1931).

[23] On a systematic use of Lockwood's differentiation between social integration and system integration (see Lockwood (1971: 125) for the formation of a general theory of society see Habermas (1981).

at the University of Freiburg. This was the work of a neo-conservative group of German and Austrian economists (partly motivated by strong social/ethical commitments). Members of the School were Franz Böhm, Walter Eucken, Alexander Rüstow, Wilhelm Röpke, Alfred Müller-Armack and Friedrich August von Hayek, who assumed Eucken's professorship in Freiburg in 1962.[24] As Karlo Tuori has accurately observed, the ordo-liberals took (or rather hijacked) the idea of an Economic Constitution (*Wirtschaftsverfassung*) from the political Left.[25] The original idea of the Economic Constitution was proposed by Social Democrats such as Hugo Sinzheimer and Franz Neumann. In their conception, the Economic Constitution was subject to *the rule of parliamentary legislation*. It was initially foreseen that parliamentary legislation and its concretization by autonomous bodies exercising rights of social self-determination should act to facilitate comprehensive democratic control of the markets.[26] In their use of the concept of an Economic Constitution, however, the ordo-liberals *turned it upside down*, and they transformed it into a *constitution enabling comprehensive control of democracy by free market competition*. In particular, the ordo-liberals diluted economic constitutionalism to a *free market ideology* that had to be realized by *competition law*. They saw the order of the free market, combined with *paternal welfare-regimes*, as an order that worked on the basis of *private–public partnerships* (later transfigured as the social market economy and Rhineland capitalism). Most importantly, though, ordo-liberalism espoused the *decoupling of the Economic Constitution from the political constitution* of the national state: the isolation and

[24] Most of the school were conservative opponents of Nazi-fascism. Böhm was a declared anti-Nazi, especially an early defender of the Jews, and a member of the resistance with close relations to Bonhoefer and Gördeler. Eucken was a conservative anti-Nazi who strongly opposed Heidegger as the first Nazi-Rektor of the University of Freiburg (over whose main entrance even in 2011 the 1936 dedication is still clearly visible). He was loosely associated with the conservative resistance. Rüstow was a member of the far-right shadow cabinet led by General Kurt von Schleicher. He engaged in a half-hearted attempt at an anti-Hitler *coup d'état*, and had to emigrate in 1933. Röpke was attached to the conservative 'revolution' (Tat-Kreis) from the early 1920s. However, he strongly opposed German fascism as early as the late 1920s, and he emigrated (as did Eucken) to Turkey in 1933. Alfred Müller-Armack was a Nazi of the first hour. Hayek took a chair at the London School of Economics (LSE) and he left the continent by 1931. He was the most radical liberal opponent of Keynes, who already had at that time a chair at the LSE. Still the best criticism of Hayek is Kelsen (1954). As a legal theorist Hayek was very close to Carl Schmitt. This point is made in Scheuerman (2004); Vatter (2010).

[25] See Tuori (2010: 16). The original idea was developed in Böhm (2010 [1933]).

[26] See in particular Neumann (1978 [1931]).

primacy of the Economic Constitution was the decisive move against the hijacked leftist idea of an Economic Constitution.

In consequence, the radical 'negation of a political constitution of Europe' became the most fundamental doctrine of ordo-liberalism once it went European (Tuori 2010: 15). The principle of decoupling the Economic Constitution from the state was progressive and regressive at the same time. It was *progressive* insofar as it led to the *establishment of a constitutional regime beyond and above the nation states*. It was *regressive* because it *reduced* constitutionalization beyond the state to the *economic sphere*, and it *decoupled constitutionalization from democratization* – with sweeping consequences.

It was the ordo-liberal idea of an Economic Constitution that finally cleared the path for the turn of Europe towards the neo-liberalism of the Chicago School. This began with the inglorious *Cassis de Dijon* decision of the ECJ in 1979, which led to the one-sided dominance of the four economic freedoms (commodities, capital, services, persons). This path was then stabilized by the one-sided anti-inflationary policies and the stability orientation of the European Central Bank, which was constitutionally institutionalized as a special regime (the EU special regimes are discussed further below) in the Treaty of Amsterdam. The lasting predominance of economic freedoms even destroyed all hopes for a positive outcome in the French Referendum on the Constitutional Treaty in 2005. This was because the negative result of the referendum was in large part the consequence of the counterproductive effects of the Bolkestein Regulation introduced by the Council of Ministers, which was designed to deregulate the market for services and was adopted just at the height of the French voting campaign. The regulation was interpreted by the French Left as a threat to the maintenance of jobs and wages, and it motivated a critical number of voters to say 'No' to the Constitutional Treaty. Finally, at present (in 2011) we are witness to the last move in that game: Brüning-style austerity policies, which run the risk of triggering a deflationary crisis.[27]

From the beginning, in sum, an evolutionary course of economic constitutionalization was pursued, which ultimately led, first, to *German hegemony* over Europe (at least on the continent); second, to the primacy of the *economic freedoms* of the Union over its political, democratic and communicative freedoms; third, to the liberation of the economic

[27] For a critical account see Somek (2008). On recent developments, see Buckel and Oberndorfer (2009).

freedoms of *big money, big banks* and *big commercial enterprises* from the national constitutional law of the democratic social-welfare state (Fossum and Menéndez 2011: 115). The latter outcome, in particular, was not intended by the ordo-liberals. Yet it was a consequence of the process of neo-liberal globalization beginning in the 1980s.

The early fundamental constitutional decision (to use Carl Schmitt's concept of a '*Grundentscheidung*') in favour of an Economic Constitution in Article 2 EEC in 1957, which established a common market on the basis of national economic and financial politics, and lacked any redistributive or regulatory policies on the European level, was pushed through against strong French resistance by the German delegation. This delegation was led by Müller-Armack (a member of the NSDAP from 1933 to 1945),[28] and was strongly supported by the then conservative US government.[29] The Treaty of Rome (alongside the autonomous European institutions of the ECJ and the Commission) set up the intergovernmental Council of Ministers. However, it stopped far short of realizing the plans of Jean Monnet, Robert Schuman and Altiero Spinelli for a federal union of Europe. Regulatory and distributive measures were excluded from European Community politics. In fact, to repeat this bitter truth, national regulative measures that contradicted the objectives of the common market could now be mitigated by the ECJ. Finally, the Reform Treaty of Lisbon consolidated the old Economic Constitution in Article 3 para. 3 Treaty of the European Union (TEU), adding the word 'social' ('highly competitive social market economy') in the (so to speak) rights part of the Treaty. However, it reinforced the dominance of global capitalism in the (much more important) European law regarding the functioning of the Union (Article 119, para. 1 Treaty on the Functioning of the European Union (TFEU)) (see Buckel and Oberndorfer 2009: 284).

The economic constitutional orientation *first* directed the European governmental regime towards *technocracy* (see Ipsen 1970). In this respect,

[28] After he joined the Nazi Party in 1933 Müller-Armack immediately published a programmatic book on the National Socialist economy. This had the title *Staatsidee und Wirtschaftsordnung im neuen Reich* (*The Idea of State and Economic Order in the New Reich*). He was involved in SS ethnic cleansing policies in Eastern Europe during his work at the *Forschungsstelle für Siedlungs- und Wohnungswesen* (the Research Centre for Inhabitation and Accommodation) in Münster, whose director he became in 1938. After 1945 he abandoned National Socialism for religion.

[29] Wegmann (2010: 94, 99, 102). On the prevalence of the ordo- and neo-liberal ideas of the Deutsche Bundesbank during the constitutional conflict over European stability and the money politics of the Central Bank see Gaitanides (2007: 553).

the political dimension was successfully repressed. *Second*, the fundamental decision of 1957 for the Economic Constitution and the implied technocratic administration marginalized the powerful wing of the CDU (the Christian Democratic Union, at that time the governing party in West Germany), which (close to Spinelli, Monnet and Schuman) supported the primarily *political* project of a *United States of Europe*. Despite the fact that it was at the top of the CDU's agenda until the 1990s, the drafting of a political constitution of Europe was postponed and suppressed again and again, even, as discussed below, after its formal invention. The reason for this was simply that one of the most fundamental ordo-liberal doctrines had now become European constitutional law: Go European, go global with the economy but *make sure that all political powers of regulation and taxation remain within the borders of the national state*!

The doctrine of the Economic Constitution paved the way for neo-liberalism because state power *and* the power of the union (and other powers of a potentially European opposition) were no longer able to increase *together* with, and on the same *scale* as, the growing *political* power and influence of global banks and global commercial corporations. In other words – *state-embedded markets began to turn into market-embedded states* (Streek 2005). The neo-liberal shift of power from the state to major shareholders was pre-determined through the formation of an Economic Constitution, and it needed only the opportunity provided by a persistent period of inflation, such as in the 1970s, to change the evolutionary path towards a society that identifies the general, and even universal, interest with the rise and fall of the profit of the major shareholders. As we will see, and this is the substance of the sixth thesis that I wish to propose, the *first repression of the political dimension of European constitutionalism has been, and will continue to be, repeated on every level of constitutionalization*. This will remain the case until the repressed dimension re-asserts itself.

In conclusion, therefore, we can see that the *development* of the European Economic Constitution was triggered by the growing need for legal norms in the common market. This problem was solved by the *structural coupling* of law and economy, which satisfied the adaptive function of *system integration* through technocratic output-legitimization. Output-legitimization compensated the lack of *social integration* at the European level.

11.5.2 Stage 2: The Juridical Constitution

The Treaty of Rome posed a new problem that was no longer simply a systemic problem alone but a problem that affected the *emancipatory dimension* of constitutional law. The emancipatory problem of *civic self-determination* came to the fore when the ECJ decided *van Gend en Loos* and *Costa* in 1963 and 1964 (and these decisions are in a way comparable with the importance of *Marbury v. Madison* for the constitutionalization of the US). The decision emphatically was described as 'the declaration of independence of Community law' (Tuori 2010: 17). The judges in 1963 and 1964 created *European citizen rights* in a risk-filled and bold teleological interpretation of the Treaties.[30] They stretched the borders of the Economic Constitution so far that it provoked a need for a Juridical Constitution of Europe or for a Constitution of Europe as Legal State (*Rechtsstaatsverfassung*). There was a kind of *developmental logic* in this move towards the Juridical Constitution: Europe's requirement for *social integration* could no longer be satisfied by output-legitimization alone. The ordo-liberal implementation of the Economic Constitution 'implied a negation of political transnationalization and constitutionalization', and this, by contrast, 'required juridical constitutionalization' (Tuori 2010: 18). Juridical constitutionalization was required to compensate for the growing *lack of input-legitimization*, which was caused by the original (and quasi-epistemic) negation of political constitutionalization.

Even after 1964, however, the decisions of the ECJ would have remained mere symbolic law if the *many national courts of first instance* had not produced endless numbers of tiny decisions all over Europe. In these decisions, European law was applied at a level quite separate from landmark political decisions for or against Europe, such as in the governments led by de Gaulle, or later by Margaret Thatcher. It was the multitude of 'national judges who made judicial decisions as European judges' (Hitzel-Cassagnes 2012: 154). As Karen Alter has shown in a series of brilliant studies, judges protected themselves from the danger that their rulings might be subject to revision on appeal by asking the ECJ for preliminary rulings (*Vorlageverfahren*) (Alter 1996; 1998). The symbolic principles of *direct effect* and *European law supremacy* (on which the ECJ insisted) were *realized by an uncontrollable multitude of lowest national courts* and – not to forget – *individual appeals* brought before these courts. In consequence, a tremendous number of single legal communicative acts were needed for the continuation of incremental constitutional evolution (Tuori 2010: 19). In this way, the emerging Juridical Constitution constitutionalized the *national courts* (that

30 See here Chalmers *et al.* (2006).

remained national and nationally constituted) in a kind of secondary constitutional act *as organs of the EU*.

In this respect, for the first time the two basic parts of modern constitutional law were partly implemented in Europe: that is, a *list of subjective rights* (direct effect) and a *system of checks and balances* that had its core in the 'unique system of judicial constitutional review which combines the German-type centralized model of constitutional court and the US-type diffused model of ordinary courts monitoring the higher law' (Tuori 2010: 18). As a result, what the many courts implemented, realized and concretized was nothing less than the *Juridical Constitution of Europe*, which solved the twofold problem of *emancipatory claims for individual European citizenship* (liberal rights), and the *structural coupling* of (*higher/European*) *law* and (*lower/national*) *law* and of *legal rights* and *legal procedures*. The formation of the Juridical Constitution quickly led to the emergence of a powerful professional discourse in European law. In consequence, a hegemonic opinion was formed which enabled the *reflexive* (self-referential) closure of the European legal system and the stabilization of its system identity and system autonomy.

In addition, the structural coupling of European law and national law facilitated the reflexive *self-determination of the European legal system through its own court*. This was later extended to the *system of correlation between highest national and European courts* (known by German lawyers as *Verfassungsgerichtsverbund* [association of constitutional courts]) (Voßkuhle 2010). In this system, the absence of a powerful parliamentary legislator has meant that the exploding dynamic of reflexive self-determination has led to a strong transfer of legislative power to the courts (which poses a real threat for democracy). Its growing legislative power allowed the ECJ to strike back the German Constitutional Court's *Solange* decision by taking a further step in the process of constitutionalization. Long before the political class of Europe created a Charter of European Rights the ECJ 'introduced the doctrine of basic rights as general principles of Community law' (Tuori 2010: 20). In so doing, it fulfilled the conditions of the *Solange* decision. Furthermore, the ECJ (in concert with the highest national courts) stabilized its legislative power through the judicial implementation and concretization of the *doctrine of proportionality*, which was extended from the review of legal acts of *executive bodies* to review of legal acts of *legislative bodies*. This contained the (once again) democratically highly problematic implication that the ECJ followed the German Supreme Court in stretching the doctrine of proportionality from a very restricted review of police law to a general review of parliamentary legislation and statutory law (Buckel and Oberndorfer 2009: 292ff.). To some degree, the ECJ completed the formal juridical constitutionalization of Europe in the last *Kadi* judgment, which claimed *European law's supremacy in respect of international law*, arguing against the UN Security Council in the same way as formerly the German Constitutional Court had argued against the ECJ in its *Solange* decision. In consequence, the doctrines of direct effect and European law supremacy did not only constitute an *independent order of European law*. In fact, via the system of preliminary rulings they also led to a Europeanization of national courts, and the European system of checks and balances caused a *division of sovereignty* between the Union and its member states *at both levels at once*: at the European Economic Community level *and* at the many national levels.

What was particularly new with the Juridical Constitution was its *emancipatory dimension*, which went beyond technocracy and the mere functional coupling of law with a technically specialized sub-system. *Technocratic output-legitimization* was supplemented with a kind of *individual legitimization* (but again bypassing *democratic* legitimization) (Möllers 2005a). Owing to its reflexive closure, the evolution of the Juridical Constitution had to satisfy the *integrative function* of society, which is not only *system* integration but also *social integration*. Despite this, however, as the Juridical Constitution was not flanked by a political constitution, this once again reinforced the *one-sided preference of the European Communities for private autonomy*. The so-called *individual legitimization* provides the citizens of Europe with *judicial remedies*. The implementation of subjective rights as legal instruments of individual citizens is not insubstantial. However, to quote Joseph Weiler: '[Y]ou could create rights and afford judicial remedies to slaves. The ability to go to court to enjoy a right bestowed on you by the pleasure of others does not emancipate you, does not make you a citizen. Long before women and Jews were made citizens they enjoyed direct effect' (1997: 503). Consequently, it is not an accident that the perfection of the Juridical Constitution of the Communities, by the end of the 1970s, went hand-in-hand with the neo-liberal turn. Europe proved itself open not only for international law, but also for the neo-liberal paradigm shift in the world economy. In cases such as *Walrave*, *Bosman*, *Viking* and *Laval* the ECJ changed its interpretation of the basic freedoms of European law from *anti-discrimination norms* to norms that *ban any constraint of free movement*, even if these constraints are imposed on the citizens of the respective country. In consequence, if I relocate a firm (a legal subject under European law) from Poland to Denmark I cannot be forced by law to maintain the high Danish wage levels, trade-union rights, employment norms, etc., for my employees. Alternatively, if I engage in a legal strike that contradicts the four freedoms (for instance because of the blockade of a major European traffic artery), freedom prevails over basic rights. In this way, *basic rights are constrained by the four basic freedoms*, and in particular by the freedoms of big money, capital etc., and not – as it should be at least in a democratic social-welfare state – the other way round (Buckel and Oberndorfer 2009: 285). A race to the social bottom is one of the likely effects of this constitutional system: ordo-liberalism is also replaced by the neo-liberal episteme in the realm of European law. Finally, and not surprisingly, in the ongoing *struggle between social classes* (and other *capital- and state-oriented conflicts*) – most notably between the European *power bloc* of loosely coupled but transnationally united executive bodies, transnational commercial and financial corporations, business and lawyer associations, and the *opposing powers* of parliaments, unions, and rainbow coalitions, consumers, enterprises without transnational potential, and countries with high social and labour law standards – the transnational power bloc clearly is the winner, and the others are the losers (Buckel and Oberndorfer 2009: 281, 287, 292). The old bourgeois one-sidedness of private autonomy (or human rights without political autonomy) has once again induced a *contradiction between private* and *public autonomy*, or between *human rights* and *democracy*, or between *judicial* and *political* policy making.[31]

To conclude this section, therefore, the development of the European Juridical Constitution was triggered by the growing need to compensate individuals for the structural negation of political constitutionalization. This problem was solved by the *structural coupling* of European law and national law, which satisfied the integrative function of *system integration* and *social integration* by adding depoliticized individual legitimization to the already working output-legitimization.

11.5.3 Stage 3: The Political Constitution

From this contradiction, we can easily – almost in a classical Hegelian dialectical move – approach the next transformative step in the *developmental logic*

[31] See Scavenius (2011). In other cases, such as the US-American history of the nineteenth century, the one-sidedness of political autonomy caused a similar contradiction between democratic self-determination and human rights. In the US-American case this was one of the origins of the Civil War.

of European incremental constitutionalization: that is, the transformation from the Juridical Constitution to the Political Constitution, which might resolve the classical contradiction of bourgeois law. *Private autonomy* without *political autonomy* is *incomplete* and must turn into its opposite: a revised heteronomy of non-egalitarian transnational class rule which is outside the reach of democratic legitimization.[32] But, as we will see, the return of the repressed dimension at the third level of incremental constitutionalization will be repressed again the moment it appears.

After the first direct election to the European Parliament in 1979, the Political Constitution of Europe began to evolve. Stimulated once more by an incremental and adaptive process of tiny legal changes, of deviant and negative communicative actions by parliament and courts, the European Parliament finally became a strong *controlling and law-shaping parliament*.[33] In a gradual process, culminating in the Lisbon Treaty, a formal *parliamentary legislative procedure* was established.[34] This bridged the growing gap between the legal and political system of the EU through the *structural coupling of law and politics*. As a result, finally, *technocratic output-legitimization* and bourgeois *individual legitimization* were supplemented with egalitarian *democratic legitimization*. Insofar as the Political Constitution constitutionalizes a specific functional system – the system which is specialized on the maintenance and accumulation of administrative and coercive power – the structural coupling of law and politics must (and here again we follow Parsons) satisfy the function of *goal attainment* within the European constitutional system. In addition, however, the political system and the public sphere cannot be reduced to a specific functional sphere existing in parallel with others. In fact, the public sphere and public law *constitute* the sphere of political communication as a democratic association of citizens – an *association politique* (Declaration of Rights of Man, 1789, Article 2). Therefore, the political system is not simply *one of many* functionally specialized social systems in a heterarchical order of social systems. To be sure, even democratic politics must satisfy the function of goal attainment, and it must strive for satisfactory conditions *for* the people. But democracy is not only government *for* the people – it is also

[32] On the logic of co-originality of private and public autonomy, see Habermas (1992).

[33] See Dann (2002); Fossum and Menéndez (2011: 123).

[34] See Bast (2010). On the special regimes of the executive agencies established under a special legislative procedure (bypassing ordinary legislative procedure) see the case study on Frontex in Rieckmann (2011).

government *by* and *through* the people (Abraham Lincoln). Therefore, the political system (at least in democracies) is focused both on the accumulation of administrative power (that is needed for goal attainment) and on the *permanent enactment of unspecialized political discourses*, which incorporate thematically open, temporally unlimited and socially inclusive *deliberation of a diffuse public*, endowed with *egalitarian procedures of decision making*. The discourse surrounding the political system cannot exclude *any* topic, it can make *everything* a subject of legislation, and it must claim democratic legitimacy for *every* binding decision. The medium of political understanding makes and changes the rules which enable the systems to work by *constraining systemic adaption, and by subjecting to normative determination the variety of goals to be attained*. Democratic legitimization *as far as it is democratic* is not in need of *procedural legitimization* that (as an effect of so-called *output-legitimization*) makes decisions acceptable *for* the people, even *without* any rational motive *by* the people to accept them (Luhmann 1983: 28, 32, 117, 119, 124). On the contrary, it needs *procedural legitimization*, which allows acceptance of binding decisions because they can be justified by *reasons* that are acceptable *by* the people and used *through* the people themselves. As a result, the whole constitutional procedure becomes government for, by and through the people. Consequently, as long as democracy remains alive, *individualized democratic legitimization* is the one and only form of legitimization for binding decisions under the Political Constitution. What is sometimes called 'individual legitimization' within a fully fledged Political Constitution is established at a higher level in the procedures of democratic legitimization, and, in consequence, is one differentiated part of it (Möllers 2005a).

Unfortunately, it is at this point that bad news arrives. Even after the invention of a political constitution in Europe, *technocratic politics, consisting in the bypassing and silencing of public opinion, trumped the emancipatory advances of parliamentary legislation*. Technocratic politics *caused a growing gap between public opinion* (that is, democratic legitimization, in this case simply measured in the decreasing number of active voters) *and parliamentary power*. In this respect, it is not technocratic politics in itself that is the problem. Modern mass democracy cannot exist without compromise, and compromise often leads to, or is even solved by, technocratic policies.[35] Furthermore, politics in complex societies relies

[35] I have to thank Gorm Harske for a discussion of this point.

on a wealth of expertise, technical and strategic knowledge and know-how, technical power and so on. So technocratic policies on their own are not the problem. The problem is the *complete repression and silencing of European public opinion in European matters*, which we have been able to observe since the beginning of the European process of incremental constitutionalization.

At the most basic level, the rhetoric and symbols of the EU are designed to silence public opinion, and so is the institutional design. For democracies, *words matter*. It makes a difference if we call a legal norm a *law* (Constitutional Treaty 2005) or a *regulation* (Lisbon Treaty 2009) – even if both have the same legal status and impact. It makes a difference if we call a legal textbook a *constitution* or a *treaty*. After the failure of the Constitutional Treaty in 2005 the differences between the words 'treaty' and 'constitution', and the words 'regulation' and 'law' have come to signify the difference between *democratic politics* and *technocratic administration*. The difference between democracy and technocracy is not only a political difference: it is also a legal difference, because democratic constitutions *forbid* the replacement of democratic politics by technocratic administration. For democracies, *symbolic forms matter*. Perhaps it makes no difference for the *judges* of the ECJ or the German Constitutional Court whether there exists a Charter of Basic Rights written in the text of the Constitutional Treaty, or if there only exists a non-visible reference in one of the many articles of the so-called Reform Treaty of Lisbon. However, it makes a difference for the *citizens* of Europe. This is once again a question of the difference between democracy and technocracy. This difference, again, is not only a political difference, but also a legal difference, because democracy will permit no '-cracy' (*kratein*) except that of the people. For democracies, moreover, *public opinion matters*. The transnational ruling class that governs Europe today has already made huge steps towards *low-intensity* democracy (Susan Marks) and *post-democracy* (Colin Crouch) (Marks 2000; Buchstein and Jörke 2003; Crouch 2008). The first step followed immediately the referendum on the Constitutional Treaty in 2005. After that, the political class of Europe ordered itself to take a two-year break from public discussion, which contributed notably to the silencing of public opinion. Then came the Reform Treaty of Lisbon with some minor changes, which all had similar implications. That is, they were designed to reduce the democratic significance of the new treaty to avoid the dangerous emergence of public opinion. Or, as Angela Merkel put it bluntly in an interview on German television on 14 May 2008: 'My friend Sarkozy and I have suggested to call it, not a constitution, but a *reform treaty* because only then can another French referendum be avoided.' The next long step was the implementation of a particular executive regime beyond the Treaties: that is, the European Stability Mechanism (ESM), imposed during the crisis of the European periphery and the financial system of the euro. This was crowned by the direct intervention of the hegemonic power of the continent to compel Greece to revoke a referendum (already announced to the Greek people) on so-called European 'aid' for and 'rescue' of Greece. The special regime of the Stability Mechanism has a long European tradition, which seems to be akin to the *secret common law* of the Union. It just needs to be made *publicly explicit* that it is not the *common law of the European citizens*, but the *particular law of the European ruling class*. We are now close – and this is the seventh thesis that I wish to propose – to approaching a European *dual state*: that is, a state marked by *public legalism* (normative state) and *backdoor prerogative rule* (prerogative state), which is distinctively *post-democratic*.[36]

The priority of technocratic politics was stabilized from the very beginning of European integration by extra-parliamentary and executively dominated special regimes, reaching from EURATOM, through the almost omniscient, and formally badly implemented, European Council, to FRONTEX. Jürgen Bast has analysed the nearly complete loss of democratic legitimization in the case of the true head of the Union, the European Council (Bast 2005: 44). The key point here can be expressed in one sentence: *The informal power of the united executive bodies of Europe (called the European Council) is the result of a soft-law regime with hard-law effects, which enables the circumvention of public opinion, legal review and parliamentary control.*[37] This informal mix of soft and hard law is characteristic of all kinds of special regimes, exemplified by the Bologna Process of the Council of Europe (acting in close co-operation with the Commission, the Council of the EU and the one informal representative of the civil society, the Bertelsmann Group).[38] If voters stay away from the ballots, no deliberative, auditive, comitological or any other brand of new and fancy 'democracy' can save real democracy (this is the case simply because there is no deliberative democracy without normatively functioning egalitarian procedures of decision making). In such a case the

[36] For a historical case study see Fraenkel (1999). On post-democracy see Crouch (2008).

[37] See chapter 14 in Brunkhorst (2012). For more general discussion of the bypassing techniques of soft law regimes, see Möllers (2005b).

[38] See chapter 14 in Brunkhorst (2012).

outbreak of a *legitimization crisis* and the *return of the repressed dimension of the constitutional system* becomes more and more likely.

By way of conclusion, therefore, we assert that the *development* of the European Political Constitution was triggered by the contradiction between subjective rights and democracy, which engendered a growing need for the public completion of private autonomy. The need was satisfied by the *structural coupling* of law and politics. However, this coupling fulfils the integrative function of *system integration* without fulfilling the need for *social integration*. The final form of the democratic normative state of Europe is thus undermined by its backdoor prerogative state that is no longer democratic.

11.5.4 Stage 4: The Social Security Constitution

The latent conflict between a democratic normative state and a pre-democratic prerogative state was not only characteristic for the first years of dictatorial fascist rule in Germany (where a *democratic* state had disappeared but a *normative* state still existed). Nonetheless, Ernst Fraenkel's theory of the dual state can be generalized to describe all *bourgeois parliamentary democracies* (all of which were socially limited democracies, usually excluding materially disadvantaged groups, women, people of colour) that existed during the nineteenth century and the first half of the twentieth century (even if only rarely in such extreme variants as Nazi Germany). The constitutional conflict between the *democratic rule of law* and a *pre-democratic prerogative state of bourgeois class rule* gave rise to socialist movements, social reforms and revolutions, which demonstrated the need for a *social concretization and realization* of the hitherto 'abstract' (to follow Hegel and Marx) Political Constitution. The present economic crisis underlines the fact that the *developmental logic* that underlay the contradictions of former bourgeois parliamentary rule of law did not vanish in the process of 'modernization' of the EU (in the sense promoted by, for example, Blair and Schröder) and its mass social-welfare democracies that developed after the 1980s. On the contrary, the contradictions that once tore the bourgeois normative state apart re-asserted themselves as a structural conflict between *democratic normative rule* and *neo-liberal post-democratic 'un-rule of law'* (O'Donnell 1999): that is to say, the *old* problem of Latin America now became the *new* problem of neo-liberal 'reformed' Europe.

The eighth thesis that I wish to propose is that the present world economic crisis at least makes the need for the *social concretization* of the abstract Political Constitution of Europe manifest. Since Maastricht, we have been able to observe the emergence of a Social Security Constitution, addressing in particular the (economically relatively cheap) emancipatory dimension of *anti-discrimination norms* (which, notably, have been subject to a neo-liberal interpretation through the constitutional organs, in particular the ECJ and the special regime of the European Council). Now, however, after the introduction of a Stability Mechanism, things have changed. Suddenly the problems of (economically expensive) *re-distribution* and *just distribution* between the regions and the social classes, between the haves and the have-nots of Europe, assume pressing significance.

At a functional level, the Social Security Constitution *couples law with social structure – and in particular the law of egalitarian rights concretization with the educational system of society*. This usually leads to an institutionalization of social struggles and a tremendous expansion of higher education across the entirety of a population. Parsons and Platt have analysed this development of social (and in particular educational) inclusion in the case of the American University (Parsons and Platt 2006). In Europe, the Bologna process reflects a similar attempt to include the whole European population in the system of higher education, and so to *enhance social mobility*. As a result, the societal function that must be satisfied by the structural coupling of law with social structure is the function of *latent pattern maintenance*. That in fact worked nicely in the US in the 1950s and 1960s. However, the time to which Parsons and Platt refer in their studies was a time of *increasing 'equality' between the social classes* of the US and the whole Western segment of the world society. *But since the neo-liberal turn of the global economy inequality has again increased dramatically*. Social mobility through educational inclusion immediately has dropped back to zero (and as a further consequence educational inclusion has begun to decrease again) (Wilkinson and Pickett 2010; Judt 2010). Owing to the great turn to austerity policies during the present world economic crisis, European politics is moving in the same direction as the US and Great Britain since the 1980s. In the European case, again the one-sided class politics of the technocratic elites will prevail despite the advances of the European Social Security Constitution. Conversely, the darker side of the *Social Constitution* that is the *Security Constitution* will blossom in the long shadow of the economic crisis. The Security Constitution *structurally couples law with the police* as a constitutive part of the *Social Security Constitution* (which binds both things, the brighter and the darker side of that special constitutional regime together – such as in the old concept of *Polizey* written with a 'y').

In this respect, therefore, we conclude that the *development* of the European Social Security Constitution is induced by the contradiction between the democratic normative Union and the post-democratic prerogative Union of Europe. The growing need for social rights is answered (however insufficiently) by the *structural coupling* of law and social security systems (including the police), which fulfils the function of latent pattern maintenance attached to *system integration*. However, the *social integration* by a new system of just distribution of wealth between the regions and social classes still lacks egalitarian and comprehensive democratic legitimization.

11.6 Crisis

The functionally sequential incremental evolution of an almost *fully fledged European constitutional system* remains reliant on the clear dominance of technocratic politics. Therefore, I can conclude my argument by setting out the ninth thesis that I wish to propose. This thesis is as follows. If the *economic crisis becomes manifest*, then the disastrous mix of *procedural democratic structures* and *post-democratic politics*, which is structurally characteristic for the EU, must lead to a *crisis of legitimization*. In all probability, we are just at the beginning of such a crisis, a crisis that is national, European and global.

The crisis – or, more exactly, the series of economic crises before the great crisis of 2008 – has deprived the national state of its most basic alternatives in economic and social policies (Streek 2010). Its capacity to act and shape the future (by using the traditional mix of governmental and intergovernmental politics) always relied on the existence of *two major instruments* to shape the economic system. That is, states were able either to pursue *regulation and control by law* (which is relatively cheap) or they were able to pursue *investment and expenditure of fiscal revenue to steer the economy or to bail out losses* (which is extremely expensive). States have now lost nearly all of their money through the bail-outs and growth programmes at the beginning of the major crisis. They are now spending the rest. However, it seems that, from the beginning of the crisis, the states were no longer able to pursue the *first alternative*: that is, to make *effective* law that allows them to control and regulate the world or at least the European economy, to nationalize or cut the big transnational commercial corporations and banks into pieces. Consequently, they were forced to spend the money. They were obliged to pursue the second alternative. The few big powerful banks and commercial enterprises which have eliminated almost all market competition now argue (as did Margaret Thatcher at a time when the political power brokers still *had* an alternative) that *there is no alternative to austerity politics.* Reagan and Thatcher are gone. But Deutsche Bank and Volkswagen still exist, and they have taken over. Even the governments and their heads of state are now in the hands of bankers and their staff of technocrats, as in Italy or Greece. They are not elected by the people, but by the European Council. In states where the bankers have not yet taken the lead, their advice resembles the advice of the old Roman Senate, or the advice of the Godfathers of the modern Mafia. It is an advice without any legally binding force. But whoever does not follow it is already a dead man, even if he leaves the room alive.

What we might most accurately call the *great neo-liberal transformation of the national state* seems unalterable, and it has at least established a very stable new hegemonial power structure in world society, which for the first time is global *and* transnational. There is no way back to national sovereignty – if there ever was one that was not doomed to end in disaster. The simple reason is that during the last thirty years the markets went global, and (as discussed) they have transformed the historical conditions in which markets were embedded by *controlling state power* – conditions that compelled Richard Nixon to the confession that 'we are all Keynesians' – into conditions in which states are *controlled by markets.* As a consequence, popular sovereignty has been *fragmented* – both beyond, as well as within, the borders of the national state (Prien 2010). Post-democracy is becoming our everyday reality. The abysmally negative dialectic underlying the constitutionalization of the EU is, as we have seen, a striking example of this great transformation that finally marginalizes democratic self-determination. Once the structures of economy and power have changed so deeply, any way back to the (at least as a useful legal fiction) undivided *sovereign* national state is closed once and for ever. The only way out that remains open consists, therefore, in the radical democratization of the already existing transnational institutions and organizations.

The 'symptomatic truth' of Europe today (using an expression of Slavoj Zizek) is that the *repression of the substantial alternatives is caused by the repression of the institutional alternatives.*[39] The winners in the process of Europeanization and globalization, the loosely united executive bodies,

[39] This is the core point in Habermas (2011).

operating in conjunction with a few big global banks and commercial enterprises, have effectively suppressed all debate on the *constitutional alternatives* between *European democratic leadership*, which is at least legitimated by European-wide public controversies, and *collective European Bonapartism*, which is enacted by the European Council and the consultant class that pretends to represent civil society: the executive boards of Deutsche Bank and the Bertelsmann Group, on the other hand. As a result of the repression of *European* constitutional and institutional alternatives, the clear and present substantial alternatives concerning economic policies are repressed as well. These alternatives are between *neo-liberal austerity policies* at the moment of an imminent global deflation crisis, and *Keynesian policies of publicly financed growth, steered in favour of the have-nots and the periphery*, designed to prevent a crisis that could become the biggest economic crash of modern capitalism.

As it seems now, however, the return of the repressed becomes more likely from hour to hour. Probably the hegemonic oppression of the Greek referendum that threatened the technocratic leadership of Europe by unleashing an uncontrollable public debate (which is at the core of all democracy that is worth that name) was the last time technocracy prevailed in Europe. Not we, the people, now *they* are at the edge – the Party of 1 per cent.

Bibliography

Albert, Mathias (2005). 'Politik der Weltgesellschaft und Politik der Globalisierung: Überlegungen zur Emergenz von Weltstaatlichkeit', in Bettina Heinz, Richard Münchand and Tyrell Hartmann (eds). *Zeitschrift für Soziologie*, special number on *Weltgesellschaft*. 223–39.

Alter, Karen (1996). 'The European Court's Political Power', *West European Politics* 19(3): 458–87.

(1998). 'Who are the "Masters of the Treaty?"', *International Organization* 52: 121–47.

Bast, Jürgen (2005). Einheit und Differenzierung der Europäischen Verfassung', in Yvonne Becker *et al.* (eds). *Die Europäische Verfassung – Verfassungen in Europa*. Baden-Baden: Nomos, pp. 34–60.

(2010). 'Europäische Gesetzgebung – Fünf Stationen in der Verfassungsentwicklung der EU', in Claudio Franzius, Franz C. Meyer and Jürgen Neyer (eds). *Strukturfragen der Europäischen Union*. Baden-Baden: Nomos, pp. 173–80.

Böckenförde, Ernst-Wolfgang (1986). *Die verfassungsgebende Gewalt des Volkes – Ein Grenzbegriff des Verfassungsrechts*. Frankfurt: Metzner.

Bogdandy, Armin von and Ingo Venzke (2009). 'In wessen Namen? Die internationale Gerichtsbarkeit diskurstheoretisch betrachtet', Lecture given in Zurich on 28 May 2009: Internationale Gerichte in Zeiten globalen Regierens. Berlin: Suhrkamp.

Böhm, Franz (2010 [1933]). *Wettbewerb und Monopolkampf. Eine Untersuchung zur Frage des wirtschaftlichen Kampfrechts und zur Frage der rechtlichen Struktur der geltenden Wirtschaftsordnung*. Baden-Baden: Nomos.

Brandom, Robert (2000). *Expressive Vernunft*. Frankfurt: Suhrkamp.

Brunkhorst, Hauke (2005). *Solidarity: From Civic Friendship to a Global Legal Community*. Cambridge, MA: The MIT Press.

(2012). *Legitimationskrisen. Verfassungsprobleme der Weltgesellschaft*. Baden-Baden: Nomos.

Buchstein, Hubertus and Dirk Jörke (2003). 'Das Unbehagen an der Demokratietheorie', *Leviathan* 31(4): 470–95.

Buckel, Sonja and Lukas Oberndorfer (2009). 'Die lange Inkubationszeit des Wettbewerbs der Rechtsordnungen – Eine Genealogie der Rechtsfälle Viking/Laval/Rüffert/Luxemburg aus der Perspektive einer materialistischen Europarechtstheorie', in Andreas Fischer-Lescano, Florian Rödl and Christoph Schmid (eds). *Europäische Gesellschaftsverfassung: Zur Konstitutionalisierung sozialer Demokratie in Europa*. Baden-Baden: Nomos, pp. 277–96.

Chalmers, Damian, Christos Hadjiemmanuil, Giorgio Monti and Adam Tomkins (eds) (2006). *European Union Law*. Cambridge: Cambridge University Press.

Chimni, Bhupinder S. (2004). 'International Institutions Today: An Imperial Global State in the Making', *European Journal of International Law* 15(1): 1–37.

Conrad, Sebastian (2008). 'Globalization Effects: Mobility and Nation in Imperial Germany, 1880–1914', *Journal of Global History* 3: 43–6.

Cooper, Ian (2011). 'Comment on Fossum and Menendez', presented at Workshop 'A Multitude of Constitutions?', Lecture given at the University of Oslo, January 2011, on file with author.

Crouch, Colin (2008). *Postdemokratie*. Frankfurt: Suhrkamp.

(2011). *Über das befremdliche Überleben des Neoliberalismus*. Frankfurt: Suhrkamp.

Dann, Philipp (2002). 'Looking through the Federal Lens: The Semi-parliamentary Democracy of the EU', *Jean-Monnet Working Paper* 5/02.

Di Fabio, Udo (1988). *Das Recht offener Staaten*. Tübingen: Mohr.

Eldredge, Niles and Stephen Jay Gould (1972). 'Punctuated Equilibria: An Alternative to Phyletic Gradualism', in Thomas J.M. Schopf (ed.). *Models in Paleobiology*. San Francisco, CA: Freeman-Cooper, pp. 82–115.

Fassbender, Bardo (2009). *The United Nations Charter as the Constitution of the International Community*. Leiden: Nijhoff.

Fischer-Lescano, Andreas (2004). *Globalverfassung. Die Geltungsbegründung der Menschenrechte im postmodernen ius gentium*. Weilerswist: Velbrück Wissenschaft.

Fischer-Lescano, Andreas and Gunther Teubner (2006). *Regime-Kollisionen*. Frankfurt: Suhrkamp.

Forsythe, Murray (1981). *Unions of States. The Theory and Practice of Confederations*. New York, NY: Holmes.

Fossum, John Eric and Augustín José Menéndez (2011). *The Constitutions Gift: Elements of a Constitutional Theory for a Democratic European Union*. Lanham, MD: Rowan & Littlefield.

Fraenkel, Ernst (1999). 'Der Doppelstaat', in Ernst Fraenkel. *Gesammelte Schriften*. Edited in 7 vols by Alexander v. Brünneck, Hubertus Buchstein and Gerhard Göhler. Vol II. Baden-Baden: Nomos.

Gaitanides, Charlotte (2007). 'Die Verfassung für Europa und das Europäische System der Zentralbanken', in Charlotte Gaitanides, Stefan Kadelbach and Gil Carlos Rodriguez Iglesias (eds). *Europa und seine Verfassung, Festschrift Zuleeg*. Baden-Baden: Nomos, pp. 550–5.

Gersick, Connie J.G. (1991). 'Revolutionary Change Theories: A Multilevel Exploration of the Punctuated Equilibrium Paradigm', *The Academic Management Review* 16(1): 10–36.

Gould, Stephen J. (1978). 'Episodic Change versus Gradualist Dogma', *Science and Nature* 2: 5–12.

(2002). *The Structure of Evolutionary Theory*. Cambridge, MA: Harvard University Press.

Gould, Stephen J. and Richard C. Lewontin (1979). 'The Spandrels of San Marco and the Panglossian Paradigm: A Critique of the Adaptationist Programme', available at: http://faculty.washington.edu/lynnhank/GouldLewontin.pdf, accessed 15 January 2014.

Häberle, Peter (1991). 'Gemeineuropäisches Verfassungsrecht', *Europäische Grundrechtezeitung* 18: 261–74.

(2009). *Europäische Verfassungslehre*, 6th edition. Baden-Baden: Nomos.

Habermas, Jürgen (1981). *Theorie des kommunikativen Handelns*. Frankfurt: Suhrkamp.

(1992). *Faktizität und Geltung*. Frankfurt: Suhrkamp.

(2011). 'Die Krise der Europäische Union im Licht einer Konstitutionalisierung des Völkerrechts'. Manuscript of a lecture given at the Humboldt University in Berlin on 16 June 2011: Zur Verfassung Europas. Ein Essay, Berlin: Suhrkamp 2011, S. 39–96.

Hitzel-Cassagnes, Tanja (2012). *Die Verfassung des Transnationalen. Reflexive Ordnungsbildung jenseits des Staates*. Stuttgart: Nomos.

Hobsbawm, Eric J. (1994). *Das Zeitalter der Extreme. Weltgeschichte des 20. Jahrhunderts*. Munich: Hanser.

Ipsen, Hans Peter (1970). *Verfassungsperspektiven der Europäischen Gemeinschaften*. Berlin: Walter de Gruyter.

Judt, Tony (2010). *Ill Fares the Land*. New York, NY: Penguin.

Kelsen, Hans (1931). *Wer soll der Hüter der Verfassung sein?* Berlin-Grunewald: Rothschild.
(1944). *Peace through Law*. Chapel Hill, NC: University of North Carolina Press.
(1954). 'Demokratie und Sozialismus', in Norbert Leser (ed.). *Demokratie und Sozialismus. Ausgewählte Aufsätze*. Wien: Verlag der Wiener Volksbuchhandlung, pp. 170–210.
Kreide, Regina (2008). *Globale Politik und Menschenrechte: Macht und Ohnmacht eines politischen Instruments*. Frankfurt: Campus.
(2009). *Globale Gerechtigkeit und Transnationales Regieren. Habilitationsschrift*. Frankfurt: Johann Wolfgang Goethe-Universität.
Kubon-Gilke, Gisela and Ekkart Schlicht (1998). 'Gerichtete Variationen in der biologischen und sozialen Evolution', *Gestalt Theory* 20(1): 48–77.
Kuhn, Thomas (1967). *Die Struktur wissenschaftlicher Revolutionen*. Frankfurt: Suhrkamp.
Lakatos, Imre (1977). 'The Methodology of Scientific Research Programmes', reprinted in *Philosophical Papers*. Vol. I. Cambridge: Cambridge University Press.
Leisering, Lutz (2007). 'Gibt es einen Weltwohlfahrtsstaat?', in Matthias Albert and Rudolf Stichweh (eds). *Weltstaat und Weltstaatlichkeit*. Wiesbaden: Westdeutscher Verlag, pp. 185–205.
Lockwood, David (1971). 'Soziale Integration und Systemintegration', in Wolfgang Zapf (ed.). *Theorien des sozialen Wandels*. Cologne: Kiepenheuer & Witsch, pp. 124–37.
Luhmann, Niklas (1983). *Legitimation durch Verfahren*. Frankfurt: Suhrkamp.
(1990). 'Verfassung als evolutionäre Errungenschaft', *Rechtshistorisches Journal* 9: 176–200.
(1997). *Die Gesellschaft der Gesellschaft*. Frankfurt: Suhrkamp.
Luther, Jörg (2011). 'The Constitution's Gift to the European Union: A Donkey or a Trojan Horse?', Lecture given at the University of Oslo, January 2011, on file with author.
Marks, Susan (2000). *The Riddle of All Constitutions*. Oxford: Oxford University Press.
Marx, Karl (1973). 'Bourgeoisie und Konterrevolution', in Karl Marx and Friedrich Engels, *Werke* in 43 vols. Berlin: Dietz. Vol. 6, pp. 102–24.
Maus, Ingeborg (1992). *Zur Aufklärung der Demokratietheorie*. Frankfurt: Suhrkamp.
(1994). 'Volkssouveränität vs. Konstitutionalismus. Zum Begriff einer demokratischen Verfassung', in Günther Frankenberg (ed.). *Auf der Suche nach der gerechten Gesellschaft*. Frankfurt: Fischer, pp. 74–83.
Mayr, Ernst (1992). 'Speciational Evolution or Punctuated Equilibria', in A. Somit and A.S. Peterson (eds). *The Dynamics of Evolution*. Ithaca, NY: Cornell University Press, pp. 21–53.

Meyer, John (2005). *Weltkultur*. Frankfurt: Suhrkamp.

Möllers, Christoph (2003). 'Verfassungsgebende Gewalt - Verfassung - Konstitutionalisierung. Begriffe der Verfassung in Europa', in Arnim v. Bogdandy (ed.). *Europäisches Verfassungsrecht*, 1st edition. Berlin: Springer, pp. 1–56.

(2005a). *Gewaltengliederung. Legitimation und Dogmatik im nationalen und internationalen Rechtsvergleich*. Tübingen: Mohr Siebeck.

(2005b). 'Transnationale Behördenkooperation', *Zeitschrift für ausländisches öffentliches Recht und Völkerrecht* 17: 351–89.

(2010). 'Lässt sich Rechtsgeltung naturalisieren?', Lecture at the annual conference of the Görres-Gesellschaft, Freiburg.

Neumann, Franz L. (1978). 'Über die Voraussetzungen und den Rechtsbegriff einer Wirtschaftsverfassung (1931)', in Franz Neumann. *Wirtschaft, Staat, Demokratie. Aufsätze 1930–1954*. Frankfurt: Suhrkamp, pp. 76–102.

O'Donnell, Guillermo (1999). 'Polyarchies and the (Un)Rule of Law in Latin America: A Partial Conclusion', in Juan Mendez, Guillermo O'Donnell and Paulo Sergio Pinheiro (eds). *(Un)Rule of Law and the Underprivileged in Latin America*. Notre Dame, IN: University of Notre Dame Press, pp. 303–37.

Osterhammel, Jürgen (2009a). *Kolonialismus*. Munich: Beck.

(2009b). *Die Verwandlung der Welt. Eine Geschichte des 19. Jahrhunderts*. Munich: Beck.

Osterhammel, Jürgen and Niels P. Petersson (2007). *Geschichte der Globalisierung*. Munich: Beck.

Parsons, Talcott (1961). 'Order and Community in the International Social System', in James N. Rosenau (ed.). *International Politics and Foreign Policy*. Glencoe, IL: The Free Press, pp. 120–9.

(1964). 'Evolutionary Universals in Society', *American Sociological Review* 29(1-6): 339–57.

Parsons, Talcott and G.M. Platt (2006). *Die amerikanische Universität*. Frankfurt am Main: Suhrkamp.

Pernice, Ingolf (2010). 'La rete europea di costituzionalità - Der Europäische Verfassungsverbund und die Netzwerktheorie', *WHI - Paper 01/10*, Humboldt University, Berlin, available at www.whi-berlin.de/documents/whi-paper0110.pdf.

Prien, Thore (2010). *Fragmentierte Volkssouveränität - Recht, Gerechtigkeit und der demokratische Einspruch in der Weltgesellschaft*. Baden-Baden: Nomos.

Report of Luxembourg *Conseil d'État* (1952), available at www.ena.lu?lang=1&doc=9644.

Rieckmann, Jana (2011). 'Problems of Legitimisation of the EU Agency "Frontex"', MA Thesis, University of Flensburg and Syddansk University.

Scavenius, Theresa (2011). 'Comment on The Constitution's Gift by Fossum and Menéndez', Lecture given at the University of Oslo, January 2011, available at: www.zaoerv.de/70_2010/70_2010_1_a_51_72.pdf, accessed 15 January 2014.

Scheuerman, William E. (2004). 'The Unholy Alliance of Carl Schmitt and Friedrich A. Hayek', *Constellations* 4: 172–88.

Schönberger, Christoph (2005). *Föderale Angehörigkeit. Habilitationsschrift*, Freiburg.

Schwarze, Jürgen (ed.) (2000). *Die Entstehung einer europäischen Verfassungsordnung*. Baden-Baden: Nomos.

Sellin, Volker (2001). *Die geraubte Revolution. Der Sturz Napoleons und die Restauration in Europa*. Göttingen: Vandenhoek.

Somek, Alexander (2008). *Individualism: An Essay on the Authority of the European Union*. Oxford: Oxford University Press.

Streek, Wolfgang (2005). 'Sectoral Specialization: Politics and the Nation State in a Global Economy', Paper presented at the 37th World Congress of the International Institute of Sociology, Stockholm.

(2010). 'Noch so ein Sieg, und wir sind verloren. Der Nationalstaat nach der Finanzkrise', *Leviathan* 38: 159–73.

Sunstein, Cass (2004). *The Second Bill of Rights*. New York, NY: Basic Books.

Taylor, Charles (2007). *A Secular Age*. Cambridge, MA: Harvard University Press.

Thornhill, Chris (2011). *A Sociology of Constitutions. Constitutions and State Legitimacy in Historical-Sociological Perspective*. Cambridge: Cambridge University Press.

Tuori, Kaarlo (2010). 'The Many Constitutions of Europe', in Kaarlo Tuori and Suvi Sankari (eds). *The Many Constitutions of Europe*. Farnham: Ashgate, pp. 3–30.

Tuori, Kaarlo and Suvi Sankari (2010).*The Many Constitutions of Europe*. Farnham: Ashgate.

Vatter, Miguel (2010). 'Foucault y la ley: la juridificación de la política en el neoliberalismo', in Vanessa Lemm (ed.). *Michel Foucault: biopolítica y neoliberalismo*. Santiago: Ediciones Universidad Diego Portales, pp. 199–216.

Voßkuhle, Andreas (2010). 'Multilevel Cooperation of the European Constitutional Courts: Der Europäische Verfassungsgerichtsverbund', *European Constitutional Law* 6: 175–98.

Wahl, Rainer (2003). *Verfassungsstaat, Europäisierung, Internationalisierung*. Frankfurt: Suhrkamp.

Wegmann, Milène (2010). 'European Competition Law: Catalyst of Integration and Convergence', in Kaarlo Tuori and Suvi Sankari (eds). *The Many Constitutions of Europe*. Farnham: Ashgate, pp. 91–107.

Weiler, J.H.H. (1997). 'To be a European Citizen – Eros and Civilisation', *Journal of European Public Policy* 4: 495–519.

Wesel, Uwe (1984). *Juristische Weltkunde: Eine Einführung in das Recht*. Frankfurt: Suhrkamp.

Wiener, Antje (2008). *The Invisible Constitution of Politics*. Cambridge: Cambridge University Press.

Wilkinson, Richard and Kate Pickett (2010). *The Spirit Level. Why Greater Equality Makes Societies Stronger*. New York, NY: Bloomsbury.

INDEX